D0908702

THE LETTERS OF

Charles and Mary Anne Lamb

Volume I • Letters of Charles Lamb • 1796–1801

ALSO EDITED BY EDWIN W. MARRS, JR.

The Letters of Thomas Carlyle to His Brother Alexander, with Related Family Letters, 1968

CHARLES LAMB AT TWENTY-THREE.
From a pencil and chalk drawing by Robert Hancock (1730–1817).
Courtesy of the National Portrait Gallery, London.

THE LETTERS OF
Charles and Mary Anne Lamb

Volume I • Letters of Charles Lamb • 1796–1801

EDITED BY EDWIN W. MARRS, JR.

CORNELL UNIVERSITY PRESS
ITHACA AND LONDON
1975

First published 1975 by Cornell University Press.
Published in the United Kingdom by Cornell University Press Ltd.,
2-4 Brook Street, London W1Y 1AA

International Standard Book Number 0-8014-0930-6
Library of Congress Catalog Card Number 75-8436
Printed in the United States of America by York Composition Co., Inc.

To

Perthenia Northcraft Marrs

and our daughters

Nancy, Lisa, and Jenny

ACKNOWLEDGMENTS

Permission to quote from *The Letters of Charles Lamb: To Which Are Added Those of His Sister, Mary Lamb,* edited by E. V. Lucas, published by J. M. Dent & Sons, Ltd., and Methuen & Company, Ltd., London, in 1935, has been granted by L. M. Cooper and R. R. Maddison of Knapp-Fishers, Solicitors and Commissioners for Oaths, London, the trustees of the will of the late E. V. Lucas; and by Associated Book Publishers, Ltd., London, through the offices of Ann Macintyre. Quotations from *Collected Letters of Samuel Taylor Coleridge,* edited by Earl Leslie Griggs, © Oxford University Press, 1956 (Volumes I and II), 1959 (Volumes III and IV), 1971 (Volumes V and VI), are by permission of Oxford University Press, Oxford. Passages from my "Some Account of the Publishing History of the Lambs' Letters, with Notes on a New Edition in Progress," in the *Charles Lamb Bulletin* of April 1973, are republished with the consent of Basil Savage, editor of the *Charles Lamb Bulletin.*

Permissions to publish the manuscript letters have been given or other courtesies regarding them extended by Lord Abinger; Dorothy Hamlen of The University of Akron Library; D. Carruthers of the Auckland Public Library; Roger W. Barrett; John Alden of the Boston Public Library; Thomas C. Bright, and William A. Dillon of the Jervis Library, Rome, New York; Norman Higham of the University of Bristol Library and Mrs. H. Marsden-Smedley (letters in the Pinney Papers); T. A. J. Burnett and H. M. T. Cobbe of The British Museum; Christine D. Hathaway of the Brown University Library (letters in the Koopman Collection); Jane D. Van Arsdale and William H. Loos of the Buffalo and Erie County Public Library; Leslie S. Clarke of The General Library, and Estelle Rebec and the director of The Bancroft Library, the University of California at Berkeley; Mrs. A. D. G. Cheyne; Robert M. Copeland of the Charles Leaming Tutt Library, Colorado College; Kenneth A. Lohf of the Butler Library,

Columbia University Libraries (a letter in the George Dunlop Collection); Jane E. Woolston and the late George H. Healey of Cornell University Library, and the Library Board of Cornell University (letters in the Wordsworth Collection); James and Helen Stevens Cox of The Toucan Press; Kenneth C. Cramer of the Dartmouth College Library; Emily Driscoll of Emily Driscoll Autographs and Manuscripts; Paul I. Chestnut, Edwin J. Hix, and Mattie Russell of the William R. Perkins Library, Duke University (letters on microfilm of the collection of Lord Abinger); the Edinburgh University Library; Mrs. William A. Cox and Laetitia Yeandle of The Folger Shakespeare Library; Michael D. C. Forrer; Arthur Freeman; Gordon T. Banks of Goodspeed's Book Shop, Inc.; Mrs. Alfred C. Harrison and Mrs. George deF. Lord, and Professor George deF. Lord; Raymond E. Hartz; William H. Bond, Suzanne Flandreau, Carolyn E. Jakeman, Janell Jensen, Mrs. Ronald Ricker, and Martha Eliza Shaw of The Houghton Library, Helen Willard of the Theatre Collection, and Carole A. Beals and Eleanor L. Nicholes of The Harry Elkins Widener Collection, Harvard University; Elizabeth B. Tritle of the Haverford College Library (letters in the Charles Roberts Collection); Arthur A. Houghton, Jr., and Mary V. Minstrell; Robert O. Dougan, Alan Jutzi, Jean F. Preston, Herbert C. Schulz, and Daniel H. Woodward of the Henry E. Huntington Library and Art Gallery; Mrs. Donald F. Hyde; Elfrieda Lang and David A. Randall of The Lilly Library, Indiana University; Frank Paluka of The University of Iowa Libraries, Iowa City, Iowa (letters in the Brewer–Leigh Hunt Collection); Frau Dr. Hille of the Universitätsbibliothek, Jena, East Germany (a letter in the Wolfgang Maximilian Collection); Francis Kettaneh; Florence S. Reeves, Basil Savage, and the late Ernest G. Crowsley of The Charles Lamb Society; H. Jack Lang; Mrs. L. V. Ledoux, and Mrs. Thomas J. Sands; David I. Masson of the Brotherton Collection, The University of Leeds (letters in the Novello Cowden Clarke subcollection); the Library of Congress (a letter in the Batchelder Autograph Collection); E. H. Seagroatt of the Hornby Library, City of Liverpool, Libraries Department; Hinda Rose of Maggs Bros., Ltd.; Glenn B. Skillin of the Maine Historical Society; Dr. Debes of the Universitätsbibliothek, Karl-Marx-Universität, Leipzig; Lowell R. Wilbur of the Public Library, Mason City, Iowa (a letter in the May Hanford MacNider Collection); Stephen T. Riley of the Massachusetts Historical Society;

James S. Ritchie of the National Library of Scotland; Richard L. Ormond of the National Portrait Gallery, London; Edwin A. Sy of the Lockwood Library, the State University of New York at Buffalo; Perry O'Neil and Joseph T. Rankin of the Arents Collections, Mrs. Charles Szladits and the late John D. Gordan of the Henry W. and Albert A. Berg Collection, Robert W. Hill and Jean R. McNiece of the Manuscripts & Archives Division (letters in the Montague Collection and Personal and Miscellaneous Papers), and John Miller and Faye Simkin, of The New York Public Library, Astor, Lenox and Tilden Foundations; D. S. Porter of the Department of Western Manuscripts, the Bodleian Library, Oxford; Mr. and Mrs. W. Hugh Peal, and Ruth Van Norman; John D. Kilbourne of The Historical Society of Pennsylvania; Gilda Hodes on behalf of The Carl and Lily Pforzheimer Foundation, Inc., and Olivia Jasper, Donald H. Reiman, and Kathleen Ritch of The Carl H. Pforzheimer Library; Frederick B. Adams, Jr., Herbert Cahoon, and C. A. Ryskamp of The Pierpont Morgan Library; Alexander P. Clark, Earle E. Coleman, and Wanda M. Randall of the Princeton University Library (letters presented to the library by Charles Scribner); Bernard Quaritch, Ltd., through the offices of Arthur Freeman; Catherine D. Hayes of The University of Rochester Library; Clive E. Driver of The Philip H. & A. S. W. Rosenbach Foundation; the late Charles J. Rosenbloom; Ronald Hall and Dr. F. Taylor of The John Rylands Library, Manchester; Mary R. Gayle of The Estelle Doheny Collection, The Edward Laurence Doheny Memorial Library, St. John's Seminary, Camarillo, California; David Satinoff; Mary Allely of the Scripps College Library; Wallace Nethery of the Hoose Library, the University of Southern California; Julius P. Barclay and Ralph W. Hansen of The Stanford University Libraries; Robert H. Taylor, and Thomas W. Blanding and Thomas V. Lange of the Robert H. Taylor Collection, Princeton, New Jersey; David Farmer of the Humanities Research Center, June Moll of the Miriam Lutcher Stark Library of The University of Texas Library, and the Faculty Committee on the Use of Historical and Literary Manuscripts, The University of Texas; Joann Karges of the Mary Couts Burnett Library, Texas Christian University (a letter in the William Luther Lewis Collection); Margaret Skerl of The Library, University College London (letters in the Rogers Papers, the gift of Professor Egon Pearson); K. A. R. Horne of The State Library of

Victoria, on behalf of the Library Council of Victoria; A. P. Burton, T. M. MacRobert, and G. M. Nash of the Victoria and Albert Museum (letters in the Forster Collection); Lorna D. Fraser of the Victoria University Library, Toronto; Mary Faith Pusey and Elizabeth Ryall of the Clifton Waller Barrett Library, the University of Virginia; Elsie T. Freeman of the Washington University Libraries, St. Louis (letters in the I. A. Stevens Collection, Rare Book Department); Hannah D. French of the Wellesley College Library; Kenneth Twinn of Dr. Williams's Trust and Dr. Williams's Library, London; D. G. Wilson; Nesta Clutterbuck and Stephen Gill of The Wordsworth Library, Grasmere; and Christina M. Hanson, Herman W. Liebert, Louisa O'Neil, and Marjorie G. Wynne of The Beinecke Rare Book and Manuscript Library, and Dorothy W. Bridgwater and Rutherford David Rogers, of Yale University Library.

Permissions to publish the illustrations have been given or other courtesies regarding them extended by T. A. J. Burnett, Mrs. A. Payne, and L. N. Peverett of The British Museum; R. E. Jones, P. J. Parr, Linda Randall, and the Syndics of the Fitzwilliam Museum, Cambridge University; the Fogg Art Museum, and William H. Bond and Carolyn E. Jakeman of The Houghton Library, Harvard University; Carey S. Bliss, Mary Lou DeLapp, Robert O. Dougan, Alan Jutzi, Robert R. Wark, and Daniel H. Woodward of the Henry E. Huntington Library and Art Gallery; Mildred Archer and S. J. McNally of the India Office Library and India Office Records, London; W. W. S. Breen of The Library of the Inner Temple, and The Masters of the Bench of the Inner Temple; Richard L. Ormond of the National Portrait Gallery, London; John P. Baker, Joseph T. Rankin, and Mrs. Charles Szladits of The New York Public Library, Astor, Lenox and Tilden Foundations; and A. P. Burton, Janet P. Steen, and Margaret Timmers of the Victoria and Albert Museum.

Among those who have helped in the searches for the letters or illustrations or with the research are Richard D. Altick; Herschel Baker; George L. Barnett; W. A. Taylor of the Birmingham Public Libraries; Robert K. Black of Robert K. Black Rare Books and Autographs; E. Cave of the Cambridge City Libraries; Irving Halpern of the Carnegie Book Shop, Inc.; Donald Missen of Christ's College Library and R. C. Smail of Sidney Sussex College Library, Cambridge University; Robert Rosenthall of the University of Chicago Library;

Dominie Rathbone of Christ's Hospital; Kathleen Coburn; Morton N. Cohen; Winifred F. Courtney; the Ministry of Defence, Whitehall; T. S. Mercer of the Ditton Historical Research Society; Francis Edwards, Ltd.; Richmond D. Williams of the Eleutherian Mills Historical Library; D. O. Pam of the Central Library, the London Borough of Enfield; Derek Brown of the District Central Library, Esher, Surrey; K. C. Newton of the Essex Record Office; Walter H. Evert; John M. Shaw of the Robert Manning Strozier Library, The Florida State University, Tallahassee; Earl Leslie Griggs; Gabriel Austin of The Grolier Club; Frederick W. Hilles; Florence Hine; John Palmer of the House of Commons; A. J. Farrington, Miss S. R. Johnson, and S. J. McNally of the India Office Library and India Office Records, London; Victor and Irene Murr Jacobs; Vilas Johnson; Carl H. Ketcham; Lee Kirby; Florence S. Reeves and Basil Savage of The Charles Lamb Society; Humphrey Lloyd; Robert D. Marshall; Cynthia Matlack; Robert F. Metzdorf; Mrs. Richard M. More; Winifred A. Myers of Winifred A. Myers (Autographs), Ltd.; John Gordon-Christian of Christ Church Library, Oxford University; Lewis Patton; Thomas L. Philbrick; Pickering and Chatto, Ltd.; Katherine Armitage and Peggy Batten of the University of Pittsburgh; Annabel F. Beddow, Mary L. Dimmick, Marcia Grodsky, George McMaster Jones, Joan Kretchun, Sally L. Rowley, Miss Lee Spanos, and Pamela S. Vance of the University of Pittsburgh Libraries; I. E. Hustwick of Bernard Quaritch, Ltd.; D. W. Allen of the Royal Doulton Potteries; H. S. Tallamy of the Library of Royal Leamington Spa; D. G. C. Allan of the Royal Society for the Encouragement of Arts, Manufacture, and Commerce; E. M. Rubenstein; Sotheby & Company; B. F. Stevens and Brown, Ltd.; the late Walter S. Taintor; Mrs. Charles Tickle; Richard C. Tobias; Benjamin H. Trask; Ralph M. Wardle; Vera Watson; K. C. Harrison of the City of Westminster Central Reference Library; John Wilson of John Wilson Autographs, Ltd.; Frank H. Sommer of the Libraries, The Henry Francis du Pont Winterthur Museum; Carl Woodring; and Joseph de Berry of Yale University Press.

Preparation of the edition has had the financial support of the Colgate University Research Council, the John Simon Guggenheim Memorial Foundation, the National Foundation on the Arts and the Humanities, the University of Pittsburgh Center for International

Studies, and the University of Pittsburgh Faculty Grants Committee. The Guggenheim Foundation awarded me a fellowship for the year 1972–1973 to provide exceptional time for research and, in 1975, a subvention to help defray the production costs of this edition.

Preparation of the edition has had the encouragement of Richard D. Altick, Morton N. Cohen, Walter H. Evert, Kenneth J. Fielding, Mr. and Mrs. Edward L. Fischer and the late Margrit Fischer, David Halliday, Robert G. Hooker, Weldon A. Kefauver, Cecil Y. Lang, Mildred Love Marrs, Mr. and Mrs. Albert Hayes Northcraft, Gordon N. Ray, Jerome L. Rosenberg, Charles Richard Sanders, Robert F. Whitman, and Carl Woodring.

The assistance of the staff of Cornell University Press, the Guggenheim Foundation, Mrs. Kretchun, Mr. McNally, Professor Marshall, Mrs. More, Mr. and Mrs. Peal, the University of Pittsburgh, Professor Ray, Miss Reeves, Mrs. Vance, and Professor Woodring has been extensive.

The help of my wife, Perthenia, extends beyond measure.

I thank all who are named, and the many not named who replied to my inquiries and requests.

E. W. M., Jr.

Pittsburgh, Pennsylvania

CONTENTS

ILLUSTRATIONS

ABBREVIATIONS

Ainger (1888) Alfred Ainger, ed. *The Letters of Charles Lamb: Newly Arranged, with Additions.* 2 vols. London and New York: Macmillan, 1888.

Ainger (1900) Alfred Ainger, ed. *The Letters of Charles Lamb: Newly Arranged, with Additions,* Vols. I–IV. Vols. IX–XII of *The Life and Works of Charles Lamb*. 12 vols. London: Macmillan, 1899–1900.

Ainger (1904) Alfred Ainger, ed. *The Letters of Charles Lamb: Newly Arranged, with Additions.* 2 vols. London and New York: Macmillan, 1904.

C. L. Charles Lamb.

CLSB *Charles Lamb Society Bulletin.* Retitled *Charles Lamb Bulletin* January 1973.

Coleridge's Letters Earl Leslie Griggs, ed. *Collected Letters of Samuel Taylor Coleridge.* 6 vols. Oxford: Clarendon Press, 1956–1971.

Coleridge's Poetical Works (1912) Ernest Hartley Coleridge, ed. *The Complete Poetical Works of Samuel Taylor Coleridge, Including Poems and Versions of Poems Now Published for the First Time.* 2 vols. Oxford: Clarendon Press, 1912.

De Quincey's Writings David Masson, ed. *The Collected Writings of Thomas De Quincey.* 14 vols. London: Black, 1896–1897.

DNB *Dictionary of National Biography.*

Fitzgerald Percy Fitzgerald, ed. *The Life, Letters and Writings of Charles Lamb*. 6 vols. London: Moxon, 1876.

Friend, The, ed. Barbara Rooke Barbara E. Rooke, ed. *The Friend, I* [and *II*], in *The Collected Works of Samuel Taylor Coleridge,* ed. Kathleen Coburn and Bart Winer. Vol. IV, Parts 1 and 2. London: Routledge & Kegan Paul; Princeton: Princeton University Press, 1969.

Godwin C. Kegan Paul. *William Godwin: His Friends and Contemporaries.* 2 vols. London: King, 1876.

Harper Henry H. Harper [and Richard Garnett], eds. *The Letters of Charles Lamb: In Which Many Mutilated Words and Passages Have*

Been Restored to Their Original Form; with Letters Never before Published and Facsimiles of Original MS Letters and Poems. 5 vols. Boston: Bibliophile Society, 1905.

Hazlitt W[illiam] Carew Hazlitt, ed. *Letters of Charles Lamb: With Some Account of the Writer, His Friends and Correspondents, and Explanatory Notes. By the Late Thomas Noon Talfourd, D.C.L., One of His Executors. An Entirely New Edition, Carefully Revised and Greatly Enlarged.* 2 vols. London: Bell, 1886.

Hazlitt's Works P. P. Howe, ed. *The Complete Works of William Hazlitt. After the Edition of A. R. Waller and Arnold Glover.* 21 vols. London and Toronto: Dent, 1930–1934.

H. C. R. on Books and Writers Edith J. Morley, ed. *Henry Crabb Robinson on Books and Their Writers.* 3 vols. London: Dent, 1938.

Lamb and the Lloyds E. V. Lucas, ed. *Charles Lamb and the Lloyds.* London: Smith, Elder, 1898.

Lives of the English Poets George Birkbeck Hill, ed. *Lives of the English Poets by Samuel Johnson, LL.D.* 3 vols. 1905. Rpt. New York: Octagon Books, 1967.

Lloyd-Manning Letters Frederick L. Beaty, ed. *The Lloyd-Manning Letters.* Bloomington: Indiana University Press, 1957.

Lucas (1905) E. V. Lucas, ed. *The Works of Charles and Mary Lamb.* 7 vols. New York: Putnam's; London: Methuen, 1903–1905.

Lucas (1912) E. V. Lucas, ed. *The Letters of Charles and Mary Lamb, 1796–1820* [and *1821–1842*]. Vols. V–VI of *The Works of Charles and Mary Lamb;* 6 vols. London: Methuen, 1912.

Lucas (1935) E. V. Lucas, ed. *The Letters of Charles Lamb: To Which Are Added Those of His Sister, Mary Lamb.* 3 vols. London: Dent and Methuen (copublishers), 1935.

Macdonald William Macdonald, ed. *Letters of Charles Lamb,* Vols. I–II. Vols. XI–XII of *The Works of Charles Lamb.* Large-paper Edition. 12 vols. London: Dent; New York: Dutton, 1903.

Manning-Lamb Letters G. A. Anderson [and P. P. Howe], eds. *The Letters of Thomas Manning to Charles Lamb.* London: Secker, 1925.

New Southey Letters Kenneth Curry, ed. *New Letters of Robert Southey.* 2 vols. New York and London: Columbia University Press, 1965.

Purnell Thomas Purnell, ed. *The Complete Correspondence and Works of Charles Lamb.* 4 vols. London: Moxon, 1870.

Rickman Orlo Williams. *Lamb's Friend the Census-taker: Life and Letters of John Rickman.* London: Constable, 1911.

Sala George Augustus Sala, ed. *The Complete Correspondence and Works of Charles Lamb*. London: Moxon, 1868.

Shelley and His Circle Kenneth Neill Cameron and Donald H. Reiman, eds. *Shelley and His Circle: 1773–1822*. 6 vols. Cambridge, Mass.: Harvard University Press, 1961–1973.

Southey's Correspondence Charles Cuthbert Southey, ed. *The Life and Correspondence of Robert Southey*. 6 vols. 1849–1850. Rpt. St. Clair Shores, Mich.: Scholarly Press [1968].

Talfourd (1837) Thomas Noon Talfourd, ed. *The Letters of Charles Lamb, with a Sketch of His Life*. 2 vols. London: Moxon, 1837.

Talfourd (1848) Thomas Noon Talfourd, ed. *Final Memorials of Charles Lamb; Consisting Chiefly of His Letters Not before Published, with Sketches of Some of His Companions*. 2 vols. London: Moxon, 1848.

TLS *Times Literary Supplement* (London).

Wordworths' Letters Ernest de Selincourt, ed. *The Letters of William and Dorothy Wordsworth*. 6 vols. Oxford: Clarendon Press, 1935–1939. 2d ed.: Vol. I, rev. Chester L. Shaver (1967); Vol. II, rev. Mary Moorman (1969); Vol. III, rev. Mary Moorman and Alan G. Hill (1970).

Wordworth's Poetical Works (1940–1949) E[rnest] de Selincourt and Helen Darbishire, eds. *The Poetical Works of William Wordsworth*. 5 vols. Oxford: Clarendon Press, 1940–1949.

Works E. V. Lucas, ed. *The Works of Charles and Mary Lamb*. 7 vols. New York: Putnam's; London: Methuen, 1903–1905.

Works (1818) *The Works of Charles Lamb*. 2 vols. London: Ollier, 1818.

The act, scene, and line numbers locating the passages from Shakespeare correspond to those in *The Riverside Shakespeare*, ed. G. Blakemore Evans *et al.* (Boston: Houghton Mifflin, 1974).

LIST OF LETTERS

INTRODUCTION

I

The children of John and Elizabeth Lamb were children as well of the Inner Temple, the medieval headquarters of the Knights Templars and Knights of St. John of Jerusalem and the seat of English law and Inn of Court where once functioned Sir Edward Coke and John Selden and even Chaucer and Gower some say. From its garden in Shakespeare's vision came the emblems for the Wars of the Roses.

Lamb was born in a ground-floor apartment at 2 Crown Office Row on February 10, 1775, and Mary presumably at another address on December 3, 1764. Their brother John, the James Elia of Elia's "My Relations," pretentious, dogmatic, remotely humane, was born on June 5, 1763. He attended Christ's Hospital from 1769 to 1778, then entered the South Sea House, and there rose from clerk to accountant. He published a pamphlet on the prevention of cruelty to animals, was married, and accumulated a collection of paintings of value. He died on October 26 and was buried at the church of St. Martin Outwich on November 7, 1821. Elizabeth, born on January 9, 1762, Samuel, baptized on December 13, 1765, a second Elizabeth, born on August 30, 1768, Edward, born on September 3, 1770, and possibly the William interred from the Temple in June 1772 at the church of St. Dunstan-in-the-West were their sisters and brothers who died in childhood.

Elizabeth, the children's mother, was born in Hitchin, Hertfordshire, in a year not determined. Her father, Edward Field, earned his living as a gardener and died in 1766. Her mother, Mary, the eldest daughter of Edward Bruton (d. 1726) and the former Elizabeth Tyrrell (d. 1745), was baptized at Kimpton on May 28, 1713, and married at Hitchin on September 14, 1736. Mrs. Field supported herself after her husband's death until hers on July 31, 1792, as the caretaker of Blakesware, the manor house near Widford of William Plumer (1687–1767), the former Elizabeth Byde (d. 1778), and their family. Elizabeth Lamb, who was living in St. Marylebone, London, before her marriage in St. Dunstan's-in-the-West on March 29, 1761, was a good mother and loved all her children, though according to Lamb she did not understand and too often neglected Mary. Mary was a good daughter and loved her. But on September 22, 1796, while helping to set the table for dinner, Mary was mastered by a lurking insanity. She began throwing forks wildly about the room, one of them wounding her father, and she seized a case knife from the table and pursued around the room her little apprentice dressmaker. When Mrs. Lamb cried out at her daughter, Mary, shrieking, turned on her mother and killed her with a knife thrust to her heart.

John, the children's father, was born in about 1725 to a Lincolnshire cobbler and his wife whose given names are not known. John Lamb went probably to the grammar school or to Christ's Hospital in Lincoln and then went to London to become a footman. He returned home a few years later to display his livery to his mother. He developed into a courageous and an independent man, brisk and happy for the most part, and came to appreciate humorous verse and the poetry of Prior and Swift. At one point he lived in Bath and at another joined a Society of Friends. In perhaps 1770 he published *Poetical Pieces on Several Occasions* and from 1772 to 1799 served as a first waiter in Inner Temple Hall. But from about 1747 to 1792 he chiefly served Samuel Salt. Salt, a shy eccentric, was a son of Vicar John Salt of Audley, Staffordshire, and for years the widower of the former Elizabeth Benson. He had become a member of the Inner Temple in 1745 and the owner of the Lambs' and his own apartments at 2 Crown Office Row in about 1768. He became a bencher, reader, and treasurer of the Inner Temple, a member of Parliament, director of the South Sea and East India companies, governor of a number of hospitals and of Christ's Hospital, and the benefactor of the Lambs. He opened his library to them, played a part in the entrances of Lamb and probably Lamb's brother into their school and businesses, and left their parents five hundred pounds in South Sea stock, two hundred pounds in cash, and a ten-pound annuity upon his death on July 27, 1792. The elder John Lamb, Elia's Lovel of "The Old Benchers of the Inner Temple," was Salt's friend, attendant, and keeper of time and books and treasury. He died querulous and palsied and was buried at the church of St. Andrew, Holborn, on April 13, 1799, beside his wife and sister, Sarah.

Sarah, the children's Aunt Hetty, a spinster and her brother's senior by ten years, completed the household. She disrupted it by a strange dark and religious character that conflicted with the sunny personalities of her brother and especially her sister-in-law. The repeated attempts of the gentlewomanly Mrs. Lamb to soften the rudeness of Sarah with attentions only vexed her. The hatred that was thus irritated into existence made them wretched before each other for twenty years and would have done so for longer had not Charles and Mary brought them finally into concord. No such trouble ever existed between Sarah and Lamb. He acknowledged in the Maria Howe story of his and Mary's *Mrs. Leicester's School: Or, the History of Several Young Ladies, Related by Themselves* (1809) that his aunt's love was for him alone and, though he was sometimes apprehensive of her, his love for his aunt nearly exceeded his combined love for his parents. His serious disposition and a spirit delicate and subject to fears and depressions kept him somewhat apart from them, and they frequently had to leave him in order to attend to Salt's needs or chose to leave him for parties or friends. At those times Lamb generally elected to be by himself, to excite his imagination from the books in Salt's chambers or liberate his thoughts by the fountain and the sundial and in the walkways of the gardens of the Temple. Yet his aunt was close when he needed her. Because of that and their profoundly harmonious natures it was usually in her lap that he sought and found solace when frightened in his solitude or the night or by the black things in illustration in Joseph Glanvill's *Philosophical Considerations Touching Witches and Witchcraft* and Thomas Stackhouse's *A New History of the Holy Bible*. She died on February 9, 1797.

Mary too watched over him and twice took him into Hertfordshire. In 1778 or 1779 they visited their grandaunt the former Anne Bruton. She, who was baptized in 1717 and married in May 1747 to James Gladman (1704–1769), had long been at the farm in Mackery End where her husband had been a yeoman. She continued there to her death on August 3, 1799, as the housekeeper of Thomas Hawkins. Mary, writing as Louisa Manners in *Mrs. Leicester's School,* told how she and her brother had wandered through the farmhouse and over its grounds, looked into the barn and stroked the pied cow, observed the thresher and the bees at their work and the milkers and the fowl, searched the woodhouse for eggs and the orchard for flowers, picked currants and gooseberries and tumbled in the hay, watched the sheep-shearing and joined in a sheepshearing supper, and taken their dinners with the field hands at a long white table before a faggot fire. Lamb mentioned those days when telling of later ones in "Mackery End, in Hertfordshire." In about 1781 Mary took him to visit their grandmother. Mary had been a guest at Blakesware before its mistress' death and so was able to leave her impressions of Mrs. Plumer as well as of Mrs. Field and the ancient mansion with marble hall of Hogarth prints and high-placed busts or hanging medallions of the twelve Caesars, room of portraits of Plumers in costumes of former times, and bedroom of old-fashioned furniture and tapestries Biblical in theme. Mary left her impressions as those of Margaret Green in *Mrs. Leicester's School.* Lamb left his fullest ones, of his grandmother and the house, in "Dream-children; a Reverie" and "Blakesmoor in H——shire."

Before Mary took him to Blakesware, the performance of Thomas Augustine Arne's opera *Artaxerxes* given with David Garrick's pantomime *Harlequin's Invasion* at Drury Lane in the evening of December 1, 1780, had in fancy taken him farther. He had attended with his elders on passes supplied by Francis Fielde (d. 1809), his godfather, supposedly Richard Brinsley Sheridan's confidant, and the oilman of High Holborn and Cavendish Square whose widow in 1812 conveyed to Lamb the Hertfordshire property of Button Snap. Lamb recalled in "My First Play" that it had transported him to a heaven beyond its spectacular Persian setting.

The schooling of Mary was limited to William Bird's Academy, a day school at 3 Bond Stables, Fetter Lane, across Fleet Street from the Temple. There she learned arithmetic and English composition from Benjamin Starkey, who became the author of *Memoirs of the Life of Benj. Starkey, Late of London, but Now an Inmate of the Freemen's Hospital, in Newcastle* (1818) and the subject of Lamb's "Captain Starkey." After she had completed her studies she began her apprenticeship as a dressmaker. The schooling of Lamb was started by Mary and then for a year or so made the responsibility of Mrs. Elizabeth Reynolds (d. 1832), who was pleased to have known Oliver Goldsmith. She was the daughter of Charles Chambers (d. 1777), who for years had been a clerk to Salt and a librarian of the Temple Society. Thus she almost surely was the Betsy Chambers of Lamb's "Epicedium: Going or Gone."

Mrs. Reynolds remained the family's good friend, and so did her friend Randal Norris (1751–1827). Both kept Lamb and Mary associated with the Temple long after they had left it. Norris, the N. R. of Lamb's "A Death-bed: In a Letter to R. H. Esq. of B——," had come to study at the Inner Temple in 1778. He became its librarian in 1784 and its subtreasurer in 1801. In that year he was married to Mrs. Field's acquaintance Elizabeth Faint (1765?–1843) of Widford in a ceremony that included Mary as a bridesmaid. In 1807 he helped to relieve the straitened circumstances in which the separation of Mrs. Reynolds from her husband had placed her by persuading the Temple Society to grant her an annuity of ten pounds. Lamb also helped her, from his own pocket but much later. When Lamb had completed his studies with her, he followed his sister into the academy in Fetter Lane and received from Bird and a Mr. Cook, who became a player at Drury Lane, instruction as slight as she had received from Starkey.

In The humble Petition (so it is styled) of the *30th. March 1781 John Lamb* of the *Inner Temple, London, Scrivener,* did humbly beseech the Right Honourable, Right Worshipful, and Worshipful the Governors of Christ's-Hospital, London, that their Worships in their usual Pity and Charity to distressed Men, poor Widows, and Fatherless Children *admit one of his* Children, named *Charles Lamb* of the Age of *Seven* Years *and Upwards,* into Christ's-Hospital, there to be Educated and Brought up among other poor Children, for *He* (who shall ever pray, etc.) *has a Wife and three Childn. and finds it difficult to maintain his Family without some Assistce.* Because Salt had already conferred the presentations allotted to him, one of his fellow governors of the school, Timothy Yeats (1713?–1792), a hop and brandy merchant of 2 St. Mary Hill, partner in Yeats and Company, and freeholder in Mortlake, Surrey, presented Lamb in September. Salt signed the bond on May 13, 1782, that guaranteed the institution payment of up to one hundred pounds for any damage the boy might do. The governors admitted him on July 17.

On October 9 he followed what had been his brother's ten- or fifteen-minute walk east on Fleet Street past Johnson and Boswell's Mitre tavern and Fetter Lane, past St. Dunstan's and the wonder of its clock, whose two life-sized wooden savages alternately struck the quarters with their knotty clubs, past Fleet Market and the debtors' prison within whose rules had lived Wycherley and Penn. Lamb walked north on Old Bailey to Newgate Street and the new prison rising from the ruins of the old, from the reign of Charles II to its burning by Lord George Gordon and his mob in the No-Popery Riots of 1780 wet, rotten, diseased, overcrowded, where had sat Penn and Defoe. From there Lamb walked east on Newgate past The Salutation and Cat into the cloisters of the old Gray Friars' monastery become by the benefaction of Edward VI in 1552, the subscription of a generous citizenry, and a charter of 1553 the charity boarding school whose students, above seven hundred and poor boys all, were clothed antiquely in blue caps and gowns, neckbands and knee breeches, and petticoats and stockings of yellow.

Lamb was clothed so on the day he entered. On that same day he witnessed with a sinking heart a first offender of the regulations in fetters. A second offender, Lamb later learned, would be locked in solitary in the dungeons. A third would have his venerable habit replaced with such a hateful cap and jacket as lamplighters wore, be ceremoniously scourged and paraded before his fellows and superiors in the noble dining hall, and then he banished to a relative, friend, or parish officer waiting outside its gate. Lamb was introduced to the daily routine. The boys rose in neat and airy dormitories to a bell at six in the summer and seven in the winter and breakfasted on bread and small beer. They attended classes in spacious rooms until eleven and had an hour's play. On Tuesdays, Thursdays, Fridays, and Sundays they dined on scanty portions of boiled beef or roast mutton. On the other days they dined on meager servings of bread and butter with either milk and water, rice milk, or pease porridge. They played until one, returned to classes until four in the winter and five in the summer, and had bread and a choice of butter or cheese for supper at six. They retired in the winter directly and in the summer at eight. The Bible was read and graces and prayers were said before meals and at bedtime, class time became church time on Sundays, and throughout the week anthems and hymns and services succeeded with monastic regularity. The boys had a vacation for a month in the summer and for approximately a half-month at Christmas and Easter. They had whole-day leaves every other Wednesday and on thirty-nine anniversaries of Christian and national events. They had half-day leaves twice a week.

But Lamb was not confined to the grounds of the school by its vacation and leave schedules, and his diet was not restricted by its kitchen. For day after day came his aunt or his parents' maid bearing her basket of tea and hot rolls and roast veal or lean loin of bacon, and Randal Norris through some now obscure influence made it possible for him to go home almost as often as he wished.

Those advantages were denied to the nine-year-old Coleridge, who in April 1782 had been sent from his mother in Ottery St. Mary to his uncle John Bowdon in London, in July to Christ's Hospital Junior School in Hertford, and in September to the establishment in London and the loneliness he remembered in "Frost at Midnight" and Lamb recalled in "Christ's Hospital Five and Thirty Years Ago." Those advantages were denied also to four others of Lamb's schoolmates who figure in that essay and the early letters. Robert Allen, handsome and cordial, quick of smile and big laugh, was born in 1772 to the Reverend Mr. Timothy Allen and his wife, of Feversham, Kent. In 1792 he proceeded from Christ's Hospital to University College, Oxford, where he earned the B.A. in 1796 and the M.A., M.B., and M.D. in 1803. He was the first friend of Coleridge at Christ's, brought him and Southey together at Oxford in 1794, and participated with them in their abortive scheme to found a pantisocracy that was to have been located at the last on land the theologian and scientist Joseph Priestley (1733–1804) owned on the banks of the Susquehanna northwest of Northumberland, Pennsylvania. In 1796 Allen was enrolled at Westminster Hospital, was married to a widow with children and an income, and lost her to consumption. In 1797 at the urgings of Anthony, later Sir Anthony, Carlisle (1768–1840), a surgeon at Westminster and from 1808 to 1824 additionally a professor of anatomy at the Royal Academy, Allen crossed to Portugal to become a deputy surgeon with England's Second Royals. He was out of the service and in London by 1802, turned to journalism after returning from Oxford in 1803, and according to Lamb's notice in "Newspapers Thirty-five Years Ago" wrote successively for the *Oracle, True Briton, Star,* and *Traveller*. He died of apoplexy in 1805.

Charles Valentine and Samuel Le Grice were the sons of the Reverend Mr. Charles (1742?–1792) and Sophia Anne (d. 1830) Le Grice, of Bury St. Edmunds, Suffolk. Charles Valentine, a wit who possibly inclined Lamb toward punning, was born in 1773. In 1792 he proceeded to Trinity College, Cambridge, where he was graduated B.A. in 1796 and received the M.A. in 1805. Between 1796 and 1799 he left for Cornwall to tutor William John Godolphin Nicholls (1789?–1815), the son of the late John William Nicholls of Trereife, Penzance, and his widow, the former Mary Ustick of Botallack. In 1799 Le Grice was married to her and ordained a deacon at Norwich. He became a priest in 1800, was the curate of Madron, Penzance, from 1806 to 1831, and inherited the Trereife estate upon his wife's death in 1821. He left a number of minor publications in prose and verse at his death in 1858. His brother, Samuel, a madcap who was like a brother to Lamb in the difficult days consequent upon the tragedy of Mary and her mother, was baptized in 1775. He was admitted to Trinity College, Cambridge, in 1794, was matriculated in 1795, but was not graduated. By 1799 he had accepted a commission in the Sixtieth Foot through the favor of Frederick Augustus, Duke of York and Albany (1763–1827). Samuel Le Grice died in 1802 of yellow fever in Jamaica.

Mild Marmaduke Thompson, to whom Lamb first sent "The Old Familiar Faces" and dedicated *A Tale of Rosamund Gray and Old Blind Margaret* (1798), was born in 1776 to Thomas Thompson, a silk merchant, and his wife, of London. In 1796 he passed from Christ's to Pembroke College, Cambridge, where he received the B.A. in 1800 and the M.A. in 1803. He was ordained a deacon and a priest at Norwich in 1800 and was recommended by Charles Simeon (1759–1836), a founder of the Church Missionary Society, to be one of the first five chaplains to the East India Company. Thompson served as a missionary in Cuddalore from 1806 to 1809 and in the Madras presidency from 1815 to 1819. In 1819 his first wife died and he went back to England. He was the rector of Brightwell, Berkshire, from 1831 to his death in 1851.

Those men when Bluecoat boys were among the Grecians, the select scholars, of the grammar division of the institution. Most of the Grecians went, and two or three of them the school customarily each year sent on endowments, to Cambridge or Oxford. They were expected to accept church orders once they had accepted their degrees. The Grecians studied under the direction of the Reverend Mr. James Boyer (1736–1814), the upper-grammar master. He had come to Christ's as a pupil in 1744 and returned in 1767 after having earned his B.A. in 1756 at Balliol College, Oxford. He retired in 1799, with a governorship of the school and a rectorate he had held from it since 1793 at Colne Engaine, Essex.

But Lamb, whom Charles Valentine Le Grice recalled for Lamb's biographer and editor Thomas Noon Talfourd as of amiable ways and gentle manners and perceptive, sensible, and indulged by all, had, perhaps as a condition of a frail constitution and a body once lame and attacked by smallpox, a stutter that unfitted him for a pulpit and thus for the station of Grecian. He was accordingly made a deputy Grecian and studied his English, Latin, Greek, and the classics under the direction of the Reverend Mr. Matthew Feild, or Field (1748?–1796), the lower-grammar master. Feild had come to Christ's as a pupil in about 1757, returned in 1776 after having earned his B.A. in 1772 and his M.A. in 1775 at Pembroke College, Cambridge, and stayed to his death. Yet Lamb, despite what must have been an acute disappointment at knowing he would never follow the Grecians into their universities and prospective bright lives, in 1820 confessed as Elia in his essay on the school that never had he been happier than during the seven years he spent in its classrooms.

His mother formally received him back into her charge on November 23, 1789. That was two years before Jesus College, Cambridge, received Coleridge, who by then was inspired recognizably and whom Lamb saw entrancing even the casual fellow in the cloisters with sweetly intoned recitations from the Greek poets or explications of the Neoplatonists. Through Salt's massive, snuff-breathing associate Thomas Coventry (1712?–1797), of Fleet Street and of North Cray, Kent—he was another of the benchers of the Inner Temple and of the governors of Christ's Hospital, an undergovernor of the South Sea Company, and late a member of Parliament—Lamb obtained employment in the countinghouse at 27 Bread Street Hill of Coventry's friend Joseph Paice (d. 1810). Paice was a merchant and a director of the South Sea Company. Because of his deference toward women, he became Lamb's example for "Modern Gallantry." The details of Lamb's position are not recorded, nor are the reasons Lamb left it and his next. That was a clerkship Paice or Salt secured for him in the examiner's department of the South Sea House, the office for Pacific trade at the junction of Threadneedle and Bishopsgate streets, where worked Lamb's brother and the Italian clerk the original Elia. A salary receipt, however, in the amount of £12 1*s*. 6*d*. for twenty-three weeks indicates Lamb began at the South Sea House on September 1, 1791, made half a guinea a week, and left on February 8, 1792.

It is reasonably certain that later in February or sometime in March he visited his grandmother and became involved in the romance, which Mrs. Field allegedly discouraged because of the insanity in the Lamb family and which ended within the next two years, with the blonde girl Lamb called Alice W——n in "New Year's Eve" and "A Chapter on Ears," Alice in "Dream-children; a Reverie," and Anna in the sonnets of 1795 and 1796. She in all likelihood was Ann Simmons of Blenheims, a hamlet near Blakesware. She became the wife of a London pawnbroker and silversmith named Bartram, or Bartrum, of Prince's Street near Leicester Square. She also became the widow with three daughters of Fitzroy Street who was known to Randal Norris' elder daughter, Jane, afterward Mrs. Arthur Tween of Widford.

Paice or Salt recommended him to his next and final employer. On April 5, 1792, the court of directors of the East India House approved his petition for appointment. Lamb, his father or brother, and Coventry and Salt's benevolent Inner Temple colleague Peter Peirson (d. 1808) would on the twenty-seventh sign the required security bond for five hundred pounds. On about the fifth Lamb walked down Fleet Street from the Temple, around St. Paul's, down Cheapside, and down Cornhill one block beyond Bishopsgate to the porticoed building stretching westward toward him on Leadenhall from Lime. He ascended its stairs to enter and take his seat before a high desk first in a row of five or six high desks on a little aisle behind a railing in one of the compartmented interiors. He commenced to drive a quill across ledgers in reckoning of the Oriental wealth freighted into East India Company warehouses from the holds of the great far-sailing East Indiamen and parceled out through auction in the East India House salesroom. Excepting overtime pay and a holiday allowance of ten pounds, he would annually earn, for example, a gratuity of £30 for his probationary first three years, a salary of £40 in 1795 and £90 in 1799, and a salary plus a gratuity totaling £120 in 1800, £480 in 1815, and £730 by the time of his retirement. On March 29, 1825, the court of directors would approve his request for retirement and authorize a pension of £450 less the deduction, nine pounds then, accumulating for Mary in an employees' survivors' fund since its establishment in April 1816.

On that same March day he would descend the stairs a last time from work and go, his small figure diminished in late years by his wonted black dress, a superannuated man after thirty-three years a clerk in the accountant general's department of the East India House.

By 1794, but conjecturally at about the time of the sale in 1793 of Salt's real estate in Crown Office Row, the family had moved a few blocks northwest of the Temple and just northeast of Drury Lane and Covent Garden theaters to 7 Little Queen Street, Holborn, where it shared a house with a Mr. and Mrs. Weight until they moved to Manchester in 1794. Notwithstanding the declining health and reduced income of the parents, the family was managing on Salt's bequest, Mr. Lamb's wages from Inner Temple Hall, and financial support from Sarah Lamb and the children. Lamb had resumed attending the theater since leaving Christ's Hospital and the prohibition of the school against it. From December 1794 into January 1795 he was spending some of his evenings in The Salutation and Cat deepening his friendship with Coleridge.

Coleridge had fallen in love with Mary Evans of London while he was still in the Bluecoat school, enlisted in and been rescued out of the Fifteenth Light Dragoons while in his second year at Cambridge, become hastily engaged to Sara Fricker (1770–1845) of Bristol, and left his college a final time. He was in town contributing the "Sonnets on Eminent Characters" to the *Morning Chronicle* and regretting his loss of Miss Evans to a betrothal or an understanding that led to her marriage to one Fryer Todd in October 1795. Coleridge was delaying his own marriage to Miss Fricker. Southey, who in the summer of 1794 had quit Balliol College, Oxford, and had become engaged and on February 14, 1795, would secretly be married to Sara Fricker's sister Edith (1774–1839), came to town in January 1795 to conduct Coleridge back to Bristol.

Southey then met Lamb and in February 1836 wrote the publisher Edward Moxon that during the winter of 1794–1795 Lamb was much in the company of James White, Lamb and Coleridge's late schoolfellow whom Lamb would celebrate in "The Praise of Chimney-sweepers" for White's yearly Smithfield suppers for sweeps. White was born in 1775 in Bewdley, Worcestershire, had been a student at Christ's from 1783 to 1790, and had become a clerk in its treasurer's office. He remained through at least February 1808 while founding in

1800 in Warwick Square the advertising agency that continues today at 72–78 Fleet Street as R. F. White and Sons, Ltd. He was married to Margaret Faulder, the daughter of a Bond Street bookseller. White died in 1820.

Sometimes Lamb joined White in his rooms to survey the development of *Original Letters, &c. of Sir John Falstaff and His Friends; Now First Made Public by a Gentleman, a Descendant of Dame Quickly, from Genuine Manuscripts Which Have Been in the Possession of the Quickly Family near Four Hundred Years,* a comic gloss of Shakespeare published in 1796 and with all the credit to White. Lamb, though, may have taken more than an incidental part in its composition, particularly of its "Dedicatyone, to Master Samuel Irelaunde," the forger of Shakespeare manuscripts William Henry Ireland (1775–1835) disguised as occasionally he disguised himself behind the name of his father.

Sometimes Lamb accompanied White to The Three Feathers, in Hand Court, to sip Burton's ale with John Mathew Gutch. Gutch was late of Christ's too and would later rent lodgings to Lamb and Mary. By printing, probably on his own presses, the selection of Wither's poems that he sent to Lamb in 1810 and expanded and issued in 1820, he prompted Lamb to write "On the Poetical Works of George Wither." Gutch was born in 1776, the eldest of the five sons and several daughters of the divine and antiquary John Gutch (1746–1831), of Oxford, and the former Elizabeth Weller. He began business life as a law stationer with a man named Anderson in Southampton Buildings, Chancery Lane, Holborn. Gutch moved to Bristol in 1803 and purchased *Felix Farley's Bristol Journal,* which he managed until 1844 and retained some interest in thereafter. Between 1800 and 1809 he was married to Mary Wheeley, a Birmingham coachmaker's daughter. From about 1810 to 1812 he conducted a second-hand bookselling concern. In 1823, having lost or been divorced from his first wife, he was married again, this time to the daughter of a Worcester banker named Lavender. Afterward Gutch started with one Alexander the London *Morning Journal.* The venture cost Gutch his savings and ended in 1829 with the suppression of the paper and convictions against the partners for libeling George IV and Lord Chancellor John Singleton Copley, Baron Lyndhurst (1772–1863). Gutch was released on his own recognizance, entered his father-in-law's bank, and following its failure in 1848 limited his activities mainly to a fellowship in the Society of Antiquaries, the Bristol newspaper, and the editing of ballads and songs about Robin Hood and of four discourses by the Oxford scholar and divine George Watson (1723?–1773). Gutch died at his home, Barbourne, near Worcester, in 1861.

II

At other times during the period 1794–1795 Lamb began to write the sonnets that would appear in the *Monthly Magazine* for 1796 and in Coleridge's *Poems on Various Subjects* (1796), *Sonnets from Various Authors* (1796), and *Poems. To Which Are Now Added Poems by Charles Lamb, and Charles Lloyd* (1797). The greater part of December 1795 and January 1796 he passed pleasantly in perhaps Baumes House, Hoxton, during his single stroke of madness. On May 27, 1796, he wrote in answer to Coleridge, who had been married to Sara Fricker on the previous October 4 and set up housekeeping in a cottage near the Bristol Channel at Clevedon, issued and guided *The Watchman* through its ten numbers from March 1 to May 13, 1796, and since late March lived in Oxford Street, Kingsdown, Bristol. Lamb included in his letter, his earliest to survive, the lines to Mary he composed in confinement. They are in atonement for some impatience and adumbrate the relationship between Lamb and Mary that from her awful act of September 22, 1796, grew to govern their lives. The relationship, whose graces and claims expressed became consequential parts of their letters, was nurtured for two and one-half years across the paths harrowed by the frenzied force that had quickened it. The relationship was nurtured then and thenceforth by the humanity and purpose especially of Lamb, who became necessarily its principal.

Lamb had entered the dining room in the trail of the fury and the midst of its wreckage. The landlord and the apprentice dressmaker were apparently moving in horror and terror, his aunt seemed to be senseless in shock on the floor, his father was in tears and bleeding from his forehead, and his mother's pierced body was caught in the chair facing the swaying form of Mary. He snatched the knife from her hand. She was led to a private asylum in Islington, where over the next eleven days a doctor, a druggist, and nurses reclaimed her from the power that possessed her. Although she grieved at the memory of what she had done and feared John would commit her to Bedlam, her judgment discriminated between lunacy and matricide to bless her with some repose. For only two moments during those days did tranquillity abandon Lamb. His sympathies and strength in the main held firm and directed him, forever he thought, from poetry and the past to the awesome responsibilities before him. He would lose his aunt to her wealthy cousin but gain, he believed, assurance of her comfort. He would leave his brother to his accustomed ease beyond the darkened household. He would economize to keep his father, himself, and their ancient maid together. He would keep Mary, for as long as he had the legal right to decide where she should be kept, under care outside a public hospital.

Although he had enjoined Coleridge not to come, Lamb pressed him for spiritual counsel and news of his family and plans. Lamb responded to Coleridge's answers with earnest arguments and a solicitude to become characteristic, with gradually renewed discussions of literature that soon involved poems of his own, and with continuing accounts of himself and those closest to him. He worked late and came home some evenings to broken suppers and weary cards with his father, who was so far sunk into senility that Samuel Le Grice had had to play cards with him even during the coroner's inquest over the corpse of Mrs. Lamb. Lamb was distressed when the relative who had appeared gracious in September summoned him in December to take back his aunt. Although she was one more worry for him during the two months more she wasted away, he was touched by the memories she stirred and her words while drifting away about being glad to be with him to die. Possibly he was given release from remorse by writing the poem on the day of her funeral.

He wrote "Sonnet to a Friend" and dedicated his portion of Coleridge's *Poems* (1797) to Mary, conducted a correspondence and almost daily conversed with her too, brought her books and Coleridge's letters, and remarked her sweet intercourse with her inmates and caretakers and her steady improvement after the scarlet fever she had contracted in January 1797. By his solemn promise to watch over her for life (the phrase is essentially Talfourd's) he persuaded the parish authorities to make her his ward. He decided to bring her out of the asylum. But he would not bring her home while their father lived, because of the pain the presence of each would inevitably arouse in the other. Shortly before or early in April he established her in a room in Hackney and began to go to her there whenever he was free.

In July 1797 he allayed the sense of isolation intensifying within him from prolonged devotion to his family by getting away for a week to the Coleridges, who were then at Nether Stowey and introduced him to the Wordsworths and others. It seems that he returned to 7 Little Queen Street only to leave it and its sad associations a last time for 45 Chapel Street, Pentonville. In August he went with Charles Lloyd for two days with the Southeys at Burton. In September and October he wrote of how changed he was by the recent past and of his mother and sister in "Written a Year after the Events" and "Written Soon after the Preceding Poem."

The radiant Christian season dawned but did not shed its light on Mary. On the eve of its advent she fell into deep darkness and had again to be led to Islington. The bleakness of the season for Lamb, resigned in near despondency as though widowed and desolate, is plain in "Written on Christmas Day, 1797" and "The Old Familiar Faces." He appreciated but declined the invitation of Coleridge to take Mary into his house and recognized the good intentions but resented the attempts of Lloyd to draw him too much from himself and his rounds. Yet he relented to proceed with Lloyd on their collection of poems called *Blank Verse* (1798) and interest him in the progress and publication of *Rosamund Gray*. Lamb spent two weeks with Lloyd and his family in Birmingham when Mary improved late in the spring of 1798, was misguided by him into alienation from Coleridge, and suspended his correspondence with Coleridge with a series of taunting questions for him to debate in the universities of Germany. In the summer and fall Lamb turned to Southey and Robert Lloyd, began *John Woodvil: A Tragedy. To Which Are Added, Fragments of Burton, the Author of the Anatomy of Melancholy* (1802), and saw Mary through two setbacks. Over the fall and winter she regained her health. In April 1799, after their father's death, Lamb was able to have her rejoin him. It was probably then that they moved into the house at 36 Chapel Street, Pentonville.

For a year their lives went smoothly. They met the mathematician and Chinese scholar Thomas Manning and William Godwin and healed the quarrel with Coleridge after he had arrived from Germany in July 1799. They welcomed him as their guest for five weeks in March and early April 1800, and they humored the authoresses who persisted in calling after he had departed to visit the Wordsworths at Grasmere and resettle with his family, first at Nether Stowey and then at Keswick. Lamb delivered "Pride's Cure," as he still called *John Woodvil,* to the home of John Philip Kemble, the actor and a manager of Drury Lane. Lamb composed at Coleridge's instigation the "Curious Fragments" supposedly from Robert Burton's commonplace book, and he contributed Thekla's song, or "Ballad from the German," to Coleridge's translations from Schiller's *Wallenstein* trilogy. Besides reading the proofs of those translations he read history while scorning, as he usually would, the history being made all around him.

In May 1800 their maid became ill and died. Mary in consequence of having anxiously waited on her for eight days relapsed. Lamb, realizing that such a dreadful concatenation of events could at any time be repeated, was left fearfully alone and depressed. He wrote Coleridge on May 12 that he almost wished Mary were dead. He wrote Manning on the seventeenth that he was reeling without her support. He tried off and on to endure the gloomy house in a neighborhood in which he now felt ostracized, but had given it up by the latter date and moved in with White. By the twentieth, it seems, he was with Gutch at 27 Southampton Buildings and with rising spirits had accepted his offer, to which Gutch's partner shortly agreed, to rent three rooms they would have to spare in midsummer and share the use of their servant. Mary, he prayed, would then be able to return to him. Over Whitsuntide he withdrew into Hertfordshire, more heavy of heart than ever. He found her miraculously well when he got back and, on June 15, took her into a home he had again prepared for them, this time within the privacy of the crowds of the city.

They stayed at Southampton Buildings until late March 1801. While there Lamb with a heart once more light sent forth in letters his jokes on Gutch and Manning. Lamb sent forth his earliest descriptions of the trials of the eccentric and author George Dyer and initial impression of the statistician John Rickman, the anecdote of an encounter with exhibitory snakes, and those first rhapsodies on London. Lamb wrote of the writer on agriculture and economics Dr. James Anderson, of the failure and its aftermath of Godwin's tragedy "Antonio," of Kemble's rejection of *John Woodvil,* of the second edition of Wordsworth and

Coleridge's *Lyrical Ballads.* Mary, with a heart perhaps equally as light, formed her raillery of him, called "Helen," sometimes called "Helen Repentant Too Late." On March 25, having sold an extra bed to cover the expenses, they moved back into the Inner Temple, into an airy fourth-floor apartment in 16 Mitre Court Buildings, where they lived for eight years.

Lamb, who had written the Epilogue to "Antonio," continued trying to help Godwin, especially in his endeavor to write for the stage. Lamb and Mary went on a holiday to Margate in September, nursed Dyer through a crisis, and marveled at the antics of Godwin that led to his marriage on December 21, 1801, to Mary Jane Clairmont. By then Lamb had rushed John Fenwick's *Albion* to its death by having had printed in that newspaper his offensive epigram on the philosopher James Mackintosh, had written briefly for the *Morning Chronicle,* and had started to contribute to the *Morning Post.* In February 1802, when the energy he spent and the frustration he was caused exceeded the value of the money he received, he stopped for slightly more than the eighteen months the paper remained in Daniel Stuart's hands. He and Mary gave themselves more freely to the parties and card games they were holding or attending, by then up to four times a week. In August they left for a month in the Lake District, whose scenery impressed even Lamb. By early 1803 they had expanded their circle of acquaintances to include the tutor and miscellaneous writer George Burnett, the retired naval captain James Burney, the philanthropist and abolitionist Thomas Clarkson and his wife, Catherine, the dramatist Thomas Holcroft, the journalist and judge John Stoddart and his sister, Sarah. To her Mary, on July 21, 1802, had written her first letter that is extant.

That good life was interrupted in the spring of 1803. Coleridge, who was visiting the Lambs, wrote his wife that Mary smiled ominously on March 25, the day after she had happened to meet a former admirer of her mother at Rickman's. On the twenty-seventh she confessed to Lamb with agony that she was falling ill. In the morning of the twenty-ninth she seized Coleridge to rave of Dyer. Coleridge alerted Lamb, ran for a coach, and escorted her to an asylum in Hoxton. She was calm behind bitter tears, for she knew, admitted, the propriety of his action. But "Charles," Coleridge concluded, was "cut to the Heart." Rickman wrote Southey that in the afternoon Lamb came in abruptly on him, sat down and cried, then fairly recovered toward evening and stayed overnight and through dinner the next day. Lamb began his letter to Coleridge of April 13, one humorous because of the comments on a montero cap and pipes and port, with the announcement that he and Mary were improving and that he expected her return within two weeks. He ended his next, to Coleridge of May 20, one largely explanatory of the arrangement of the contents of what became Coleridge's *Poems* (1803), with a postscript that reads, "Mary sends love from home."

Her illness left her weak and dejected into July. Lamb comforted her and until then kept her from company. Early in that same month he took her to the theater with Southey, Rickman, and Rickman's sister, Mary. Two weeks later Lamb took Mary on vacation to the Isle of Wight with James and Sarah Burney and their son, Martin Charles, and to Portsmouth to see Fenwick before he turned himself over to the authorities in London for indebtedness. In September Mary reported to Sarah Stoddart that Lamb was unwell. In November he owned he was and showed himself so by his inability to review the first two volumes of Godwin's life of Chaucer and his attendant irritability toward the Godwins on the subject of the arrested review.

By mid-March 1804 Lamb had severed his connection, re-established the previous fall, with the *Morning Post.* Although poorer, he and Mary were happier free of a commitment that had become another annoyance. They saw a little of Coleridge before he sailed in April for Malta to join Stoddart and his bride, the former Isabella Moncreiff, and his sister. Lamb sent Dorothy Wordsworth two new poems by Mary in June. At about the same time, Mary instructed Sarah Stoddart in the ways of men and women by explaining a foolish act of Lamb and her quiet management of him. In the summer came a month at Richmond, from where they toured up and down the Thames. In the autumn they passed many hours with John and Mary Hazlitt in Great Russell Street while William Hazlitt, whom the Lambs had met in March 1803, painted his portrait of Lamb. Lamb served the Wordsworths in the late winter and early spring of 1805 by involving himself in the investigations of the sinking of the East Indiaman *Earl of Abergavenny.* John Wordsworth, their brother and its captain, was among the hundreds who were lost. Mary held back her expression of sympathy and her sonnet in which she wished Coleridge home to soothe the anguished Wordsworths until May 7 for fear of intruding on their sorrow. On June 3 her grief overwhelmed her. Lamb had her confined and sought again seclusion in the country.

On June 14, 1805, he answered a letter Dorothy Wordsworth had written to Mary and disclosed his compassion and wretchedness. Presumably near the end of July he notified Manning of Mary's convalescence and signified his improved state by the tone of his letter and by his work on "A Farewell to Tobacco." On September 18 Mary wrote from home of her own improved state to Sarah Stoddart, who was lately back from Malta to care for her mother. Mary confirmed her expressions of better health by telling of her inquiries at the admiralty office concerning the elder Mrs. John Stoddart's pension. Yet even after outings to Egham and the vicinity of Harrow, Lamb and Mary continued to be nervous and unlike their former selves. Lamb felt tortured at his office and could not get to work on a farce he wanted to write. Mary was dissatisfied with whatever she did and could not escape the haunting thought that she might be insane. They struggled to console each other and were helped by Manning's arrival in town in November and Miss Stoddart's visit in January and February 1806.

On January 7, 1806, Lamb wrote Hazlitt incomparably of the stir for Lord Nelson's funeral. On February 1 Lamb sent William and Mary Wordsworth's son John *The King and Queen of Hearts: With the Rogueries of the Knave, Who Stole Away the Queen's Pies* (1806), which Lamb had recently written. It was the first of several similar books he and Mary would write for the Godwins' Juvenile Library. By February 19 he had taken the room in which he escaped in the evening from callers to write "Mr. H——: A Farce in Two Acts." Two days later Mary carried the manuscript to Richard Wroughton, an actor and a manager of Drury Lane. On June 26 Lamb informed Wordsworth of its acceptance in a letter that reveals his excitement and contains his design for the ticket of admission.

In May Lamb had seen Manning off for Portsmouth and Canton, was presently to spend his vacation at home with Mary in order to complete their *Tales from Shakespear. Designed for the Use of Young Persons* (1807), and in August greeted Coleridge, broken in health but at least returned from Malta and his wanderings about Italy. They took him in for about ten days, tried to reunite him with his family, and continued to look forward to the performance of "Mr. H——."

They counted on its success despite Lamb's misgivings, yet accommodated themselves to their disappointments when, with Hazlitt and the diarist Henry Crabb Robinson, in the evening of December 10 they saw and heard it hissed and shouted almost off the stage. Lamb joined in the hissing and the next day insisted on sparing Mary the difficulty of reporting the failure to Wordsworth and Sarah Stoddart. He wrote Miss Stoddart that because a "smoking man must write smoky farces" and because he was swearing off tobacco, he and Mary must thrive.

Apparently they did for six months. He proceeded with his research for *Specimens of English Dramatic Poets, Who Lived about the Time of Shakspeare: With Notes* (1808) and she proceeded presumably with *Mrs. Leicester's School.* Her malady overtook her while they were the guests of the Clarksons at Bury St. Edmunds in June 1807. Mary was submissive when Lamb hurried her away, but she became so violent at Chelmsford that he had to obtain assistance. He bound her arms with a borrowed waistcoat in order to resume their journey, and in the hours borne before they reached the Hoxton asylum he listened through his exhaustion as she declined through hers into the misery of a manic-depressive. It was late July at the earliest before he was permitted so much as to see her. But probably by the close of the summer she was participating in the activities of those evenings when Lamb had their friends in for cribbage or whist. She became caught up in the wedding plans of Hazlitt and Sarah Stoddart and on May Day 1808 was a bridesmaid at the wedding. Lamb perpetrated an elaborate hoax on Hazlitt, founded on his dying to bachelorhood, and was nearly expelled from the wedding ceremony because of the laughter its solemnity caused him.

Before the end of 1808 Lamb and Mary saw the publication of his *The Adventures of Ulysses* and *Specimens of English Dramatic Poets* and their *Mrs. Leicester's School.* Near the beginning of 1809 they began their *Poetry for Children, Entirely Original* (1809). Before the end of March 1809 they vacated 16 Mitre Court Buildings at the request of the landlord, who wanted their apartment for himself. They put up in Hazlitt's former lodgings at 34 Southampton Buildings until June 3. Then, with a maid and new curtains and chairs, they moved into the seven rooms on the third and fourth floors of 4 Inner Temple Lane that were to become their home for the next eight years.

Mary could not sleep right in the new place, and Lamb could not get comfortable. On June 5 she fell ill under the burden of novelty and fatigue. After seeing her into the asylum, he was helpless to prevent his feeling of dislocation from deteriorating into desolateness. Two days later he as of old wrote Coleridge to write to him. On June 13, in the first of several thoughtful letters to the senior Charles Lloyd on his translations from Homer and Horace, Lamb desired the news to be conveyed to Robert Lloyd that Mary was getting well. Although she came home in mid-July, she did not regain strength till October. It gathered in her during that month, when she and her brother, with his cards partner Edward Phillips and Martin Burney, paid the visit that had been postponed since her illness recurred to the Hazlitts at Winterslow and from there walked abroad in golden weather to spots prehistoric and medieval in Wiltshire. The experience, whose afterglow was enhanced by Lamb's unexpected increase in income and Mary's encouraging their apartment into a home, carried them through the remainder of 1809 and back to Winterslow in July 1810. But tiring coach journeys and a stay of two to three weeks in an area then depressed by a bank failure upset him and ended in confinement early in August for her.

Too soon after she was discharged late in September 1810, a visit from Dorothy Wordsworth, callers, and problems with maids imperiled her recovery. Lamb placed her and to some extent himself under the care of Dr. George Leman Tuthill and for a time kept her largely sequestered. Lamb and Tuthill had no sooner restored her to where she was well enough to venture out than an excess of the exciting and worrisome Coleridge and her hearing suddenly in his presence, in the evening of March 6, 1811, of George Burnett's death in a workhouse brought her gradually to surrender to her disorder. On the eighth her distressing manner of conversation moved Godwin to speak of it two days later to Coleridge. On the fourteenth Coleridge informed the miniaturist and author Mary Matilda Betham of Godwin's report and the subsequent one by Coleridge and Southey's businessman friend John James Morgan, that early in the morning of March 9 Lamb had had to take Mary to an asylum in the country. On May 11 Robinson noted in his diary his gratification at finding her home when on that day he dropped in on Lamb. (Edith J. Morley's edition of Robinson's diary—*Henry Crabb Robinson on Books and Their Writers* [1938]—is the edition referred to or quoted from throughout this Introduction.)

Robinson's entries for February 26 and May 9, 1812, and for June 11 and October 15, 1813, established the approximate periods of her next two illnesses. The entry for February 5, 1812, when she called Robinson's attention to William Gifford's brutal characterizations in the *Quarterly Review* of Lamb's praises of John Ford in *Specimens of English Dramatic Poets* as the "blasphemies of a poor maniac" and of Lamb as an "unfortunate creature [for whom] every feeling mind will find an apology in his calamitous situation," may indicate a cause of the earlier illness. Neither illness is mentioned in the few extant letters of those years. During that period Lamb wrote the Prologue to Coleridge's *Remorse. A Tragedy, in Five Acts* (1813), "Recollections of Christ's Hospital" for the *Gentleman's Magazine,* and "Confessions of a Drunkard" for *The Philanthropist.* He was ending the series of essays he had begun in the latter half of 1811 for *The Reflector* of John and Leigh Hunt and, after its failure, beginning his association with their *Examiner.*

In the spring of 1814 he wrote the Epilogue to James Kenney's *Debtor and Creditor: A Comedy, in Five Acts* (1814). For a few days in late summer he took Mary to Harrow and strolling alongside the Thames. In October, as a favor to Wordsworth and Southey, he devoted three weeks of his vacation to composing a review of Wordsworth's *Excursion* that Gifford mutilated before he published it in the *Quarterly.* On December 12, only eight days after the appearance of "On the Melancholy of Tailors" in *The Champion,* Lamb went back on his recent agreement with its editor, John Scott, occasionally to send him an essay for it. The "very particular circumstances" (the language is from the letter to Scott) that prevented Lamb from proceeding were almost certainly connected with Mary. For on December 11 Robinson had learned of and remarked in his diary on her fatigue from writing "On Needle-work" for the *New British Lady's Magazine.* About a week later he learned of her having been confined. On December 28 Lamb ended a letter to Wordsworth with "Mary keeps very bad." From January 23 through February 8, 1815, Robinson repeatedly recorded in his diary that Lamb was in poor spirits and harassed by the duties of his office. On February 19 Robinson dined out with them both and observed that Mary was not alarmingly thin and pale and that Lamb was most agreeable.

The Lambs enjoyed the company of William and Mary Wordsworth and her sister Sara Hutchinson in London from early May well into June 1815. The Lambs made the most of Whitsuntide in mid-May by going off with the lawyer and miscellaneous writer Barron Field to see the house and gardens at Luton Hoo of John Stuart, third Earl of Bute, the Norman cathedral and Francis Bacon's estates in St. Albans, and the farm in Mackery End and their relatives nearby. It was the excursion and visit that, with the pleasure he felt then, Lamb recollected in 1821 in "Mackery End, in Hertfordshire." In addition he and Mary took advantage of the Saturday in mid-August reserved as the feast day of the East India House clerks by using it and the Sunday and Monday following to tour Cambridge, to the especial delight of Mary. She was in fine health and wrote enthusiastically of the adventures to friends. But on September 13 she crumbled.

The violence and unexpectedness of this attack bewildered Lamb and shook his health. He thought of going into rooms, of quitting the East India House, and of his complaints about his work there as a cause of her collapse. But he remained and in his time at home did what he could to see Mary Matilda Betham's *Lay of Marie* through the press. His weeks of long days and nights without Mary had ended by November 20, when Robinson heard she was back. That evening Robinson called and engaged her, her brother John, and Martin Burney in whist. Lamb was cheerful doubtlessly then. He was so buoyant at Christmas that he wrote Manning of Mary's death and other wild fictions and did not expose them until the next day. In his letter of April 26, 1816, which with that of the ninth tells of Coleridge having come to town from Calne with John Morgan and found a haven with Dr. James Gillman and his family at Highgate, Lamb wrote Wordsworth that even the East India House had become less oppressive to him than it had been.

The year 1816 was the first since 1808 in which Mary was free from illness. For almost a third of it she and Lamb lived out of the city. They vacationed for a month during June and July at John and Mary Morgan's in Calne, seeing Marlborough, Chippenham, Bristol, and Bath. Then they went into lodgings that Mary and Charlotte Brent, Mrs. Morgan's sister, had found in the London suburb of Dalston (at 14 Kingsland Row if the lodgings were those whose address Mary gave in a letter of 1821 to Marianne Ayrton, the wife of the music critic and impresario William Ayrton). Lamb and Mary went into them as a trial measure to counter the ennui Lamb particularly had experienced after coming back into the Temple. They re-entered the Temple after ten weeks, refreshed from waking and roaming among rural scenes and keeping the hours Lamb was away from his office quietly to themselves. "I do think I could live in the country entirely, at least I thought so while I was there," Mary wrote Sara Hutchinson in November, "but since I have been at home I wish to live and die in the Temple where I was born."

They lived there one more year. For about a month of it, from perhaps April 27 to May 24, 1817, according to unpublished and published entries in Robinson's diary (the earlier date is cited in Ernest C. Ross's *The Ordeal of Bridget Elia: A Chronicle of the Lambs* [Norman: University of Oklahoma Press, 1940], p. 127), Mary was in an asylum. For probably another month, during the summer, the Lambs and Mrs. Morgan were at Brighton. On November 21 Lamb and Mary explained to Dorothy Wordsworth that because their apartment had become dirty and was out of repair and because living in chambers had become inconvenient, they had uprooted themselves from their native ground and were at ease over a brazier's shop at 20 Russell Street, Covent Garden, Lamb's favorite section of town. Next door above the corner of Number 21 and Bow Street was once Will's Coffee-house, in its great day the court of Dryden and a sometime resort of Pope. Next door on the ground floor of Number 19 or below them at Number 20 was once Barker's bookshop, where Lamb, as he remembered in 1823 in "Old China," had after ten o'clock on a Saturday night during hard times made the purchase of a folio Beaumont and Fletcher that required him to wear his brown suit threadbare in consequence. Rear windows looked out on Covent Garden Theatre, and front ones on Drury Lane. Around below streamed life's parade, fascinating to Mary and fulfilling them both by its sounds.

There Lamb acted finally on a thought that had been with him since at least September 1816 by collecting those of his and Mary's writings that Charles and James Ollier would publish as *The Works of Charles Lamb* in June 1818. On June 18, 1818, he wrote the Olliers, naming a few friends to whom he wanted gift copies sent. Then he was off to Birmingham for a month with the Lloyds. His way of expressing himself in his letters before and after the trip suggests that Mary did not accompany him. Marianne Hunt's mention of an illness to Mary Shelley on July 14 suggests why. On August 4 Leigh Hunt in his portion of that letter reported that Mary was improving. (The Hunts' letter is in *Shelley and His Circle,* VI, especially 608 and 612.) On October 26 Lamb in his letter to Southey indicated that she was home. Her disorder did not afflict her again until late in the summer of 1820.

To her and Lamb in the period intervening came occasions for writing letters that are among their best. In 1819 are Lamb's to Gutch on the acting of Frances Kelly, to Wordsworth in lines and words alternately in black and red ink concerning Wordsworth's *Peter Bell, a Tale in Verse* and John Hamilton Reynolds' *Peter Bell, a Lyrical Ballad,* to Manning on the East India House clerk Thomas Bye and his reduction in salary for coming in drunk one morning, to Wordsworth on his *The Waggoner* and the downfall of Bye, to Miss Kelly in July proposing marriage and acknowledging her refusal, to Henry Dodwell or John Chambers at the East India House on the giantess Lamb and Mary encountered in August in Cambridge, to Dorothy Wordsworth on the Wordsworths' son William following the day he spent in November with the Lambs. In 1820 is Lamb's letter to Coleridge in red ink regarding Charles Lloyd. In 1820 are Mary's letters from suburban Stoke Newington in March to Miss Kelly on studying Latin and French and to Mary Sabilla Novello, the wife of the organist and composer Vincent Novello, on living out of town in the spring. Lamb's of May through August 1820 show the Lambs shifting between Russell Street and Dalston, show them in Cambridge from mid-July to mid-August, and awaiting the *London Magazine* of August for the essay on the South Sea House, the first essay signed "Elia." Lamb's letters of September 1 and 2 tell of Mary having just fallen ill. Robinson's diary for November 4 tells that by then she had recovered and gives the opinion that she had done so in less time than usual because she had been kept in the Dalston lodgings rather than in an asylum.

Except for about a week in mid-November for welcoming William, Mary, and Dorothy Wordsworth back from the Continent, Lamb and Mary did not return to their Russell Street residence until shortly after Christmas. With them for most of January 1821 was twelve-year-old Emma Isola, the orphan they had probably met in Cambridge the summer before and informally came to adopt. She was now on vacation from school and had come to visit them from Cambridge, where she lived with her aunt Miss Humphreys. In March the Lambs began shifting again between Russell Street and Dalston. In late May they left Russell Street for a month's holiday in Margate. Near the end of September they became tied to Dalston by the breakdown of Mary, apparently because of the decline of their brother. Lamb informed her of John's death, which occurred on October 26, when she could be only vaguely sensitive to it. He thereby permitted her to comprehend by degrees what could shock her into a relapse if concealed till she regained her reason. She recovered just prior to November 18, Robinson noted then in his diary, and two days later Lamb notified Rickman of their having removed to town.

What Lamb complained of to Wordsworth on March 20, 1822, as "a certain deadness to every thing" that dated from about the time of their loss, moved them during the winter almost to bury themselves back in Dalston and in the spring to decide on a trip to France. They embarked in the morning of June 18, with a French guide and Sarah James, Mary's nurse. Precisely fourteen months later Mrs. Shelley wrote Leigh Hunt from Paris of the story James Kenney and his wife, the former Louisa Holcroft, told her, that at Amiens Mary "was taken ill in her usual way, and Lamb was in despair, he met however with some acquaintances, who got Miss L. into proper hands & L. came on to Versailles and staid with the Kenny's, going on very well, if the French wine had not been too good for him" (Frederick L. Jones, editor, *The Letters of Mary W. Shelley* [Norman: University of Oklahoma Press, 1944], I, 254–255). Lamb went to Paris with Kenney's fellow dramatist John Howard Payne and, assured of the care and recovery of Mary, returned to London in mid-August to work. Mary went on to Versailles with Miss James, saw Paris with Mrs. Kenney and Robinson and Payne, and in the evening of September 6 rejoined her brother at home. Their only other outing of the year was to Richmond for a few days at its end.

Lamb by then had seen to the revisions for *Elia. Essays Which Have Appeared under That Signature in the London Magazine*. John Taylor and James Augustus Hessey published it in January 1823. Since the appearance of his *Works* (1818) Lamb had continued to write for various periodicals—*The Champion,* for example, *The Examiner, The Indicator,* the *Morning Chronicle,* the *New Times.* After 1823 he would write for others—*The Athenaeum,* for example, *Blackwood's*

Magazine, the *Englishman's Magazine,* the *New Monthly Magazine, The Reflector, The Spectator, The Times.* But by those writings republished in 1823 from the *London* and in 1833 from the *London* primarily, he became most widely known.

On February 16, 1823, Robinson recorded that Mary was resting from an attack, provoked it seems by a toothache, that had lasted at most for two days. She and Lamb shortly had the company of Mrs. Coleridge and her daughter, Sara. Lamb on April 4 had a dinner with Coleridge, Gillman, Robinson, the poets Thomas Moore and Samuel Rogers, Sara Hutchinson, and William and Mary Wordsworth at the Gloucester Place residence of Mrs. Wordsworth's cousin Thomas Monkhouse and his wife, Jane. In about a week the Wordsworths left for Belgium and Holland and the Lambs migrated to Dalston. From there, on April 25, Lamb wrote to Miss Hutchinson the letter that is graphically descriptive of Mary's poor penmanship. On June 6 the Lambs and Sarah James went away for nine days near Tunbridge Wells and for the rest of their month at Hastings. Before they went Lamb merrily left at his office his "Rules and directions to be observed by Mr Chambers at the end of June 1823 (applicable to any month when I am absent) concerning deposits, voucher, Error Ledger, and other circumstances of Mr Lamb's department of the Journal system; to obviate the inconvenience of my absence." After they returned Lamb found that their homes and the town seemed alien.

On July 24 he wrote John and Mary Hazlitt's daughter Mary of his sister busy about moving into a white cottage with six rooms and a garden behind on Colebrook Row beside the New River in Islington. Although the affair was easy, it caused her to fall ill: "Tell your Mother," Randal Norris wrote his daughters, Elizabeth and Jane, on August 6 (in a letter in E. V. Lucas' *At the Shrine of St. Charles: Stray Papers on Lamb Brought Together for the Centenary of His Death in 1834* [London: Methuen, 1934], p. 19), "that the Lambs have taken a House in Colebrook Row, Islington, have left Russell Street and will leave Dalston very soon where Mary is and Miss James. She has been ill but is recovering. Mr. Lamb thinks it was occasioned by [merely] thinking of the removal, for she had no trouble in it." Lamb was settled in Colebrook Cottage by September 6, Mary joined him on the eighth, and they were receiving their friends before long. Mary received Dyer in November. He stopped in one bright afternoon on his way to dine with the author Anna Letitia Barbauld. He walked out, forgetting to put his spectacles on, directly into the New River.

Strength returned slowly to Mary. A cold suspended Lamb for weeks in lethargy and stirred him to describe it greatly to the poet Bernard Barton on January 9, 1824. In mid-April the Lambs declined to go with the stockbroker and writer Thomas Allsop and his wife to Reigate for want of time and because of the presence of Manning and soon of Emma Isola and because they expected Wordsworth and his wife. Lamb promised that he and Mary would accompany the Allsops anywhere during his vacation in the summer. But then he kept her much to himself and, mindful above all to keep her well, took her on no lengthy excursions. In November, with the same regard for her welfare, he decided not to take her on a visit they had planned to the Thomas Monkhouses' at Ramsgate. He and Mary thereby forestalled past the end of the year a recurrence of her affliction. That winter she had the obstinate cold and once again a toothache.

Her protracted discomfort worried and wore him out. The unusually persistent annoyances he was experiencing at his office convinced them both that he was no longer fit for business. He obtained certificates attesting to his failing health from Gillman and Tuthill and on February 7, 1825, tendered his resignation. On his way home from work on March 29 he placed in Robinson's mailbox a note that reads, "I have left the d——d India house for Ever! give me great joy." On April 6 he wrote the following and more to Wordsworth:

Here am I then after 33 years slavery, sitting in my own room at 11 oClock this finest of all April mornings a freed man. . . . I came home for ever on Tuesday in last week. The incomprehensibleness of my condition overwhelm'd me. It was like passing from life into Eternity. Every year to be as long as three, i.e. to have three times as much real time, time that is my own, in it! I wandered about thinking I was happy, but feeling I was not. But that tumultuousness is passing off, & I begin to understand the nature of the gift. Holydays, even the annual month, were always uneasy joys. Their conscious fugitiveness—. The craving after making the most of them—. Now when all is holyday, there are no holydays. I can sit at home in rain or shine without a restless impulse for walkings. I am daily steadying, & shall soon find it as natural to me to be my own master, as it has been irksome to have had a master. Mary wakes every morning with an obscure feeling that some good has happened to us.

The tumultuousness, though it subsided momentarily, did not pass off. It issued, rather, in what he called a nervous fever involving insomnia and pain. To remedy it and escape from the callers who aggravated it, he and Mary in July let their cottage to the author and bookseller William Hone and somewhat joined and somewhat succeeded the Allsops in their lodgings at a Mrs. Leishman's, probably a Mrs. G. R. Leishman's, on Chase Side in Enfield. They were successful to the extent that he was able to write a few pieces, "The Pawnbroker's Daughter: A Farce" included, and to invite Hone up in August. But in September, during their first weekend home, a recurrence of the condition so severe as to require the application of leeches to Lamb's temples drove them, this time with Sarah James, back to Enfield. In a house that now seemed deserted and melancholy without the Allsops, anxiety and nursing took their toll of Mary. Lamb and Miss James brought her home deprived of her reason near the end of the month. Lamb put himself under daily medical attention until sometime in October. Early in December he sent out a few words saying that he and Mary could, with care, see their friends.

He and Mary came down with colds in the first two weeks of January 1826. His intermittently impaired his hearing and shut him largely indoors into May. He wrote most of the "Popular Fallacies" for Henry Colburn's *New Monthly Magazine* during that period. He wrote them all to earn extra money. But discovering ways possible to manage without it, he stopped doing them by September. Then, wanting some regular occupation, he started reading the perhaps two thousand plays David Garrick had bequeathed to the British Museum. Lamb's reading resulted in the extracts and elucidations published in Hone's *Table Book* for 1827 and the few not published till later.

On January 20, 1827, Lamb wrote Robinson of the dying of Randal Norris. Lamb requested Robinson's assistance for the family while reminiscing about the plain old-fashioned manners of the last person to call him Charley and keep him attached to the Inner Temple. In the spring, after visits from Emma Isola and Frances Kelly, Lamb and Mary returned to Mrs. Leishman's. In the summer Emma returned to them there. Lamb began to teach her Latin so that she might qualify as a governess and to inquire about proper households for her. He also began to collect verses from friends for her album and to see Moxon falling in love with her. Lamb wrote but Covent Garden refused "The Wife's Trial; or, the Intruding Widow." With Mary he was weighing their dull but placid life in the village against their excess of company in Islington.

In August they decided to go back to Colebrook Cottage in early fall. But in September they gave it up for a convenient yellowish house of recent construction next to the residence and insurance office of Thomas Westwood on Chase Side in Enfield. They remained at Mrs. Leishman's while their maid, Becky, took charge of the moving. On September 30 they moved in. An entrance they had looked forward to was, however, sad. For increasing excitement had in the previous evening badly overset Mary. Lamb brought in Becky's sister to try to take care of her and canceled their invitations. In the months that followed he saw Emma leave and Mary begin to rise in health but sink once more because of the leaving and coming of nurses. He saw in dispiritment the fringes of winter before her recovery was certain. Apparently they had the comfortable Christmas for which they had hoped and shared it only with Emma.

Mary was soon well. Lamb complained of nervousness and poor health into the spring of 1828. Emma departed in April to serve as the governess in the family of the Reverend Mr. Williams of Fornham. The clouds of loneliness under which the Lambs drooped were dispersed by the arrival of good guests, warm weather, and the season's colors and by a dinner they attended for Wordsworth at Thomas and Rachel Talfourd's in May. It was August before they revisited London, to the pleasure of Frances Kelly, the poet Thomas Hood, and his wife, Jane. It was near the end of September before Emma could revisit the Lambs. Martin Burney, Coleridge, and once Keats's good friend Charles Cowden Clarke and his bride, the former Mary Victoria Novello, were among others who came to Enfield that fall. Emma came back in the first week of January 1829 and stayed for about three weeks. She came back again in the last week of May and was reunited with her former schoolmate Maria Fryer, whom the Lambs had invited as a surprise for Emma in return for the surprise of herself. But Mary was unable to welcome them. The prospect of their visit, conjoined with the loss of Becky to marriage, the imposition of a new maid, and perhaps the death of John Bates Dibdin, a son of the proprietor of Sadler's Wells Theatre Charles Dibdin, the younger, had compelled an attack a few days in advance of their appearance. Lamb, for everyone's sake but his own, had placed Mary in an asylum in the London borough of Fulham.

The presence of Emma and Miss Fryer lightened then intruded upon his desolateness. At first he could but shortly could not accept other company. Yet when the girls had gone, in early July, he felt so forlorn that he accepted an offer to stay in town with Rickman. Ten days where companions had too long ago lived returned him to the refuge of solitude in Enfield. He told Barton on July 25, 1829, of having become "convinced that I was better to get home to my hole at Enfield, & hide like a sick cat in my corner." He added that Mary, whom he had recently seen, was "looking better in her health than ever, but sadly rambling, and scarce showing any pleasure in seeing me, or curiosity when I should come again." She was home by the middle of August and well enough at its end for Lamb to ask Charles Ryle, of the audit department of the East India House, and his wife out for a day. Then ensued a relapse and the extended tendance of a doctor. Furthermore, they either felt or were obliged to give up their house and were reluctant to take another. Lamb, depressed and desperate, sold their furniture and arranged for their board and lodging next door at the Thomas Westwoods'. Mary, relieved of the responsibility of housekeeping, improved remarkably within a week after their move toward the end of October. They both were restored by mid-November and had Emma for her Christmas vacation.

Emma caught a cold on the way back to Fornham near the end of January 1830 that developed into cerebrospinal meningitis. Lamb dared neither to take Mary on the road nor to leave her behind in her state of anxiety. Thus, in spite of their desire to do otherwise, there was nothing they could do but endure their distress until Mrs. Williams released them from it with good news on March 1. Emma was able to have Lamb come for her in about a month and to resume her position in May. In June he was able to distribute copies of his *Album Verses, with a Few Others,* which Moxon, who had recently quit Longman's to establish his own firm, had issued as his first publication. In the beginning of July Lamb and Mary fled some discomfort in Enfield to lodgings at their old address of 34 Southampton Buildings, Chancery Lane, Holborn. The move almost immediately caused her to become ill. He removed her to an asylum, remained in the lodgings for as long as his hope remained for her recovery in London, and toward mid-

November returned with her to the Westwoods'. She began to mend in the familiar quiet and could enjoy Emma for the holidays.

The Lambs were housebound by snow and slush for the first two months or so of 1831. They were worried by having heard only once from Emma since her departure. In March she came to them in need of rest and was kindly dismissed by Mrs. Williams. Then their lives went well. They entertained moderately. Emma in the summer and again in the fall went away to the homes of others. Lamb wrote several poems and essays, among them those for the *Englishman's Magazine* while Moxon possessed it, from August to its collapse in October. Also that year Lamb wrote and Moxon published *Satan in Search of a Wife; with the Whole Process of His Courtship and Marriage, and Who Danced at the Wedding by an Eye Witness.*

In February 1832 Elizabeth Reynolds' death and a cold Mary caught as a result of the hurried trip into London she and Lamb made to pay their respects deepened the melancholy they were experiencing, in part because of the absence of Emma. In addition they had come to feel persecuted by the sour disposition of Mrs. Westwood. Lamb learned that Emma had left Miss Fryer's home, in Chatteris, for Miss Humphrey's, in Cambridge, and on March 1 wrote her of their troubles and of Mary's need for her. Robinson found Emma with the Lambs and everyone in fair health and a good mood when he called on March 8. About two months later Mary broke down. Lamb placed her with Frederick and Ann Walden, who took in mental patients, at Bay Cottage, Church Street, Edmonton. He then began virtually to fall apart.

Throughout his manhood there were periods, often of stress, in which he drank excessively. Shortly after he had on this occasion confined Mary he drank more in one day than in any other in his life. Having told Moxon that, he in the same letter implored Moxon to come out to restrain him. Lamb became drunk at a dinner party that included Emma and Robinson at the Talfourds' on May 26. He slept there in his clothes that night and the next and, not knowing what else to do, went to pound on Robinson's door on the two following mornings. "Yet in the midst of this half-crazy irregularity," Robinson recorded on May 28, 1832, "he was so full of sensibility that speaking of his sister he had tears in his eyes—and he talked about his favourite poems with his usual warmth, praising Andrew Marvell extravagantly."

On July 23 Robinson walked to Enfield and noted that Lamb was in fine health, full of praise for Emma, and capable of speaking of Mary with composure. On August 24 Lamb wrote Robinson that Mary was looking forward to playing cards with him and thereby suggested she was home. Robinson went to Enfield on September 25. "I found them on the whole comfortable," reads his entry, "but Miss Lamb bore sad marks of her late illness, looked very low indeed and thin, but when she spoke her voice was strong and the rubbers that we played gave her pleasure."

In April 1833 Lamb, probably by paying thirty pounds, overcame John Taylor's threat of an injunction for copyright infringement and so left Moxon free to bring out *The Last Essays of Elia: Being a Sequel to Essays Published under That Name*. Later in the month Emma and Moxon became engaged to be married. The Westwoods and the Lambs contracted influenza. In early May the disease and possibly the help Mary gave to Mrs. Westwood caused Mary to suffer an attack that required her removal to the Waldens'. Because the duration of her illnesses had lengthened to the extent that half her life was dead to him (as Lamb expressed it to Wordsworth near the end of the month), and the other half was filled with dread of the next attack and removal, he decided that she should no longer live with him but that he should live with her. He arranged for the Waldens to accept him and Mary as boarders and without regret left Enfield. He arranged for Emma to spend the time till her wedding either with Moxon's family or with the Misses Buffams, of late the Lambs' landladies at 34 Southampton Buildings. On July 30 he gave her away in marriage. Mary was too ill to attend and, apparently, either had become confused about the event or had not been told its date. But the "dreary blank of *unanswered questions,*" she wrote to Moxon and Emma about a week later, "which I ventured to ask in vain, was cleared up on the wedding-day by Mrs W—— taking a glass of wine; and, with a total change of countenance, begged leave to drink Mr. and Mrs. Moxon's health.— It restored me, from that moment: as if by an electrical stroke: to the entire possession of my senses.— I never felt so calm and quiet after a similar illness as I do now. I feel as if all tears were wiped from my eyes, and all care from my heart." Lamb added that never "was such a calm, or such a recovery."

In two or three months her calm gave way to despondency. On the last day of the year her despondency broke up into violence. On February 14, 1834, Lamb sought to still Maria Fryer's concern for him. "In one word, be less uneasy about me," he wrote.

I bear my privations very well. I am not in the depths of desolation, as heretofore. Your admonitions are not lost upon me. Your kindness has sunk into my heart. Have faith in me. It is no new thing for me to be left to my Sister. When she is not violent, her rambling chat is better to me than the sense and sanity of this world. Her heart is obscured, not buried; it breaks out occasionally; and one can discern a strong mind struggling with the billows that have gone over it. I could be no where happier than under the same roof with her. Her memory is unnaturally strong—& from ages past, if we may so call the earliest records of our poor life, she fetches thousands of names and things, that never would have dawned upon me again; & thousands from the 10 years she lived before me. What took place from early girlhood to her coming of age principally, lives again (every important thing, and every trifle) in her brain with the vividness of real presence. For 12 hours incessantly she will pour out without intermission **all her past life,** forgetting nothing, pouring out name after name to the Waldens! as a dream; sense & nonsence; truths & errors huddled together; a medley between inspiration & possession.

In March, however, he was desolate. Instances of his drinking and mention of the destruction he was causing himself are in Robinson's diary entry for the twentieth. In May, after perhaps a seven years' silence, Lamb heard from Manning. On May 10 Lamb wrote him that though Mary continued now and then to be violent, he hoped she was recovering. Lamb, though sad, sounds improved. On June 7 Robinson drove out to Edmonton and saw them "more comfortable than I have seen [them] together for a long time." Mary was soon able to accompany her brother again on his monthly trip, habitual for almost a year, to dine at the British Museum with one of its officials, the translator Henry Francis Cary. That summer his son Francis Stephen Cary began his portrait of Lamb and Mary.

Coleridge's death, in the morning of July 25, 1834, stunned the Lambs. Neither of them went to the funeral. In August, it seems, Lamb called at Highgate to express himself to James and Anne Gillman. He insisted on giving five guineas to Harriet Macklin, the Gillmans' maid and Coleridge's nurse, so affected was he by her feelings for his old friend. On November 21 he inscribed a reflection in the personal literary album of James Keymer, an admirer of Lamb and a friend of the historian and biographer John Forster, at Forster's request. Forster published it in his memorial of Lamb in the *New Monthly Magazine* of February 1835, and Lucas republished it in *Works* (I, 351–352) as "The Death of Coleridge: In the Album of Mr. Keymer." It begins:

When I heard of the death of Coleridge, it was without grief. It seemed to me that he long had been on the confines of the next world,—that he had a hunger for eternity. I grieved then that I could not grieve. But since, I feel how great a part he was of me. His great and dear spirit haunts me. I cannot think a thought, I cannot make a criticism on men or books, without an ineffectual turning and reference to him. He was the proof and touchstone of all my cogitations. He was a Grecian (or in the first form) at Christ's Hospital, where I was deputy Grecian; and the same subordination and deference to him I have preserved through a life-long acquaintance.

The eulogy ends:

He was my fifty years old friend without a dissension. Never saw I his likeness, nor probably the world can see again. I seem to love the house he died at more passionately than when he lived. I love the faithful Gilmans more than while they exercised their virtues towards him living. What was his mansion is consecrated to me a chapel.

Coleridge had been reading his *Poetical Works* (1834) before he died. In the margin opposite "This Lime-tree Bower My Prison," addressed to Lamb originally and composed while Lamb was with him at Nether Stowey in July 1797, Coleridge had penciled "Ch. and Mary Lamb—dear to my heart, yea, as it were my Heart.— S. T. C. Æt. 63; 1834——1797–1834 = 37 years!" He stipulated in his will that a plain gold mourning ring and a lock of his hair be presented "to my oldest Friend, & ever-beloved Schoolfellow, Charles Lamb, and in the deep and almost life-long affection, of which this is the slender record, his equally beloved Sister Mary Lamb, will know herself to be included" (*Coleridge's Letters,* VI, 1000). Lamb, according to Forster, never got over Coleridge's death.

On November 18, 1834, Robinson noted Moxon's report that Mary had fallen ill. On December 22 Lamb wrote his last letter, to George Dyer's wife, asking about a book he may have left in her parlor when he was there on the eighteenth. Also on the twenty-second, while in the course of his daily walk or returning from a tavern, he stumbled against a stone, fell, and hurt his face. His wounds seemed not to be serious, but erysipelas developed. In the evening of the twenty-sixth Ryle informed Talfourd, the coexecutors of Lamb's will, that Lamb was in danger. In the morning of the twenty-seventh Talfourd went to him, discovered him extremely weak and nearly insensible, and failed to get his attention. Within an hour, faintly murmuring the names of friends, Lamb painlessly died. Mary remarked on his beauty in sleep—nothing more. He was buried from the Waldens' in the afternoon of January 3, 1835, in the presence of a few, underneath the place in Edmonton churchyard he had pointed out to Mary.

She had become conscious of his death by then, but did not feel it until her illness passed in mid-February 1835. She accepted her loss with unexpected composure and said she wished but feared she could not afford to move into and live in town. Moxon, Robinson, Ryle, and Talfourd wanted her to move, to reside with Sarah James and near friends, and assured Mary she had sufficient money. Lamb, to everyone's amazement, had left her an estate worth between fifteen hundred and two thousand pounds, a portion of which Ryle and Talfourd would invest for her to yield an annual return of ninety to one hundred and twenty pounds. Moreover, on the application of Ryle and Talfourd, the directors of the East India House resolved in March to provide her with a lifetime annuity of one hundred and twenty pounds in consideration of Lamb's contributions to the Regular Widows', or East India House Clerks', Fund. Mary, grieving and bemoaning her inability to cry when Robinson visited her on March 10, insisted that living in London was beyond her means. Her affliction overcame her in May and held her till perhaps November. It overcame her in January 1836 and held her till close to mid-May. On the fourteenth she told Robinson she was tired of Edmonton and ready to go to Miss James. Mary only wanted and felt certain of obtaining Ryle's approval, but nothing came of her plan. In November she told Robinson the thought of it was painful and, though she was uncomfortable at the Waldens', she would spend the winter there.

In Robinson's diary and in the last chapter of Ross's *The Ordeal of Bridget Elia* (see p. xlviii, above), a chapter constructed to a considerable extent from Robinson's papers in Dr. Williams's Trust, Dr.

Williams's Library, London, are the other reliable facts of her final years. In 1837 she was not ill and would not move. In about October 1838 she had an attack that lasted apparently into July 1839. During that time Robinson proposed to Ryle and Talfourd that they move her either to the home of Miss James or to that of her sister Mrs. Parsons. Talfourd was willing until Ryle informed him that Mary was violent and persuaded him that they had not the legal right and could expect trouble from the Waldens. Talfourd consulted her physician, Dr. J. Vale Asbury. He was opposed to moving her ever, for he thought he could help her and knew of the solace she found in strolling in Edmonton churchyard. Talfourd was impressed enough with Asbury to commit her to his care and guarantee his fees. On August 29, 1839, Robinson noted her deterioration in his diary:

I had an early dinner and then I walked to Edmonton, where I stayed more than two hours with some difficulty to fill up the time. Poor dear Mary Lamb was ten months ill lately and these severe attacks have produced the inevitable result. Her mind is gone, at least it is become inert. She has still her excellent heart—is kind and considerate and her judgment is sound—nothing but good feeling and good sense in all she says; but still no one would discover what she once was. She hears ill and is slow in conception. She says she bears solitude better than she did. She is afraid to come to town, lest she should suffer under a renewal of her periodical alienation of mind. She did not press me to stay till the last coach, and so after a few games of piquet I took the seven o'clock stage.

Robinson's letters to Wordsworth of July 25 and December 14, 1840, show she was ill at least once and possibly twice in 1840.

In June 1841 Lamb's biographer the poet Bryan Waller Procter, acting partly in his capacity as a metropolitan commissioner of lunacy, called on her unannounced. He found her neglected, subject to excitement by Mrs. Walden's foul temper, and anxious to move. Through Procter's intercession she was settled by July 14 in Mrs. Parsons' home, at 41 Alpha Road, Regent's Park, where she had a room on the ground floor for herself and her books and a bedroom up two pairs of stairs. She could visit with friends and, as Robinson came to believe, possibly did so to excess. She was ill in 1841 from perhaps October to December. She was ill in 1842 from perhaps February to August, though she received Wordsworth and Robinson in May. On October 3, 1842, she wrote her last two extant letters, to Emma Moxon and

Jane Tween, Mrs. Randal Norris' daughter. (On July 25, 1843, Sarah James wrote the last letter in this edition for Mary, to express Mary's sorrow and shock to Mrs. Tween over the death of her mother.) On March 19, 1843, Robinson noted that Mary was woefully changed—"a mere wreck of herself"—and deaf. In August he thought she was better. In October she dislocated her shoulder. The accident shocked her out of the darkness into which she had lapsed and caused her friends to become displeased with her lack of protection. Mrs. Talfourd spoke of her displeasure to Mrs. Parsons in April 1844. Later in the year Mrs. Parsons and Mary moved into a more comfortable house, at 40 Alpha Road.

The calls Robinson paid Mary on December 10, 1845, and July 11, 1846, were made particularly difficult by her having become inarticulate. In February 1847 Moxon informed Robinson that she rarely recognized anyone and had been put to bed. On May 20 she died. A small company was conveyed to Edmonton churchyard on May 28, 1847, to see her placed in the grave of Charles Lamb.

III

The first edition of Lamb letters, Thomas Noon Talfourd's *The Letters of Charles Lamb, with a Sketch of His Life,* was published in 1837, less than three years after Lamb's death. A few letters had already appeared, as part of Procter's "Recollections of Charles Lamb," in *The Athenaeum* of January 24 and February 7, 1835. The second edition, Talfourd's *Final Memorials of Charles Lamb; Consisting Chiefly of His Letters Not before Published, with Sketches of Some of His Companions,* came out in 1848, a little more than a year after the death of Mary.

What is known of the making of those editions is given principally in the portions of the letters of Talfourd and Wordsworth and the letters and diary entries of Robinson that Robert S. Newdick incorporated in *The First Life and Letters of Charles Lamb: A Study of Thomas Noon Talfourd as Editor and Biographer* (Columbus: Ohio State University, 1935), pp. 19–43. On February 12, 1835, Robinson expressed in his diary his dissatisfaction with Procter's choice of letters for "Recollections of Charles Lamb." On February 13 Robinson wrote Wordsworth of a decision to prepare an edition of them. On February

16 Barron Field wrote Robinson of his preference for Southey as the editor over himself, Moxon, Talfourd, and Forster. But Moxon or Robinson, probably, approached Talfourd. During the next two years Talfourd, with the assistance mainly of Charles Valentine Le Grice, Moxon, Robinson, Southey, and Wordsworth in gathering the letters and details of Lamb's life, constructed *The Letters of Charles Lamb, with a Sketch of His Life*. Talfourd dedicated it to Mary. Edward Moxon published it, in two volumes, in 1837.

In its Preface, which he dated June 26, 1837, Talfourd explained his procedure and plans:

> The recentness of the period of some of the letters has rendered it necessary to omit many portions of them, in which the humour and beauty are interwoven with personal references, which, although wholly free from any thing which, rightly understood, could give pain to any human being, touch on subjects too sacred for public exposure. Some of the personal allusions which have been retained, may seem, perhaps, too free to a stranger; but they have been retained only in cases in which the Editor is well assured the parties would be rather gratified than displeased at seeing their names connected in life-like association with one so dear to their memories.
>
> The italics and capitals are invariably those indicated by the MSS. It is to be regretted that in the printed letters the reader must lose the curious varieties of writing with which the originals abound, and which are scrupulously adapted to the subjects. The letters are usually undated. Where the date occurs, it has generally been given; and much trouble has been necessary to assign to many of the letters (the post-marks of which are not legible) their proper place, and perhaps not always with complete success.
>
> Many letters yet remain unpublished, which will further illustrate the character of Mr. Lamb, but which must be reserved for a future time, when the Editor hopes to do more justice to his own sense of the genius and the excellences of his friend, than it has been possible for him to accomplish in these volumes. [I, ix–x]

Then Talfourd presented 180 letters. I arrive at the number, as I do at every such, by disregarding the numbering in the editions, recombining those letters and portions that Talfourd and his successors disjoined to form two letters or more, and separating those they joined to form one letter. I count as letters each letter and discrete portion, as well as the excerpts from other letters quoted in preliminaries, textual narratives or notes, and reference matter.

Joseph Cottle in *Early Recollections; Chiefly Relating to the Late Samuel Taylor Coleridge, during His Long Residence in Bristol* (1837; revised as *Reminiscences of Samuel Taylor Coleridge and Robert Southey,* 1847); Thomas Hood in "Literary Reminiscences. No. IV," in *Hood's Own* (1838); Anne Mathews in *Memoirs of Charles Mathews, Comedian* (1838); N. P. Willis in *The Corsair,* 1 (March 1839), 27; E. S. in "Recollections of George Dyer," in the *Mirror of Literature, Amusement, and Instruction,* 38 (December 1841), 310–311; and Henry Cary in *Memoir of the Rev. Henry Francis Cary* (1847) presented a few more letters. Robinson reported in his diary and to his brother Thomas that on October 13 and 14, 1847, he spoke with Talfourd of others. "He read to me," reads the entry of the fourteenth, "some letters by Charles Lamb on the tragical event which threw a cloud over both his sister and himself. I have given a decided opinion that these letters ought to be made public, both for his and her sakes, though they reveal the fact that even he was once in confinement. The additional volume of letters will be of great interest, beyond even the preceding. They will supply an apology for all one wishes away in his delightful works." The entry of February 6, 1848, states that Robinson called on Talfourd "and gave him all those letters of Lamb to Wordsworth which I thought might, without giving offence, be printed. I found Talfourd at work on Lamb's papers, and I believe he will complete his publication of Lamb's *Letters* with the love with which he began it." Talfourd completed his *Final Memorials of Charles Lamb; Consisting Chiefly of His Letters Not before Published, with Sketches of Some of His Companions* during the next six months. He dedicated it to Wordsworth. Edward Moxon published it, in two volumes, in 1848.

In its Preface, which he dated July 1848, Talfourd reminded his readers of the references in his first Preface "to letters yet remaining unpublished, and to a period when a more complete estimate might be formed of the singular and delightful character of the writer than was there presented." He announced the arrival of that period and proceeded so:

Several of his friends, who might possibly have felt a moment's pain at the publication of some of those effusions of kindness, in which they are sportively mentioned, have been removed by death; and the dismissal of the last, and to him the dearest of all, his sister, while it has brought to her the repose she sighed for ever since she lost him, has released his biographer from a difficulty which has hitherto prevented a due appreciation of some of his noblest qualities. Her most lamentable, but most innocent agency in the event which consigned her for life to his protection, forbade the introduction of any letter, or allusion to any incident, which might ever, in the long and dismal twilight of consciousness which she endured, shock her by the recurrence of long past and terrible sorrows; and the same consideration for her induced the suppression of every passage which referred to the malady with which she was through life at intervals afflicted. Although her death had removed the objection to a reference to her intermittent suffering, it still left a momentous question, whether even then, when no relative remained to be affected by the disclosure, it would be right to unveil the dreadful calamity which marked one of its earliest visitations, and which, though known to most of those who were intimate with the surviving sufferers, had never been publicly associated with their history. When, however, I reflected that the truth, while in no wise affecting the gentle excellence of one of them, casts new and solemn lights on the character of the other; that while his frailties have received an ample share of that indulgence which he extended to all human weaknesses, their chief exciting cause has been hidden; that his moral strength and the extent of his self-sacrifice have been hitherto unknown to the world; I felt that to develope all which is essential to the just appreciation of his rare excellence, was due both to him and to the public. While I still hesitated as to the extent of disclosure needful for this purpose, my lingering doubts were removed by the appearance of a full statement of the melancholy event, with all the details capable of being collected from the newspapers of the time, in the "British Quarterly Review," and the diffusion of the passage, extracted thence, through several other journals. After this publication, no doubt could remain as to the propriety of publishing the letters of Lamb on this event, eminently exalting the characters of himself and his sister, and enabling the reader to judge of the sacrifice which followed it.

I have also availed myself of the opportunity of introducing some letters, the objection to publishing which has been obviated by the same great healer, Time; and of adding others which I deemed too trivial for the public eye, when the whole wealth of his letters lay before me, collected by Mr. Moxon from the distinguished correspondents of Lamb, who kindly responded to his request for permission to make the public sharers in their choice epistolary treasures. The appreciation which the letters already published, both in this country and in America—perhaps even more remarkable in America than in England—have attained, and the interest which the lightest fragments of Lamb's correspondence, which have accidentally appeared in other quarters, have excited, convince me that some letters which I withheld, as doubting their worthiness of the public eye, will not now be unwelcome. There is, indeed, scarcely a note—a *notelet*—(as he used to call his very little letters) Lamb ever wrote, which has not some tinge of that quaint sweetness, some hint of that peculiar union of kindness and whim, which distinguish him from all other poets and humorists. I do not think the reader will complain that—with some very slight exceptions, which personal considerations still render necessary—I have made him a partaker of *all* the epistolary treasures which the generosity of Lamb's correspondents placed at Mr. Moxon's disposal.

When I first considered the materials of this work, I purposed to combine them with a new edition of the former volumes; but the consideration that such a course would be unjust to the possessors of those volumes induced me to present them to the public in a separate form. In accomplishing that object, I have felt the difficulty of connecting the letters so as to render their attendant circumstances intelligible, without falling into repetition of passages in the previous biography. My attempt has been to make these volumes subsidiary to the former, and yet complete in themselves; but I fear its imperfection will require much indulgence from the reader. The italics and capitals used in printing the letters are always those of the writer; and the little passages sometimes prefixed to letters, have been printed as in the originals. [I, vii–xii]

Now Talfourd presented 102 letters, 82 of them new and 20 undesignated portions he had withheld from some of the letters in his former volumes. In his two editions, then, Talfourd introduced a total of 262 letters.

The catalogues and bibliographies show that Talfourd's editions were republished, one edition or the other, separately or combined, by W. T. Amies of Philadelphia (1879); D. Appleton and Company of New York and Geo. S. Appleton of Philadelphia (1848 and 1849); A. C. Armstrong of New York (1885 and 1886); Bell and Daldy of London (1867 and 1870); Henry G. Bohn and Company of London (1837); Cassell and Company, Ltd., of London (1911); Colonial Press Company of Boston (no date); Crosbie, Nichols, Lee and

Company of Boston (1860); H. W. Derby of New York (1861); Derby and Jackson of New York (1857, 1858, 1859, and 1861); Dana Estes and Company of Boston (no date); Harper and Brothers of New York (1838, 1839, 1847–1848, 1850, 1851, 1852, 1855, 1864, and 1868); W. P. Hazard of Philadelphia (1837?, 1854, 1855, 1856, 1857, and 1885); Moxon (1840, 1841, 1842, 1848, 1849, 1850, 1855, 1859, and 1865); G. Routledge and Sons of New York (1867); Sheldon and Company of New York (1863 and 1865); William Veazie of Boston (1863); and W. J. Widdleton of New York (1868).

Additional letters were introduced in Lucy Barton and Edward FitzGerald's *Selections from the Poems and Letters of Bernard Barton* (1849); Tom Taylor's *Life of Benjamin Robert Haydon, Historical Painter, from His Autobiography and Journals* (1853); Peter George Patmore's *My Friends and Acquaintances* (1854); George Daniel's "An Inedited Letter of Charles Lamb," in the *Illustrated London News* of October 20, 1855; Mary Cowden Clarke's "Recollections of Mary Lamb. By One Who Knew Her," in the *National Magazine*, 3 (1858), 360–365; Mary Balmanno's *Pen and Pencil* (1858), which has a facsimile of a letter; George William Curtis' "Notes of Charles Lamb to Thomas Allsop," in *Harper's New Monthly Magazine*, 20 (1859), 88–97; the anonymous "My Friend's Library," in the *Atlantic Monthly*, 8 (1861), 440–447; Thornton Hunt's *The Correspondence of Leigh Hunt* (1862); J. E. Babson's *Eliana: Being the Hitherto Uncollected Writings of Charles Lamb* (1864); Mary Cowden Clarke's *The Life and Labours of Vincent Novello* (1864); and *Charles Lamb: His Friends, His Haunts, and His Books* (1866), by the novelist and biographer Percy Hethrington Fitzgerald (b. 1834), who within ten years became Lamb's editor.

Moxon's company planned the third edition of the letters in the early sixties. According to the stories of its development in William Carew Hazlitt's letters in *The Athenaeum* of November 2 and 30, 1867, and a letter by the Moxon firm in the issue of November 23, the firm first engaged Procter to prepare both the edition and what became his *Charles Lamb: A Memoir* (1866) and engaged Hazlitt—the grandson of the essayist—when Procter defaulted as editor. Disagreements arose between Hazlitt and the company over money and the quality of the manuscript, on which Hazlitt had worked for possibly two years and submitted in the fall of 1866. The parties separated in

1867, and the embittered Hazlitt, who for the time being gave up the work, commented publicly on the affair afterward in his *Mary and Charles Lamb: Poems, Letters, and Remains: Now First Collected, with Reminiscences and Notes* (1874), pp. 15–17, in his published edition of the letters (see below), and in his *The Lambs: Their Lives, Their Friends, and Their Correspondence. New Particulars and New Material* (1897), pp. 83–93. The journalist and novelist George Augustus Henry Sala (1828–1896) succeeded Hazlitt and edited the volume of 223 letters, arranged according to addressee rather than chronologically as Talfourd had arranged those in his editions, that E. Moxon and Company released in 1868 as the first volume of the projected three- or four-volume *The Complete Correspondence and Works of Charles Lamb* and then withdrew, presumably because Sala retired from the project. An inscription inside the cover of a Sala volume owned in 1902 by J. Rogers Rees of Llandaff, Wales, and presently by the Yale University Library asserts on the authority of an (unidentified) autograph letter that Matthew Arnold was offered the editorship of what I consider another, the fourth, edition. Its editorship went, however, to the drama critic and novelist Thomas Purnell (1834–1889). He, with the assistance of Emma Isola Moxon, in effect completed *The Complete Correspondence and Works of Charles Lamb.* E. Moxon, Son and Company issued it, in four volumes, in 1870. Also in 1870 the Moxon company issued a one-volume edition of the letters only. The Purnell edition has Purnell's prefatory essay on Lamb's life and genius in place of Sala's. Neither the Sala nor the Purnell edition has a statement of editorial policy. The Purnell edition has Sala's arrangement and assembly of letters and 114 more letters. The Purnell edition includes among its 337 letters 78 not in Talfourd's editions and excludes 3 letters of the 262 in Talfourd's editions.

Other letters published shortly before and in the first half of the seventies are in the anonymous "Charles Lamb in the Temple," in the *Pall Mall Gazette* of September 22, 1869; Thomas Sadler's edition of the *Diary, Reminiscences, and Correspondence of Henry Crabb Robinson, Barrister-at-Law, F.S.A.* (1870); John Payne Collier's *An Old Man's Diary, Forty Years Ago* (1871–1872); Mary Cowden Clarke's "Some Letters of Charles Lamb; with Reminiscences of Himself Awakened Thereby," in the *Gentleman's Magazine,* N.S. 11 (1873), 617–630; and Hazlitt's *Mary and Charles Lamb: Poems,*

Letters, and Remains: Now First Collected, with Reminiscences and Notes (1874). Percy Fitzgerald edited the fifth edition, *The Life, Letters and Writings of Charles Lamb.* E. Moxon and Company published it, in six volumes, in 1876. It is shown to have been republished by T. and A. Constable of London as the Enfield Edition (1876?); Gibbings and Company, Ltd., of London and J. B. Lippincott Company of Philadelphia as the Temple Edition (1895); W. W. Gibbings and Company of London as the Temple Edition (1891, 1892, 1895, 1897, and 1903); The Navarre Society of London as the Enfield Edition (1924); and John Slark of London (1882–1884 and 1886).

Fitzgerald was the last editor to arrange the letters according to addressee. He was the first editor to praise and re-use Talfourd's life of Lamb, though he revised it as required to join its parts and supplemented it with notes. He was also the first editor to write in this manner (I, ix–xii):

Thus much for the Life. The Letters, as is well known, were edited by Serjeant Talfourd in accordance with his peculiar views; being cut up, altered, and dealt with in very summary fashion. Many of the passages seem to have been suppressed, for no apparent reason: as, for instance, "A word of your healths will be richly acceptable;" "Love and respects to Edith." Others again are altered as offending the editor's fastidious taste: such as Lamb's humorous execrations—"damn him!" being always changed to "hang him!" or such a sentence as "gone sick and died and putrified," changed to "was buried;" while others, as the "Right Reverend tears of Earl Nelson," or "Hurra, boys! down with the Atheists!" are cautiously omitted. So careful was the editor, that where a name might be guessed from the initial, he substituted another, so as not to suppress merely, but to send the reader off on a wrong scent. Passages, too, where Lamb reproaches himself with little excesses in drink and extravagance, are also suppressed, such as "wasting away the little we have, which my wise conduct has already encroached on one-half;" and "Last Sunday, . . . inspired with new rum, I tumbled down and broke my nose." These are only a few specimens; for the whole was carried out in the most thorough fashion.

When some years ago a complete issue of the Correspondence was prepared, the letters were compared with the originals, and most of the suppressed passages restored; while the fragments of letters which the editor had divided, were brought together. I should have been glad to have collated them afresh; but, unfortunately, the originals have disappeared.

The present edition will be found the most complete that has yet been offered to the public, and is certainly the first that has claims to being styled "edited." It contains forty new letters, besides some twenty more that have been collected from various sources. Many of these are of a very trifling kind—mere notelets, as they are called; but still all are characteristic, and offer some little turn of thought which the reader would not like to lose.

Fitzgerald remarked on his handling of Lamb's public writings and his discoveries of new pieces among them. He concluded in part with an acknowledgment to Forster, to whom he dedicated the work and was indebted for "the twenty-five letters and 'notelets,' which are now first published in the Correspondence. To make the collection of Lamb's Letters complete seems to be impossible. A whole series addressed to Wordsworth remains unpublished. Each year brings to light a fresh contribution; and even, as I write [this Preface is dated November 1875], new Memoirs are announced, containing new letters. By the time, however, that this edition shall be completed, I hope to have arranged that nearly all the letters in print shall be included. Should this be found impossible, the *locale* of such letters will be indicated, so that the reader may, at least, know where to look for them." The Fitzgerald edition includes among its 451 letters (counting the 2 added to the Enfield and Temple editions) 116 not in Purnell's edition and excludes 2 letters of the 337 in Purnell's.

Letters published in the last half of the seventies and the first half of the eighties are in C. Kegan Paul's *William Godwin: His Friends and Contemporaries* (1876); Richard Henry Stoddard's *The Life, Letters and Table Talk of Benjamin Robert Haydon* (1876); Coventry Patmore's edition of Procter's *An Autobiographical Fragment and Biographical Notes* (1877); Charles and Mary Cowden Clarke's *Recollections of Writers* (1878); M. Betham-Edwards' "Letters of Coleridge, Southey, and Lamb to Matilda Betham," in *Fraser's Magazine,* 18 (1878), 73–84; Betham-Edwards' *Six Life Studies of Famous Women* (1880); J. Fuller Russell's "Charles Lamb," in *Notes and Queries,* 6th Ser., 4 (1881), 223–224 and 363–364; R. S. Chilton's "Some Letters of Charles Lamb to John Howard Payne," in the *Century Illustrated Monthly Magazine,* 24 (1882), 927–930; and the anonymous "Letters of Charles Lamb," in *The Athenaeum* of April 12, 1884. Then followed Hazlitt's *Letters of Charles Lamb: With Some Account of the Writer, His Friends and Correspondents, and Explanatory Notes. By the Late Thomas Noon Talfourd, D. C. L., One of His Executors. An Entirely New Edition, Carefully Revised and Greatly Enlarged.* George Bell and Sons of London published it, in two volumes, in 1886.

"The basis of the two volumes now offered to the public," Hazlitt opened his Preface (dated November 1885), "is the Selection of letters made by Mr. Justice Talfourd in 1837, and the 'Final Memorials' published under his care eleven or twelve years later. The correspondence was in each case accompanied by a biographical and explanatory narrative which, looking at the intimacy which subsisted between Charles Lamb and the writer, and the agreeable style in which it was composed, has been thought deserving of preservation. But as two chronological Series have here been digested into one, the necessity was created of revising the text of the connecting biography in such a way as to blend the two accounts, and to reconcile a variety of contradictions, repetitions, and mistakes. To a considerable extent, the practice has been followed of including new letters and new notes between brackets; but to have carried such a principle thoroughly out would have involved at least half the book in its operation: so extensive have been the additions of fresh material and the correction of old. Whatever lucidity or zeal my judicial predecessor may have possessed on the bench, he does not seem to have carried much into the study. His inaccuracy and slovenliness are little less than miraculous" (I, vii).

Hazlitt observed that it was nearly twenty years since he first undertook to edit the letters, defended his decision then to arrange them according to addressee, and subjoined this passage, relative to the editions—which Hazlitt considered as one, as his, edition—of Sala, Purnell, and Fitzgerald (the brackets are Hazlitt's):

"The Complete Correspondence and Works of Charles Lamb" [edited by W. C. Hazlitt], 8vo, E. Moxon and Co., Dover Street, 1868, 4 vols. This edition was issued without my name, and with those of two or three persons in succession, who had next to nothing to do with it. I did not even see the proofs, which were superintended by a Mr. D. C. Higgs; and the text and notes abound with blunders. The date and even arrangement in various copies seem to differ, as the book passed through sundry booksellers' hands; and the series eventually extended to six volumes, with the two last of which I had no concern whatever. [I, xiv, note 2]

One of Hazlitt's reasons for now ordering the letters chronologically was "to utilize the running commentary of Mr. Justice Talfourd, which is certainly recommended by its agreeable and conciliatory tone, though rather too indiscriminate in its laudation of persons—not to say fulsomely euphuistic, and redolent to excess of a benevolent, yet rather lamentable *camaraderie*." He went on:

I have permitted myself to make only such alterations in the text of this thread of letterpress as the writer himself must often have seen fit to do with improved knowledge, or as the amalgamation of the two series of correspondence, and embodiment of extensive additions, positively necessitated. But the imperfect state of the undertaking, and the very numerous errors of arrangement and fact which have hitherto disfigured it, as well as what is termed the Fitzgerald edition, would have rendered anything less than a careful recension of the whole matter an unsatisfactory compromise; and a farther point, in which I have ventured to depart from former lines, is in the distribution of the letters for the first time into Three Books, making as many epochs in the career of Lamb: his correspondence with Coleridge in the closing years of the eighteenth century, which places before us, almost Montaigne-like, the thoughts and joys, and sorrows, of one young man to another—two such as are never to be again beheld: his letters to that same Coleridge between the opening of the new century and the institution of the "London Magazine" in 1820, when the writer found it possible and better to have more friends than one, and to draw into the circle of his correspondents and sympathizers the Wordsworths, Southey, the Hazlitts, and Chinese Manning: and lastly those which he exchanged mainly with the men to whom his obscurity and poverty were little more than a tradition. [I, xv–xvi]

Hazlitt commended Talfourd's narrative as intelligent, genial, and useful, but was disturbed at finding misstatements, incorrect dating, and the need silently to correct punctuation, orthography, and grammar. For though Talfourd "somewhat self-complacently dwells on the advantages of an academical training, and almost laments that his friend should have lacked them, he does not seem to have brought back from the University even an average conversance with the laws of English composition; and it is edifying to compare with the style and matter of the Judge who prided himself on having been to College those of the Clerk who had by misadventure owed all his learning to a charity school, and was merely a man of genius!" Hazlitt saw it as his duty to leave Talfourd "unmolested," yet saw fit to add that had Talfourd not "been what he was in relation to his subject," Hazlitt should have cut far more than he did from Talfourd's biographical essay, which Hazlitt charged "not merely with excrescences, but with declarations of opinion on religious points" (I, xvi–xvii) with which he altogether disagreed. Hazlitt thought some might regret the circumstances that precluded his printing all the letters extant, but assured them that many of the omissions are "wholly unimportant, and chiefly curious as samples of handwriting." He mentioned that the notes are Talfourd's, but "with indispensable corrections, and with additions derived from every quarter" (I, xviii–xix) conceivable to him. He thanked those who had helped him, pointed to letters Talfourd had overlooked, and closed with praises for Lamb and himself. Hazlitt's edition, the sixth, includes among its 488 letters 55 not in Fitzgerald's edition and excludes 18 letters of the 451 in Fitzgerald's.

The seventh edition, the first of three by the writer and divine Alfred Ainger (1837–1904) titled *The Letters of Charles Lamb: Newly Arranged, with Additions,* Macmillan and Company of London and New York issued, in its Eversley Series, in two volumes, in 1888. In his Introduction, which he dated November 1887, Ainger recounted the instances and features of the existing editions. He believed Hazlitt's edition to have an advantage over the editions since Talfourd's because of Hazlitt's reversion to a chronological ordering of the letters. But he believed it improper of Hazlitt to have republished under Talfourd's name Talfourd's work extensively revised. Ainger chose not to use Talfourd's narrative. He criticized Fitzgerald and Hazlitt for their excessively severe criticism of Talfourd's methods and recalled the considerations Talfourd was constrained to heed. Still, Ainger conceded that Talfourd should not have proceeded as he did in his second edition: "This was, beyond all question, a grave error of judgment, and the consequence was that if Talfourd's former work had of necessity a 'scrappy' character, for reasons that were entitled to all respect, the second work was more fragmentary still" (I, xvii). He defended Talfourd's deletion of expletives and other unfashionable expressions and of passages referring to living persons and intimate confidences of Lamb to himself. But Ainger admitted that Talfourd's work has a second serious defect:

It certainly could never have been an easy task to determine the dates of Lamb's various letters. He rarely dated a letter, especially in early life, and postmarks are too often torn or illegible. To arrange the Letters, therefore, in anything like chronological order must have been, as it is still, matter of great difficulty. But Talfourd, we must agree, might have come something nearer to success. Even where the postmarks existed, he does not seem to have noticed them, or to have cared for any more precise reference to a letter than that it was written "about this time." Sometimes, even in the absence of both date and postmark, references in the Letters to incidents in the lives of Lamb or his correspondent might have saved the editor from many errors. [I, xviii–xix]

Ainger remarked on his own additions and corrections and on his own deletions of dozens of short letters so trivial that they would insult the memory of Lamb and his readers if Ainger were to have included them. After writing of the qualities of Lamb and his letters generally, he returned to a discussion of their earliest editor and his detractors:

In certain respects I have tried to improve upon Talfourd's method as an editor of these Letters. But I have little sympathy with those who have spoken slightingly of the obligations he has laid upon all lovers of Charles Lamb. Least of all can I understand the covert charges against him of having, in the interest of his friend, over-coloured his virtues or concealed any of his frailties or foibles. When Talfourd put together the *Final Memorials* after the death of Mary Lamb in 1847, he attempted a fresh estimate of Lamb's character, as affected by the evidence of facts then for the first time published to the world. He headed these last pages, "Lamb fully known." I believe that those who know Lamb best must acknowledge both the generosity and the discriminating justice of this estimate. It may be true that a certain daintiness, a certain hothouse flavour, in Talfourd's style is a little out of keeping with his subject, but it certainly is not for the critical fashions of this age to look back scornfully on the "preciosity" of forty years since. But if Talfourd wraps up his judgments with something of an over-elegant elaboration, these judgments appear to me for the most part admirable. And although the number of Lamb's collected letters has largely grown in the last forty years, and his scattered writings have been collected and published, no record has "leaped to light" which need in any degree modify the estimate then formed. [I, xxvi]

Ainger's first edition includes among its 414 letters 27 not in Hazlitt's edition and excludes 101 letters of the 488 in Hazlitt's.

Letters published between 1889 and the end of the century are in Peter William Clayden's *Rogers and His Contemporaries* (1889); William Knight's *The Life of William Wordsworth* (1889); Hazlitt's "Some Unpublished Letters of Charles and Mary Lamb," in the *Atlantic Monthly,* 67 (1891), 145–160; I. A. Taylor's "On Autographs. II," in *Longman's Magazine,* 18 (1891), especially 141; James Dykes Campbell's "A Letter of Charles Lamb," in *The Athenaeum* of June 13, 1891; David Douglas' *Familiar Letters of Sir Walter Scott* (1891); the anonymous "Unpublished Letters of Charles and Mary Lamb," in the *Cornhill Magazine,* N.S. 19 (1892), 610–623; John Hollingshead's *My Lifetime* (1895); Mrs. James T. Fields's *A Shelf of Old Books* (1895), which has a facsimile of the letter in the *Atlantic Monthly* of 1861, mentioned above; George Birkbeck Hill's *Talks about Autographs* (1896); Hazlitt's *The Lambs: Their Lives, Their Friends, and Their Correspondence. New Particulars and New Material* (1897); Curtis Guild's *A Chat about Celebrities* (1897); E. V. Lucas' "Charles Lamb and Robert Lloyd; Some Unpublished Letters," in the *Cornhill Magazine,* 77 (1898), 595–605 and 734–745, which Lucas expanded into *Charles Lamb and the Lloyds* (1898); Lucas' "A New Lamb Letter," in *The Academy,* 57 (1899), 373; and Hazlitt's *Lamb and Hazlitt: Further Letters and Records Hitherto Unpublished* (1899). Edward Verrall Lucas (1868–1938), journalist, essayist, critic, was to become the Lambs' best and most devoted editor and biographer.

The eighth edition, Ainger's second edition of *The Letters of Charles Lamb: Newly Arranged, with Additions,* Macmillan and Company, Ltd., of London published, as the last four volumes of its twelve-volume Edition de Luxe of Ainger's *The Life and Works of Charles Lamb,* in 1900. The eighth edition contains Ainger's original Introduction and a "Preface to the Present Edition," which Ainger dated Christmas 1899 and which, except for certain of his expressions of thanks, reads thus:

The present edition of Charles Lamb's Letters makes no claim to be complete. Indeed, no such result is attainable at the present moment, or at any future time. There may be, and probably are, many letters of Lamb's dispersed throughout the world, which have never seen the light of print. I myself know of a whole series, of great interest, in the possession of a family who, for reasons satisfactory to themselves, will not consent to their publication. In the meantime, however, I am glad to have been able to make some important additions to the collection originally edited by me. The very interesting series of letters to Robert Lloyd and his father, contained in the volume *Charles Lamb and the Lloyds,* edited by Mr. E. V. Lucas, are now, by arrangement with the publishers, Messrs. Smith and Elder, included in these volumes, and inserted in their proper places. For various other letters I am indebted to the courtesy of friends and correspondents. . . . Certain letters which I was constrained in my previous edition to place in the Notes, because they had reached me too late for insertion in the text, are now placed there in their due position. Others again, the exact dates of which have been discovered since my former edition was published, have been rearranged in chronological order; and as I have been able to correct many misreadings and misprints in the text, and to embody in the Notes much new information of interest, I hope I may claim that the present edition, though far from perfect, is a real improvement on its predecessor. [IX, or I, xxxiii–xxxiv]

In revising the text for this large-paper edition of Lamb's Life, Works, and Letters, I have seen no reason to depart from the principle on which I had previously acted, of not including among his writings certain fragments which had been left as such by their author, because he had (to repeat a sentence of my own already printed) "tired of his task, or found that he had misconceived his powers." Accordingly, a brief chapter of a proposed novel, and a half-written version in prose of a poem by Thomas Hood, will still be missed by those critics who habitually search first in such a collection for what has been omitted. And once again, I would venture to submit that in editing the letters of a distinguished author, it is at once a disrespect to his memory and an affront to his readers to include Notes, of three lines long, containing an invitation to supper, or a reminder of some outstanding engagement. [IX, or I, xxxv]

Ainger's second edition includes among its 446 letters 32 not in Ainger's first edition and excludes no letters of the 414 in Ainger's first.

Before the ninth edition appeared, six other letters had—two are in Adrian H. Joline's *Meditations of an Autograph Collector* (1902) and four, included in my volumes, are in undetermined issues of *Harper's New Monthly Magazine* and the *National Review.* William Macdonald, editor of the Turner House Classics and the Temple Autobiographies, prepared the ninth edition. J. M. Dent & Company of London and E. P. Dutton & Company of New York published the *Letters of Charles Lamb,* as the final two volumes of their twelve-volume standard and large-paper editions of *The Works of Charles Lamb,* in 1903. It is shown to have been republished by Dent and Dutton in 1907 and 1925, though the last date is questionable.

In his Preface Macdonald credited Talfourd with having had the opportunity and ability to write a lasting biography of Lamb and attacked him for his "folly" in having produced instead "two brilliant fragments, two exquisite pieces of plausible and perfunctory stop-gap,—and each of them was felt to be, in the most essential sense, obsolete—no longer enough, no longer good for the time—the day after its publication. The instant that each was read the world felt that, excellent though this was, more than this was wanted. The position of those two books, consequently, is as unique as it is pathetic. They are a classic, and yet they are an impossible classic. The world cannot well, nor would willingly, let them die; and yet nobody thinks of reprinting them. They only reappear as the material built into somebody else's work" (XII, or II, xvi–xvii).

Macdonald recited the occasions for and some instances of the "momentous and criminal sins of omission" (XII, or II, xviii) of Talfourd, his disregard of dates and his careless dating, and his procedures that resulted in inconvenience to readers of his second edition. Macdonald mentioned Sala's and Purnell's editions. Then he pointed to a defect in Fitzgerald's edition and considered the improvements in and shortcomings of the later editions:

> The great defect of that edition, as regards the letters, was the arrangement into groups, the chronological order beginning afresh with each correspondent. This defect was amended, in different ways, in both Mr Hazlitt's edition of 1886 and in Canon Ainger's of 1888. Mr Hazlitt arranged the letters in one chronological series, but retained the Talfourd biography, or commentary, gloss, disquisitions—one knows not quite what to call it—but he added a great deal, and the book is fully more Hazlitt's than Talfourd's. Canon Ainger, on the other hand—working after Hazlitt—gave the letters themselves, divested of all accompaniments and encumbrances, and supplied the needful notes at the end of each volume. But his chronological order was merely that of Mr Hazlitt, with scarce a new date fixed or an error corrected. One could very easily show that the

second of these two editors had not taken much pains about this matter, and that he set his face resolutely against a certain class of correspondence which was likely to keep a faithful editor out o' bed at night, as it has kept me many a night till four in the morning. But both of these editions are valuable, and each of them is preferable to the other in some respect. Canon Ainger had some opportunities not accorded to Mr Hazlitt; but he has worked under the difficulties that belong to a position of great social and moral importance, and has, consequently, sacrificed Lamb to considerations that are, to say the least, a little special and personal. What I mean will reveal itself to anyone who will compare the true text of the Dibdin letters, now for the first time given to the world, with the version of them to be found in the Eversley Edition—where we have what remains of Lamb's private correspondence after it has been submitted to what one has no choice but to call an ecclesiastical censorship of wit and humour. [XII, or II, xxiii–xxiv]

The first aim of Macdonald was to make his edition as complete as possible. "Suffice it that this edition has prospered so far in its leading aim that the reader is here put in possession of 589 letters of Charles Lamb, as against 417 in the Eversley, and 449 in the Fitzgerald Editions. It is true that this excess of almost 50 per cent. over the number of letters in the Eversley Edition is partly made up by the inclusion of many brief notes which Canon Ainger preferred to exclude—as I also would have preferred to exclude them had I considered my own convenience, and time, and profit, and much waste of eyesight, and electric units, and temper" (XII, or II, xxv).

Macdonald's second aim was "to insist upon, and use all possible means and arguments to secure, perfect fulness and fidelity of the text. This has always been difficult of attainment in regard to Lamb's letters, and even the most tiresome and insistent editor may have to be content, in the end, with something less than what seems to him absolutely indispensable. The forces against which he has to contend came into the field early, and it will be long before they are completely routed from every rood, perch, cranny, and corner of it. Nevertheless, good words have their weight with the better intelligences, and I can congratulate myself on having secured the withdrawal of a veto placed upon certain passages in some of the letters of an important series. 'Your argument is perfectly sound,' I have been told; and consent, at first withheld, has been magnanimously accorded against the grain and bias of personal feeling and personal taste. The glory in such a case belongs to the conquered" (XII, or II, xxv–xxvi). Examples of the superiority of Macdonald's mind and work over the minds and works of his predecessors follow.

Macdonald's third aim was the "effecting of a nearer approach to correctness in the chronological order of the Letters" (XII, or II, xlvi). Examples follow. After those he wrote: "Not to exhaust the catalogue of my achievements, so leaving nothing unknown and magnificent, let me say, generally, that in every main section of the correspondence I think I may claim to have made the way easier for the Reader who is in the habit of remembering what he read on the preceding page, and who desires to find the contents of the page that follows in a concatenation accordingly. To be sure, a very great deal remains to be done; a good deal which even I could do with a few weeks or a few days or even a few hours more at my disposal for the attempt" (XII, or II, xlix–l).

After making other excuses, Macdonald then wrote:

> To come to the very lame and impotent conclusion of this discourse, I must express my regret that want of time has made it absolutely impossible that this editor should have attempted to equip these volumes with such a complement of Notes as he would have wished to supply. In the absolute inability of achieving anything in that direction that was worth doing I seriously considered whether I did not owe it to myself to let these volumes go without any, even the meagrest pretence of note-writing. However, I decided to append a few scattered explanations of the kind that an editor with a bad memory might permit himself to indite when time was wanting in which to look up information or verify references. I ought to say that the same conditions of pressure in the getting out of these volumes have compelled me to be very thankful for the ample assistance rendered in such matters as proof-reading, etc., by some of the members of the staff of Aldine House. Some of the early sheets of the first volume were not read by me at all, but I have only noticed one place which betrays the absence of the editorial eye. And that is not a mistake of this edition, but a stereotyped blunder of forty to sixty years of age, which by that intermission of vigilance has been allowed to make, I hope, its last appearance in decent type. [XII, or II, l–li]

Macdonald's edition includes among its 581 letters 155 not in Ainger's second edition and excludes 20 letters of the 446 in Ainger's second.

Lucas' "Lamb's Letters on the Death of John Wordsworth," in *The Athenaeum* of February 6, 1904, and Major S. Butterworth's "A Lamb Letter," in the *Academy and Literature,* 67 (1904), 72, appeared at about the time of the tenth edition, Ainger's third edition of *The Letters of Charles Lamb: Newly Arranged, with Additions.* Macmillan and Company, Ltd., of London and the Macmillan Company of New York issued it, in two volumes, again in the Eversley Series, in 1904. It has the "Preface to the Edition de Luxe (1900)" and a "Prefatory Note to the Present Edition (1904)," which Ainger dated October 1903 and in which he explained he was able to admit about twenty new letters from Lamb to John Rickman in addition to all the letters in his work of 1900. Ainger's third edition includes among its 464 letters 38 not in Macdonald's edition and excludes 155 letters of the 581 in Macdonald's.

It is shown that Ainger's editions, of 1888, 1900, or 1904, were republished by A. C. Armstrong and Son of New York (1888 twice, 1891, 1894, 1896, 1897, and 1904); Bigelow, Brown of New York (1928?); C. T. Brainard Publishing Company of Boston (1900? and 1912?); The Edinburgh Society (1888); R. H. Hinkley of Boston (1902–1903 and on an unspecified date); International Publishing Company of New York (in the 1890s and perhaps twice in 1900); Jefferson Press of Boston and New York (sometime in the 1900s); Lamb Publishing Company of New York (1888, 1899?, 1899, 1908, 1912?, and perhaps on two other occasions in the 1900s); Macmillan and Company of London and New York (1888, 1891, 1894, and 1897); Pafraets Book Company of Troy, New York (1888–1889, 1888 and 1889, and 1902–1903); and an unspecified Boston firm (sometime after 1909).

The letters in Ernest Betham's *A House of Letters* (1905) appeared at about the time of the eleventh edition, *The Letters of Charles Lamb: In Which Many Mutilated Words and Passages Have Been Restored to Their Original Form; with Letters Never before Published and Facsimiles of Original MS Letters and Poems.* Henry Howard Harper (1871–1953), secretary of the Bibliophile Society, wrote the "Prefatory," which he dated November 26, 1904, and the Introduction. Richard Garnett (1835–1906), biographer, critic, poet, and keeper of printed books at the British Museum, wrote the "Notes on Facsimile Letters." The Bibliophile Society of Boston printed 470 copies of the work, most of them on Dutch handmade paper, a few on Japanese vellum, in five volumes, for its members in 1905.

In the first part of his Introduction Harper rehearsed the failings of the editions of Talfourd, Sala, Purnell, and Fitzgerald—their omissions, excisions, corruptions, incorrect datings, and imperfect or improper orderings of letters. He remarked that neither Fitzgerald nor Hazlitt included the collections of letters to the William Ayrtons, John Bates Dibdin, the Lloyds, and Rickman (there are letters to Rickman in those editions) and only some of the letters to Manning. Harper remarked that of the letters to those, Ainger in 1888 included only the letters to Dibdin, and in 1904 additionally some of the letters to Manning, Rickman, and the senior Charles Lloyd. Harper also remarked that, in part because of the increasing difficulty of collecting and publishing the letters after the appearance of Hazlitt's edition particularly, Ainger and Macdonald were especially liable to perpetuate the mistakes of earlier editors while making their own. Among Harper's examples and comments are these (the brackets are Harper's):

In the very first letter in the second volume of Mr. Macdonald's edition, we find a startling aggregation of blunders, which could have resulted only from the grossest ignorance and carelessness of some copyist to whom the letter, which is to Mrs. Ayrton, was probably intrusted for transcription. It is incredible that the transcribed copy was ever compared with the original, or that the editor paid any attention whatever to it. The letter is dated, at the close, "Cov[ent] Gar[den] 23 Jan. 1821"; whereas, this has been transposed, as well as transmuted, and placed at the beginning of the letter as,—"Coogar, 23 Jan. 1821." In this letter, Lamb says: "My sister desires me, as being a more expert penman than herself," etc. ("penman" is plainly written), and the printed copy has it "person" instead of "penman"; by which the meaning of the sentence is totally perverted. Again, beginning with the fifth line, the original reads: "I like to write that word *Fanny*. I do not know but it was one reason of taking upon me this pleasing task." By changing words and interposing a comma in the printed copy, the pleasing little complimentary turn of the remark is converted into a ridiculous state of uncertainty. In the seventh and eighth lines "William and Frances" is printed, "William and Francis," by which the sex of Frances (Fanny) is changed from feminine to masculine. The printed copy has three other slight errors.

In a letter dated February 25, 1809, to Robert Lloyd, Lamb tells him that he is "worthy to be mentioned with Claudian's *Old Man of Verona*."

Mr. Macdonald gives it, "Claudian's old Mare of Verona." This curious inadvertency almost provokes a suspicion that even Mr. Macdonald had been guilty of playing horse with Lamb's text. The mistake is evidently not chargeable to negligence on the part of the printer, because the absence of italics or quotation marks would indicate that the editor did not grasp the sense of the comparison, and it never occurred to him that Lamb referred to something written by Claudian. [I, 14–15]

In an undated letter to Manning, written in the spring of 1803, the following passage is omitted entirely: "Lloyd has written to me, and names you. I think a letter from Maison Magnan (is *that* a Person or a Thing?) would gratify him. G. Dyer is in love with an idiot, who loves a doctor, who is incapable of loving anything but himself,—a puzzling circle of perverse providences! A maze as un-get-out-again-able as the house which Jack built."

Possibly this last excision may have been pardonable in Talfourd's first edition, but Lamb's reputation as a classic is too securely established to admit of any meddling with his text in the present age. It is inconceivable that Canon Ainger should have countenanced such omissions in his edition, seeing that he had ample facilities for comparison of the Manning series (which seems to have suffered in the hands of editors nearly as much as the Coleridge series), for he says, "the autographs of the Manning letters have been in my hands, through the kindness of their owner, the Rev. C. R. Manning," etc. The cases here cited, however, are mere trivialities in comparison with the wholesale slaughtering process inflicted upon many of the letters, even in the most recent editions.

In the Dent edition of 1903, Mr. Macdonald has probably approached completeness of text more nearly than any of his predecessors. In his preface he shows himself to be thoroughly awake to the necessity of "perfect fulness and fidelity of the text," but he was unfortunately compelled to rely too much upon the untrustworthy texts of Ainger, Hazlitt, and others before them, except for the new letters which he had in hand; and indeed many of these are not faithfully transcribed, as we have already seen. A collation of the two latest and most complete editions of the letters with the original MSS., with the corrections pencilled in the margins of the books, has resulted in making the volumes appear extremely ridiculous, when viewed in the light of any pretence to completeness. The corrected pages resemble a proof-reader's first corrected copy from type set up by an apprentice in a job-printing office. In many places the marginal spacings were insufficient to admit the requisite interpolations, and it was necessary to insert extra sheets. [I, 16–17]

This much may be said for Mr. Macdonald, however; he generally followed the text, where he had access to the original MSS., and such deviations as we have discovered, in cases where these were actually in his hands, appear to have resulted from lack of due care in transcribing, and hasty, if not careless, editing. The same cannot be said of Canon Ainger, who, we believe, did not pretend to give the full text without modifications. In some places the editors seem to wander entirely from the text, while in other parts, lines are actually given *verbatim*. [I, 20–21]

If any further collateral proof be required in order to show the immediate necessity of a new and more complete edition of Charles Lamb's letters, the purpose of the present edition may become more plainly evident and justifiable when it is known that by comparing the two latest editions of the letters, it has been discovered that the Macdonald edition . . . contains one hundred and sixty-one letters which do not appear in the latest Ainger edition . . . while the latter edition contains forty-two letters not included in the former. All of these are now given, together with several not appearing in either of these two, or any previous edition. Also, in the present edition we have restored upwards of five thousand words omitted entirely from the text of letters in the supposedly complete editions, and rehabilitated nearly three thousand words and sentences which have been changed from their original state, either by accident or intent. In a single letter, that of August 14, 1800, to Coleridge, sixty-three corrections have been made.

It is always easy to criticise others, however, for what they have done, and more particularly for what they have left undone. In recent years a great deal has been accomplished by editors in the way of supplying dates, placing the letters in convenient arrangement, providing comprehensive indices, and elucidating obscure passages in the text by explanatory notes; and if there are still some deficiencies, it remains for us to remedy them to the best of our ability and be thankful for what has already been achieved, rather than waste time in bewailing the shortcomings of preceding editions. [I, 22–23]

Harper and Garnett did not always "slavishly" adhere to Lamb's punctuation, capitalization, and other such matters. They hoped that by the lengths to which they and the Bibliophile Society had gone to make their work complete, accurate, and attractive, Lamb's "aggrieved spirit . . . [might] be tranquillized in some measure" (I, 24). Harper devoted the second part of his Introduction to an analysis of the characteristics of Lamb and the contents especially of the letters. To that he annexed "Contemporary Notices of Charles Lamb," one notice by Moxon dated January 27 and the other from *The Mirror* of January 24, 1835. The edition, which is attractive, includes among its 746 letters 284 not in Ainger's third edition and excludes 2 letters of the 464 in Ainger's third.

The twelfth edition comprises the final two volumes of Lucas' *The Works of Charles and Mary Lamb,* which G. P. Putnam's Sons of New York and Methuen & Company of London published, in seven volumes, during the period 1903–1905. In this edition Lucas could not, understandably, take into account the work of Harper and Garnett. Three paragraphs in Lucas' Preface (dated November 20, 1904) to the two volumes are especially relevant to the publishing history of the Lambs' letters:

> In this edition of the correspondence of Charles Lamb, that of his sister, Mary Lamb, is for the first time included. In it also appear for the first time between seventy and eighty letters, many of them of the highest importance; and it is the first edition to take note in chronological order of those letters printed by other editors that are not available for the present volumes: a step which should, I think, add to the biographical value of the work. [VI, v]
>
> Owing to the curious operations of the law of copyright, it will not for at least forty-two years be possible for any one edition of Lamb's correspondence to contain all the letters. To-day, in order to possess a set complete down to the present time, one must purchase at least nine, and possibly more, works, amounting to many volumes—among them *Charles Lamb and the Lloyds,* of which I was the editor, but which I am debarred from using. It is in order, to some extent, to meet the difficulty thus set up, and to cover the whole ground of the correspondence, that I have in the notes drawn attention to every important letter distributed over these many other volumes. I am, however, perfectly aware that only for a brief period will this list be exhaustive, since new letters continually come to light, while there are, I understand, at this moment in private collections in America many letters that have not yet been printed, forty-two years' copyright in which may date from the day they are published—for the benefit not of any descendants of the Lambs (for they left none) but of those who happen to possess them. [VI, vi]

In acknowledging the kindnesses of some of his contributors, Lucas mentioned new or newly transcribed letters to Ayrton, Coleridge,

Dibdin, Charles Wentworth Dilke, Moxon, and the Wordsworths. This paragraph follows:

> The Barton letters and all other letters at the British Museum have been copied afresh, and so have those in the Dyce and Forster collection at South Kensington, at the Bodleian and National Portrait Gallery. But although great care has been taken, I am not prepared, in the face of the fatality that indissolubly associates editors of Lamb with inaccuracy, to guarantee a single line. In printing from the original documents I have sometimes altered the punctuation—but only as little as might be to assist the sense at the first reading. In great part I have left the letters as Lamb wrote them, often retaining his peculiarities of spelling and punctuation, unexpected capitals and still more unexpected small initials. I trust that no one will resent this literalness. Now and then, very reluctantly, I have had to omit a sentence or paragraph on account of a freedom beyond modern taste, while on two or three occasions a reference of a personal character has been deleted as possibly hurtful to the susceptibilities of living people. But the total amount of omissions from the letters available for the present edition does not equal one quite short missive; and a number of round epithets and passages will be discovered in it that other editors, with more courage than I can muster, have suppressed. [VI, viii]

In the Contents Lucas starred the new letters and new collations or restorations and gave the sources of his texts. This edition includes among its 590 letters 27 not in Harper and Garnett's edition and excludes 183 letters of the 746 in Harper and Garnett's.

The letters first published in Bertram Dobell's "Some Unpublished Letters of Charles Lamb," in *The Athenaeum* of May 5, 1906, and Walter Jerrold's *Thomas Hood: His Life and Times* (1907) preceded the appearance of the thirteenth edition, Lucas' *The Letters of Charles and Mary Lamb, 1796–1820* [and *1821–1842*]. Methuen & Company, Ltd., of London published the two volumes as the final ones of its six-volume edition of Lucas' *The Works of Charles and Mary Lamb* in 1912. It is shown that Macmillan republished both the entire edition and the letters only in 1913. In his Preface Lucas noted his inclusion of all of Mary's letters—forty-five according to his count—and his references to or abstracts of the letters in previous editions that he was prevented from using because of continuing copyright restrictions. He noticed the completeness of Harper and Garnett's edition, his failure to obtain permission to republish a large number of letters from it, and the restraints imposed by and judgments regarding English copyright law that still kept him from republishing sixteen letters from his *Lamb and the Lloyds*. He wrote, as an example of other difficulties, of letters that passed through Sotheby's while his work was passing through the press. Of his work, he wrote that it "has been revised throughout and in it will be found much new material. I have retained from the large edition only such notes as bear upon the Lambs and the place of the letters in their life, together with such explanatory references as seemed indispensable. For the sources of quotations and so forth the reader must consult the old edition" (V, vii). But in the Contents he again gave the sources of his texts. This edition includes among its 604 letters 13 not in Lucas' first edition and excludes 1 of the 590 letters in Lucas' first.

Preceding the appearance of the fourteenth edition are the letters first published in Harry B. Smith's *A Sentimental Library: Comprising Books Formerly Owned by Famous Writers, Presentation Copies, Manuscripts, and Drawings* (1914), which has facsimiles of letters; S. M. Ellis' "Some New Charles Lamb Letters," in the *Saturday Review,* 119 (1915), 596–597 and 625–626; Mrs. G. A. Anderson's "Some Unpublished Letters of Charles Lamb," in the *London Mercury,* 7 (1922), 36–45; facsimiles in W. K. Bixby's *Charles Lamb: A Letter regarding Roast Pig to William Hazlitt and a Letter on Friendship to Robert Lloyd, Together with a Dissertation on Roast Pig* (1922), Luther A. Brewer's *Some Lamb and Browning Letters to Leigh Hunt* (1925; reprinted 1969), and Oxford University Press's *Seven Letters from Charles Lamb to Charles Ryle of the East India House, 1828–1832* (1931); John Howard Birss's "A New Letter of Charles Lamb," in *Notes and Queries,* 161 (1931), 363; Thomas Ollive Mabbott and John Howard Birss's "Some Uncollected Letters of Charles Lamb," in *Notes and Queries,* 165 (1933), 296–298; R. C. Bald's "A New Letter from Charles Lamb," in *Modern Language Notes,* 49 (1934), 511–513; facsimiles in *Piccadilly Notes. Charles Lamb Centenary Number,* No. 13 (1934), 407–408, a sales catalogue of Henry Sotheran, Ltd.; and L. E. Holman's *Lamb's "Barbara S——": The Life of Frances Maria Kelly, Actress* (1935).

Lucas' *The Letters of Charles Lamb: To Which Are Added Those of His Sister, Mary Lamb* is the fourteenth and last edition. J. M. Dent & Sons, Ltd., of London and Methuen & Company, Ltd., of

London published it, in three volumes, in 1935. Yale University Press republished it in the same year. AMS Press, Inc., of New York reprinted it in 1968. Here are portions of the first three pages of the Introduction, which Lucas dated July 1935:

The present edition of the letters of Charles Lamb is the first to bring all the known material into one work: a desirable condition, made possible by Mr. Hugh Dent's enthusiasm and by his firm's acquisition of the residuary legatee's rights, by the courtesy of collectors, and by the friendly co-operation of other publishers. Thus not only do these three volumes contain all the letters in the editions of Talfourd, of Percy Fitzgerald, of Bohn's Library [Hazlitt's edition], of Ainger, of W. Carew Hazlitt [his other works on the Lambs, of 1874, 1897, 1899, mentioned above], of Everyman's Library, based on the labours of William Macdonald, of the Boston Bibliophile Society, 1905, and of my own in its latest form, 1912, but also whatever has come to light since their day.

That Lamb wrote many more letters than we possess is made evident by the leanness of certain years—say, for instance, from 1809 to 1818, while there is nothing preceding those to Coleridge beginning with 27th May 1796, when the writer was twenty[-one], marvellously preserved by their not too orderly recipient, although there would, for instance, have been at least an acknowledgment, but probably much more, of Coleridge's lines *To a Friend, Together with an Unfinished Poem,* sent to Lamb, who was the friend indicated, in December 1794. We know also, from references here and there, that other letters must have been written, and from time to time some of them will, I feel sure, emerge. Meanwhile, here is as complete a harvest as now can be.

When, more than thirty years ago, I was first engaged in this most agreeable of tasks, there was less concentration. The correspondence with Coleridge, for example, was in London, the property of the late Mrs. Arthur Morrison; the Moxon letters were at Rowfant; the Rickman letters were in England, but, through copyright restrictions, inaccessible to me, while the Manning letters belonged to an American collector who refused to let them be seen. Since then, however, all these treasures passed into the hands of one wealthy and omnivorous collector, Henry E. Huntington of Pasadena, who has since died, and they are now in the Huntington Library there [properly San Marino], the property in perpetuity of the State of California, for any one to examine in comfort.

America indeed (although, in a moment of petulance, Lamb once vowed he would write only for antiquity) now possesses most of his MSS. At Pasadena there are more than two hundred of the letters, all of which are in this edition. Lamb's considerable correspondence with Wordsworth belongs now, by bequest, to the University of Texas, and is incorporated here; in the Pierpont Morgan Library, now vested in the City of New York, there are some thirty letters, which I have been allowed to copy; in the Folger Shakespeare Library in Washington I found a dozen; and so forth. And then there are the private collectors. . . . Since private ownership frequently changes, I have marked the home only of such letters as are safely at rest in institutions, but I hope that there are no omissions in the list of acknowledgments that follows. . . .

What England retains, beyond the Bernard Barton correspondence in the British Museum, bequeathed by Mrs. Edward FitzGerald, and the [Alexander] Dyce and Forster treasures at the Victoria and Albert Museum, I am unable to report; for public requests for such information have yielded almost no results, the most important being, I think, the full text of the letter of 25th May 1820 to Dorothy Wordsworth which I received from Miss Emma Hutchinson. The letters to Southey, still in Talfourd's transcription, should, for instance, be somewhere, but I know of only two, and there are many others the present traditional text of which badly needs collating with their originals. . . .

As to the value and importance of these letters, their good sense, their wit, their humanity, their fun, their timeliness and timelessness, I have nothing fresh to say: the book is the evidence. I would, however, remark that the chronological arrangement and annotations constitute a new biography of this unique and fascinating figure in English literature, and probably the best loved. [I, v–vii]

Lucas wrote a few words on the fullness of his annotations, on his inclusion of Lamb's short letters, on Lamb's odd spellings. Lucas paid tribute to the researches of Mrs. Gertrude Alison Anderson (1875–1924) by giving over most of the remainder of the Introduction to appreciations of her by her son—Basil Anderson—and by the poet and scholar Edmund Blunden (1896–1974). The edition includes among its 1,027 letters 424 not in Lucas' second edition and also includes 229 not in any of the editions. It excludes 1 of the 604 letters in Lucas' second edition and also excludes 6 letters in other publications.

Early to make known some of its weaknesses were E. G. B. in "Notes on 'The Letters of Charles and Mary Lamb,'" *Notes and Queries,* 180 (1941), 329–332; B. in "Letters of Charles Lamb," *Notes and Queries,* 184 (1943), 248–249; and George L. Barnett in "Dating Lamb's Contributions to the *Table Book,*" *Publications of the Modern*

Language Association of America, 60 (1945), 602–605. Professor Barnett later exposed many more: first, in "A Critical Analysis of the Lucas Edition of Lamb's Letters," *Modern Language Quarterly,* 9 (1948), 303–314, defects mainly in the transcriptions of the letters in the Berg Collection, The New York Public Library; and then, in "Corrections in the Text of Lamb's Letters," *Huntington Library Quarterly,* 18 (1955), 147–158, defects in the transcriptions of the letters in The Huntington Library. In his 1948 article Barnett concluded that he had "no desire to trample on the esteem in which the memory of E. V. Lucas is generally held."

I have previously added my word of praise for his admirable annotations and good intentions for a task whose difficulty I do not minimize. My concern is rather with the text of Charles Lamb's letters. The examples given of various types of errors are not confined to any one portion of the three volumes, nor are they limited to a particular collection of letters. In the main the letters concerned are in collections that Mr. Lucas visited, and, while we are not told on whose authority the texts are put forth, where the location is given the implication is that Lucas saw the original. But I have shown that the mere listing of the locations of some of the originals cannot be regarded as proof that they have been the sources for his texts. Furthermore, indications are that many, if not most, of the letters are based on previous and faulty editions, and that Lucas has failed to avoid the tendency of editors of Lamb's letters to perpetuate errors and to inaugurate others by overzealous emendation, excessive editing, and downright carelessness.

While some Lamb lovers have found the Lucas edition perfectly adequate for their shelves, and while there is no doubt that it is the best edition to date, it cannot be the final text for scholars who demand accuracy in every detail. In short, we do not yet possess a definitive edition of the letters of Charles Lamb.

Barnett's 1955 article begins:

Some time ago I called attention to the numerous types of errors in the so-called "standard" edition of the correspondence of Charles Lamb. Examples were given of faulty dating, erroneous location of manuscripts, incorrect transcription of text, and misinformation in the notes. While many errors were the result of following previous, faulty readings, many others were inaugurated. The examples were taken from all three volumes of this edition and were not confined to any one collection of manuscripts.

It was concluded that we cannot call the Lucas edition a definitive one but one that must be used with suspicion and caution. The present paper is not concerned with presenting additional proof of these findings; none is needed. Its purpose is to correct Lucas' text of those letters whose original manuscripts are preserved at the Henry E. Huntington Library.

The article ends:

In the twenty years since the appearance of Lucas' edition of 1,021 letters written by Charles and Mary Lamb, it has become clearly evident that the text is unreliable and the dating inaccurate in a large number of cases. The locations of the manuscripts of more than half the total number of letters are omitted. Presumably the text of these is based on previous editions, and in the case of those manuscripts that have been lost, we may never be certain of the accuracy or completeness of the printed version; indeed, the faults in transcriptions that can be checked should make us aware of the strong possibility of other errors. Certainly, when a new or revised edition of Lamb's correspondence is called for, dependence on available original manuscripts should be insisted on. In the meantime, the correction of the text of a substantial portion of the corpus, facilitated by the unparalleled collection at the Huntington Library, should be of service to scholars of the Romantic Period.

Evidence of Lucas' poor treatment of letters at Harvard is presented by Carl Woodring in "Charles Lamb in the Harvard Library," *Harvard Library Bulletin,* 10 (1956), 208–239 and 367–402; at the Victoria and Albert Museum, by P. F. Morgan in "On Some Letters of Charles Lamb," *Notes and Queries,* N.S. 3 (1956), 531–532; and at the British Museum and the Bodleian, by Duane Schneider in "The Lucas Edition of Lamb's Letters: Corrections and Notes," *Notes and Queries,* N.S. 21 (1974), 171–174. Evidence of similar treatment of other letters is presented by P. P. Howe, for example, in "Lamb and Hazlitt," *TLS* of September 26, 1935; T. O. Mabbott in "Notes on Two Letters of Charles Lamb," *Notes and Queries,* 189 (1945), 37; and Wallace Nethery in "Charles Lamb to Janus Weathercock," *Notes and Queries,* 207 (1962), 182–183.

Letters or portions published at about the time or since the publication of Lucas' edition of 1935 are in Robert S. Newdick's *The First Life and Letters of Charles Lamb: A Study of Thomas Noon Talfourd as Editor and Biographer* (1935); Lucas' "An Unpublished Letter of Charles Lamb," in the *TLS* of February 13, 1937; M. A. de Wolfe

Howe's "Lamb to Hazlitt: A New-found Letter," in *The Spectator,* 161 (1938), 237–238, and the *CLSB* of March 1952; "Olybrius' " "Complete Text of a Letter of Charles Lamb," in *Notes and Queries,* 174 (1938), 28; "Olybrius and Co.'s" "An Uncollected Letter of Lamb," in *Notes and Queries,* 175 (1938), 437–438 (shown to be in Lucas' edition by V. Rendall's "An Uncollected Letter of Lamb," in *Notes and Queries,* 176 [1939], 64); John H. Birss's "Lamb on Revisions: An Uncollected Letter," in *American Notes and Queries,* 2 (1942), 83–84, and *Notes and Queries,* 183 (1942), 286 (republishes with corrections the letter published in Curtis Guild's *A Chat about Celebrities* [1897], referred to above); Jeremiah Stanton Finch's "Charles Lamb's 'Companionship . . . in Almost Solitude,' " in the *Princeton University Library Chronicle,* 6 (1945), 179–199; Richard D. Altick's *The Cowden Clarkes* (1948); Reginald L. Hine's *Charles Lamb and His Hertfordshire* (1949); George L. Barnett's "Charles Lamb to John Britton: An Unpublished Letter," in the *Modern Language Quarterly,* 13 (1952), 353–355 (gives complete the letter given in part in John H. Birss's "A New Letter of Charles Lamb," in *Notes and Queries,* 173 [1937], 278); M. K. Joseph's *Charles Aders: A Biographical Note, Together with Some Unpublished Letters Addressed to Him by S. T. Coleridge and Others, and Now in the Grey Collection, Auckland City Library* (1953); Basil Willey and Paul M. Zall's "Another Unpublished Letter of Charles Lamb," in the *CLSB* of March 1954; Barnett's "Charles Lamb and the Button Family: An Unpublished Poem and Letter," in the *Huntington Library Quarterly,* 19 (1956), 191–195; Vera Watson's "Thomas Noon Talfourd and His Friends," in the *TLS* of April 20 and 27, 1956; Carl Woodring's "Charles Lamb in the Harvard Library," in the *Harvard Library Bulletin,* 10 (1956), 208–239 and 367–402; Barnett's "Charles Lamb's Part in an Edition of Hogarth," in the *Modern Language Quarterly,* 20 (1959), 315–320, and the *CLSB* of July 1960; Earl Leslie Griggs's edition of the *Collected Letters of Samual Taylor Coleridge,* III (1959), 220 (republished in Barbara E. Rooke's edition of *The Friend* [1969], I, lv); John R. Barker's "Some Early Correspondence of Sarah Stoddart and the Lambs," in the *Huntington Library Quarterly,* 24 (1960), 59–69 (presents the same letters presented in John R. Barker's "The First Mrs. Hazlitt: And Some New Lamb Letters," in the *CLSB* of September 1961); David V. Erdman's "Reliques of the Contemporaries of William Upcott, 'Emperor of Autographs,' " in the *New York Public Library Bulletin,* 64 (1960), 581–587; Woodring's "Lamb Takes a Holiday," in the *Harvard Library Bulletin,* 14 (1960), 253–264; T. C. Skeat's "Letters of Charles and Mary Lamb and Coleridge," in the *British Museum Quarterly,* 26 (1962–1963), 17–21; W. Braekman's "Two Hitherto Unpublished Letters of Charles and Mary Lamb to the Morgans," in *English Studies,* 44 (1963), 108–118 (gives the same letters given by Skeat and also Mary's portion of a letter written by her and Lamb); David Bonnell Green's "Charles Lamb, Bradbury and Evans, and the Title of *The Last Essays of Elia,*" in *English Language Notes,* 1 (1963), 37–40; Green's "Three New Letters of Charles Lamb," in the *Huntington Library Quarterly,* 27 (1963), 83–86, and the *CLSB* of March 1964; Barnett's *Charles Lamb: The Evolution of Elia* (1964; includes the letter mentioned in Newman I. White's "Unpublished Letters," in the *TLS* of September 10, 1938); Green's "A New Letter of Charles Lamb to Basil Montagu," in the *Huntington Library Quarterly,* 31 (1968), 199–200; Carl E. Ketcham's "The Death of Wordsworth's Brother John: Manuscript Materials in the Cornell–Dove Cottage Collection," in the *Cornell Library Journal* (Spring 1970), pp. 25–43 (presents complete the letter quoted in part in Frank Prentice Rand's *Wordsworth's Mariner Brother* [1966]); and James T. Wills's "New Lamb Material in the Aders Album: Jacob Götzenberger and Two Versions of 'Angel Help,' " in the *Harvard Library Bulletin,* 22 (1974), 406–413.

IV

The present edition includes all available letters of Charles and Mary Anne Lamb. Notices are provided for the few extant manuscript letters that are unavailable. Over 7 percent of the more than 1,150 letters in the present edition have not previously been published. Over 11 percent are not in the preceding edition. About 80 percent of the letters in the present edition are transcriptions of original manuscripts, copies, or facsimiles held by the persons and institutions listed in the Acknowledgments. The holders were found through advertisements, announcements, and letters of inquiry to collectors, dealers, librarians, and persons interested in Lamb scholarship in Asia, Australia, Europe, New Zealand, and North America. The Huntington Library collection, the largest, has approximately two hundred manuscript letters. Mr. W. Hugh Peal's collection, the second largest, has approximately one hundred. Collections of ten or more but fewer than sixty are held by Lord Abinger, The British Museum, Brown University, The Folger Shakespeare Library, Harvard University, The University of Leeds, the State University of New York at Buffalo, The New York Public Library, The Pierpont Morgan Library, Princeton University, The Rosenbach Foundation, Mr. Robert H. Taylor, The University of Texas, the Victoria and Albert Museum, Dr. Williams's Trust and Dr. Williams's Library, and Yale University.

In none of the letters of the present edition have the Lambs' words been willfully excluded or the Lambs' language willfully altered. The red ink and sketches, the asterisks and punctuation marks, the fanciful letter layout and ink blots to which Lamb calls attention, and what Talfourd called "the curious varieties of writing with which the originals abound, and which are scrupulously adapted to the subjects" are either reproduced or indicated by varieties of type. The placement of such formal parts of the letters as headings, salutations, complimentary closes, signatures, and postscripts is, except when content or meaning might be affected, regularized:

1. The place of composition is assigned in square brackets when it is not given in the original letter or when it is different from that indicated in the part title and running head.

2. The date or conjectured date of composition is assigned in square brackets when the date is not given in the original letter. An assigned date is explained when necessary. When a date is given at the beginning of an original letter and another is given either at its end or on its address leaf, the date line at the head of the printed letter shows both the beginning and completion dates of the letter—June 30[–July 1], 1814, for instance; the date at the end or on the address leaf of the original letter is set flush left at the end of the printed letter. When dates are given at the beginning, within, and at the end or on the address leaf of an original letter, the beginning and completion dates are shown on the printed letter as above. The internal dates are set flush left when they are written at the end of a portion of a letter and flush right when they are written at the beginning of a portion of a letter. A conjectured assigned date is shown this way: [May ?6, 1800]

when the day is in question, [?May 6, 1800] when the month, [May 6? 1800] when the day and the month, [May 6 ?1800] when the year, or [May 6, 1800?] when the whole. An assigned date derived from a postmark is normally neither questioned nor explained.

3. The salutation is always separated from the body of the letter even when it is run into the body of the original letter.

4. Paragraphs are always indented even though some in the original letters are indicated only by spacings.

5. Superior characters and most interlinear writings are lowered, important or interesting cancellations restored in angle brackets, illegible cancellations of one manuscript line or more noted, and locutions torn away or illegible indicated by ellipses in square brackets and their extent noted.

6. The many locutions written larger than those near them, in most instances apparently for emphasis, are printed in boldface or, when underscored, in boldface italic. Where locutions are not obviously but are suggestively larger than those near them, I have relied on my understanding of the characteristics of the Lambs' handwriting and on my perception of the Lambs' general manner of expression in deciding whether to have such locutions printed in boldface. The several locutions written in huge characters are printed in large boldface. Locutions however much larger than normal in the original letters are not represented when they are written over other locutions to correct or cancel them or, except in extraordinary cases, when they appear in addresses, salutations, complimentary closes, or signatures.

7. Also not represented are underscorings in addresses, dates, and signatures; punctuation following addresses, dates, and signatures; lines across pages drawn (needlessly) to separate parts of a letter; and carets. Misplaced carets are disregarded altogether.

8. Some marks of punctuation, for the most part periods after existing dashes that apparently end sentences within paragraphs, have been silently added. Quotations and parentheses have been silently closed.

9. The American conventions of punctuation in conjunction with closing quotations marks have been observed, parentheses substituted for virgules employed as parentheses, and dashes standardized to one-em, two-em, and three-em lengths.

10. Misspellings have been corrected, within them in square brackets or in the notes, when words other than those intended or when non-

words whose senses are not clear result—"boat" for "boa[s]t," for example, or "cout" for "cou[r]t"—or when they probably would be misconstrued as the editor's or a typographer's errors.

11. The complimentary close is always separated from the body of the letter even when it is run into the body of the original letter. A complimentary close expanded over a few lines may be compressed into fewer.

12. The signature is always separated from the body of the letter or the complimentary close even when it is run into one or the other in the original letter.

13. Postscripts are set as paragraphs where postscripts normally belong, no matter where they appear on the original, and in the order in which they seem to have been written.

14. Lamb's glosses are set as notes at the end of the letter, no matter where they appear on the original, and in the same type face and size as the rest of the letter. They are marked by asterisks, daggers, or other such symbols, regardless of how Lamb marked them.

15. In an unnumbered note, or source note, to each letter is the name of the holder of the original manuscript, copy, or facsimile, or the source of the published text used when an original manuscript, a copy, or a facsimile is unavailable or has not been recovered. The text used whenever possible in such instances is Lucas' of 1935, unless another seems clearly more faithful to the Lambs' ways. The presentation of such previously published letters conforms to that of the other letters in the placement of parts and in such matters as the substitution of roman for italic type in dates, the deletion of unnecessary or irregular editorial intrusions, and the deletion of punctuation following addresses, dates, and signatures. All previously published letters are designated, as well as their locations in the fourteen principal editions or in the work in which they first or most completely appear if they are not in any of those editions.

16. Foreign expressions are translated, in the notes, if they are not in *The American College Dictionary* (New York: Random House, 1949).

PART I

Letters 1–27

7 Little Queen Street, Holborn

May 27, 1796—June 29, 1797

1. *Charles Lamb to Samuel Taylor Coleridge*

[May 27, 1796]

Dear C—

make yourself perfectly easy about May.[1] I paid his bill, when I sent your clothes. I was flush of money, & am so still to all the purposes of a single life, so give yourself no further concern about it. The money would be superfluous to me, if I had it.

With regard to Allen,—the woman he has married has some money, I have heard about £200 a year, enough for the maintenance of herself & children; one of whom is a girl **nine years old!** so Allen has dipt betimes into the cares of a family. I very seldom see him, & do not know whether he has given up the Westminster hospital.

When Southey becomes as modest as his predecessor Milton, & publishes his Epics in duodecimo I will read 'em,—a Guinea a book is somewhat exorbitant, nor have I the opportunity of borrowing the **work.**[2] The extracts from it in the Monthly Review & the short passages in your Watchman seem to me much superior to any thing in his partnership account with Lovell———

Your poems[3] I shall procure forthwith. There were noble lines in what you inserted in one of your Numbers from Religious musings, but I thought them elaborate. I am somewhat glad you have given up that Paper—it must have been dry, unprofitable, & of "dissonant mood" to your disposition. I wish you success in all your undertakings, & am glad to hear you are employed about the Evidences of Religion. There is need of multiplying such books an hundred fold in this philosophical age to *prevent* converts to Atheism, for they seem too tough disputants to meddle with afterwards—. I am sincerely sorry for Allen, as a family man particularly———

Le Grice[4] is gone to make puns in Cornwall. He has got a tutorship to a young boy, living with his Mother a widow Lady. He will of course initiate him quickly in "whatsoever things are lovely, honorable, & of good report." He has cut Miss Hunt compleatly,—the poor Girl is very ill on the Occasion, but he laughs at it, & justifies himself by saying "she does not see him laugh!" Coleridge, I know not what suffering scenes you have gone through at Bristol,—my life has been somewhat diversified of late. The 6 weeks that finished last year & began this your very humble servant spent very agreeably in a **mad house at Hoxton—.** I am got somewhat rational now, & **dont bite any one.** But **mad** I was—& many a vagary my imagination played with **me,**[5] enough to make a **volume** if all **told**— ———

My Sonnets I have extended to the **Number of nine** since I saw you, & will some day communicate to you———

I am beginning a poem in blank **verse,** which if I finish I publish———

White[6] is on the eve of publishing (he took the hint from **Vortigern**) Original letters of Falstaff Shallow &c—a copy you shall have when it comes out. They are without exception the best imitations I ever saw— ———

Coleridge it may convince you of my regards for you when I tell you my head ran on you in my madness as much almost as on another Person,[7] who I am inclined to think was the more immediate cause of my temporary frenzy—. The sonnet I send you has small merit as poetry but you will be curious to **read** it when I tell you it was written in my prison house in one of my lucid Intervals

to my sister

If from my lips some angry accents fell,
  Peevish complaint, or harsh reproof unkind,
  Twas but the Error of a sickly mind,
And troubled thoughts, clouding the purer well,
  & waters clear, of Reason: & for **me**
  Let this my verse the poor atonement be,
My verse, which thou to praise: wast ever inclined
  Too highly, & with a partial eye to see
No Blemish: thou to me didst ever shew
  Fondest affection, & woudst oftimes lend
An ear to the desponding, love sick Lay,
  Weeping my sorrows with me, who repay
But ill the mighty debt, of love I owe,
  Mary, to thee, my sister & my friend———

With these lines, & with that sisters kindest remembrances to C— I conclude—

Yours Sincerely
Lamb

Your conciones ad populum[8] are the most eloquent politics that ever came in my way.

Write, when convenient—not as a task, for here is nothing in this letter to **answer**——

You may inclose under cover to me at the India house what letters you please, for they come post free.— —[9]

We cannot send our remembrances to Mrs. C—not having seen her, but believe me our best good wishes attend you both———

My civic & poetic compt's to Southey[10] if at Bristol—. Why, he is a very Leviathan of Bards—the small minow I—

MS: Henry E. Huntington Library; by permission of The Huntington Library, San Marino, Calif. Pub.: Talfourd (1848), I, 4–7; Sala, I, 1–4; Purnell, I, 1–4; Fitzgerald, I, 287–290; Hazlitt, I, 88–91; Ainger (1888), I, 1–3; Ainger (1900), I, 1–4; Macdonald, I, 1–3; Ainger (1904), I, 1–3; Harper, II, 3–6; Lucas (1905), VI, 1–3; Lucas (1912), V, 1–3; Lucas (1935), I, 1–3. Address: Mr. Coleridge/ Bristol. Postmark: May 27, 1796.

1. William May, according to the London directory of 1808, of The Salutation and Cat. He was probably its landlord and had retained Coleridge's belongings as surety against a bill Coleridge left unpaid when he left the inn in January 1795 for The Angel, in St. Martin's le Grand, Newgate Street. The letter Lamb is answering has not been recovered. As a rule I shall not call attention to letters to the Lambs that have not been recovered. For Robert Allen, mentioned below, see the Introduction, p. xxxi.

2. Southey's *Joan of Arc, an Epic Poem,* which Joseph Cottle (1770–1853), the Bristol bookseller, author, and friend and benefactor of Coleridge and Southey, had published earlier this year in quarto and which established Southey's reputation as a writer. It is favorably noticed in the *Monthly Magazine,* 2d Ser., 19 (April 1796), 361–368. Its passages at Book II, 431–433, IV, 484–504, and VII, 320–331, are given in *The Watchman,* No. 1 (March 1, 1796), 19 and 27–28. On p. 27 of *The Watchman* Coleridge, borrowing from Mark Akenside's "Notes on the Two Books of the Odes," *Poems* (1772), p. 344, described it as "a poem which exhibits fresh proof that great poetical talents and high sentiments of liberty do reciprocally produce and assist each other." (For Coleridge's contribution of fifty-nine lines to Book I, three hundred sixty-one to Book II, ten to Book III, and nine to Book IV see *Coleridge's Poetical Works* [1912], I, 131, and II, 1027–1030, and *Joan of Arc,* p. vi.) Robert Lovell (1770?–1796), below, of whose death on May 3 from "a putrid fever" (*Coleridge's Letters,* I, 207) Lamb was still unaware, was a brother-in-law of Coleridge and Southey by his marriage to Mary Fricker (1771–1862) on January 20, 1794. He was their collaborator in planning a pantisocracy and in writing *The Fall of Robespierre. An Historic Drama* (1794), though Southey had to rewrite Lovell's unsuitable third act in addition to writing his own second act. Lovell was Southey's collaborator in the composition of *Poems: Containing The Retrospect, Odes, Elegies, Sonnets, &c.* (1795). Besides his widow, Lovell left a son, Robert, Jr. Lovell's (unidentified) father and brother reluctantly provided for both as a consequence of the entreaties of Southey. Accounts of Lovell are in *The Observer, Part 1st Being a Transient Glance at about Forty Youths of Bristol* (Bristol: n.p. [1795]), p. 16, and in M. Ray Adams, *Studies in the Literary Backgrounds of English Radicalism, with Special Reference to the French Revolution* (1947; rpt. New York: Greenwood Press, 1968), pp. 130–140.

3. *Poems on Various Subjects* (1796), which contains, as Effusions VII and XI–XIII, Lamb's "As when a child on some long winter's night," "Was it some sweet device of Faery," "Methinks how dainty sweet it were, reclin'd," and "O! I could laugh to hear the midnight wind" (*Works,* V, 3–4). The volume also contains Coleridge's acknowledgment that Lamb composed the last four lines of Effusion XIV—"Thou gentle Look, that didst my soul beguile." That the first of those four sonnets is by Lamb is suggested by its publication above his name in *Poems on Various Subjects* and in Coleridge's *Poems* (1797). That it is by Coleridge is suggested by its publication above his initials in the *Morning Chronicle* of December 29, 1794, by its presence in his *Poems* (1803), and by its absence from Lamb's *Works* (1818). Probably it was written by them conjointly. The "noble lines," mentioned following, from Coleridge's "Religious Musings. A Desultory Poem, Written on Christmas Eve, in the Year of Our Lord, 1794" are among lines 260–357 and 206–225, which are in *The Watchman,* Nos. 2 and 4 (March 9 and 25, 1796), 45–47 and 101. Coleridge gave up that paper for lack of income after No. 10 (May 13, 1796) and gave up also his employment on "Evidences of Religion." The phrase "dissonant mood" is from Milton, *Samson Agonistes,* line 662.

4. Charles Valentine Le Grice. (See the Introduction, pp. xxxi–xxxii.) The quotation following is from Philippians 4:8. Miss Hunt has not been identified.

5. One, according to Lucas (1935), I, 4, and *Works,* V, 286, was that he was Young Norval, or Douglas, of the tragedy *Douglas,* by John Home (1722–1808). Lamb's nine sonnets, referred to below, include the four mentioned in note 3 and "When last I roved these winding wood-walks green," "We were two pretty babes, the youngest she," "A timid grace sits trembling in her eye," "If from my lips some angry accents fell" (given as "to my sister" below), and "Sonnet." The poem in blank verse is "The Grandame," the surviving porton of a projected longer work. It was first published in Charles Lloyd's *Poems on the Death of Priscilla Farmer* (1796). See *Works,* V, 7–8, 14, and 5–6.

6. James White. (See the Introduction, pp. xxxv–xxxvi.) William Henry Ireland's pseudo-Shakespearean *Vortigern and Rowena,* mentioned following, had been unsuccessfully produced at Drury Lane on April 2, 1796.

7. Possibly Ann Simmons. See the Introduction, p. xxxiv.

8. *Conciones ad Populum. Or Addresses to the People* (1795).

9. Because of the franking privilege still granted even to the clerks of the East India House. Payment upon delivery was otherwise the custom until the penny post was instituted on January 10, 1840.

10. Southey had returned this month from a stay of six months in Spain and Portugal.

2. *C. L. to Coleridge*

Tuesday [Monday] night [May 30—
Tuesday evening, May 31, 1796]

I am in such violent pain with the head ach that I am fit for nothing but transcribing, scarce for that. When I get your poems & the Joan of Arc I will excercise my presumption in giving you my opinion of 'em. The Mail does not come in before tomorrow (Wednesday)[1] morning. The following sonn[e]t was composed during a walk down into Hertfordshire early in last summer.

The lord of light shakes off his drowsy hed:*
  Fresh from his couch up springs the lusty Sun,
  And girds himself his mighty race to run.
Meantime, by truant love of rambling led,
  I turn my back on thy detested walls,
Proud City, & thy sons I leave behind,
A selfish, sordid, money-getting kind,
  who shut their ears, when holy Freedom calls.
I pass not thee so lightly, humble spire,
  That mindest me of many a pleasure gone,
  of merrier days, of love & **Islington,**
Kindling anew the flames of past desire;
  And I shall muse on thee, slow journeying on
To the green plains of pleasant Hertfordshir[e.]

The last line is a copy of **Bowles's** "to the green hamlet in the peaceful plain."[2] Your ears are not so very fastidious—many people would not like words so prosaic & familiar in a sonnet as Islington & Hertfordshire. The next was written within a day or two of the last, on revisiting a spot, where the scene was laid of my 1st sonnet "that mock'd my step with many a lonely glade"

When last I roved these winding wood walks green,
  Green winding walks, & pathways shady-sweet,
  oftimes would **Anna** seek the silent scene,
Shrouding her beauties in the lone retreat.
  No more I hear her footsteps in the shade:
Her image only in these pleasant ways
Meets me, **self-**wandring where in better days
  I held free converse with my fair haird maid.
I pass'd the little cottage, which she loved,
  The cottage which did once my **all** contain:
  It spake of days that neer must come again,
Spake to my heart & much my heart was **moved.**
  "Now fair befall thee, gentle maid," said I,
  And from the cottage turn'd me, with a sigh—

The next retains a few lines from a sonnet of mine, which you once remarked had no "body of thought" in it. I agree with you, but have preserved a part of it, & it runs thus. I flatter myself you will like it.

A timid grace sits trembling in her **Eye,**
As loth to meet the rudeness of men's sight,
Yet shedding a delicious lunar light,
That sleeps in kind oblivious extacy
The care-craz'd mind, like some still melody;
Speaking most plain the thoughts which do possess
Her gentle sprite, peace & meek quietness,
And innocent† loves,† & maiden purity.
A look whereof might heal the cruel smart
of changed friends, or fortune's wrongs unkind;
Might to sweet deeds of Mercy move the heart
Of him, who hates his brethren of mankind.
Turned are those beams from me, who fondly **yet**
Past joys, vain loves, & buried hopes regret.

The next & last I value most of all. Twas ⟨written⟩ composed close upon the heels of the last in that very wood I had in mind when I wrote "Methinks how dainty sweet."

We were two pretty babes, the youngest she,
The youngest & the loveliest far, I ween,
And **Innocence** her name. The time has been,
We two did love each others' company;
Time was, we two had wept t' have been apart.
But when, with shew of seeming good beguild,
I left the garb & manners of a child,
And my first love for Man's society,
Defiling with the world my virgin heart,
My loved companion dropt a tear, & **fled,**
And hid in deepest shades her awful **head.**
Beloved, who can tell me where **Thou art,**
In what delicious **Eden** to be found,
That I may seek **thee** the wide world around.

Since writing it I have found in a poem by Hamilton of Bangour these 2 lines to happiness

Nun sober & devout, where art thou **fled**
To hide in shades thy meek contented **head.**[3]

Lines eminently beautiful, but I do not remember having re'd 'em previously, for the credit of my 10th & 11th lines. Parnell has 2 lines (which probably suggested the **above**) to **Contentment**

> Whither ah! whither art thou **fled**
> To hide thy meek contented‡ **head.**———

Cowley's exquisite Elegy on the death of his friend Harvey suggested the phrase of **"we two"**

> "Was there a tree that did not know
> The love betwixt **us two?**———[4]

So much for acknowledged plagarisms, the confession of which I know not whether it has more of **Vanity** or **Modesty** in it. As to my blank verse I am so dismally slow & steril of ideas (I speak from my heart) that I much question if it will ever come to any issue. I have hitherto **only** hammerd out a few indepent Unconnected Snatches, not in a capacity to be sent. I am very ill, & will rest till I have read your poems—for which I am very thankful. I have one more favor to beg of you, that you never mention Mr. May's affair in any sort, **much** less *think* of repaying. Are we not flocci-nauci[5]-what d'ye call-em-ists? . . ———

We have just learnd, that my poor brother has had a sad accident, a large stone blown down by yesterday's high wind has bruised his leg in a most shocking manner—he is under the care of Cruikshanks.[6]

Coleridge, **there** are 10000 objections against my paying you a visit at Bristol—it cannot be, **else**—but in this world tis better not to think too much of **pleasant possibles,** that we may not be out of humour with **present insipids.** Should any thing bring you to London, you will recollect No. 7 Little-Queen St. Holborn—

I shall be too ill to call on Wordsworth[7] myself but will take care to transmit him his poem, when I have **read it.** I saw Le Grice the day before his departure, & mentioned incidentally his "teaching the young idea how to shoot"—knowing him & the probability there is of people's having a propensity to **pun** in his compy. you will not wonder that we both stumbled on the **same pun at once, he** eagerly anticipating **me,—** "he would teach him to shoot!"— Poor Le Grice! if wit alone would entitle a man to respect &c. he has written a very witty little pamphlet[8] lately, satirical upon college declamations; when I send White's book, I will add that. I am sorry there should b[e] any difference between you & Southey. "Between you two there should be peace." tho' I mus[t] say I have borne him no good will since he spirited you away from among **us.** What is become of **Moschus?** You sported some of his Sublimities I see in your Watchman. Very decent things. So much for tonight from your afflicted head achey sore throatey humble Servant

C Lamb

Tuesday eve

of your Watchman, the Review of Burke[9] was the best prose, I augurd great things from the 1st number. There is some exquisite poetry interspersed. I have re-read the extract from the Religious musings & retract whatever invidious there was in my censure of it as elaborate. There are times, when one is not in a disposition thoroughly to relish good writing. I have re-read it in a more favorable **moment** & hesitate not to pronounce it sublime. If there be any thing in it approachg. to tumidity (which I meant not to infer in elaborate (I meant simply labord)) it is the Gigantic hyperbole by which you describe the Evils of existing Society. Snakes Lions hyenas & behemoths[10] is carrying your resentment beyond bounds. The pictures of the Simoom—of frenzy & ruin—of the whore of Babylon & the "cry of the foul spirits disherited of Earth"—& the "strange beatitude which the good man shall recognize in heaven"—as well as the particulazizing of the children of wretchedness—(I have unconsciously included every part of it) form a **variety** of uniform excellence. I hunger & thirst to read the poem complete. That is a capital line in your 6th No. "this dark freeze coated, hoarse, teeth chatteri[n]g Month"[11]—they are exactly such epithets as Burns would have stumbled **on,** whose poem on the ploughd up daisy you seem to have had in **mind.** Your complaint that your readers some thought there was too much some too little original matter in your Nos. reminds me of **poor dead Parsons** in the Critic—"too little incident! give me leave to tell you, Sir, there is too much incident." I had like to have forgot thanking you for that exquisite little morsel the 1st sclavonian **Song.**[12] The expression in the 2d "more happy to be unhappy in hell" is it not **very quaint?** Accept my thanks in common with those of all who love good poetry for the Braes of Yarrow. I congratulate you on the enemies you must have made by your splendid invective against the barterers in "human flesh & sinews." Coleridge, you will rejoyce to hear that Cowper is recoverd from his lunacy, & is employ'd on his translation of the Italian &c poems of **Milton,** for an edition where **Fuseli** presides as designer.[13] Coleridge, to an idler like myself to write & receive letters are both very pleasant, but I wish not to break in upon your valuable time by expecting to hear very frequently from you. Reserve that obligation for your moments of lassitude, when you have nothing **else** to do; for your **loco-restive** & all your idle propensities of course have given way to the duties of providing for a family. The mail is come in but no parcel, yet this is Tuesday.[14] Farewell then till to morrow, for a nich & a nook I must leave for criticisms. By the way I hope you do not send your own only copy of Joan of Arc; I will in that case return it immediately.— **Your** parcel *is* come, you have been *lavish* of your presents. Wordsworth's poem I have hurried thro' **not** without delight. Poor Lovell! my heart almost accuses me for the light manner I spoke of him above, not dreaming of his death. My heart bleeds for your accumulated troubles, God send you thro' em with patience. I **conjure** you dream not that I will ever think of being repaid! the very word is galling to the ears. I have red all your Rel: Musings with uninterrupted feelings of profound admiration. You may safely rest your fame on it. The best remaing. things are what I have before **read,** & they lose nothing by my recollection of your manner of reciting 'em, for I too bear in mind the "voice the look"[15] of absent friends, & can occasionally **mimic** their manner for the amusement of those who have seen 'em. Your empassiond manner of recitation I can recall at any time to mine own heart, & to the ears of the bystanders. I rather *wish* you had left the Monody on C. concluding as it did abruptly. It had more of **Unity.**— The conclusion of your R. Musings I fear will entitle you to the reproof of your Beloved woman, who wisely will not suffer your fancy to run **riot,** but bids you walk humbly with your **God.**[16] The very last words "I exercise my young noviciate thot. in ministeries of heart-stirring song" tho' not now new to me, cannot be enough admired. To speak politely, they are a well turnd compliment to Poetry. I hasten to read Joan of Arc. &c. I have read your lines at the beginng. of 2d book, they are worthy of Milton, but in my mind yield to your Rel. Musgs. I shall read the whole carefully & in some future letter take the liberty to particularize my opinions of it. of what is new to me among your poems next to the Musings, that beginning **"My pensive Sara"**[17] gave me most pleasure: the lines in it I just alluded to are most exquisite—they made my sister & **self** smile, as conveying a pleasing picture of Mrs. C. checquing your wild wandrings, which we were so fond of hearing you indulge when **among us.** It has endeared us more than any thing to your good Lady; & your own **self-reproof** that follows delighted us. Tis a charming poem throughout (you have well remarkd that "charming, admirable, exquisite" are words expressive of feelings, more than conveying of ideas, else I might plead very [w]ell want of room in my paper as ex[c]use for **generalizing.**). I want room to tell you how we are charmed with your verses in the Manner of Spencer[18] — &c. &c. &c. &c &c

I am glad you resume the Watchman—change the Name, leave out all articles of **News** & whatever things are peculiar to **News Papers,** & confine yourself to Ethics, verse, criticism, or rather do not confine yourself—. Yet[19] your plan be as diffuse as the Spectator, & I'll answer for it **the work prospers.** If I am vain enough to think I can be a contributor, rely on my inclinations. Coleridge, in reading your R. Musings I **felt** a transient superiority over you, **I *have* seen priestly.**[20] I love to see his name repeated in your writings. I love & honor him **almost profanely.** You would be charmed with his *sermons,* if you never read em,— You have doubtless read his books, illustrative of the doctrine of **Necessity.** Prefixed to a late work of his, in answer to **Paine** there is a preface given an account of the **Man** & his services to **Men,** written by Lindsey, his dearest friend,—well worth your reading—

forgive my prolixity, which is yet too brief for all I could wish to say,—God give you comfort & all that are of your household———. Our loves & best good wishes to Mrs. C—

C Lamb

*drowsy hed I have met with I think in Spencer. Tis an old thing, but it rhymes with led. & rhyming covers a multitude of licences. [The expression is in *The Faery Queene,* I, ii, 5, and also in James Thomson's *The Castle of Indolence,* I, 46.—Ed.]

†Cowley uses this phrase with a somewhat different meaning; I meant loves of relatives friends &. [The phrase is in Abraham Cowley's "The Muse," line 14.—Ed.]

‡an odd Epithet for Contentment in a poet so "poetical" as Parnell. [The epithet is in "A Hymn to Contentment," lines 7–8, by Thomas Parnell (1679–1718).—Ed.]

MS: Huntington Library. Pub.: Talfourd (1837), I, 28; Talfourd (1848), I, 8–19; Sala, I, 4–12; Purnell, I, 4–12; Fitzgerald, I, 290–298; Hazlitt, I, 91–98; Ainger (1888), I, 3–10; Ainger (1900), I, 4–14; Macdonald, I, 4–11; Ainger (1904), I, 3–10; Harper, II, 6–16; Lucas (1905), VI, 5–10; Lucas (1912), V, 5–11; Lucas (1935), I, 5–11. Address: S. T. Coleridge/Bristol. Postmark: June 1, 1796.

1. Tuesday, as Lamb's later dating and the postmark indicate. The sonnet following is titled "Sonnet" in *Works,* V, 14.

2. William Lisle Bowles (1762–1850), "To a Friend," line 14. Lamb's last line is closer to "The fruitful fields of pleasant Hertfordshire," in *A Tale of Two Swannes* (1590), line 14, by William Vallans (fl. 1578–1590). Lamb next quotes his own "Was it some sweet device of Faery," line 2.

3. William Hamilton (1704–1754), "To the Countess of Eglintoun, with 'The Gentle Shepherd,' " lines 75–76.

4. "On the Death of Mr. William Hervey," lines 43–44.

5. Literally, from *floccus* ("a lock of wool") and *naucus* ("a trifle"), but the beginning of a rule in old Latin grammars under which are listed words "of no account." Lamb may be recalling an expression of William Shenstone (1714–1763)—"flocci-nauci-nihili-pili-fication of money"—in Shenstone's *Works,* Vol. III: James Dodsley, ed., *Letters to Particular Friends* (1769), Letter XXI. Lamb may be alluding to the pantisocrats. See Letter 21, below, near the reference to note 13.

6. William Cumberland Cruikshank (1745–1800), the anatomist who had attended Samuel Johnson in his final illness.

7. Wordsworth was at this time living with his sister, Dorothy, at Racedown Lodge, Birdsmoorgate, Dorsetshire. He and Coleridge had met during Wordsworth's five weeks in Bristol in September and October 1795. Wordsworth and Lamb met in July 1797, at the Coleridges' at Nether Stowey. The poem Lamb mentions following is "Guilt and Sorrow; or Incidents upon Salisbury Plain," which Wordsworth in early March had sent to Cottle, who gave it to Coleridge, who sent it to Lamb, who returned it to Wordsworth. The quotation following is from James Thomson, *The Seasons,* "Spring," line 1149.

8. Charles Valentine Le Grice's *A General Theorem for a ******* Coll. Declamation* (1796). One of the causes of the difficult relations between Coleridge and Southey, referred to below, had arisen in the fall of 1795, when Southey, pressed by his uncle the Reverend Mr. Herbert Hill (1750–1828) to enter the church but deciding instead to study law, deserted the advocates of pantisocracy. Another may have arisen in January 1795, when Southey had "spirited" Coleridge not just from London but also into a marriage for which Coleridge had not been anxious. Peace came between the two (Lamb's quotation is from *Paradise Lost,* X, 924) in 1797 and lasted until Coleridge's departure for Malta in 1804 and the disintegration of the Coleridges' marriage. Then Southey gave his sympathy and support to Mrs. Coleridge, but remained as helpful as he could to her husband. Moschus is Lovell, who so signed his contributions to *Poems: Containing The Retrospect, Odes, Elegies, Sonnets, &c.* Two of Lovell's poems, called by Coleridge "sublime and truly original," reappear in *The Watchman,* No. 5 (April 2, 1796), 132.

9. "Review of Burke's Letter to a Noble Lord," *The Watchman,* No. 1 (March 1, 1796), 16–23.

10. In lines 272–275. The simoom and its effect, following, are in lines 269–270,

the whore of Babylon is in 323–338, the quotations are in 327–329 and 352–355, and the "particulazizing of the children of wretchedness" is in 276–301.

11. Coleridge's "Lines on Observing a Blossom on the First of February, 1796," line 3, in *The Watchman,* No. 6 (April 11, 1796), 164, reminds Lamb of Robert Burns's "To a Mountain Daisy on Turning One Down with the Plough in April, 1786." William Parsons (1736–1795), below, whom Lamb mentioned again in "On Some of the Old Actors" and "On the Artificial Comedy of the Last Century" (*Works,* II, 134 and 146), was the original Sir Fretful Plagiary of Richard Brinsley Sheridan's *The Critic* and thus the first to speak publicly its lines next quoted, inaccurately, from I, i, 282–289.

12. "Song of a Female Orphan," the first of three Esthonian ballads that Coleridge transformed into prose for *The Watchman,* No. 9 (May 5, 1796), 271–273. He had italicized the expression in the second, "Song of the Haymakers," that Lamb finds not quaint. "Song. The Braes of Yarrow," next mentioned, is by John Logan (1748–1788). It is in *The Watchman,* No. 3 (March 17, 1796), 79–80. Coleridge's "On the Slave Trade," to which Lamb refers as "splendid invective" and by what seems to be a paraphrase of "barterers of human blood," from "Religious Musings," line 180, is in *The Watchman,* No. 4 (March 25, 1796), 100–109.

13. Cowper never fully recovered from his attack of insanity in 1787, when he attempted to hang himself, and was thereafter subject to states of stupor and delusions in which he heard strange voices and was possessed by strange fancies. His *Latin and Italian Poems of Milton* was published with illustrations by the sculptor and draftsman John Flaxman (1755–1826) in 1808. *Cowper's Milton* was published in 1810. The forty-seven illustrations that the painter and author Henry Fuseli (Johann Heinrich Fuessli, 1741–1825) had executed partly for the former work were exhibited from 1799 to 1800 as a Milton Gallery in rooms that had been recently vacated by the Royal Academy in Pall Mall.

14. On which Lamb continues to write, despite his farewell.

15. If Lamb is quoting from Coleridge's letter, as it appears, then Coleridge had echoed Bowles's "Thy look and voice," from "Picture of a Young Lady," line 14. Lamb complains below about the thirty-six lines that Coleridge had added to the "Monody on the Death of Chatterton" for *Poems on Various Subjects* since its composition in 1790 and publication in Lancelot Sharpe, ed., *Poems, Supposed to Have Been Written at Bristol, by Thomas Rowley, and Others, in the Fifteenth Century* (1794).

16. Coleridge's "The Eolian Harp: Composed at Clevedon, Somersetshire," line 52. Lamb next quotes from "Religious Musings," lines 411–412.

17. Effusion XXXV in *Poems on Various Subjects.* Coleridge retitled it "The Eolian Harp" for *Sibylline Leaves* (1817).

18. "Lines in the Manner of Spenser." Coleridge did not resume *The Watchman.*

19. "Let" must have been intended.

20. Joseph Priestley, whom Lamb possibly had seen while Priestley was officiating as morning preacher at the Gravel Pit, Hackney, between 1791 and his emigration to America in the spring of 1794. Lamb, who was reared a Unitarian by Sarah Lamb, and Coleridge, who was at this time still a convinced Unitarian, were understandably attracted to Priestley as one of the fathers of Unitarianism and because of his superior mind and humanitarian principles. Coleridge paid tribute to him in Effusion IV (later called "Priestley") of *Poems on Various Subjects* and in "Religious Musings," lines 371–376. The sermons of Priestley, mentioned following, were published during the period 1788 to 1797. His *The Doctrine of Philosophical Necessity, Illustrated* was published in 1777, *A Free Discussion of the Doctrines of Materialism, and Philosophical Necessity, in a Correspondence between Dr. Price, and Dr. Priestley* in 1778, and *A Letter to Jacob Bryant . . . in Defence of*

Philosophical Necessity in 1780. His *Letters to the Philosophers and Politicians of France . . . on Religion* (1793) was republished first as *A Continuation of the Letters . . .* (1794) and then, under the editorship of the Unitarian Theophilus Lindsey (1723–1808), as *An Answer to Mr. Paine's Age of Reason* (1795).

3. *C. L. to Coleridge*

Wednesday [June 8—Friday, June 10, 1796]

With Joan of Arc I have been delighted, amazed. I had not presumed to expect any thing of such excellence from Southey. Why the poem is alone sufficient to redeem the character of the age we live in from the imputation of degenerating in Poetry, were there no such beings extant as Burns & Bowles, Cowper & ——— fill up the blank how you please, I say nothing. The subject is well chosen. It opens well. To become more particular, I will notice in their order a few passages, that chiefly struck me on perusal.— Page 26 "Fierce & terrible Benevolence!"[1] is a phrase full of grandeur & originality. The whole context made me feel *possess'd,* even like Joan herself. Page 28. "it is most horrible with the keen sword to gore the finely fibred human frame" & what follows pleased me mightily. In the 2d. book the first forty lines,[2] in particular, are majestic & high-sounding. Indeed the whole vision of the palace of Ambition & what follows are supremely excellent. Your simile of the Laplander "by Niemi's lake, or Balda Zhiok, or the mossy stone of Solfar Kapper"—will bear comparison with any in Milton for **fullness of circumstance & lofty-pacedness of Versification.** Southey's similes, tho' many of em are capital, are all inferior. In one of his books the simile of the **Oak** in the Storm occurs I think four times![3] To return, the light in which you view the heathen deities is accurate & beautiful. Southey's personifications in this book are so many fine & faultless pictures. I was much pleased with your manner of accounting for the reason why Monarchs take delight in **war.** At the 447th line you have placed Prophets & Enthusiasts cheek by jowl, on too intimate a footing for the dignity of the former. Necessarian-like-speaking it is correct. Page 98 "Dead is the Douglas, cold thy warrior frame, illustrious Buchan" &c are of kindred excellence with Gray's "Cold is Cadwallo's tongue" &c. How famously the **Maid** baffles the Doctors,[4] Seraphic and Irrefragable "with all their trumpery." 126 page the procession, the appearances of the **Maid,** of the Bastard son of Orleans & of **Tremouille,** are full of fire & fancy, & exquisite melody of versification. The personifications from **line** 303 to 309 in the heat of the battle had better been omitted, they are not very striking & only encumber. The converse which Joan & Conrade hold on the Banks of the Loire is altogether beautiful. page 313 the conjecture that in Dreams "All things are that seem"[5] is one of those conceits which the Poet delights to admit into his creed—a creed, by the way more marvellous & mystic than ever athanasius dream'd of. Page 315 I need only ***mention*** those lines ending with "She saw a serpent gnawing at her heart"!!! They are good imitative lines "he toild & toild, of toil to reap no end, but endless toil & never ending woe." 347 page **Cruelty** is such as Hogarth might have painted her. page 361 All the passage about **Love** (where he seems to confound conjugal love with Creating & Preserving **love**) is very confused & sickens me with a load of useless personifications. **Else,** that 9th book is the finest in the **volume,** an exquisite combination of the ludicrous & the terrible,—I have never read either even in translation, but such as I conceive to be the manner of Dante & Ariosto. The 10th book is the most languid. On the whole, consider[i]ng the celerity wherewith the ⟨book⟩ poem was finish'd I was astonish'd at the infrequency of weak lines. I had expected to find it **verbose.** Joan, I think, does too little in Battle—Dunois, perhaps, the same—Conrade too much. The anecdotes interspersed among the battles refresh the mind very agreeably, & I am delighted with the very many passages of simple pathos abounding throughout the poem—passages which the author of "Crazy Kate"[6] might have written.— Has not Master Southey spoke very slightingly in his preface & disparagingly of **Cowper's Homer?**—what makes him reluctant to give **Cowper his fame?** And does not Southey **use** too often the expletives **"did" & "does"?** they have a good effect at times, but are too inconsiderable or rather become blemishes, when they mark a style. On the whole, I expect Southey **one** day to rival Milton. I already deem him equal to Cowper, & superior to all living **Poets Besides.** what says Coleridge? The "Monody on Henderson"[7] is *immensely good;* the rest of that little volume is *readable & above mediocrity.* I proceed to a more pleasant task,—pleasant because the poems are **yours,** pleasant because you impose the task on me, & pleasant, let me add, because it will confer a whimsical importance on me to sit in judgment upon your rhimes. First tho' let me thank you again & again in my own & my sister's name for your invitations. Nothing could give us more pleasure than to **come,** but (were there no other reasons) while my Brother's leg is so bad it is out of the question. Poor fellow, he is very feverish & light headed, but Cruikshanks has pronounced the symptoms favorable, & gives us every hope that there will be no need of **amputation.** God send, **not.** We are necessarily confined with him the afternoon & evening till very late, so that I am **stealing** a few minutes to **write** to you. Thank you for your frequent letters, you are the only **correspondent** & I might add the only friend I have in the world. I go no where & have no acquaintance. **Slow of speech,** & reserved of manners, no one seeks or cares for my society & I am left alone. Allen calls very occasionally, as tho' it were a duty rather, & seldom stays **ten minutes.** Then judge how thankful I am for your **letters.** Do not, however, burthen **yourself** with the correspondence. I trouble you again so soon, only in obedience to your injunctions. Complaints apart, **proceed** we to our **task.** I am called away to tea, thence must wait upon my brother, so must delay till to morrow. Farewell—

Thursday[8]

I will first notice what is new to me. 13th page. "The thrilling tones that concentrate the soul" is a nervous line, & the 6 first lines of page 14 are very pretty. the 21st effusion a perfect thing. That in the manner of Spencer is very sweet, particularly at the **close.** the 35th effusion is most exquisite—that line in particular "And tranquil muse upon tranquillity." It is the very reflex pleasure that distinguishes the tranquillity of a thinking being from that of a shepherd—a modern one I would be understood to mean—a Dametas;[9] one that keeps other people's sheep. Certainly, Coleridge, your letter from Shurton Bars has less merit than most things in your volume; personally, it may chime in best with your own feelings, & therefore you love it best. It has however great merit. In your 4th Epistle that is an exquisite paragraph & fancy-full of "A stream there **is** which rolls in lazy flow" &c. &c. "Murmu[r]s sweet undersong mid jasmin bowres" is a sweet line & so are the 3 next. the concluding simile is far-fetch'd. "tempest-honord" is a quaint-ish phrase. of the Monody on H.[10] I will hereonly notice these lines, as superlatively excellent!

That energetic one "Shall I not praise thee, Scholar, Christian, friend." like to that beautiful climax of Shakespear "King, Hamlet, Royal Dane, **Father.**" "Yet Memory turns from little **Men** to thee." "& sported careless round their fellow child." The whole, I repeat it, is immensely good. Yours is a Poetical family. I was much surpriz'd & pleased to see the signature of **Sara** to that elegant composition, the 5th Epistle.[11] I dare not *criticise* the Relig. Musings, I like not to *select* any part where all is excellent. I can only admire; & I thank you for it in the name of Christian, as well as a Lover of good Poetry. Only let me ask, is not that thought & those words in **Young, "Stands in the Sun"?**[12] or is it only such as Young in one of his *better moments* might have writ? "Believe, thou, O My Soul, Life is a vision shadowy of truth, & vice & anguish & the wormy grave Shapes of a dream!" I thank you for these lines, in the name of a **Necessarian,** & for what follows in next paragraph in the name of a child of **fancy. After all you can nor ever will write** any thing, with which I shall be so delighted as what I have heard yourself repeat. You came to Town, & I saw you at a time when your heart was yet bleeding with recent wounds. Like yourself, I was sore galled with disappointed **Hope.** You had "many an holy lay, that mourning soothed the mourner on his way."[13] I had ears of sympathy to drink them in, & they yet vibrate pl[e]asant on the sense. When I read in your little volume your 19th Effusion. or the 28th. or 29th. or what you call the "Sigh." I think I hear *you* again. I image to myself the little smoky room at the Salutation & Cat, where we have sat together thro' the winter nights, beguiling the cares of life with Poesy. When you left London, I felt a dismal **void** in my heart, I found myself cut off at one & the same time from two most dear to me. "How blest with **ye** the Path could I have trod"[14] "of Quiet life." In your conversation you had blended so many pleasant fancies, that they cheated me of my grief. But in your absence, the tide of melancholy rushd in again, & did its worst **Mischief** by overwhelming my Reason. I have recoverd. But feel a stupor that makes me indifferent to the hopes & fears of this life. I sometimes wish to intro[d]uce a religious turn of mind, but habits are strong things, & my religious fervors are confined alas to some fleeting moments of occasional solitary devotion—. A correspondence, opening with you has roused me a little from my lethargy, & made me conscious of existence. Indulge me in it. I will not be very troublesome. at some future time I will amuse you with an account as full as my memory will permit of the strange turn my **phrensy** took. I look back upon it **at times** with a gloomy kind of **Envy.** For while it lasted I had many many hours of pure happiness. Dream not Coleridge, of having tasted all the grandeur & wildness of **Fancy,** till you have **gone mad.** All now seems to me **vapid;** comparatively so. Excuse this selfish digression—

Your **Monody**[15] is so superlatively excellent, that I can only wish it perfect, which I cant help feeling it is **not** quite. Indulge me in a few conjectures. What I am going to propose would make it more compress'd & I think energic. tho' I am sensible at the expence of many beautiful lines. Let it begin "Is this the land of song-ennobled line" & proceed to "Otway's famish'd form." Then "Thee Chatterton" to "blaze of Seraphim." **Then** "clad in nature's rich array" to "orient day" **then** "but soon the scathing lightning" to "blighted land." Then "Sublime of **thought"** to **"his bosom glows."** then "but soon upon *his* poor unshelterd head Did Penury her sickly Mildew shed, & soon are fled the charms of early grace & Joys wild gleams that lightned oer his face!" Then "Youth of tumultuous soul" to "sigh" as before. The **rest may all stand** down to "gaze upon the waves below." What follows now may come next, as **detached verses, suggested by the Monody** rather than a part of it. They are indeed in **themselves very sweet** "And we at sober eve would round thee throng, Hanging enraptured on thy **stately song"**—in particular perhaps. If I am obscure you may understand me by counting lines, I have proposed omitting **24 lines.** I feel that thus comprest it would gain energy. but think it most likely you will not agree with me, for who shall go about to bring opinions to the Bed of Procrustes[16] & introduce among the Sons of Men a Monotony of identical feelings. I only propose with diffidence. Reject, you, if you please with as little remorse as you would the color of a coat or the pattern of a buckle where our fancies differ'd. The lines "Friend to the friendless &c."[17] which you may think "rudely disbranched" from the Chatterton will patch in with the Man of Ross, where they were once quite at **Home** with 2 more which I recollect, "& oer the dowried virgin's snowy cheek bad[e] bridal love suffus[e] his blushes meek!" very beautiful. The Pixies is a perfect thing. and so are the lines on the spring page 28. The epitaph on an infant like a Jack of lanthorn has danced about (or like Dr. Forster's scholars) out of the Morng. Chron. into The Watchman & thence back into your Collection. It is very pretty, & you seem to think so, but may be have oe'r looked it[s] chief **merit,** that of filling up a whole page. I had once deemd Sonnets of unrivalld use that way, but your epitaphs I find are the more diffuse. Edmund[18] still holds its place among your best **verses.** "Ah! fair delights" to **"roses round"** in your Poem calld **Absence** recall (none more forcibly) to my mind the tones in which *you recited it.* I will not notice in this tedious (to you) manner verses which have been so long delightful to me, & which you already know my opinion of. of this kind are Bowles,[19] Priestly, & that **most exquisite & most Bowles-like** of all, the 19th Effusion. It would have better ended with **"agony of care."** the 2 last lines are obvious & unnecessary & you need not now make 14 lines of it, now it is re-christend from a Sonnet to an Effusion. Schiller might have written the 20 effusion. Tis worthy of him in any sense. I was glad to meet with those lines[20] you sent me, when my Sister was so ill. I had lost the Copy. & I felt not a little proud at seeing my name in your **verse.** The complaint of Ninathoma (1st stanza in particular) is the **best** or only **good** imitation of Ossian I ever saw—your "restless gale" excepted. "To an infant" is most sweet—is not "foodful" tho', very harsh! would not **"dulcet"** fruit be less harsh, or some other friendly bi-syllable. in Edmund "Frenzy fierce-eyed child"[21] is not so well as frantic—tho' that is an epithet adding nothing to the meaning. "Slander *couching*" was better than squatting. In the Man of Ross It *was a* better line thus "If neath this roof thy wine-chear'd moments pass" than as it stands **now. Time** nor nothing can reconcile me to the **concluding 5 lines of Kosciusko** call it any thing you will but **sublime.** in my 12th Effusion[22] I had rather have seen what I wrote myself, tho' they bear no comparison with your exquisite line, **"On** rose-leafd beds amid your faery bowers" &c.— I love my sonnets because they are the reflected images of my own feelings at different times. To instance, in the 13th "How reason reeld" &.—, are good lines but must spoil the whole **with me,** who know it is only a fiction of yours & that the rude dashings did in fact **not rock** me to **repose.** I grant the same objection applies not to the former sonnet, but still I love my own **feelings.** They are dear to **memory,** tho' they now & then wake a sigh or a tear.[23] "Thinking on divers things fore done." I charge you, Col. **spare my ewe lambs—&**

tho' a Gentleman may borrow six lines in an epic poem (I should have no objection to borrow 500 & without acknowledging) still **in** a Sonnet—**a personal poem** I do not **"ask my friend** the aiding verse." I would not wrong your feelings by proposing any improvements (Did I think myself capable of suggesting **em**) in such personal poems as "Thou bleedest my poor heart"[24]—**od so** I am catchd I have already **done** it—but that simile I propose abridging would not **change** the feelings or introduce any alien ones. Do you **understand me?** in the 28th however & in the "Sigh" & that composed at Clevedon, things that come from the heart direct, not by the medium of the fancy, I would not suggest an Alteration. When my blank verse is finished or any long fancy-poems "propino tibi alterandum cut-up-andum abridg-andum" just what you will with it—but spare my **Ewe lambs!** that to Mrs. Siddons now you were welcome to improve, if it had been worth it. but I say unto you again Col. spare my **Ewe lambs.**——— ——

I must confess were they mine I should **omit** in **Editione secund:**[25] Effusions 2—3 because satiric, & below the dignity of the poet of religious **Musings.** 5.—7—half of the 8th——that written in early Youth as far as **"Thousand eyes"**— tho' I part not unreluctantly with that lively line "Chaste Joyance dancing in her bright-**blue Eyes"** & one or 2 more just thereabouts—. But I would substitute for it that sweet poem called "Recollection" in the 5th No. of the watchman,[26] better I think than the remainder of this poem, tho' not differing materially. As the poem now stands it look[s] altogether **confused. And do not omit** those lines upon the "early blossom" in your 6th No. of the Watchman. & I would omit the 10th Effusion—or what would do better alter & improve the last **4 lines.** In fact, I suppose if they were mine I should **Not omit omit 'em.** But your **verse** is for the **most part so exquisite,** that I like not to see **aught of meaner matter** mixed with it. Forgive my petulance & often I fear ill founded criticisms, & forgive me that I have by this time made your eyes & head ach with my long letter. But I cannot forego hastily the **pleasure & pride**[27] of thus conversing with **you.**— You did not tell me whether I was to include the Conciones ad Populum in my remarks on your **poems.** They are not unfrequently **sublime,** & I think you could not do better than to turn 'em into **verse,**—if you have nothing else to **do.** Allen I am sorry to say is a *confirmed* atheist. Stodart[28] or

Stothard a cold hearted well bred conceited disciple of Godwin does him **no good.** His wife has several daughters (**one** of em as old as himself) surely there is something **unnatural** in such a marriage. How I sympathise with you **on the dull duty of a review[er,]** & he[ar]tily **damn** with you **Ned Evans**[29] & the **Prosodist.** I shall however wait impatiently for the Articles in the **Crit. Rev.** next month, because they are *yours.* **Young Evans** (W. Evans a branch of a family you were **once** so intimate with) Is come into our office, & sends his love to you. Coleridge, I devoutly wish that Fortune, who has made sport with you so long, may play one freak more, throw you into London or some spot near it, & there snug-ify you for life. Tis a selfish but natural wish for me, cast as I am "on life's wide plain, friendless."[30] Are you acquainted with Bowles? I see by his last Elegy (written at Bath) you are near **neighbours.** And I can think I see the groves again"—"Was it the voice of thee"—"Twas not the voice of thee, my buried friend"—"who dries with her dark locks the tender tear"—are touches as true to nature as any in his other Elegy, written at the hot wells, about poor **Russell** &c—. You are doubtless acquainted with **it**—
Thursday

Friday 10th June

I do not know that I entirely agree with you in your stricture—upon my Sonnet to Innocence.[31] To men, whose hearts are not quite deadend by their commerce with the world, **Innocence** (no longer familiar) becomes an **awful idea.** So I felt, when I wrote it. Your other censures (qualified & sweeten'd tho' with praises somewhat extravagant) I perfectly coincide with. Yet I chuse to retain the—word **"lunar"**—indulge a **"lunatic"** in his loyalty to his mistress the moon. I have just been reading a most pathetic copy of verses on Sophia Pringle, who was hanged & burn'd for coining. **One** of the strokes of pathos (which are very many, all somewhat obscure) is "She lifted up her guilty forger to heaven" **a note** explains by forger her right hand with which she forged or coined the base metal! For pathos read bathos. You have put me out of conceit with my blank verse by your Religious Musings. I think it will come to nothing. I do not like 'em enough to send 'em. I have just been reading a book, which I may be too partial to as it was the delight of my childhood, but I will recommend it to you.— it is **Isaac Walton's complete Angler!"** All the scientific part you may omit in reading. The dialogue is very simple, full of pastoral beauties & will charm you. Many pretty old verses are interspersed. This letter, which would be a week's work reading only,[32] I do not wish you to **answer** it in less than a month. I shall be **richly content** with a letter from you some day early in July—tho' if you get any how *settled* before then pray let me know it immediately—'twould give me such **satisfaction.** Concerning the unitarian chapel, the salary is the only scruple that the most rigid moralist would admit as **valid.** Concerning the tutorage—is not the salary low, &—absence from your family unavoidable? **London**—is the only fostering soil for **Genius.—**

Nothing more occurs just now, so I will leave you in mercy **one** small white spot empty below[33] to repose your eyes upon, fatigued as they must be with the **wilderness** of words they have by this time painfully travell'd thro'. God love you, Coleridge & prosper you thro' life, tho' mine will be loss, if your lot is to be cast at Bristol or at Nottingham or any where but **London—.** Our loves to Mrs. C———

C. L.

MS: Huntington Library. Pub.: Talfourd (1837), I, 26, 27, and 28; Talfourd (1848), I, 19–36; Sala, I, 12–25; Purnell, I, 12–25; Fitzgerald, I, 298–311; Hazlitt, I, 99–109; Ainger (1888), I, 10–21; Ainger (1900), I, 14–29; Macdonald, I, 11–22; Ainger (1904), I, 10–21; Harper, II, 16–31; Lucas (1905), VI, 13–21; Lucas (1912), V, 13–22; Lucas (1935), I, 13–22. Address: S. T. Coleridge/ Bristol. Postmark: June 10, 1796.

1. In I, 375. The word "possessed" (see below) is in I, 380. The quotation from p. 28 is in I, 408–409.

2. The lines are Coleridge's, as are II, 41–140, 144–147, 223–265, 273–285, and 292–452. Southey omitted all of them after the first edition of the poem. Coleridge first reused them in "The Visions of the Maid of Orleans. A Fragment," which prior to its appearance in the *Morning Post* of December 26, 1797, Lamb in Letter 21 dissuaded him from including in *Poems* (1797), but in Letter 22 for the most part praised. Coleridge next reused them in "The Destiny of Nations: A Vision," lines 127–277. (See *Coleridge's Poetical Works* [1912], I, 131 and 136, and David V. Erdman, "Unrecorded Coleridge Variants," *Studies in Bibliography,* 11 [1958], esp. 151–153.) The vision of the palace of Ambition (see below) is in *Joan of Arc,* II, 136–210, and the simile of the Laplander in II, 64–80.

3. The oak, not always in the storm, occurs five times in the poem—in IV, 95 and 335; VII, 447 and 580–581; and X, 403. The reasons why monarchs delight in war, referred to below, are given in II, 371–380. Prophets are placed near enthusiasts in II, 447–448. The quotation from p. 98 is from III, 132–133, and judged comparable to Thomas Gray's "The Bard," line 29.

4. In III, 308–505. "Seraphic, Subtile, or Irrefragable" is in III, 245. The next

quotation is from *Paradise Lost,* III, 475. The events described as on p. 126 are in IV, 48–92. The personifications are in VI, 303–309. The converse between Joan and Conrade is in IV, 264–319.

5. From IX, 10. The next quotation is from IX, 39, and the one following that from IX, 424–425. The description of Cruelty is at IX, 621–630, and that of Love at IX, 887–934.

6. In Cowper's *The Task,* I, 534–556. Southey in his Preface to *Joan of Arc* (p. vi) accused Cowper in his translation *Homer's Iliad and Odyssey* (1791) of having "stripped him [Homer] naked."

7. Cottle's "Monody on the Death of John Henderson, A.B., of Pembroke College, Oxford," which is in Cottle's "little volume" called *Poems* (1795; 2d ed., 1796).

8. Five lines preceding are canceled. Lamb now turns to *Poems on Various Subjects* and praises as nervous and pretty "To the Rev. W. J. Hort while Teaching a Young Lady Some Song-tunes on His Flute," lines 10 and 17–22; as perfect "Lines: Composed while Climbing the Left Ascent of Brockley Coomb, Somersetshire, May 1795"; as sweet "Lines in the Manner of Spenser"; and as exquisite "The Eolian Harp," particularly line 38.

9. In Milton's "Lycidas," line 36, and a stock figure in pastoral poetry. The letter from Shurton Bars, mentioned following, is "Lines Written at Shurton Bars, near Bridgewater, September 1795, in Answer to a Letter from Bristol." Epistle IV is "To the Author [Cottle] of Poems Published Anonymously at Bristol in September 1795," from which Lamb quotes lines 11 and 24 and remarks about the quaint compound in line 45.

10. Cottle's "Monody on the Death of John Henderson," which Coleridge commended in Epistle IV and whose lines 4 (like *Hamlet,* I, iv, 44–45), 12, and 64 Lamb commends especially.

11. Mrs. Coleridge's "The Silver Thimble. The Production of a Young Lady, Addressed to the Author [Cottle] of the Poems Alluded to in the Preceding Epistle."

12. "Religious Musings," line 111, which reminds Lamb of Edward Young's *The Complaint; or, Night Thoughts,* V, 190–191. Lamb next quotes from "Religious Musings," lines 395–398, and thanks Coleridge additionally for lines 402–419.

13. *Poems on Various Subjects,* p. vii. Effusions XIX, XXVIII, and XXIX, referred to following, are "On a Discovery Made Too Late," "The Kiss," and "Imitated from Ossian." "The Sigh" was Effusion XXXII.

14. Bowles, "In Memoriam," line 1. "Quite life" is (at the least) from *Anything for a Quiet Life,* by Thomas Middleton (1570?–1627).

15. "Monody on the Death of Chatterton." Lamb's proposals for it, which Coleridge rejected, are concerned with its 1796 version, lines 23–32, then 9–14, then 50–57, then 60–61, then 33–40, then 58–59 and 62–63, and then 64–67. The expression "gaze upon the waves below" is from line 108. "And we . . . stately song" forms lines 131–132.

16. The fabled robber of Attica who mutilated his victims to make them conform to the length of his bed.

17. "Monody on the Death of Chatterton," lines 41–46, which Coleridge had transferred from and would later transfer back to "Lines: Written at the King's Arms, Ross, Formerly the House of the 'Man of Ross.'" The quotation "rudely disbranched" is from "Religious Musings," line 266, and the one after it from the earlier versions of the "Man of Ross," lines 9–10. The "Pixies," mentioned below, is "Songs of the Pixies." The poem beginning on p. 28 is "Lines: To a Beautiful Spring in a Village." The four-line "Epitaph on an Infant" reminds Lamb, by its dance from the *Morning Chronicle* of September 23, 1794, to *The Watchman,* No. 9 (May 5, 1796), 270, then to *Poems on Various Subjects,* of the dance of the scholars from Britain to France to Spain and back again in the untitled nursery

rhyme about Dr. Forster, or Faustus. See *The Oxford Dictionary of Nursery Rhymes,* ed. Iona and Peter Opie (Oxford: Oxford University Press, 1951), p. 168.

18. "Lines on a Friend Who Died of a Frenzy Fever Induced by Calumnious Reports." It is "Absence. A Farewell Ode on Quitting School for Jesus College, Cambridge," lines 9–16, that prompts Lamb's fond recollection. Lamb's "tedious (to you)," below, is an adaptation of Coleridge's "Tedious to thee," from "To a Friend [Lamb], Together with an Unfinished Poem," line 5.

19. "To the Rev. W. L. Bowles," which with "Priestley," "To the Honourable Mr. Erskine," "Burke," "Koskiusko," "Pitt," "Mrs. Siddons," and "To Earl Stanhope" (to mention those that Lamb mentions below) form in part the "Sonnets on Eminent Characters." Effusion XIX, finally titled "On a Discovery Made Too Late" but from time to time called "Sonnet," Lamb would have end at line 12. Effusion XX is "To the Author of 'The Robbers.' "

20. "To a Friend, Together with an Unfinished Poem," in which "Charles" appears in line 19 and which when sent to Lamb almost certainly accompanied the then unfinished "Religious Musings." By "restless gale," below, Lamb means "Imitated from Ossian," in which the expression occurs in line 5. The harsh "foodful" remains in "To an Infant," line 7.

21. "Lines on a Friend Who Died of a Frenzy Fever Induced by Calumnious Reports," line 17, which earlier read "Frenzy, frantic." Its line 19 contains "Slander squatting," next, which earlier read "Slander couching." Lamb prefers the "Man of Ross," line 11, as it was earlier and is elsewhere to its counterpart line 5 in *Poems on Various Subjects.*

22. Lamb's "Methinks how dainty sweet it were, reclin'd," the sestet of which Coleridge had altered from

> Or we might sit and tell some tender tale
> Of faithful vows repaid by cruel scorn,
> A tale of true love, or of friend forgot;
> And I would teach thee, lady, how to rail
> In gentle sort, on those who practise not
> Or love or pity, though of woman born [*Works,* V, 4]

to

> But ah! sweet scenes of fancied bliss, adieu!
> On rose-leaf beds amid your faery bowers
> I all too long have lost the dreamy hours!
> Beseems it now the sterner Muse to woo,
> If haply she her golden meed impart,
> To realise the vision of the heart.

In Effusion XIII, mentioned below—Lamb's "O! I could laugh to hear the midnight wind"—Coleridge changed the concluding lines from

> To be resolv'd into th' elemental wave,
> Or take my portion with the winds that rave [*Works,* V, 4]

to

> How Reason reel'd! What gloomy transports rose!
> Till the rude dashings rock'd them to repose.

23. Cf. Anna Letitia Barbauld (1743–1825), "Ode to Life," line 26, in *Sourcebook of Poetry,* comp. Al Bryant (Grand Rapids, Mich.: Zondervan, 1968). The quotation following is from Robert Burton, *The Anatomy of Melancholy,* "The Author's Abstract of Melancholy," line 2. Southey in *Joan of Arc,* IV, 195 (206 in standard ed.), may have provided Lamb with the epithet and pun "ewe lambs." The next quotation is from Coleridge's "To a Friend, Together with an Unfinished Poem," line 4.

24. "On a Discovery Made Too Late." Effusion XXVIII, mentioned following, is "The Kiss," and "that composed at Clevedon" is "The Eolian Harp." The Latin-

English translates, "I shall give it to you to be altered, cut up, and abridged." The poem to the actress Mrs. Sarah Siddons (1755–1831) is that on which Lamb and Coleridge probably collaborated, "As when a child on some long winter's night."

25. *Poems* (1797): Effusions II and III are "Burke" and "Pitt" and are not in it. Effusion V is "To the Honourable Mr. Erskine" and is not in it. Effusion VII is "Mrs. Siddons" and is in it. Effusion VIII is "Koskiusko" and is not in it. (Effusion VI, if Lamb means to include it, is "To Richard Brinsley Sheridan, Esq." and is not in it.) "Written in Early Youth, the Time, an Autumnal Evening," later retitled "Lines: On an Autumnal Evening," remains intact in it, even though Lamb would part with its first seventy lines, though reluctantly with line 24 and perhaps another nearby.

26. April 2, 1796, p. 133. The poem reappears revised and retitled "Sonnet [V and IV]: To the River Otter" in *Sonnets from Various Authors* (1796) and *Poems* (1797). "[Lines.] On Observing a Blossom on the First of February 1796," mentioned below, from *The Watchman,* No. 6 (April 11, 1796), 164–165, is in *Poems* (1797). Effusion X, "To Earl Stanhope," does not reappear until *Poems* (1803).

27. From Burns's "A Rose-bud, by My Early Walk," line 14.

28. John, later Sir John, Stoddart (1773–1856), who became a judge and journalist, and Hazlitt's brother-in-law through Hazlitt's marriage in 1808 to his sister, Sarah. His father, John (d. 1805?), was a naval lieutenant who for some years had been living in retirement with his wife and daughter on St. Anne's Street, Salisbury, and would remove to the small property he acquired in the neighboring village of Winterslow, Wiltshire. Stoddart received his early education at the grammar school in Salisbury Close, where the assistant master was Coleridge's brother Edward (1760–1843). Stoddart proceeded in 1790 to Christ Church, Oxford, from where he was graduated B.A. in 1794 and earned the B.C.L. in 1798 and the D.C.L. in 1801. In 1801 he became a member of the College of Advocates. Shortly before August 1803 he went with his bride to Malta to serve as the king's and admiralty advocate until 1807. He practiced in Doctors' Commons after his return and from 1812 to 1816 worked as a leader writer for the *Times.* In 1817 he started a rival paper, successively called the *New Times,* the *Day and New Times,* the *New Times,* and the *Morning Journal,* which ran until May 1830. He relinquished his editorship of it in 1826, when he was knighted and returned to Malta as chief justice and justice of the vice-admiralty court. He retired to England in 1840, devoted himself to philology and history, and died at his home, in Brompton Square, London. Among his publications are translations of Schiller's *Fiesco* (1796) and *Don Carlos* (1798), both done in collaboration with the German grammarian and medalist Georg Heinrich Noehden (1770–1826), and of a work by the French satiric poet Joseph Despaze (1776–1814), *The Five Men; or, a Review of the . . . Executive Directory of France* (1797). Stoddart also published *Remarks on the Local Scenery and Manners of Scotland during the Years 1799 and 1800* (1801), legal writings, and essays on grammar, history, and philology in the 1848, 1850, and 1858 editions of the *Encyclopaedia Metropolitana.* He was married in 1803 to Isabella Moncreiff (d. 1846), the elder daughter of Sir Henry Moncreiff, eighth baronet, later Sir Henry Moncreiff Wellwood of Tulliebole (1750–1827), a Scottish divine who since 1793 had been chaplain to George III. Her writings, published under the pseudonym Martha Blackford, include *The Eskdale Herd-boy* (1819); *The Scottish Orphans* (1822) and its sequels, *Arthur Monteith* (1822) and *Arthur Monteith . . . To Which Is Added the Young West Indian* (2d. ed., 1823); *Annals of the Family McRoy* (1823); and *The Young Artist* (1825) and its sequel, *William Montgomery* (1829). The Stoddarts' children were Henry Moncreiff, who according to the *DNB* died while a pupil at the Charterhouse, London; John Frederick (1806?–1839), who in 1827

became a member of the Scottish bar and in 1836 a judge in Ceylon; William Wellwood (1810?–1856), an acquaintance of Thackeray and a tutor, an officer, and chaplain of St. John's College, Oxford, from 1832, and vicar of Charlbury, Oxfordshire, from 1853, to his death; twins (b. 1808 or 1809), one of whom may have been Henry Moncreiff; a daughter who died in infancy in 1804; a daughter whom Mary Lamb called "little Missy" in 1807, in Vol. II, Letter 216; Mary; and Isabella. When Stoddart met William Godwin, mentioned below, I cannot say. Lamb met Godwin in 1800 and discovered him to be decent, well behaved, and with "neither horns nor claws" (Letter 59). The antecedent of the pronoun opening Lamb's next sentence is "Allen."

29. Mrs. Jane West (1758–1852), *The History of Ned Evans: A Tale of the Times* (4 vols.; 1796), which is (anonymously) noticed in the *Critical Review,* 18 (November 1796), 341. Presumably the prosodist is Mrs. West. The articles alluded to in the next sentence are the reviews of *Joan of Arc* and *Poems on Various Subjects* anticipated for and published in the *Critical Review,* 17 (June 1796), 182–192 and 209–212. (There is nothing about or recognizably by Coleridge in its July issue.) William Evans, referred to as W. Evans below, entered the East India House in May 1796, was in receipt of salary from the accountant general's office from May 1797, and left before the June quarter 1808, when his name was omitted from the salary list. According to Lamb here, he was related to the family of Thomas Evans (d. 1814), the only son of the widow Mrs. Charlotte Evans, who had befriended Coleridge while he was at Christ's Hospital. Thomas had entered Christ's in 1784, had in 1788 or 1789 introduced Coleridge to his sisters—Elizabeth, Anne, and Mary (the last was the eldest, with whom Coleridge had fallen in love)—and by 1806 was Lamb's co-worker at the East India House. That the India Office Library, India Office Records has no information on him suggests he did not long remain.

30. "At Oxford, 1796," lines 7–8, by Bowles, whose "Elegiac Stanzas Written during Sickness at Bath," lines 21, 13, 17, and 76, Lamb quotes below and compares to Bowles's "Elegy Written at the Hotwells, Bristol, July, 1789." The last laments the death of Thomas Russell (1762–1788) of Winchester College and New College, Oxford, author of *Sonnets and Miscellaneous Poems* (1789). When Coleridge was a boy he had once seen Bowles, who at the time of this letter was rector of Chicklade, Wiltshire. By his *Sonnets Written Chiefly on Picturesque Spots during a Tour* (1789) Coleridge was strongly influenced. But Coleridge did not meet him until September 1797, when he took "Osorio. A Tragedy" (see Letter 25, note 4) to Bowles's house at Donhead St. Mary, Wiltshire.

31. "We were two pretty babes, the youngest she." Coleridge's strictures probably had to do with Lamb's concept of innocence departing in shame as maturity comes. But Coleridge accepted Lamb's explanation here, for when he published the poem in *Sonnets from Various Authors* he appended to its eleventh line a note that reads, "Innocence which while we possess it, is playful, as a babe, becomes AWFUL when it has departed from us.— This is the sentiment of the line, a fine sentiment and nobly expressed" (p. 7). The word "lunar," below, is in "A timid grace sits trembling in her eye," line 3. Sophia Pringle and the verses on her have not been identified.

32. For, besides its length and detail, it is written in a miniscule hand on less than two folio sheets. See *Coleridge's Letters,* I, esp. 210 and 255, for expressions in addition to the expression to which Lamb alludes below about Coleridge's becoming a Unitarian minister. See I, 219 and 226–233, for the invitation Coleridge had received in May to tutor the children of Mrs. Elizabeth Evans of Darley Abbey, Derbyshire. She, the daughter of the inventor Jedediah Strutt (1726–1797) and the widow of William Evans (d. 1795), had proposed £150 annually and wished him to live in her residence. He was interested, but her (unidentified)

father-in-law and brothers were opposed to the idea, and by August she had deferred to them. She gave him £95 and gave Mrs. Coleridge her children's baby clothes for their trouble.

33. Which he filled with his oversized initials.

4. *C. L. to Coleridge*

Monday Night [June 13—
Thursday, June 16, 1796]

Unfurnished at present with any sheet-filling subject, I shall continue my letter gradually and journal-wise. My second thoughts entirely coincide with your comments on 'Joan of Arc,' and I can only wonder at my childish judgment which over-looked the 1st book and could prefer the 9th: not that I was insensible to the soberer beauties of the former, but the latter caught me with its glare of magic,—the former, however, left a more pleasing general recollection in my mind. Let me add, the 1st book was the favourite of my sister—and *I* now, with Joan, often 'think on Domremi and the fields of Arc.'[1] I must not pass over without acknowledging my obligations to your full and satisfactory account of personifications. I have read it again and again, and it will be a guide to my future taste. Perhaps I had estimated Southey's merits too much by number, weight, and measure. I now agree completely and entirely in your opinion of the genius of Southey. Your own image of melancholy[2] is illustrative of what you teach, and in itself masterly. I conjecture it is 'disbranched' from one of your embryo 'hymns.' When they are mature of birth (were I you) I should print 'em in one separate volume, with 'Religious Musings' and your part of the 'Joan of Arc.' Birds of the same soaring wing[3] should hold on their flight in company. Once for all (and by renewing the subject you will only renew in me the condemnation of Tantalus), I hope to be able to pay you a visit (if you are then at Bristol) some time in the latter end of August or beginning of September for a week or fortnight; before that time, office business puts an absolute veto on my coming.

> 'And if a sigh that speaks regret of happier times appear,
> A glimpse of joy that we have met shall shine and dry the tear.'[4]

Of the blank verses I spoke of, the following lines are the only tolerably complete ones I have writ out of not more than one hundred and fifty.

[——— On the green hill top,
Hard by the house of prayer, a modest roof,
And not distinguish'd from its neighbour barn,
Save by a slender-tapering length of spire,
The Grandame sleeps: a plain stone barely tells
The name and date to the chance passenger.
For lowly born was she, and long had eat
Well-earn'd, the bread of service;—her's was else
A mounting spirit, one that entertain'd
Scorn of base action, deed dishonorable,
Or aught unseemly. I remember well
Her reverend image: I remember too,
With what a zeal she serv'd her Master's house;
And how the prattling tongue of garrulous age
Delighted to recount the oft-told tale;
Or anecdote domestic: Wise she was,
And wond'rous skill'd in genealogies,
And could in apt and voluble terms discourse
Of births, of titles, and alliances;
Of marriages and intermarriages;
Relationships remote, or near of kin;
Of friends offended, family disgraced,
Maiden high born, but wayward, disobeying
Parental strict injunctions, and regardless
Of unmix'd blood, and ancestry remote,
Stooping to wed with one of low degree:
But these are not thy praises: and I wrong
Thy honor'd memory, recording chiefly
Things light or trivial. Better 'twere to tell,
How with a nobler zeal, and warmer love,
She serv'd her *heavenly Master*. I have seen,
That reverend form bent down with age and pain,
And rankling malady: yet not for this
Ceas'd she to praise her Maker, or withdraw
Her trust from him, her faith, and humble hope;

So meekly had she learn'd to bear her cross;
For she had studied patience in the school
Of Christ; much comfort she had thence deriv'd,
And was a *follower* of the NAZARENE.]

That I get on so slowly you may fairly impute to want of practice in composition, when I declare to you that (the few verses which you have seen excepted) I have not writ fifty lines since I left school. It may not be amiss to remark that my grandmother (on whom the verses are written) lived housekeeper in a family the fifty or sixty last years of her life—that she was a woman of exemplary piety and goodness—and for many years before her death was terribly afflicted with a cancer in her breast which she bore with true Christian patience. You may think that I have not kept enough apart the ideas of her heavenly and her earthly master but recollect I have designedly given in to her own way of feeling—and if she had a failing, 'twas that she respected her master's family too much, not reverenced her Maker too little. The lines begin imperfectly, as I may probably connect 'em if I finish at all,—and if I do, Biggs[5] shall print 'em in a more economical way than you yours, for (Sonnets and all) they won't make a thousand lines as I propose completing 'em, and the substance must be wire-drawn.

Tuesday Evening, June 14, 1796

I am not quite satisfied now with the Chatterton, and with your leave will try my hand at it again. A master joiner, you know, may leave a cabinet to be finished by his journeyman when his own hands are full. To your list of illustrative personifications,[6] into which a fine imagination enters, I will take leave to add the following from Beaumont and Fletcher's 'Wife for a Month;' 'tis the conclusion of a description of a sea-fight;—'The game of *death* was never played so nobly; the meagre thief grew wanton in his mischiefs, and his shrunk hollow eyes smiled on his ruins.' There is fancy in these of a lower order from 'Bonduca;'—'Then did I see these valiant men of Britain, like boding owls creep into tods of ivy, and hoot their fears to one another nightly.' Not that it is a personification; only it just caught my eye in a little extract book I keep,[7] which is full of quotations from B. and F. in particular, in which authors I can't help thinking there is a greater richness of poetical fancy than in any one, Shakspeare excepted. Are you acquainted with Massinger? At a hazard I will trouble you with a passage from a play of his called 'A Very Woman.' The lines are spoken by a lover (disguised) to his faithless mistress. You will remark the fine effect of the double endings. You will by your ear distinguish the lines, for I write 'em as prose. 'Not far from where my father lives, *a lady,* a neighbour by, blest with as great a *beauty* as nature durst bestow without *undoing,* dwelt, and most happily, as I thought then, and blest the house a thousand times she *dwelt in.* This beauty, in the blossom of my youth, when my first fire knew no adulterate *incense,* nor I no way to flatter but my *fondness;* in all the bravery my friends could *show me,* in all the faith my innocence could *give me,* in the best language my true tongue could *tell me,* and all the broken sighs my sick heart *lend me,* I sued and served; long did I serve this *lady,* long was my travail, long my trade to *win her;* with all the duty of my soul I **served her.'** 'Then she must love.' 'She did, but never me: she could not *love me;* she would not love, she hated,—more, she *scorn'd me;* and in so poor and base a way *abused me* for all my services, for all my *bounties,* so bold neglects flung on me'—'What out of love, and worthy love, I *gave her* (shame to her most unworthy mind,) to fools, to girls, to fiddlers and her boys she flung, all in disdain of me.'[8] One more passage strikes my eye from B. and F.'s 'Palamon and Arcite.' One of 'em complains in prison: 'This is all our world; we shall know nothing here but one another, hear nothing but the clock that tells our woes; the vine shall grow, but we shall never see it,' &c. Is not the last circumstance exquisite? I mean not to lay myself open by saying they exceed Milton, and perhaps Collins, in sublimity. But don't you conceive all poets after Shakspeare yield to 'em in variety of genius? Massinger treads close on their heels; but you are most probably as well acquainted with his writings as your humble servant. My quotations, in that case, will only serve to expose my barrenness of matter. Southey in simplicity and tenderness, is excelled decidedly only, I think, by Beaumont and F. in his[9] 'Maid's Tragedy' and some parts of 'Philaster' in particular, and elsewhere occasionally; and perhaps by Cowper in his 'Crazy Kate,' and in parts of his translation, such as the speeches of Hecuba and Andromache. I long to know your opinion of that translation. The Odyssey especially is surely very Homeric. What nobler than the appearance of Phœbus at the beginning of the Iliad—the lines ending with 'Dread sounding, bounding on the silver bow!'[10]

I beg you will give me your opinion of the translation; it afforded me high pleasure. As curious a specimen of translation as ever fell into my hands, is a young man's in our office, of a French novel.[11] What in the original was literally 'amiable delusions of the fancy,' he proposed to render 'the fair frauds of the imagination!' I had much trouble in licking the book into any meaning at all. Yet did the knave clear fifty or sixty pounds by subscription and selling the copyright. The book itself not a week's work! To-day's portion of my journalising epistle has been very dull and poverty-stricken. I will here end.

Tuesday Night

I have been drinking egg-hot and smoking Oronooko (associated circumstances, which ever forcibly recall to my mind our evenings and nights at the Salutation); my eyes and brain are heavy and asleep, but my heart is awake; and if words came as ready as ideas, and ideas as feelings, I could say ten hundred kind things. Coleridge, you know not my supreme happiness at having one on earth (though counties separate us) whom I can call a friend. Remember you those tender lines of Logan?

'Our broken friendships we deplore,
And loves of youth that are no more;
No after friendships e'er can raise
Th' endearments of our early days,
And ne'er the heart such fondness prove,
As when we first began to love.'[12]

I am writing at random, and half-tipsy, what you may not *equally* understand, as you will be sober when you read it; but *my* sober and *my* half-tipsy hours you are alike a sharer in. Good night.

'Then up rose our bard, like a prophet in drink,
Craigdoroch, thou'lt soar when creation shall sink.'

Burns.

Thursday

I am now in high hopes to be able to visit you, if perfectly convenient on your part, by the end of next month—perhaps the last week or fortnight in July. A change of scene and a change of faces would do me good, even if that scene were not to be Bristol, and those

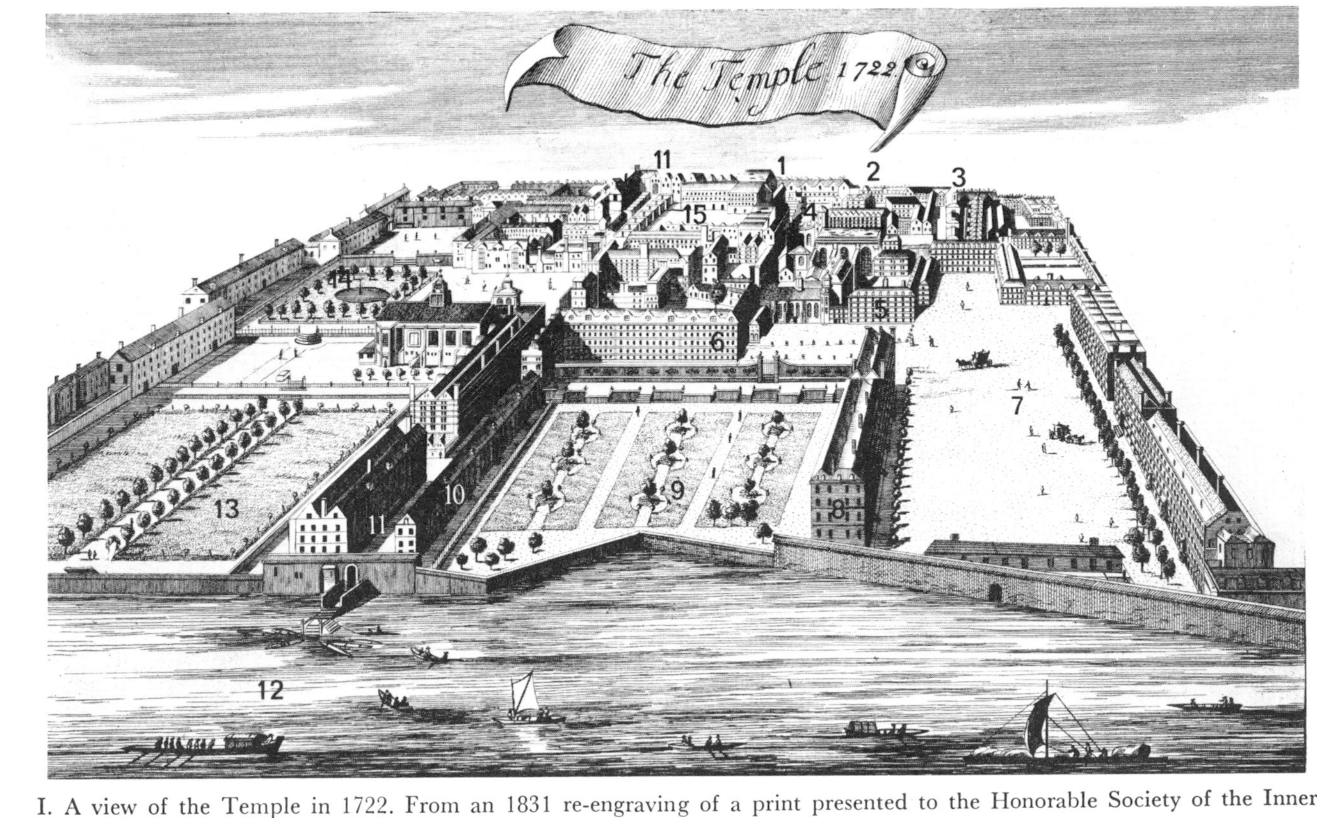

I. A view of the Temple in 1722. From an 1831 re-engraving of a print presented to the Honorable Society of the Inner Temple. Courtesy of The Masters of the Bench of the Inner Temple.

Key: 1—Inner Temple Lane; 2—Fleet Street; 3—Mitre Court Buildings; 4—Temple Church; 5—Inner Temple Hall; 6—Crown Office Row; 7—King's Bench Walk; 8—Paper Buildings; 9—Inner Temple Garden; 10—Harecourt Buildings; 11—Middle Temple Lane; 12—River Thames; 13—Middle Temple Garden; 14—Fountain Court; 15—Hare Court.

II. A perspective view of the Temple next the riverside in 1741. From an engraving by the Swiss artist J. Maurer. Courtesy of The Masters of the Bench of the Inner Temple.

III. Christ's Hospital (from the cloisters) in 1804. From an engraving by James Sargant Storer (1771–1853). Courtesy of the Victoria and Albert Museum.

IV. The writing school of Christ's Hospital in 1816. From an aquatint by Joseph Constantine Stadler (fl. 1780–1816). Courtesy of the Victoria and Albert Museum.

faces Coleridge's and his friends. In the words of Terence, a little altered, 'Tædet me hujus quotidiani mundi.'[13] I am heartily sick of the every-day scenes of life. I shall half wish you unmarried (don't show this to Mrs. C.) for one evening only, to have the pleasure of smoking with you, and drinking egg-hot in some little smoky room in a pot-house, for I know not yet how I shall like you in a decent room, and looking quite happy. My best love and respects to Sara notwithstanding.

Yours sincerely,
Charles Lamb

MS: unrecovered. Text, headed "(*Apparently a continuation of a letter the first part of which is missing*)": Lucas (1935), I, 26–30. Also pub.: Talfourd (1837), I, 35–43; Sala, I, 26–31; Purnell, I, 26–31; Fitzgerald, I, 312–317; Hazlitt, I, 109–114; Ainger (1888), I, 21–26; Ainger (1900), I, 29–36; Macdonald, I, 22–27; Ainger (1904), I, 21–26; Harper, II, 31–37; Lucas (1905), VI, 26–30; Lucas (1912), V, 26–30. The first sentence in the letter may mean that Lamb had begun elsewhere, but it may also mean that he is beginning by declaring his intention either to continue the substance of the previous letter or to write of whatever comes to him as he goes along, though he has nothing important in mind.

1. *Joan of Arc,* IV, 290.

2. In "Melancholy. A Fragment," which Coleridge must have included in his letter to Lamb, for it was first published in the *Morning Post* of December 12, 1797. Coleridge wrote it when he was nineteen. If it had been "disbranched" ("Religious Musings," line 266) from an embryo hymn, it was one that later perished with the rest of the hymns in embryo at the time of this letter.

3. Cf. *Cymbeline,* V, v, 471, and Milton's "Il Penseroso," line 52. For revealing the secret of the gods Tantalus, below, was made to stand in water that receded whenever he bent to drink it and beneath fruit-laden branches that were blown from him whenever he reached to grasp them.

4. Cowper's "To the Rev. Mr. Newton. An Invitation into the Country," lines 21–24. Below I have inserted Lamb's "The Grandame" from Coleridge's *Poems* (1797) to present a semblance of the original of this letter. The poem as it appears in Lloyd's *Poems on the Death of Priscilla Farmer* is in Lucas (1905), VI, 30–31. See my Introduction, pp. xxv–xxvi, for Lamb's grandmother Mary Field.

5. Nathaniel Biggs of Bristol, the printer of some of the early works of Coleridge, Wordsworth, Lloyd, and Southey. In 1798 he joined Cottle and, using the imprint "Biggs and Cottle," printed, for example, *Lyrical Ballads.* From 1799 to 1801 he was still operating in Bristol, using the imprints "Biggs and Cottle" and "Biggs and Co." He printed Coleridge's *Poems* (1803) as N. Biggs of Crane Court, Fleet Street, London. By 1809 he was at 1 Gough Square, London, as a printer and wholesale stationer.

6. In "Monody on the Death of Chatterton." The quotation, below, from Francis Beaumont and John Fletcher's *Wife for a Month* is from V, i, 348–350, and that from their *Bonduca* is from I, i, 111–114. The latter quotation Lamb in 1808 included in *Specimens of English Dramatic Poets, Who Lived about the Time of Shakspeare: With Notes* (*Works,* IV, 322).

7. But later this year destroyed. A similar book, of about fifty pages and mainly in Mary's hand, is in the Huntington Library.

8. Philip Massinger, *A Very Woman,* IV, iii, 185–199, 208–214, and 225–228.

The quotation following, from Beaumont and Fletcher's *The Two Noble Kinsmen* (which Lamb identifies as "Palamon and Arcite"), is from II, ii, 43–46. Both passages are in *Specimens of English Dramatic Poets* (*Works,* IV, 350–351 and 340).

9. Should be "their."

10. The *Iliad,* I, 60, a line for whose singularity Cowper apologized.

11. Jean-Claude Gorjy, or Gorgy (1753–1795), *Sentimental Tablets of the Good Pamphile, Written in the Months of August, September, October, and November 1789* (1791), which was translated under that title in 1795 by Peter Solomon du Puy (d. 1829). He was appointed a clerk in the accountant general's office in 1786, in receipt of salary from 1789, given an allowance as a Dutch translator from 1800, and retired in 1829. Lamb was one of the subscribers for his book.

12. John Logan's "Ode on the Death of a Young Lady," lines 31–36. The quotation in the next paragraph is from Burns's "The Whistle," lines 65–66.

13. *Eunuchus,* II, iii, 6, which Lamb translates in his next sentence.

5. *C. L. to Coleridge*

[Wednesday, June 29—
Friday evening, July 1, 1796]

The first moment I can come I will, but my hopes of coming yet a while yet hang on a ticklish thread. The coach I come by is immaterial as I shall so easily by your direction find ye out. My mother is grown so entirely helpless (not having any use of her limbs) that Mary is necessarily confined from ever sleeping out, she being her bed fellow. She thanks you tho' & will accompany me in spirit. Most exquisite are the lines from Withers.[1] Your own lines introductory to your poem on **Self** run smoothly & pleasurably, & I exhort you to continue 'em. What shall I say to your Dactyls? They are what you would call good **per se** but a parody on some of 'em is just now suggesting itself & you shall have it rough & **unlicked.** I mark with figures the lines parodied.

4 Sorely your Dactyls do drag along limp-footed.
5 Sad is the measure that hangs a clog round 'em so,
6 Meagre, & languid, proclaiming its wretchedness.
1 Weary, unsatisfied, not little sick of em,
11 Cold is my tired heart, I have no charity,
2 Painfully trav'lling thus over the rugged road.

7 O begone, Measure, half Latin half English, then.

12 Dismal, your Dactyls are, God help ye, rhyming **Ones.**

I ***possibly*** may not come this fortnight—therefore all thou hast to do is **not** to look for me any particular day, only to write word immediately if at any time you quit Bristol, lest I come & Taffy[2] be not at home. I ***hope*** I can come in a day or two. But young Savory of my **office** is suddenly taken ill in this very nick of time & I must officiate for him till he can come to w[ork a]gain. Had the Knave gone sick & d[i]ed & putrefied at any other t[ime,] philosophy might have afforded me comfort, but just now [I have] no patience with him. **Quarles**[3] I am as great a stranger [to as] I was to **Withers.** I wish you would try & do something to [bring] our elder bards into more general fame. I writhe with indignation, [whe]n in books of Criticism, where common place quotation is heaped upon quotation, I find no mention of such men as Massinger or B. & Fl. men with whom succeeding Dramatic Writers (otway alone excepted) can bear no manner of Comparison. Stupid Knox hath noticed none of 'em among his extracts.

Thursday

Mrs. C. can scarce guess how she has gratified me by her very kind letter & sweet little poem.[4] I feel that I *should* thank her in rhyme, but she must take my acknowledgment at present in plain honest prose. The uncertainty in which I yet stand whether I can come or no damps my spirits, reduces me a degree below prosaical, & keeps me in a suspense that fluctuates between hope & fear. **Hope** is charming, lively, blue-eyed wench, & I am always glad of her company, but could dispense with the visitor she brings with her, her younger sister, **fear,** a white liver'd-lilly-cheeked, bashful palpitating, awkward hussey that hangs like a green girl[5] at her sister's apronstrings & will go with her whithersoever ***she* goes.** For the life & soul of me I could not improve those lines in your poem on *the Prince* & Princess so I changed them to what you bid me & left 'em at Perry's. I think 'em altogether good, & do not see why you were sollicities about *any* alteration. I have not yet seen, but will make it my business to see, today's chronicle for your verses on Horne Took. Dyer stanza'd him in one of the papers, tother day but I think unsuccessfully: Tooke's friends' meeting was I suppose a dinner **of condolence. .** I am not sorry to find you (for all Sara)[6] immersed in clouds of smoke & metaphysic. You know I had a sneaking kindness for this last noble science, & you taught me some smattering of it. I look to become no mean proficient under your tuition. **Coleridge, what do you mean by saying you wrote to me about Plutarch & Porphyry,—**[7]I received no such letter, nor rememb[e]r no syllable of the matter, yet am not apt to forget any part of your epistles, least of all an injunction like that. I will cast about for 'em, tho' I am a sad hand to know what books are worth, & both those worthy gentlemen are alike **out of my line.** To-morrow I shall be less suspensive & in better cue to write, so good bye at present

Friday evening

that execrable aristocrat & knave Richardson[8] has given me an absolute refusal of leave! The *poor man* cannot guess at my disappointment. Is it not hard, this "dread dependance on the low bred mind"? Continue to write to me tho', & I must be content———. Our loves & best good wishes attend upon you both—

Lamb

Savory did return, but there are 2 or 3 more ill and absent, which was the plea for refusing me. I will never commit my peace of mind by depending on such a wretch for a favor in future, so shall never have heart to ask for holidays again. The man next him in office, **Cartwright,**[9] furnished him with the objections.——

C Lamb

MS: Huntington Library. Pub.: Talfourd (1848), I, 37–41; Sala, I, 32–35; Purnell, I, 32–35; Fitzgerald, I, 318–321; Hazlitt, I, 115–117; Ainger (1888), I, 26–28; Ainger (1900), I, 36–39; Macdonald, I, 27–30; Ainger (1904), I, 26–28; Harper, II, 38–41; Lucas (1905), VI, 32–34; Lucas (1912), V, 31–33; Lucas (1935), I, 31–33. Address: Mr. Coleridge/Bristol. Postmark: July 1, 1796.

1. George Wither, or Withers (1588–1667), the poet and pamphleteer of whom Lamb wrote in "On the Poetical Works of George Wither" (*Works,* I, 181–184). Unknown are the lines by him that Coleridge had sent to Lamb. Unknown too is the poem on Self, mentioned next. "To a Friend, Together with an Unfinished Poem" and "Melancholy. A Fragment" have been suggested as the latter work. A third possibility, if one considers Lamb's remarks in Letter 2, near the reference to note 17, and the allusion in this letter, at the reference to note 6, is "The

Eolian Harp." Only the third stanza is Coleridge's in Southey's "The Soldier's Wife. Dactylics," which appears in Southey's *Poems* (1797), p. 81, so:

Weary way-wanderer languid and sick at heart
Travelling painfully over the rugged road,
Wild-visag'd Wanderer! ah for thy heavy chance!

Sorely thy little one drags by thee bare-footed,
Cold is the baby that hangs at thy bending back,
Meagre and livid and screaming its wretchedness.

Woe-begone mother, half anger, half agony,
As over thy shoulder thou lookest to hush the babe,
Bleakly the blinding snow beats in thy hagged face.

Thy husband will never return from the war again,
Cold is thy hopeless heart even as Charity—
Cold are thy famish'd babes—God help thee, widow'd One.

2. Unidentified, but conjecturally a maid or neighbor of the Coleridges. There were two Savorys (see below) in the accountant general's office—William, who received his appointment in 1792, was in receipt of salary from 1795, and left in 1805; and Thomas Kingsman, who was appointed in 1796, in receipt of salary from 1799, and released in 1805. A stain on the manuscript obscures the locutions in brackets. They are supplied from Lucas (1935), I, 32.

3. Francis Quarles (1592-1644), the author, among other works, of *Emblems* (1635) and *The Virgin Widow* (1649). Passages from the latter are in "Extracts from the Garrick Plays" (*Works,* IV, 420–421 and 585). It was Lamb who was to bring the "elder bards into more general fame," principally in the work just cited, the *Specimens of English Dramatic Poets,* and the essay on Wither, and also in "Characters of Dramatic Writers, Contemporary with Shakspeare" (*Works,* I, 40–56). Knox, labeled at the end of the paragraph, was Vicesimus Knox (1752–1821), the miscellaneous writer and the compiler of *Elegant Extracts* (1789).

4. Unidentified and probably unrecovered.

5. *Hamlet,* I, iii, 101. The poem on the prince and princess (mentioned following), on the separation between George, Prince of Wales, and Princess Caroline, is "On a Late Connubial Rupture in High Life." James Perry (1756–1821), the founder in 1782 of the *European Magazine* and since 1789 proprietor and editor with James Gray, or Grey (d. 1796), of the *Morning Chronicle,* rejected the piece. Perry also rejected the poem on the politician and philologist John Horne Tooke (1736–1812)— "Verses Addressed to J. Horne Tooke and the Company Who Met on June 28th, 1796, to Celebrate His Poll at the Westminster Election." (Tooke lost, to Charles James Fox [1749–1806] and Alan Gardner, first Baron Gardner [1742–1809].) George Dyer (1755–1841), about whose character and eccentricities Lamb in these letters and in "Oxford in the Vacation" and "Amicus Redivivus" (*Works,* II, 7–12 and 209–213) was wondrously more specific than he was in locating or identifying here Dyer's (unlocated and unidentified) stanzas on Tooke, was the son of John, a Bridewell shipwright and lighterman. Two charitable women sent Dyer first to a charity school and, in 1762, to Christ's Hospital. There he was befriended and guided by the classical scholar and physician Anthony Askew (1722–1774), became a Grecian—a superior student—and remained until 1774. In that year he entered Emmanuel College, Cambridge, attracted the favorable attention of its master, Richard Farmer (1735–1797), and was graduated B.A. in 1778. In 1779 he became an usher at the grammar school in Dedham, Essex. In about 1781 he returned to Cambridge and nearby Chesterton to tutor the children of the dissenting minister and hymn writer Robert Robinson (1735–1790). Robinson led him into Unitarianism and association with the Cambridge dissenters, among them Dyer's close friend the reformer and scientific

writer William Frend (1757–1841), in their struggle against the imposition of religious and political disabilities. Having to give up whatever hope he might have held for preferment, Dyer retired briefly to Swavesay, near Cambridge. From perhaps 1783 to 1785 he was an usher with John Clarke (1757–1820), the father of Charles Cowden Clarke, at the school in Northampton conducted by the divine and educator John Collett Ryland (1723–1792). Dyer went to London in 1792. He was living in Carey Street, Lincoln's Inn Fields, in 1794, when he met Coleridge. Probably through Coleridge he came to meet Lamb and Southey. In about 1795 Dyer removed to humble and, as it turned out, permanent lodgings at 1 Clifford's Inn, Fleet Street. In 1802 he became the tutor of the sons of Charles Stanhope, third Earl Stanhope (1753–1816), a statesman and man of science who named Dyer one of his executors and legatees. Dyer left him in 1802. Afterward he added enough to his small annuity by working as a hack for booksellers and as an occasional instructor in Greek and Latin to earn at best a modest living. He contributed to the *Analytical Review,* the *Christian Reformer,* the *Critical Review,* William Hone's *Every Day Book,* the *Gentleman's Magazine,* the *Monthly Magazine,* James Anderson's *Recreations in Agriculture, Natural History, Arts and Miscellaneous Literature,* John and Leigh Hunt's *Reflector,* and the Delphin classics of Greece and Rome, issued by Abraham John Valpy (1787–1854) in 141 volumes from 1819 to 1830. Editing the series cost Dyer his eyesight shortly after the publication of its last volume. Among his books are studies of the poor, of Cambridge University (see Letter 86, note 11) and the University of London and dissenting colleges, of the English constitution, *Poems, Consisting of Odes and Elegies* (1792), *Memoirs of the Life and Writings of Robert Robinson* (1796), *The Poet's Fate* (1797), *Poems* (1801), *Poems and Critical Essays* (2 vols.; 1802), and *Poetics: Or a Series of Poems, and of Disquisitions on Poetry* (2 vols.; 1812). On May 3, 1824, Dyer was married to Mrs. Honour Mather (1761–1861), his laundress and the widow of a solicitor. She had been living in rooms opposite his own and did lovingly look after him till the end of his life. Major S. Butterworth in "Charles Lamb: Some New Biographical and Other Details," *The Bookman,* 60 (July 1921), 167, identified Dyer's father and corrected the information current until then that he was a Wapping watchman.

6. As in "The Eolian Harp," lines 49–64, in its final version.

7. Or Porphyrius (233–304?), a Greek historian and Neoplatonist.

8. William Richardson (d. 1798) had joined the East India House in 1760, been made deputy accountant general in 1778, and accountant general in 1785. The quotation following is from "Monody on the Death of Chatterton," line 98.

9. Charles Cartwright (d. 1825) had come into the East India House in 1773, succeeded Richardson as deputy accountant general in 1785 and would succeed him as accountant general in 1798, and was retired in 1822.

6. *C. L. to Coleridge*

[Tuesday,] The 5th July
[—Thursday, July 7], 1796

[To Sara and Her Samuel

Was it so hard a thing? I did but ask
A fleeting holy day. One little week,
Or haply two, had bounded my request.

What if the jaded Steer, who all day long
Had borne the heat and labour of the plough,
When Evening came and her sweet cooling hour,
Should seek to trespass on a neighbour copse,
Where greener herbage waved, or clearer streams
Invited him to slake his burning thirst?
That Man were crabbed, who should say him Nay:
That Man were churlish, who should drive him thence!

A blessing light upon your heads, ye good,
Ye hospitable pair. I may not come,
To catch on Clifden's[1] heights the summer gale:
I may not come, a pilgrim, to the 'Vales
Where Avon winds,' to taste th' inspiring waves
Which Shakespere drank, our British Helicon:
Or, with mine eye intent on Redcliffe towers,
To drop a tear for that Mysterious youth,[2]
Cruelly slighted, who to London Walls,
In evil hour, shap'd his disastrous course.

Complaints, begone; begone, ill-omen'd thoughts—
For yet again, and lo! from Avon banks
Another 'Minstrel'[3] cometh! Youth beloved,
God and good angels guide thee on thy way,
And gentler fortunes wait the friends I love.

C. L.]

the 6th July

Substitute in room of that last confused & incorrect Paragraph, following the words "disastrous course," these lines.

* ⟨With better hopes, I trust, from Avon's Vales
This other "Minstrel" cometh. Youth endear'd,
God & good Angels guide thee on thy road,
And gentler fortunes 'wait the friends I love.⟩

Let us **prose**

What can I do, till you send word what priced & placed house you should like.[4] Islington possibly you would not like, to me 'tis Classical ground. Knights bridge is a desireable situation for the air of the Parks. St. George's fields is convenient for its contiguity to the **Bench. Chuse.** But are you really coming to town? The hope of it has entirely disarmed my petty disappointment of its **nettles.** Yet I rejoice so much on my own account, that I fear I do not feel enough pure satisfaction on yours. Why, surely the joint editorship of the Chron: must be a very comfortable & secure living for a man. But should not you read french, or do you? & can you write with sufficient moderation, as tis call'd, when one suppresses the one half of what one feels, or could say, on a subject, to chime in the better with popular lukewarmness?—. Whites "letters" are near publication. Could you **review 'em** or get 'em **reviewed?**[5] are you not connected with the **Crit: Rev:?** His frontispiece is a good conceit, Sir John learning to dance, to please Madam Page, in dress of doublet &c from the upper half, & modern pantaloons with shoes &c of the 18th Century from the lower half.— & the whole work is full of goodly quips & rare fancies, "all deftly masqued like hoar **antiquity**"[6]—much superior to D*r* Kenrick's "Falstaff's Wedding," which you may have seen.— Allen sometimes laughs at Superstition & Religion & the like. A living fell vacant lately in the **gift of the Hospital.** White informed him that he stood a fair chance for it. He scrupled, & scrupled about it,—& at last (to use his own words) "tamperd" with *Godwin* to know whether the thing was **honest** or **not.** *Godwin* said nay to it, & Allen rejected the living! Could **the blindest Poor Papish** have bowed more **servilely** to his **Priest** or **Casuist?** Why sleep the Watchman's answers to that *Godwin?* I beg you will not delay to alter, if you mean to keep, those last lines[7] I sent you. Do that, & read these for your pains—

To the Poet Cowper

Cowper, I thank my God, that thou art heal'd.
Thine was the sorest malady of all;
And I am sad to think, that it should light
Upon the worthy head! But thou art heal'd,
And thou art yet, we trust, the destin'd Man,
Born to reanimate the Lyre, whose chords
Have slumber'd & have idle lain so long,
To the immortal sounding of whose strings
Did Milton frame the stately-paced verse;

Among whose wires with lighter finger playing,
Our elder Bard, Spenser, a gentle Name,
The Lady muses' dearest darling child,
Elicited the deftest tunes yet heard
In Hall or Bower, taking the delicate Ear
of Sidney, & his peerless maiden Queen,

Thou, then, take up the mighty Epic strain,
Cowper, of England's Bards the wisest & the Best
1796

I have read your climax of praises in those 3 reviews.[8] These mighty spouters out of panegyric waters have, 2 of em, scatter'd their fray even upon **me!** & the waters are cooling & refreshing. Prosaically, the Monthly Reviewers have made indeed a large **article** of it & done you justice. The Critical have in their wisdom selected not the very best specimens, & notice not, except as one name on the muster role, the "Religious Musings." I suspect Master Dyer to have been the writer of that **article,** as the Substance of it was the very remarks & the very language he used to me **one day.** I fear you will not **accord** entirely with my sentiments of Cowper, as *exprest* above, (perhaps scarcely just) but the poor Gentleman has just recover'd from his Lunacies, & that begets pity, & pity love, & love admiration, & then it goes hard with **People** but they **lie! Have you read** the Balad call'd "Leonora"[9] in the 2d No. of the **"Monthly Magazine"?—.** If you have—!!!!!!!!!!!!!! there is another fine song from the same Author (Berger) in the 3d No. of scarce inferior **merit**—& (vastly below these) there are some happy **specimens of English Hexameters** in an imitation of Ossian in the 5th No.— For your Dactyls I am sorry you are so sore about 'em—a very Sir **Fretful—.** In good troth the Dactyls are good Dactyls, but their measure is **naught. Be** not yourself "half anger half agony"[10] if I pronounce your **darling** lines not to be the best you **ever wrote** in all your **life,**—you have written much.

for the alterations[11] in those lines let 'em run thus. .

I may not come, a pilgrim, to the Banks
of *Avon, lucid stream,* to taste the Wave[†]

which Shakspere drank, our British Helicon;
or with mine eye &c &c
To muse, in tears,‡ on that mysterious youth &c.

Then the last paragraph alter thus

Complaint begone; begone, unkind reproof:§
Take up, my song, take up a merrier strain,
For yet again, & lo! from Avon's Vales
another Minstrel cometh! Youth *endear'd,*
God & good angels &c. as before——

Have a care, good Master poet, of the Statute de Contumelia,[12] what do you mean by calling Madame Mara harlots' & naughty things? The goodness of the verse would not save you in a court of Justice. But are you really coming to town?

Coleridge, a Gentleman called in London lately from Bristol, & enquired whether there were any of the family of a Mr. Chambers[13] living—this Mr. Chambers he said had been the making of a friend's fortune who wished to make some return for it. He went away without seeing her ⟨learning whether any of that family was living or not⟩. Now a Mrs. Reynolds—a very intimate friend of o[urs]—whom you have seen at our house, is the only daughter & all that survives, of Mr. Chambers—& a very little supply would be of service to her, for she married very unfortunately & has parted with her Husband. Pray, find out this Mr. Pember[14] (for that was the Gentleman's friend's name) he is an Attorney & lives at Bristol. Find him out, & acquaint him with the circumstances of the case, & offer to be the medium of supply to Mrs. Reynolds if he chuses to make her a present. She is in very distrest circumstances. Mr. Pember, Attorney, Bristol.— Mr. Chambers lived in the Temple. Mrs. Reynolds his daughter was my schoolmistress & is in the room at this present writing.—This last circumstance induced me to write so soon again—I have not further to add—. Our loves to Sara.

C Lamb

Thursday

*No: vide 3d page of this epistle [See my note 11.—Ed.]
†(inspiring wave) was too common place

‡(better than "drop a tear")

§(better refer to my own "complaint" solely th[an] half to that & half to Chatterton, as in your copy, which creates a confusion—"ominous fears" &c.) [Apparently the reading in the poem sent separately (I presume) and in 1797 revised to "ominous thoughts, away!"—Ed.]

MS, save "To Sara and Her Samuel": The Folger Shakespeare Library, Washington, D.C. Pub.: Talfourd (1848), I, 43–48; Sala, I, 35–39; Purnell, I, 35–39; Fitzgerald, I, 321–324; Hazlitt, I, 118–121; Ainger (1888), I, 28–31; Ainger (1900), I, 40–44; Macdonald, I, 30–33; Ainger (1904), I, 28–31; Harper, II, 42–48; Lucas (1905), VI, 35–39; Lucas (1912), V, 34–38; Lucas (1935), I, 34–38. Address: Mr. Coleridge/Bristol. Postmark: July 7, 1796. The poem and its date are from Lucas (1935), I, 34–35. In his 1905 edition (VI, xi) Lucas cites a facsimile of the original of the poem as his source. His additional comments and conclusions—that the poem is postmarked July 5, 1796, and was thus sent separately from the letter, and that it was cut from the top of and thus sent with the letter (Lucas [1905], VI, 35, and *Works,* V, 288)—contradict themselves and the content and manuscript of the letter, which has nothing cut from it. What may have been the case, as the letter generally and Lamb's last note and Lucas' remarks particularly suggest, is that Lamb sent two copies of the poem, one separately and the other with and as part of this letter. The poem as revised for the *Monthly Magazine,* 3 (January 1797), 54–55, is in *Works,* V, 15.

1. Should be either Clevedon's or Clifton's. Two other errors follow: the Gloucestershire-Somersetshire Avon is confused with that in Shakespeare's Warwickshire, and Helicon, the Grecian mountain of inspiration, is employed for Hippocrene, a spring on it.

2. Thomas Chatterton, who was baptized in St. Mary Redcliffe, Bristol, in 1752; went to London on April 24, 1770; and poisoned himself in desperation over his poverty on August 25, 1770.

3. Chatterton in Coleridge's "Monody on the Death of Chatterton," line 44, but Coleridge here.

4. Perry of the *Morning Chronicle* had in late June or early July invited Coleridge through Dr. Thomas Beddoes (1760–1808), a Bristol physician and the father of the poet Thomas Lovell Beddoes (1803–1849), to write regularly for him from London and possibly replace James Gray as his coeditor. Coleridge wrote Perry his acceptance and alerted Lamb to his need for a house, but the plan fell through. By "the Bench," below, Lamb designates King's Bench Prison.

5. White's *Original Letters, &c. of Sir John Falstaff and His Friends* is (anonymously) noticed in the *Monthly Review,* N.S. 21 (November 1796), 356, and in the *Critical Review,* 20 (June 1797), 234–237. Lamb praised it in Leigh Hunt's *Examiner* of September 5 and 6, 1819 (*Works,* I, 191–195). For the frontispiece and portions of the reviews see the edition of Charles Edmund Merrill, Jr. (New York and London: Harper, 1924), frontispiece and pp. 20–24.

6. "Monody on the Death of Chatterton," line 155. The miscellaneous writer William Kenrick (1725?–1779) wrote the comedy *Falstaff's Wedding* (1760).

7. Presumably "The Grandame." For the minor revisions Lamb made in "To the Poet Cowper" for the *Monthly Magazine,* 2 (December 1796), 889, see *Works,* V, 14–15.

8. Of *Poems on Various Subjects,* in the *Monthly Review,* N.S. 20 (June 1796),

194–199; the *Critical Review,* 17 (June 1796), 209–212; and the *Analytical Review,* 23 (June 1796), 610–612. The *Monthly* calls Lamb's contributions "of no inferior merit." The *Critical* calls them "very beautiful." The *Analytical* reports only that for "two or three pieces in this volume, Mr. C. acknowledges his obligation to friends."

9. Or "Lenore" (1773), by Gottfried August Bürger (1748–1794). It was translated by William Taylor (1765–1836) for the *Monthly Magazine,* 1 (March 1796), 135–137. Bürger's "The Lass of Fair Wone" and a transversion of Ossian's (properly James Macpherson's) *Carthon* called "English Hexameter Exemplified" are in the *Monthly Magazine,* 1 (April and June 1796), 223–224 and 404–405. For Sir Fretful, below, see Letter 2, note 11.

10. Southey, "The Soldier's Wife," line 7, which is Coleridge's line.

11. To which in his first note Lamb directs Coleridge.

12. The "law against calumny," possibly a reference to Coleridge's "Lines Composed in a Concert-room," esp. line 3: "Heaves the proud Harlot her distended breast." Mrs. Gertrude Elizabeth Mara (1749–1833), a popular singer who performed in London from 1784 to 1787 and from 1790 to 1802, is not named in the poem as it appears in the *Morning Post* of September 24, 1799, but may have been in the version Coleridge perhaps sent to Lamb. Its date of composition, however, has been conjectured as 1799. See *Coleridge's Poetical Works* (1912), I, 324.

13. Charles Chambers, the father of Mrs. Elizabeth Reynolds. See the Introduction, pp. xxviii–xxix.

14. Unidentified.

7. *C. L. to Coleridge*

[September 27, 1796]

My dearest friend—

White or some of my friends or the public papers by this time may have informed you of the terrible calamities that have fallen on our family. I will only give you the outlines. My poor dear dearest sister in a fit of insanity has been the death of her own mother. I was at hand only time enough to snatch the knife out of her grasp. She is at present in a mad house, from whence I fear she must be moved to an hospital. God has preserved to me my senses,—I eat and drink and sleep, and have my judgment I believe very sound. My poor father was slightly wounded, and I am left to take care of him and my aunt.[1] Mr. Norris of the Bluecoat school has been very kind to us, and we have no other friend, but thank God I am very calm and composed, and able to do the best that remains to do. Write,—as religious a letter as possible—but no mention of what is gone and done with—with me the former things are passed away,[2] and I have something more to do that to feel——

God almighty

have us all in
his keeping.——

C. Lamb

mention nothing of poetry. I have destroyed every vestige of past vanities of that kind. Do as you please, but if you publish, publish mine (I give free leave) without name or initial, and never[3] send me a book, I charge you, you[r] own judgment will convince you not to take any notice of this yet to your dear wife.—You look after your family,—I have my reason and strength left to take care of mine. I charge you don't think of coming to see me. Write. I will not see you if you come. God almighty love you and all of us——

MS: unrecovered. Text: Lucas (1935), I, 39–40. Also pub.: Talfourd (1848), I, 51–53; Sala, I, 39–41; Purnell, I, 39–41; Fitzgerald, I, 325–326; Hazlitt, I, 123–124; Ainger (1888), I, 32; Ainger (1900), I, 44–45; Macdonald, I, 33–34; Ainger (1904), I, 32; Harper, II, 49–50; Lucas (1905), VI, 41; Lucas (1912), V, 39–40. Postmark: September 27, 1796.

1. This account of the tragedy of Thursday, September 22, is in the *Morning Chronicle* of Monday, September 26:

> On Friday afternoon the Coroner and a respectable Jury sat on the body of a Lady in the neighbourhood of Holborn, who died in consequence of a wound from her daughter the preceding day. It appeared by the evidence adduced, that while the family were preparing for dinner, the young lady seized a case knife laying on the table, and in a menacing manner pursued a little girl, her apprentice, round the room; on the eager calls of her helpless infirm mother to forbear, she renounced her first object, and with loud shrieks approached her parent.
>
> The child by her cries quickly brought up the landlord of the house, but too late—the dreadful scene presented to him the mother lifeless, pierced to the heart, on a chair, her daughter yet wildly standing over her with the fatal knife, and the venerable old man, her father, weeping by her side, himself bleeding at the forehead from the effects of a severe blow he received from one of the forks she had been madly hurling about the room.
>
> For a few days prior to this the family had observed some symptoms of insanity in her, which had so much increased on the Wednesday evening, that her brother early the next morning went in quest of Dr. Pitcairn [see the next letter]—had that gentleman been met with, the fatal catastrophe had, in all probability, been prevented.
>
> It seems the young Lady had been once before, in her earlier years, deranged, from the harassing fatigues of too much business.—As her carriage towards her mother was ever affectionate in the extreme, it is believed that to the increased attentiveness, which her parents' infirmities called for by day and night, is to be attributed the present insanity of this ill-fated young woman.
>
> It has been stated in some of the Morning Papers, that she has an insane brother also in confinement—this is without foundation.
>
> The Jury of course brought in their Verdict, *Lunacy*.

The Whitehall *Evening Post* (presumably of September 26 also, though I have not seen the paper and quote from Lucas [1935], I, 41) adds that the "above unfortunate young person is a Miss Lamb, a mantua-maker, in Little Queen-street, Lincoln's-inn-fields. She has been, since, removed to Islington mad-house [possibly Fisher House]." Mr. and Mrs. Norris—she is mentioned in the next letter—were probably Philip (d. 1806) and his wife, Sally, of Castle Street, Holborn. He was a builder and surveyor associated with Christ's Hospital (the Bluecoat school), at least indirectly through his brother Richard, Jr. (d. 1792), and their father, Richard (d. 1779), both surveyors for the school. See Phyllis G. Mann's "Mr. Norris of the Bluecoat School," in the *CLSB* of September 1953, March 1954, and July 1955.

2. Revelations 21:4. The word "that" following is a mistake for "than." Texts of Coleridge's letter, of September 28, are among the few letters or texts of letters from Coleridge to Lamb (see below, Letter 95, note 1) that survive:

> Your letter, my friend, struck me with a mighty horror. It rushed upon me and stupified my feelings. You bid me write you a religious letter. I am not a man who would attempt to insult the greatness of your anguish by any other consolation. Heaven knows that in the easiest fortunes there is much dissatisfaction and weariness of spirit; much that calls for the exercise of patience and resignation; but in storms like these, that shake the dwelling and make the heart tremble, there is no middle way between despair and the yielding up of the whole spirit unto the guidance of faith. And surely it is a matter of joy that your faith in Jesus has been preserved; the Comforter that should relieve you is not far from you. But as you are a Christian, in the name of that Saviour, who was filled with bitterness and made drunken with wormwood, I conjure you to have recourse in frequent prayer to 'his God and your God'; the God of mercies, and father of all comfort. Your poor father is, I hope, almost senseless of the calamity; the unconscious instrument of Divine Providence knows it not, and your mother is in heaven. It is sweet to be roused from a frightful dream by the song of birds and the gladsome rays of the morning. Ah, how infinitely more sweet to be awakened from the blackness and amazement of a sudden horror by the glories of God manifest and the hallelujahs of angels.
>
> As to what regards yourself, I approve altogether of your abandoning what you justly call vanities. I look upon you as a man called by sorrow and anguish and a strange desolation of hopes into quietness, and a soul set apart and made peculiar to God! We cannot arrive at any portion of heavenly bliss without in some measure imitating Christ; and they arrive at the largest inheritance who imitate the most difficult parts of his character, and, bowed down and crushed underfoot, cry in fulness of faith, 'Father, thy will be done.'
>
> I wish above measure to have you for a little while here; no visitants shall blow on the nakedness of your feelings; you shall be quiet, and your spirit may be healed. I see no possible objection, unless your father's helplessness prevent you, and unless you are necessary to him. If this be not the case, I charge you write me that you will come.
>
> I charge you, my dearest friend, not to dare to encourage gloom or despair. You are a temporary sharer in human miseries that you may be an eternal partaker of the Divine nature [see below, Letter 10, note 1]. I charge you, if by any means it be possible, come to me.
>
> I remain your affectionate
> S. T. Coleridge
> [*Coleridge's Letters,* I, 238–239]

3. It is noted in Lucas (1935), I, 41, that "and never" was possibly canceled. Coleridge apparently had already invited Lamb to contribute to *Poems* (1797), which contains, under the heading "Poems, by Charles Lamb, of the India-

House," "As when a child on some long winter's night," "Was it some sweet device of Faery," "Methinks how dainty sweet it were, reclin'd," "O! I could laugh to hear the midnight wind," "The Grandame," "When last I roved these winding wood-walks green," "A timid grace sits trembling in her eye," "If from my lips some angry accents fell," "We were two pretty babes, the youngest she," "Childhood," "The Sabbath Bells," "Fancy Employed on Divine Subjects," "The Tomb of Douglas," "To Charles Lloyd. An Unexpected Visitor," and "A Vision of Repentance." They are dedicated, "with all a brother's fondness," to Mary, "the author's best friend and sister," and are in *Works,* V, 3–13. Lamb's concern for Mrs. Coleridge, following, was because of her having given birth on September 19 to David Hartley (d. 1849).

8. *C. L. to Coleridge*

[October 3, 1796]

My dearest friend,

your letter was an inestimable treasure to me. It will be a comfort to you, I know, to know that our prospects are somewhat brighter. My poor dear dearest sister, the unhappy & unconscious instrument of the Almighty's judjments to our house, is restored to her senses; to a dreadful sense & recollection of what has past, awful to her mind & impressive (as it must be to the end of life) but temper'd with religious resignation, & the reasonings of a sound judgment, which in this early stage knows how to distinguish between a deed committed in a transcient fit of frenzy, & the terrible guilt of a Mother's murther. I have seen her. I found her this morning calm & serene, far very very far from an indecent forgetful serenity; she has a most affectionate & tender concern for what has happend. Indeed from the beginning, frightful & hopeless as her disorder seemed, I had confidence enough in her strength of mind, & religious principle, to look forward to a time when *even she* might recover tranquillity. God be praised, Coleridge, wonderful as it is to tell, I have never once been otherwise than collected, & calm; even on the dreadful day & in the midst of the terrible scene I preserved a tranquillity, which bystanders may have construed into indifference, a tranquillity not of despair; is it folly or sin in me to say that it was a religious principle that *most* supported me? I allow much to other favorable circumstances. I felt that I had something else to do than to regret; on that first evening my Aunt was laying insensible, to all appearance like one dying,—my father, with his poor forehead plaisterd over from a wound he had received from a daughter dearly loved by him, & who loved him no less dearly,—my mother a dead & murder'd corpse in the next room—yet was I wonderfully supported. I closed not my eyes in sleep that night, but lay without terrors & without despair. I have lost no sleep since. I had been long used not to rest in things of sense, had endeavord after a comprehension of mind, unsatisfied with the "ignorant present time,"[1] & this kept me up. I had the whole weight of the family thrown on me, for my brother, little disposed (I speak not without tenderness for him) at any time to take care of old age & infirmities had now, with his bad leg, an exemption from such duties, & I was now **left alone.** One little incident may serve to make you understand my way of managing my mind. Within a day or 2 after the fatal **one,** we drest for dinner a tongue, which we had had salted for some weeks in the house. As I sat down a feeling like **remorse** struck me,—this tongue poo[r] Mary got for **me,** & can I partake of it **now,** when she is far **away**—a thought occurrd & relieve[d] me,—if I give into this way of feeling, there is not a chair, a room, an object in our rooms, that will not awaken the keenest griefs, I must rise above such weaknesses—. I hope this was not want of true feeling. I did not let this carry me tho' too far. On the very 2d day (I date from the day of **horrors**) as is usual in such cases there were a matter of 20 people I do think supping in our **room—.** They prevailed on me to eat *with them* (for to eat I never refused) they were all making merry! in the room,—some had come from friendship, some from busy curiosity, & some from **Interest;** I was going to partake with **them,** when my recollection came that my poor dead mother was lying in the next room, the very next room, a mother who thro' life wished nothing but her children's welfare—indignation, the rage of grief, something like remorse, rushed upon my mind in an agony of emotion,—I found my way mechanically to the adjoing room, & fell on my knees by the **side** of her coffin, asking forgiveness of heaven, & sometimes of her, for forgetting her **so soon.** Tranquillity returned, & it was the only violent emotion that master'd me, & I think it did me good.———

I mention these things because I hate concealment, & love to give a faithful journal of what passes within **me.** Our friends have been very good. Sam LeGrice[2] who was then in town was with me the 3 or 4 first days, & was as a brother to me, gave up every hour of his time, to the very hurting of his health & spirits, in constant attendance & humoring my poor father. Talk'd with him, read to him, play'd at cr[ib]bage with Him (for so **short** is the old man's recollection, that he was playing at cards, as tho' nothing had happened, while the Coroner's Inquest was sitting over the way!) Samuel wept tenderly when he went away, for his Mother wrote him a very severe letter on his loitering so long in town, & he was forced to go. Mr. Norris of Christ Hospital has been as a father to me, Mrs. Norris as a Mother, tho' we had few claims on them. A Gentleman brother to my God-mother,[3] from whom we never had right or reason to expect any such assistance, sent my father twenty pounds,—& to crown all these God's blessings to our family at such a time, an old Lady, a cousin of my father & Aunts, a Gentlewoman of fortune, is to take my Aunt & make her comfortable for the short remainder of her days.———

My Aunt is recover'd & as well as ever, & highly pleased at thoughts of going,—& has generously given up the interest of her little money (which was formerly paid my Father for her board) wholely & solely to my **Sister's** use. Reckoning this we have, **Daddy & I** for our two selves & an old maid servant to look after him, when I am out, which will be necessary, £170 or £180 (rather) a year out of which we can spare 50 or 60 at least for Mary, while she stays at Islington, where she must & shall stay during her father's life for his & her comfort. I know John will make speeches about it, but she shall not go into an **hospital.** The good Lady[4] of the Mad house, & her daughter, an elegant sweet behaved young Lady, love her & are taken with her amazingly, & I know from her **own** mouth she loves them, & longs to be with them as much———. Poor thing, they say she was but the other morning saying, she knew she must go to **Bethlem** for life; that one of her brother's would have it so, but the other would wish it Not, but he obliged to go with the stream; that she had often as she passed **Bedlam** thought it likely "here it may be my fate to end my days"—conscious of a certain flightiness in her poor head oftentimes, & mindful of more than one severe illness of that Nature before. A Legacy of £100[5] which my father will have at **Xmas,** & this 20 I mentioned before with what is in the house, will much more than set us **Clear,**—if my father, an old servant maid, & I cant **live** & live **comfortably** on £130 or £120 a year we ought to burn by slow fires, & I almost would, that Mary might not go into an hospital. Let me not leave one unfavorable impression on your mind respecting my Brother. Since this has happened he has been very kind & brotherly; but I fear for his mind,[6]—he has taken his ease in the world, & is not fit himself to struggle with difficulties, nor has much accustomed himself to throw himself into their way,—& I know his language is already, "Charles, you must take care of yourself, you must not abridge yourself of a single pleasure you have been used to" &c &c. & in that style of talking. But you, a necessarian, can respect a difference of mind, & love what *is amiable* in a character not perfect. He has been very good, but I fear for his mind. Thank God, I can unconnect myself with him, & shall manage all my father's monies in future myself, if I take charge of Daddy, which poor John has not even hinted a wish, at any future time even, to share with me——

The Lady at this Mad house assures me that I may dismiss immediately both Doctor[7] & Apothecary, retaining occasionally an opening draught or so for a while, & there is a less expensive establishment in her house, where she will only not have a room & nurse to herself for £50 or guineas a year—the outside would be 60—. You know by œconomy how much more, even, I shall be able to spare for her comforts———

She will, I fancy, if she stays, make one of the family, rather than of the patients, & the old & young ladies I like exceedingly, & she loves dearly, & they, as the saying is take to her very extraordinaryily, if it is extraordinary that people who see my sister should love her. Of all the people I ever saw in the world my poor sister was most & throughly devoi[d] of the least tincture of selfishness—. I will enlarge upon her qualities, poor dear dearest soul, in a future letter for my own comfort, for I understood her throughly; & if I mistake not in the most trying situation that a human being can be found in, she will be found (I speak not with sufficient humility, I fear, but humanly & foolishly speaking) she will be found, I trust, uniformly great & amiable; God keep her in her present Mind, to whom be thanks & praise for all his dispensations to mankind———

Lamb

Coleridge, continue to write, but do not for ever offend me by talking of sending me cash; sincerely & on my soul we do not want it. God love you both—

Send me word, how it fares with Sara. I repeat it, your letter was & will be an inestimable treasure to **me**; you have a view of what my situation demands of me like my own view; & I trust a just one—

These mentioned good fortunes & change of prospects had almost brought my mind **over** to the extreme the very opposite to **Despair**; I was in danger of making myself too happy; your letter brought me back to a view of things which I had entertained from the beginning; I hope (for Mary I can[8] answer) but I hope that *I* shall thro' life never have less recollection nor a fainter impression of what has happened than I have now; tis not a light thing, nor meant by the Almighty to be received lightly; I must be serious, circumspect, & deeply religious thro' lif[e;] & by such means may *both* of us escape madness in future if it so pleases the Almighty—

I will write again very Soon; do you directly—

MS: Huntington Library. Pub.: Talfourd (1848), I, 53–62; Sala, I, 41–47; Purnell, I, 41–47; Fitzgerald, I, 326–332; Hazlitt, I, 124–129; Ainger (1888), I, 33–37; Ainger (1900), I, 45–52; Macdonald, I, 34–39; Ainger (1904), I, 33–37; Harper, II, 53–60; Lucas (1905), VI, 43–47; Lucas (1912), V, 42–46; Lucas (1935), I, 42–46. Address: Mr. Coleridge/Bristol. Postmark: October 3, 1796.

1. *Macbeth,* I, v, 57.
2. See the Introduction, pp. xxxi–xxxii.
3. Both unidentified, as is the cousin of the senior John and Sarah Lamb.
4. Unidentified, as is her daughter.
5. Presumably part of Samuel Salt's bequest. See the Introduction, p. xxvi.
6. So far as is known, it was always sound.
7. Probably David Pitcairn (1749–1809), who practiced in London from 1779 and whose surname is given in the report of the tragedy in the *Morning Chronicle,* but perhaps William Cruikshank, who had been treating the younger John Lamb's injured leg. The apothecary has not been identified.
8. Should apparently be "can't."

9. *C. L. to Coleridge*

[October 17, 1796]

My dearest friend,

I grieve from my very soul to observe you in your plans of life, veering about from this hope to the other, & settling no where. Is it an untoward fatality (speaking humanly) that does this for you?, a stubborn irresistible concurrence of events? or lies the fault, as I fear it does, in your **own** mind? You seem to be taking up splendid schemes of fortune only to lay them down again, & your fortunes are an ignis fatuus[1] that has been conducting you, in thought, from Lancaster Court, Strand, to somewhere near Matlock, then jumping across to Dr. Somebody's whose sons' tutor you were likely to be, & would to God, the dancing demon *may*[2] conduct you at last in peace & comfort to the "life & labors of a cottager." You see from the above awkward playfulness of fancy that my spirits are not quite depress'd; I should ill deserve God's blessings, which since the late terrible event have come down in Mercy upon us, if I indulged regret or querulousnes,—Mary continues serene & chearful,—I have not by me a little letter[3] she wrote to me, for tho' I see her almost every day yet we delight to write to one another (for we can scarce see each other but in company with some of the people of the house), I have not the letter by me but will quote from memory what she wrote in it. "I have no bad terrifying dreams. At midnight when I happen to awake, the nurse sleeping by the side of **me,** with the noise of the poor mad people around me, I have no fear. The spirit of my mother seems to descend, & smile upon me, & bid me **live** to enjoy the life & reason which the Almighty has given me—. I shall see her again in heaven; she will then understand me better, my Grandmother too will understand me better, & will then say no more as she used to Do, "Polly, what are those poor crazy moyther'd brains of yours thinkg. of always?"— Poor Mary, my mother indeed *never understood* her right. She loved her, as she loved us all with a **Mother's love,** but in opinion, in feeling, & sentiment, & disposition, bore so distant a resemblance to her daughter, that she never understood her right. Never could believe how much *she* loved her—but met her caresses, her protestations of filial affection, too frequently with coldness & **repulse,**— Still she was a good mother, God forbid I should think of her but *most* respectfully, ***most*** affectionately. Yet she would always love my brother above Mary, who was not worthy of one tenth of that affection, which Mary had a right to claim. But it is my Sister's gratifying recollection, that every act of duty & of love she could pay, every kindness (& I speak true, when I say to the hurting of her health, & most probably in great part to the derangement of her senses) thro' a long course of infirmities & sickness, she could shew her, **she ever did.** I will some day, as I promised enlarge to you upon my Sister's excellencies; twill seem like exaggeration, but I will do it. At present **short letters** suit my **state of mind best. So take** my kindest wishes for your comfort and establishment in life [an]d for Sara's welfare and comforts with you. God love you; God love us all—

C. Lamb

MS: Huntington Library. Pub.: Talfourd (1848), I, 62–65; Sala, I, 47–49; Purnell, I, 47–49; Fitzgerald, I, 332–334; Hazlitt, I, 130–131; Ainger (1888), I, 38–39; Ainger (1900), I, 52–55; Macdonald, I, 40–41; Ainger (1904), I, 38–39; Harper, II, 60–62; Lucas (1905), VI, 48–49; Lucas (1912), V, 47–48; Lucas (1935), I, 46–48. Address: Mr Coleridge/Bristol. Postmark: October 17, 1796.

1. Which had conducted Coleridge in thought from Perry and the *Morning Chronicle* in London, to Mrs. Evans and her children at Darley Abbey near Matlock, to the opening of a day school at Derby on the suggestion of Dr. Peter Crompton of Derby and Liverpool and the promised tuition of his three sons if Coleridge would agree, and to living by literature and husbandry at Nether Stowey, Somersetshire. He acted on the last idea and with Mrs. Coleridge and their son and maid settled in the cottage shortly before January 6, 1797.

2. Underscored twice. The quotation, following, may be from Coleridge's letter.

3. Unrecovered, like the other letters that passed between Charles and Mary at this time.

10. *C. L. to Coleridge*

Sunday Evening, October 24 [23], 1796

Coleridge,

I feel myself much your debtor for that spirit of confidence and friendship which dictated your last letter. May your soul find peace at last in your cottage life! I only wish you were *but* settled. Do continue to write to me. I read your letters with my sister, and they give us both abundance of delight. Especially they please us two, when you talk in a religious strain,—not but we are offended occasionally with a certain freedom of expression, a certain air of mysticism, more consonant to the conceits of pagan philosophy, than consistent with the humility of genuine piety. To instance now in your last letter—you say, 'it is by the press, that God hath given finite spirits both evil and good (I suppose you mean *simply* bad men and good men) a portion as it were of His Omnipresence!' Now, high as the human intellect comparatively will soar, and wide as its influence, malign or salutary, can extend, is there not, Coleridge, a distance between the Divine Mind and it, which makes such language blasphemy? Again, in your first fine consolatory epistle you say, 'you are a temporary sharer in human misery, that you may be an eternal partaker of the Divine Nature.'[1] What more than this do those men say, who are for exalting the man Christ Jesus into the second person of an unknown Trinity,—men, whom you or I scruple not to call idolaters? Man, full of imperfections, at best, and subject to wants which momentarily remind him of dependence; man, a weak and ignorant being, 'servile' from his birth 'to all the skiey influences,'[2] with eyes sometimes open to discern the right path, but a head generally too dizzy to pursue it; man, in the pride of speculation, forgetting his nature, and hailing in himself the future God, must make the angels laugh. Be not angry with me, Coleridge; I wish not to cavil; I know I cannot *instruct* you; I only wish to *remind* you of that humility which best becometh the Christian character. God, in the New Testament (*our best guide*), is represented to us in the kind, condescending, amiable, familiar light of a *parent:* and in my poor mind 'tis best for us so to consider of Him, as our *heavenly* Father, and our *best Friend,* without indulging too bold conceptions of His nature. Let us learn to think humbly of ourselves, and rejoice in the appellation of 'dear children,'[3] 'brethren,' and 'co-heirs with Christ of the promises,' seeking to know no further.

I am not insensible, indeed I am not, of the value of that first letter of yours, and I shall find reason to thank you for it again and again long after that blemish in it is forgotten. It will be a fine lesson of comfort to us, whenever we read it; and read it we often shall, Mary and I.

Accept our loves and best kind wishes for the welfare of yourself and wife, and little one. Nor let me forget to wish you joy on your birthday[4] so lately past; I thought you had been older. My kind thanks and remembrances to Lloyd.

God love us all, and may He continue to be the father and the friend of the whole human race!

C. Lamb

MS: unrecovered. Text: Lucas (1935), I, 48–49. Also pub.: Talfourd (1837), I, 29–31; Sala, I, 49–50; Purnell, I, 49–50; Fitzgerald, I, 334–335; Hazlitt, I, 132–133; Ainger (1888), I, 39–41; Ainger (1900), I, 55–59; Macdonald, I, 41–43; Ainger (1904), I, 39–41; Harper, II, 63–65; Lucas (1905), VI, 49–50; Lucas (1912), V, 48–50.

1. See Letter 7, note 2. "Divine Nature" is from 2 Peter 1:4.

2. *Measure for Measure,* III, i, 9.

3. Ephesians 5:1. For "co-heirs with Christ of the promises," following, see Romans 8:17 and Ephesians 3:6.

4. October 21, when Coleridge had turned twenty-four. Charles Lloyd (1775–1839) was the eldest of perhaps fifteen children born to Charles (1748–1825), of Birmingham and suburban Bingley House, a Quaker, banker, philanthropist, and translator of Horace and Homer, and his wife, Mary (1750–1821), the daughter of James and Priscilla Farmer, also of Bingley House. Lloyd was privately educated by a Mr. Gilpin, entered his father's bank, left it in 1794 to study medicine in Edinburgh, left Edinburgh before 1795 to live with Wordsworth's friend the Quaker Thomas Wilkinson (1751–1836) at Yanwath, Cumberland, and there wrote *Poems on Various Subjects* (1795). He returned to Birmingham before January 1796, met Coleridge (who was in town soliciting subscribers for *The Watchman*), and so admired him that he arranged to live with and be instructed by him for eighty pounds annually. He moved in with the Coleridges a day or two after the birth of David Hartley Coleridge in September. By the end of the year Lloyd had published *Poems on the Death of Priscilla Farmer* and by his erratic temperament had caused Coleridge to refuse him further tuition, though Coleridge permitted him to remain as a lodger. In January 1797 Lloyd went to London and introduced himself to Lamb. In February Lloyd followed the Coleridges to Nether Stowey. In mid-March he left there for Lichfield to be treated for seizures by Dr. Erasmus Darwin (1731–1802), a grandfather of the naturalist. Lloyd was with Southey at Burton and Bath in August and September and spent the winter of 1797—1798 with James White in London. During the latter period appeared his *Edmund Oliver* (1798), which is dedicated to Lamb. Its hero's imitation of Coleridge's adventure in the army, fits of love, and personal characteristics widened the breach between Lloyd and Coleridge that had been opened when Coleridge published "Sonnets Attempted in the Manner of Contemporary Writers," in the *Monthly Magazine,* 4 (November 1797), 374, which consists of three sonnets burlesquing Coleridge's own, Lamb's, and Lloyd's in *Poems* (1797). (See Letter 33, source note.) Also during that period Lloyd, probably to Coleridge's displeasure, collaborated with Lamb on *Blank Verse* (see Letter 40, note 3), which contains Lamb's "To Charles Lloyd," "Written on the Day of My Aunt's Funeral," "Written a Year after the Events," "Written Soon after the Preceding Poem," "Written on Christmas Day, 1797," "The Old Familiar Faces," and "Composed at Midnight" (*Works,* V, 19–25). In August 1798 Lloyd was admitted to Caius College, Cambridge, where he formed an enduring friendship with Thomas Manning. (See Letter 53, source note, and the *Lloyd-Manning Letters.*) In April 1799 Lloyd was married to Sophia (d. 1830), a daughter of the Samuel Pembertons of Birmingham. (See Letter 29.) They began married life, with a dowry of ten thousand pounds from Mr. Pemberton and an annual income of two hundred from Mr. Lloyd, at Penrith, Cumberland. There Lloyd wrote *Isabel* (1809 and 1820—see Letter 51, note 5). In the fall they moved into the home of a Mr. Styles in Jesus Lane, Cambridge, and shortly after to Barnwell, nearby. In April 1800 they removed to Mr. Lloyd's farm at Olton Green, near Birmingham; in November to Ambleside, Westmorland; and before June 1802 into the house called Old Brathay, outside Ambleside. There they received the Wordsworths, the Southeys, and De Quincey, and there Lloyd translated specimens from Ovid's *Metamorphoses* (1811) and, despite declining health, *The Tragedies of Vittorio Alfieri* (1815). He was placed under a doctor's care in Birmingham in 1815 and in The Retreat, an asylum in York, in 1816. He escaped in 1818 to De Quincey, who was living in Dove Cottage, Grasmere, and then to Old Brathay. Although Lloyd was returned to the asylum, he soon recovered sufficiently to be released. He went to London, where he was joined by his wife and children in 1820. He published, among other works, *Nugæ Canoræ* (1819), *Desultory Thoughts in London* (1821), *Poetical Essays on the Character of Pope* (1822), and, his last work, *Poems* (1823). He afterward passed recurrently into insanity and eventually into a sanitarium at Chaillot, near Versailles, where he died. His and his wife's

children were Charles Grosvenor (1800–1840), James Farmer (1801–1881), Owen (1803–1838), Edward (1804–1865), Arthur, Mary, Sophia, Priscilla, Agatha, and Louisa.

11. *C. L. to Coleridge*

[East India House]
October 28, 1796

My dear Friend,

I am not ignorant that to be a partaker of the Divine Nature is a phrase to be met with in Scripture: I am only apprehensive, lest we in these latter days, tinctured (some of us perhaps pretty deeply) with mystical notions and the pride of metaphysics, might be apt to affix to such phrases a meaning, which the primitive users of them, the simple fishermen of Galilee for instance, never intended to convey. With that other part of your apology I am not quite so well satisfied. You seem to me to have been straining your comparing faculties to bring together things infinitely distant and unlike; the feeble narrow-sphered operations of the human intellect and the everywhere diffused mind of Deity, the peerless wisdom of Jehovah. Even the expression appears to me inaccurate—portion of omnipresence—omnipresence is an attribute whose very essence is unlimitedness. How can omnipresence be affirmed of anything in part? But enough of this spirit of disputatiousness. Let us attend to the proper business of human life, and talk a little together respecting our domestic concerns. Do you continue to make me acquainted with what you were doing, and how soon you are likely to be settled once for all.

I have satisfaction in being able to bid you rejoice with me in my sister's continued reason and composedness of mind. Let us both be thankful for it. I continue to visit her very frequently, and the people of the house are vastly indulgent to her; she is likely to be as comfortably situated in all respects as those who pay twice or thrice the sum. They love her, and she loves them, and makes herself very useful to them. Benevolence sets out on her journey with a good heart, and puts a good face on it, but is apt to limp and grow feeble, unless she calls in the aid of self-interest by way of crutch. In Mary's case, as far as respects those she is with, 'tis well that these principles are so likely to cooperate. I am rather at a loss sometimes for books for her,—our reading is somewhat confined, and we have nearly exhausted our London library. She has her hands too full of work to read much, but a little she must read; for reading was her daily bread.

Have you seen Bowles's new poem on 'Hope?'[1] What character does it bear? Has he exhausted his stores of tender plaintiveness? or is he the same in this last as in all his former pieces? The duties of the day call me off from this pleasant intercourse with my friend—so for the present adieu.

Now for the truant borrowing of a few minutes from business. Have you met with a new poem called the 'Pursuits of Literature?'[2] From the extracts in the 'British Review' I judge it to be a very humorous thing; in particular I remember what I thought a very happy character of Dr. Darwin's poetry. Among all your quaint readings did you ever light upon Walton's 'Complete Angler?' I asked you the question once before; it breathes the very spirit of innocence, purity, and simplicity of heart; there are many choice old verses interspersed in it; it would sweeten a man's temper at any time to read it; it would Christianise every discordant angry passion; pray make yourself acquainted with it. Have you made it up with Southey yet? Surely one of you two must have been a very silly fellow, and the other not much better, to fall out like boarding-school misses; kiss, shake hands, and make it up?

When will he be delivered of his new epic? *Madoc,*[3] I think, is to be the name of it; though that is a name not familiar to my ears. What progress do you make in your hymns? What Review are you connected with? If with any, why do you delay to notice White's book? You are justly offended at its profaneness; but surely you have undervalued its *wit,* or you would have been more loud in its praises. Do not you think that in *Slender's* death and madness there is most exquisite humour, mingled with tenderness, that is irresistible, truly Shakspearian?[4] Be more full in your mention of it. Poor fellow, he has (very undeservedly) lost by it; nor do I see that it is likely ever to reimburse him the charge of printing, etc. Give it a lift, if you can. I suppose you know that Allen's wife is dead, and he, just situated as he was, never the better, as the worldly people say, for her death, her money with her children being taken off his hands. I am just now wondering whether you will ever come to town again, Coleridge; 'tis among the things I dare not hope, but can't help wishing. For myself, I can live in the midst of town luxury and superfluity, and not long for them, and I can't see why your children might not hereafter do the same. Remember, you are not in Arcadia when you are in the west of England, and they may catch infection from the world without visiting the metropolis. But you seem to have set your heart upon this same cottage plan; and God prosper you in the experiment! I am at a loss for more to write about; so 'tis as well that I am arrived at the bottom of my paper.

God love you, Coleridge!—Our best loves and tenderest wishes await on you, your Sara, and your little one.

MS: unrecovered. Text: Lucas (1935), I, 50–52. Also pub.: Talfourd (1837), I, 31–34; Sala, I, 51–53; Purnell, I, 51–53; Fitzgerald, I, 336–338; Hazlitt, I, 134–136; Ainger (1888), I, 41–43; Ainger (1900), I, 57–61; Macdonald, I, 43–46; Ainger (1904), I, 41–43; Harper, II, 65–68; Lucas (1905), VI, 51–53; Lucas (1912), V, 50–52.

1. "Hope: An Allegorical Sketch."

2. Thomas James Mathias (1754?–1835), *Pursuits of Literature. A Satirical Poem in Four Dialogues* (1794–1797). The reviewer of its Part the First in not the *British* but the *Critical Review,* 18 (September 1796), 47–51, remarked that at the "elegant, though (it must be confessed) somewhat whimsical, poem of Dr. [Erasmus] Darwin, our satirist has a stroke—" and quoted Mathias' characterization of Darwin's *Botanic Garden and the Loves of the Plants:*

What?—from the Muse, by *cryptogamic* stealth
Must I purloin her native sterling wealth?
In filmy, gawzy, gossamery lines,
With *lucid* language, and most dark designs,
In sweet *tetrandryan, monogynian* strains,
Pant for a *pystill* in botanic pains;
On the luxurious lap of Flora thrown,
On beds of yielding vegetable down,
Raise lust in pinks; and with unhallow'd fire
Bid the soft virgin violet expire?

3. Southey completed the first version in 1797 but did not publish the poem until 1805. Coleridge (to answer Lamb's second question below) was intending to become connected with the *Critical Review* and the *New Monthly Magazine.* He did write for the former in February 1797.

4. See White's *Original Letters, &c. of Sir John Falstaff,* ed. Merrill, pp. 147–150.

12. *C. L. to Coleridge*

November 8, 1796

My Brother, my Friend,—

I am distrest for you, believe me I am; not so much for your painful, troublesome complaint, which, I trust, is only for a time, as for those anxieties which brought it on, and perhaps even now may be nursing its malignity.[1] Tell me, dearest of my friends, is your mind at peace, or has anything, yet unknown to me, happened to give you fresh disquiet, and steal from you all the pleasant dreams of future rest? Are you still (I fear you are) far from being comfortably settled? Would to God it were in my power to contribute towards the bringing of you into the haven where you would be![2] But you are too well skilled in the philosophy of consolation to need my humble tribute of advice; in pain and in sickness, and in all manner of disappointments, I trust you have that within you which shall speak peace to your mind. Make it, I entreat you, one of your puny comforts, that I feel for you, and share all your griefs with you. I feel as if I were troubling you about *little* things; now I am going to resume the subject of our two last letters, but it may divert us both from unpleasanter feelings to make such matters, in a manner, of importance. Without further apology, then, it was not that I did not relish, that I did not in my heart thank you for, those little pictures of your feelings which you lately sent me, if I neglected to mention them. You may remember you had said much the same things before to me on the same subject in a former letter, and I considered those last verses[3] as only the identical thoughts better clothed; either way (in prose or verse) such poetry must be welcome to me. I love them as I love the Confessions of Rousseau, and for the same reason: the same frankness, the same openness of heart, the same disclosure of all the most hidden and delicate affections of the mind: they make me proud to be thus esteemed worthy of the place of friend-confessor, brother-confessor, to a man like Coleridge. This last is, I acknowledge, language too high for friendship; but it is also, I declare, too sincere for flattery. Now, to put on stilts, and talk magnificently about trifles—I condescend, then, to your counsel, Coleridge, and allow my first Sonnet[4] (sick to death am I to make mention of my sonnets, and I blush to be so taken up with them, indeed I do)—I allow it to run thus, *'Fairy Land'* &c. &c., as I[5] last wrote it.

The Fragments I now send you I want printed to get rid of 'em; for, while they stick bur-like to my memory, they tempt me to go on with the idle trade of versifying, which I long—most sincerely I speak it—I long to leave off, for it is unprofitable to my soul; I feel it is; and these questions about words, and debates about alterations, take me off, I am conscious, from the properer business of *my* life. Take my sonnets once for all, and do not propose any re-amendments, or mention them again in any shape to me, I charge you. I blush that my mind can consider them as things of any worth. And pray admit or reject these fragments, as you like or dislike them, without ceremony. Call 'em Sketches, Fragments, or what you will, but do not entitle any of my *things* Love Sonnets, as I told you to call 'em; 'twill only make me look little in my own eyes; for it is a passion of which I retain *nothing;* 'twas a weakness, concerning which I may say, in the words of Petrarch (whose life is now open before me), 'if it drew me out of some vices, it also prevented the growth of many virtues, filling me with the love of the creature rather than the Creator, which is the death of the soul.'[6] Thank God, the folly has left me for ever; not even a review of my love verses renews one wayward wish in me; and if I am at all solicitous to trim 'em out in their best apparel, it is because they are to make their appearance in good company. Now to my fragments. Lest you have lost my Grandame, she shall be one. 'Tis among the few verses I ever wrote (that to Mary[7] is another) which profit me in the recollection. God love her,—and may we two never love each other less!

These, Coleridge, are the few sketches I have thought worth preserving; how will they relish thus detached? Will you reject all or any of them? They are thine: do whatsoever thou listest with them. My eyes ache with writing long and late, and I wax wondrous sleepy; God bless you and yours, me and mine! Good night.

C. Lamb

I will keep my eyes open reluctantly a minute longer to tell you, that I love you for those simple, tender, heart-flowing lines with which you conclude your last, and in my eyes best, sonnet[8] (so you call 'em),

> So, for the mother's sake, the child was dear,
> And dearer was the mother for the child.

Cultivate simplicity, Coleridge, or rather, I should say, banish elaborateness; for simplicity springs spontaneous from the heart, and carries into daylight its own modest buds and genuine, sweet, and clear flowers of expression. I allow no hot-beds in the gardens of Parnassus. I am unwilling to go to bed, and leave my sheet unfilled (a good piece of nightwork for an idle body like me), so will finish with begging you to send me the earliest account of your complaint, its progress, or (as I hope to God you will be able to send me) the tale of your recovery, or at least amendment. My tenderest remembrances to your Sara.—

Once more good night.

MS: unrecovered. Text: Lucas (1935), I, 53–56. Also pub.: Talfourd (1837), I, 43–48; Sala, I, 54–57; Purnell, I, 54–57; Fitzgerald, I, 339–342; Hazlitt, I, 136–139; Ainger (1888), I, 43–46; Ainger (1900), I, 61–65; Macdonald, I, 46–49; Ainger (1904), I, 43–46; Harper, II, 69–72; Lucas (1905), VI, 54–56; Lucas (1912), V, 54–56.

1. On Saturday night, November 5, Coleridge wrote of his first attack of neuralgia and the beginning of his drug addiction to his friend the tanner Thomas Poole (1765–1837) of Nether Stowey:

> I wanted such a letter as your's—: for I am very unwell. On Wednesday night I was seized with an intolerable pain from my right temple to the tip of my right shoulder, including my right eye, cheek, jaw, & that side of the throat——I was nearly frantic—and ran about the House naked, endeavouring by every means to excite sensations in different parts of my body, & so to weaken the enemy by creating a division. It continued from one in the morning till half past 5, & left me pale & fainty.—It came on fitfully but not so violently, several times on Thursday—and began severer threats towards night, but I took between 60 & 70 drops of Laudanum, and *sopped* the Cerberus just as his mouth began to open. On Friday it only *niggled;* as if the Chief had departed as from a conquered place, and merely left a small garrison behind, or as if he evacuated the Corsica, & a few straggling pains only remained; but *this morning* he returned in full force, & his Name is Legion!—Giant-fiend of an hundred hands! with a shower of arrowy Death-pangs he transpierced me, & then he became a Wolf & lay gnawing my bones.——I am not mad, most noble Festus!—but in sober sadness I have suffered this day more bodily pain than I had before a conception of—. My right cheek has certainly been placed with admirable exactness under the focus of some invisible Burning-Glass, which concentrated all the Rays of a Tartarean Sun.—My medical attendant decides it to be altogether nervous, and that it originates either in severe application, or excessive anxiety.—My beloved Poole! in excessive anxiety, I believe, it might originate!——I have a blister under my right-ear, and I take 25 drops of Laudanum every five hours: the ease & *spirits* gained by which have enabled me to write you this flighty, but not exaggerating, account——. With a gloomy wantonness of Imagination I had been coquetting with the hideous *Possibles* of Disappointment—I drank fears, like wormwood; yea, made myself drunken with bitterness! for my ever-shaping & distrustful mind still mingled gall-drops, till out of the cup of Hope *I almost poisoned* myself with Despair!
>
> [*Coleridge's Letters,* I, 249–250]

2. Cf. Psalms 107:30.

3. Certainly "Sonnet: To a Friend [Lloyd], Who Asked, How I Felt When the Nurse First Presented My Infant to Me," probably "To a Friend [Lamb] Who Had Declared His Intention of Writing No More Poetry," and possibly those associated

with the former: "Sonnet: On Receiving a Letter Informing Me of the Birth of a Son," "Sonnet: Composed on a Journey Homeward; the Author Having Received Intelligence of the Birth of a Son, Sept. 20, 1796," "Sonnet[: To Charles Lloyd]," "To a Young Friend on His Proposing to Domesticate with the Author. *Composed in* 1796," and "Addressed to a Young Man [Lloyd] of Fortune."

4. "Was it some sweet device of Faery." Its first line in Coleridge's *Poems on Various Subjects* and *Sonnets from Various Authors* reads, "Was it some sweet device of faery land." In *Poems* (1797) it reads, "Was it some sweet Delight of Faery."

5. Possibly a mistake for "you." About Lamb's "Fragments" (dwelt on next), the poems in *Poems* (1797), see Letter 7, note 3.

6. Susanna(h) Dobson (d. 1795), *The Life of Petrarch. Collected from Mémoires pour la vie de Petrarch* (2d ed.; 1776), I, 327.

7. "If from my lips some angry accents fell."

8. "Sonnet: To a Friend Who Asked, How I Felt When the Nurse First Presented My Infant to Me."

13. *C. L. to Coleridge*

November 14, 1796

Coleridge,

I love you for dedicating your poetry to Bowles.[1] Genius of the sacred fountain of tears, it was he who led you gently by the hand through all this valley of weeping, showed you the dark green yew trees and the willow shades where, by the fall of waters, you might indulge an uncomplaining melancholy, a delicious regret for the past, or weave fine visions of that awful future,

> When all the vanities of life's brief day
> Oblivion's hurrying hand hath swept away,[2]
> And all its sorrows, at the awful blast
> Of the archangel's trump, are but as shadows past.

I have another sort of dedication in my head for my few things, which I want to know if you approve of, and can insert. I mean to inscribe them to my sister. It will be unexpected, and it will give her pleasure; or do you think it will look whimsical at all? As I have not spoke to her about it, I can easily reject the idea. But there is a monotony in the affections, which people living together or, as we do now, very frequently seeing each other, are apt to give in to: a sort of indifference in the expression of kindness for each other, which demands that we should sometimes call to our aid the trickery of surprise. Do you publish with Lloyd or without him? in either case my little portion may come last, and after the fashion of orders to a country correspondent I will give directions how I should like to have 'em done. The title-page to stand thus:—

Poems,
Chiefly Love Sonnets
by
Charles Lamb, of the India House.

Under this title the following motto, which, for want of room, I put over leaf, and desire you to insert, whether you like it or no. May not a gentleman choose what arms, mottoes, or armorial bearings the herald will give him leave, without consulting his republican friend, who might advise none? May not a publican put up the sign of the Saracen's Head, even though his undiscerning neighbour should prefer, as more genteel, the Cat and Gridiron?

(Motto)

This beauty, in the blossom of my youth,
When my first fire knew no adulterate incense,
Nor I no way to flatter but my fondness,
In the best language my true tongue could tell me,
And all the broken sighs my sick heart lend me,
I sued and served. Long did I love this lady.

Massinger[3]

The Dedication

The few following poems,
Creatures of the fancy and the feeling
In life's more vacant hours,
Produced, for the most part, by
Love in idleness,
Are,
With all a brother's fondness,
Inscribed to
Mary Ann Lamb,
The author's best friend and sister.

This is the pomp and paraphernalia of parting, with which I take my leave of a passion which has reigned so royally (so long) within me; thus, with its trappings of laureatship, I fling it off, pleased and satisfied with myself that the weakness troubles me no longer. I am wedded, Coleridge, to the fortunes of my sister and my poor old father. Oh! my friend, I think sometimes, could I recall the days that are past, which among them should I choose? not those 'merrier days,'[4] not the 'pleasant days of hope,' not 'those wanderings with a fair hair'd maid,' which I have so often and so feelingly regretted, but the days, Coleridge, of a *mother's* fondness for her *school-boy.* What would I give to call her back to earth for *one* day, on my knees to ask her pardon for all those little asperities of temper which, from time to time, have given her gentle spirit pain; and the day, my friend, I trust will come; there will be 'time enough'[5] for kind offices of love, if 'Heaven's eternal year' be ours. Hereafter, her meek spirit shall not reproach me. Oh, my friend, cultivate the filial feelings! and let no man think himself released from the kind 'charities' of relationship: these shall give him peace at the last; these are the best foundation for every species of benevolence. I rejoice to hear, by certain channels, that you, my friend, are reconciled with all your relations.[6] 'Tis the most kindly and natural species of love, and we have all the associated train of early feelings to secure its strength and perpetuity. Send me an account of your health; *indeed* I am solicitous about you. God love you and yours.

C. Lamb

MS: unrecovered. Text: Lucas (1935), I, 56–58. Also pub.: Talfourd (1837), I, 48–52; Sala, I, 57–60; Purnell, I, 57–60; Fitzgerald, I, 342–345; Hazlitt, I, 139–141; Ainger (1888), I, 46–49; Ainger (1900), I, 65–68; Macdonald, I, 49–51; Ainger (1904), I, 46–49; Harper, II, 73–76; Lucas (1905), VI, 57–59; Lucas (1912), V, 57–59.

1. Coleridge changed his mind and dedicated *Poems* (1797) to his brother George (1764–1828), since 1794 a schoolmaster and chaplain priest in Ottery St. Mary. For "fountain of tears," following, see Aeschylus, *Agamemnon* (tr. Hugh Lloyd-Jones), line 887.

2. Bowles, "On Mr. Howard's Account of Lazarettos," lines 143–144. The next couplet is from his "The Grave of Howard," lines 73–74.

3. *A Very Woman,* IV, iii, 190–192 and 195–197. Lamb's title, motto, and dedication are in *Poems* (1797), pp. 215 and 216.

4. Lamb's "The Lord of Life shakes off his drowsihed," line 11. The next quotation is from Coleridge's "The Gentle Look," line 9, and the next from Lamb's "Was it some sweet device of Faery," line 3.

5. John Dryden, "To the Pious Memory of the Accomplish'd Young Lady, Mrs. Anne Killigrew," line 14. Lamb next quotes from its line 15.

6. In Ottery St. Mary. Coleridge had paid an overdue visit there in August.

V. East India House circa 1800. From a watercolor by Thomas Malton (1748–1804). Courtesy of the India Office Library and India Office Records, London.

VI. House at 7 Little Queen Street, Holborn, in 1903. From a pencil drawing by Herbert Railton (1858–1910). By permission of The Huntington Library, San Marino, California.

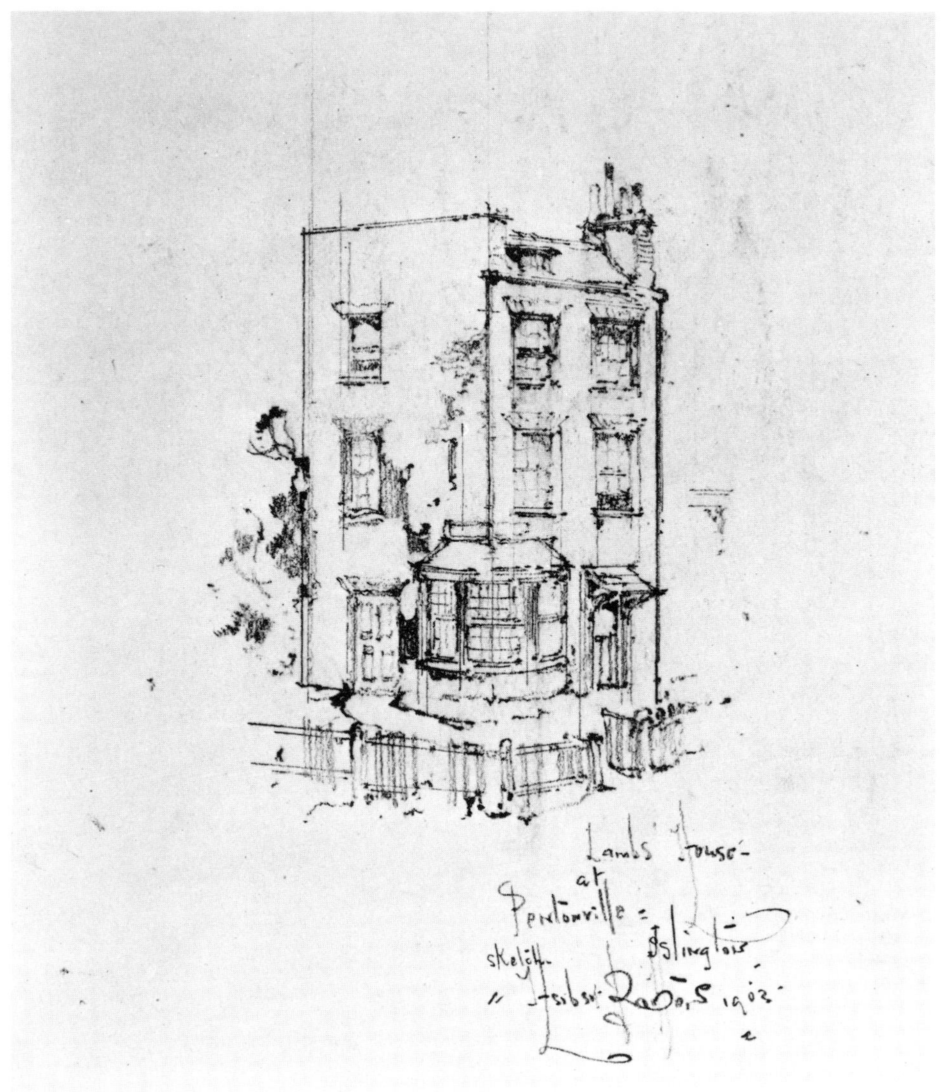

VII. House at 45 Chapel Street, Pentonville, in 1903. From a pencil drawing by Herbert Railton (1858–1910). By permission of The Huntington Library, San Marino, California.

my dear fellow, (N.B. mighty familiar of late!)

for me to come to Cambridge now is one of G-d Almighty's Impossibilities; metaphysicians tell us Even He can work nothing which implys a contradiction. I can explain this by telling you that I am engaged to do double Duty (this hot weather!) for a man who has taken advantage of this very weather to go & cool himself in "green retreats" all the month of August.—

But for You to come to London instead! — muse upon it, revolve it, cast it about in your mind — I have a Bed at your command — You shall drink Rum, Brandy, Gin, Aquavitæ, Usquebaugh, or Whiskey a nights — & for the after-dinner-Trick I have 8 Bottles of genuine Port which mathematically divided gives 1/7 for every day You stay, provided You stay a week. Hear John Milton sing,

"Let Euclid rest & Archimedes pause."

21st Sonnet—

& elsewhere,

What neat repast shall feast us, light & choice,
Of Attic Taste, with wine,* whence we may rise
To hear the Lute well touch'd, or artful voice
Warble immortal notes & Tuscan air?

Indeed the Poets are full of this pleasing Morality—

Veni cito, Domine Manning! —

N.B. I lives at No 27 Southampton Buildings Holborn

+ We Poets! generally give light dinners. Think upon it C Lamb

Excuse the Paper. — it is all I have —

* no doubt the Poet here alludes to Port wine — 38/- the dozen

VIII. Facsimile of a letter from Charles Lamb to Thomas Manning, August 11, 1800 (Letter 78). By permission of The Huntington Library, San Marino, California.

14. *C. L. to Coleridge*

[Begun at the East India House]
Thursday night [December 1, 1796]

I have delay'd writing thus long, not having by me my copy of your poems, which I had lent. I am not satisfied with all your intended omissions. Why omit 40: 63: 84:[1] above all, let me protest strongly against your rejecting the "Complaint of Ninathoma" 86. The words, I acknowledge, are Ossian's, but you have added to them the **"Music of Caril."** If a vicarious substitute be wanting sacrifice (& twill be a piece of self-denial *too*) the **Epitaph** on an **Infant** of which its Author seems so proud, so tenacious: Or, if your heart be set on *perpetuating* the four-line-wonder,[2] I'll tell you what do: sell the copywright of it at **Once** to a country statuary; commence in this manner Death's prime poet laureat; & let your verses be adopted in every village round instead of those hitherto famous **ones** "afflictions sore long time I bore, Physicians were in vain"—: I have seen your last very beautiful poem[3] in the **Monthly Magazine**—write thus, & you most generally have written thus, & I shall never quarrel with you about **simplicity—**. With regard to my lines "Laugh all that weep" &c.—I would willingly sacrifice them, but my portion of the volume is so ridiculously little, that in honest truth I can't spare them: as things are, I have very slight pretensions to participate in the **title-page—**. White's book is at length reviewed in the **Monthly;**[4] was it your doing, or Dyer's to whom I sent him? or rather do you not write in the **Critical?** for I observed in an Article of this Month's a line quoted out of *that* sonnet on Mrs. Siddons "with eager wondrin'g & perturb'd delight"—& a line from *that* sonnet would not readily have occurred to a stranger. That Sonnet, Coleridge, brings afresh to my mind the time when you wrote those on Bowles, Priestly, Burke—'twas 2 Christmas[e]s ago—& in that nice little smoky room at the Salutation, which is even now continually presenting itself to my recollection, with all its associated train of pipes, tobacco, Egghot, welch Rabbits, metaphysics & **Poetry—. Are** we *never*[5] to meet again? How differently I am circumstanced **now—**. I have never met with any one, never shall meet with any **one,** who could or can compensate me for the top of your **Society**—I have no one to talk all these matters about too—I lack friends, I lack books to supply their absence—. But these complaints ill become me: let me compare my present situation, prospects, & state of mind, with what they were but 2 months back—*but* 2 months—. **O** my friend, I am in danger of forgetting the **awful lessons** then presented **to me**—remind me of them, remind me of my Duty. Talk seriously with me when you do write. I thank you, from my heart I thank you for your sollicitude about my Sister. She is quite well,—but must not, I fear, come to live with us **yet** a good while. In the first place, because at **present** it would hurt her, & hurt my father, for them to be together: secondly from a regard to the world's good report, for I fear, I fear, tongues will be busy *whenever* that event takes place. Some have hinted, **one** man[6] has prest it on me, that she should be in perpetual confinement what she hath done to deserve, or the necessity of such an hardship I see not; do you? I am starving at the India house, near 7 oClock without my dinner, & so it has been & will be almost all the **week**—. I get home at night oe'r wearied, quite faint—& then to **Cards** with my father, who will not let me enjoy a meal in peace—but I must conform to my situation, & I hope I am, for the most part, not unthankful—

I am got home at last, & after repeated games at Cribbage have got my father's leave to write awhile: with difficulty got it, for when I expostulated about playing any more, he very aptly replied, "if you wont play with me, you might as well not come home at all!" The argument was unanswerable, & I set to afresh—. I told you, I do not approve of your omissions. Neither do I quite coincide with you in your arrangements: I have not time to point out a better, & I suppose some self-associations of your own have determined their place as they now stand. Your beginning indeed with the **Joan of Arc** lines I coincide entirely with:[7] I love a splendid **outset,**—a magnificent **Portico**—& the Diapason is **Grand**—the Religious Musings—when I read them, I think how poor, how unelevated, unoriginal, my blank verse is, "Laugh all that weep" especially, where the subject demanded a grandeur of conception: & I ask what business they have among yours—but Friendship covereth a multitude of defects.—Why omit 73?[8] At all events, let me plead for those former pages,—40. 63. 84. 86. I should like, for old acquaintance sake to spare 62. 119

would have made a figure among *Shenstone's* Elegies: *you* may admit it or reject, as you please. In the Man of Ross let the old line stand as it used "wine-cheer'd moments" much better than the lame present one. 94 change the harsh word "foodful" into "dulcet" or if [n]ot too harsh "nourishing." 91 "moveless" is that as good as "moping"—? 8 would not it read better omitting those 2 lines last but 6 about Inspiration—. I want some loppings made in the Chatterton; it wants but a little to make it rank among the finest irregular **Lyrics** I ever read. Have you time & inclination to go to work upon it—or is it too late—or do you think it needs none? Don't reject those verses in one of your Watchmen—"Dear native brook"[9] &c nor, I think, those last lines you sent me, in which "all effortless" is without doubt to be preferred to "inactive." If I am writing more than ordinarily dully 'tis that I am stupified with a tooth ache. 37 would not the 4 concluding lines of the 1st paragraph be well omitted—& it go on ***"So*** to sad sympathies" &c. in 40 if you retain it "wove" the learned Toil is better than "urge" which spoils the personification. Hang it, do not omit 48. 52. 53. what you do retain tho' call **Sonnets** for God's sake & not effusions,—spite of your ingenious anticipation of ridicule in your **Preface—**. the 5 last lines of 50 are too good to be lost, the rest is not much worth—. My tooth becomes importunate—I must finish.—pray, pray, write to me: if you knew with what an anxiety of joy I open such a long packet as you last sent me, you would not grudge giving a few minutes now & then to this intercourse (the **only** intercourse, I fear we two shall ever have) this conversation with your friend—such I boast to be called—

God love you & yours. Write me when you move, lest I direct wrong——

Has Sara no poems to publish? those lines 129[10] are probably too light for the volume where the Religious Musings are—but I remember some very beautiful lines addrest by somebody at Bristol to somebody at London

God bless you once more

C Lamb

MS: Koopman Collection, Brown University Library, Providence, R.I. Pub.: Talfourd (1848), I, 66–71; Sala, I, 60–64; Purnell, I, 60–64; Fitzgerald, I, 345–349; Hazlitt, I, 142–145; Ainger (1888), I, 49–52; Ainger (1900), I, 68–73; Macdonald, I, 51–55; Ainger (1904), I, 49–52; Harper, II, 76–81; Lucas (1905),

VI, 60–62; Lucas (1912), V, 59–62; Lucas (1935), I, 59–62. Address: Mr. Coleridge/Bristol. Postmark: December 2, 179[6].

1. "Absence. A Farewell Ode on Quitting School for Jesus College, Cambridge," "Sonnet: To the Autumnal Moon," and "Imitated from Ossian," which begin or are on pages 40, 63, and 84 in *Poems on Various Subjects* and, like "The Complaint of Ninathóma" (page 86), are not in *Poems* (1797). For "Music of Caril," below, cf. James Macpherson, *Fingal,* Books V and VI, and "The Death of Cuthullin."

2. "Epitaph on an Infant," which is in *Poems* (1797). Lamb sarcastically recommends it below as a substitute for the epitaph that reads (according to Lucas [1935], I, 62),

> Afflictions sore long time I bore,
> Physicians were in vain;
> Till Heaven did please my woes to ease,
> And take away my pain.

Lamb used the first two lines of "Epitaph on an Infant" in "A Dissertation upon Roast Pig" (*Works,* II, 124).

3. "Reflections on Having Left a Place of Retirement," which as "Reflections on Entering into Active Life. A Poem Which Affects Not to Be Poetry" is in the *Monthly Magazine,* 2 (October 1796), 732. The quotation following is from a poem of Lamb's not recovered.

4. See Letter 6, note 5. The next quotation, from Coleridge and Lamb's "As when a child on some long winter's night," line 3, is in the *Critical Review,* 18 (November 1796), 286. Those sonnets mentioned below are among "Sonnets on Eminent Characters." See Letter 3, note 19.

5. Underscored twice.

6. Perhaps Lamb's brother.

7. *Poems* (1797) opens with "Ode on the Departing Year," not with the lines from *Joan of Arc* that, with others, form "The Destiny of Nations."

8. "Lines in the Manner of Spenser," which is in *Poems* (1797). (For 40, 63, 84, and 86 see above, note 1.) "Genevieve" and "[Lines.] To a Friend in Answer to a Melancholy Letter," here numbered 62 and 119, are not in *Poems* (1797). There "cheer'd moments," below, is retained in the "Man of Ross," line 5; "foodful" in "To an Infant," line 7; "moveless," for the 1794 "moping," in "To a Young Ass: Its Mother Being Tethered near It," line 8; and the passage at lines 122–123 in "Monody on the Death of Chatterton."

9. "Sonnet: To the River Otter," the revision of "Recollection," the latter of which is in *The Watchman,* No. 5 (April 2, 1796), 133–134. The quotation "all effortless," following, is from "Addressed to a Young Man of Fortune," line 15, a poem not in *Poems* (1797) and whose reading "inactive" must have been unique to Lamb's copy. Lines 11–14 were retained in "To a Young Lady with a Poem on the French Revolution," whose line 15 begins, "Thus to sad sympathies." Omitted, like "Absence. A Farewell Ode" (in which "urge," in line 3, Coleridge never changed), were the sonnets to Priestley, Koskiusko, Lafayette, and Sheridan, here numbered 40, 48, 52, 53, and 50. Coleridge argued for the term "Effusions" in *Poems on Various Subjects,* pp. ix–x, but substituted "Sonnets" for it in *Poems* (1797).

10. "The Silver Thimble. The Production of a Young Lady, Addressed to the Author of the Poems Alluded to in the Preceding Epistle." The lines next alluded to (mentioned also in Letter 5, at the reference to note 4) have not been identified.

15. *C. L. to Coleridge*

London
the 5th Decemr. 96

To a young Lady
going out to India[1]

Hard is the heart, that does not melt with ruth,
When care sits cloudy on the brow of Youth,
When bitter griefs the *female* bosom swell,
And Beauty meditates a fond farewell
To her loved native land, and early home,
In search of peace thro' "stranger climes to roam."*

The Muse, with glance prophetic, sees her stand,
Forsaken, silent Lady, on the strand
Of farthest India, sickening at the roar
Of waves slow-beating, dull, upon the shore;
Stretching, at gloomy intervals, her eye
O'er the wide waters vainly, to espy
The long-expected bark, in which to find
Some tidings of a world she has left behind.

In that sad hour shall start the gushing tear
For scenes her childhood loved; now doubly dear;
In that sad hour shall frantic memory awake
Pangs of remorse for slighted England's sake,
And for the sake of many a tender tye
Of Love or Friendship pass'd too lightly by.

Unwept, unpitied, midst an alien race,
And the cold looks of many a stranger face,
How will her poor heart bleed, & chide the day,
That from her country took her, far away.—

Coleridge, the above has some few decent lines [in] it, & in the paucity of my portion of your volume may as well be inserted; I would also wish to retain the following if only to perpetuate the memory of so exquisite a pleasure as I have often received at the performance of the tragedy of Douglas, when Mrs. Siddons has been the Lady **Randolp.**[2] Both pieces may be inseted between the sonnets & the sketches—in which latter, the last but one of them, I beg you to alter the words "pain & want" to "pain & grief" this last being a more familiar & ear-satisfying combination. Do it I beg of you. To understand the following, if you are not acquainted with the play, you should know that on the death of Douglas his mother threw herself down a rock; & that at that time **Scotland** was busy in repelling the **Danes**———

The tomb of Douglas[3]
see the Tragedy of that name

When her son, her Douglas died,
To the steep rock's fearful side
Fast the frantic mother hied—

Oer her blooming warrior dead
Many a tear did Scotland shed,
And shrieks of long and loud lament
From her Grampian hills she sent.

Like one awakening from a trance,
She met the shock of Lochlin's[†] lance;
On her rude invader foe
Return'd an hundred fold the blow;
Drove the taunting spoiler home:
  Mournful thence she took her way,
To do observance at the tomb,
  Where the Son of Douglas lay.

Round about the tomb did go
In solemn state and order slow,
Silent pace, and black attire,
Earl, or Knight, or good Esquire,
Whoe'er by deeds of valo[u]r done
In battle had high honors won;
Whoe'er in their pure veins could trace
The blood of Douglas' noble race.

with them the flower of minstrels came,
And to their cunning harps did frame
In doleful numbers piercing rhimes,
Such strains as in the olden times
Had sooth'd the spirit of **Fingal**
Echoing thro' his fathers' hall.

"Scottish Maidens, drop a tear
Oer the beauteous Hero's bier.
Brave youth, and comely 'bove compare,
All golden shone his burnish'd hair;
Valour and smiling courtesy
Play'd in the sunbeams of his eye.
Closed are those eyes that shone so fair,
And stain'd with blood his yellow hair!"
Scottish Maidens, drop a tear
O'er the beaute*ous* Hero's bier!

"Not‡ a tear, I charge you, shed.
For the false Glenalvon dead;
Unpitied let Glenalvon lie,
Foul stain to arms and chivalry."

"Behind his back the traitor came,
And Douglas died without his fame."

⟨"Scottish Maidens, drop a tear
Oer the beauteous hero's bier."⟩

⟨"Bending, Warrior, oer thy grave,⟩
Young light of Scotland early spent!
Thy country thee shall long lament,
⟨*Douglas, "Beautiful and **Brave!"***⟩§
And oft, to after times shall tell,
*In Hope's sweet prime my **Hero** fell"*||

"Thane or Lordling, think no scorn
of the poor and lowly-born.
In brake obscure or lonely dell
The simple floweret prospers well:
The *gentler* virtues, cottage-bred,

Thrive best beneath the humble shed.
Low-born# Hinds, opprest, obscure,
Ye who patiently endure
To bend the knee and bow the head,
And thankful eat *another's bread;*—**
Well may *ye* mourn: your best friend dead,
'Till Life with Grief together end:
He would have been the poor man's friend."

"Bending, Warrior, o'er thy grave,
  Young light of Scotland early spent!
  Thy country thee shall long lament,
Douglas, "*Beautiful and* ***Brave!***"††
And oft to after times shall tell,
In Life's young prime my ***Hero*** *fell*"‡‡

At length I have done with verse-making—. Not that I relish other people's poetry less,—their's comes from 'em without effort, mine is the difficult operation of a brain scanty of ideas, made more difficult by disuse. I have been reading the "task" with fresh delight. I am glad you love **Cowper.** I could forgive a man for not enjoying **Milton,** but I would not call that man my friend, who should be offended with the "divine chit-chat of Cowper."[4] Write to me.— God love you & yours—

C. L.

is "***morbid wantonness*** of woe" a good and allowable phrase?

*Bowles ["The Dying Slave," line 27.—Ed.]
†Denmark
‡new paragraph
§(Ital:)
||(Italics)
#⟨(another paragraph begins here)⟩
**(Ital:)
††(Ital:)
‡‡(Italics)

MS: Huntington Library. Pub.: Talfourd (1848), I, 72; Sala, I, 64; Purnell, I, 64; Fitzgerald, I, 349; Hazlitt, I, 146; Ainger (1888), I, 52; Ainger (1900), I, 73; Macdonald, I, 55; Ainger (1904), I, 52; Harper, II, 81–85; Lucas (1905),

VI, 64–66; Lucas (1912), V, 64–66; Lucas (1935), I, 63–66. Address: Saml. T. Coleridge/Bristol. Postmark: December 6 [1796].

1. In *Works,* V, 16, but not (see below) in *Poems* (1797). The lady has not been identified. The last three words of line 1 are from Milton, "Lycidas," line 163.

2. A role Sarah Siddons first performed in London, at Drury Lane, on December 22, 1783. She played Lady Randolph six more times during that season and three times in the season 1784–1785. Productions of *Douglas* were given additionally in December 1787 and October 1796, but the records do not give its performers. Coleridge did not in *Poems* (1797) make the alteration in Lamb's "Fancy Employed on Divine Subjects," line 10, that Lamb requests below.

3. In *Works,* V, 9–11, and in *Poems* (1797).

4. From Coleridge's letter to Lamb, as Lamb makes clear in Letter 17, near the reference to note 6. The quotation in the postscript is from Coleridge's "Addressed to a Young Man of Fortune," line 1, which in its published version reads, "fantastic wantonness of woe."

16. *C. L. to Coleridge*

[December 9, 1796]

I am sorry: I cannot now relish your poetical present[1] so thoroughly as I feel it deserves—but I do not the less thank Lloyd & you for it. In truth Coleridge, I am perplexed & at times almost cast down—I am beset with perplexities—the old Hag of a wealthy relation, who took my Aunt off our hands in the beginning of trouble, has found out that she is "indolent & mulish" I quote her own words, & that her attachment to us is so strong that she can never be happy apart—the Lady with delicate Irony remarks, that if I am not an **Hypocrite!** I shall rejoyce to receive her again,—& that it will be a means of making me more fond of home, to have so dear a friend to come home to!—the fact is she is jealous of my Aunt's bestowing any kind recollections on us while she enjoys the patronage of her roof—she says she finds it inconsistent with her own "ease & tranquillity" to keep her any longer—& in fine summons me to fetch her home—. Now much as I should rejoyce to transplant the poor old creature from the chilling air of such patronage, yet I know how straiten'd we are already, how unable already to answer any demand which sickness or any extraordinary expence may make—. I know this, & all unused as I am to struggle with perplexities I am somewhat non plusd to say no worse—this prevents me from a through **relish** of what Lloyd's kindness & yours have furnish'd me with; I thank you tho' from my heart,— & feel myself not quite **alone** in the earth———

Before I offer, what alone I have to offer, a few obvious remarks, on the poems you sent me, I can but notice the odd coincidence of two young men, in one age, carolling their grandmothers. Love,—what L. calls the "feverish & romantic tye"[2] hath too long domineerd over all the charities of home: the dear domestic tyes of father, brother, husband—. The amiable & benevolent Cowper has a beautiful passage in his Task—some natural & painful reflections on his deceased parents: & Hayley's sweet lines to his mother are notoriously the best things he ever wrote—. Cowper's lines some of them are

How gladly would the man recall to life
The boy's **neglected sire,**—a mother too!
That softer name, perhaps more gladly still,
Might he demand them at the gates of Death—

I cannot but smile to see my Granny so gayly deck'd forth: tho' I think, whoever alter'd "thy" praises to "her" praises: "thy" honor'd memory to "her" honor'd memory,[3] did wrong—they best exprest my feelings. There is a pensive state of recollection in which the mind is disposed to apostrophize the departed objects of its attachment, & breaking loose from grammatical precision changes from the 1st to the 3d & from the 3d to the 1st person, just as the random fancy or the feeling directs. Among Lloy'ds sonnets 6th. 7th. 8th. 9th. 11th. are eminently beautiful—. I think him too lavish of his expletives—the *dos* & the *dids* when they occur too often bring a quaintness with them along with their simplicity, or rather air of antiquity, which the patrons of them seem desirous of conveying—. The Lines on Friday[4] are very pleasing—"Yet calls itself in pride of Infancy woman or man" &c. "Affection's tottering troop"—are prominent beauties—. Another time, when my mind were more at ease, I would be more particular in my remarks,—& I would postpone them now, only I want some diversion of mind. The "Melancholy man" is a charming piece of poetry: only the "whys" with submission are too many—. Yet the questions are too good to be any of 'em omitted. . for those lines of yours[5] page 18 omitted in magazine, I think the 3 first better retain'd—the 3 last, which are somewhat "simple" in the most affronting sense of the word, better omitted—to this my taste directs me,—I have no claim to prescribe to yours. "Their slothful loves & dainty sympathies"—is an exquisite line, but you knew *that* when you wrote 'em, & I trifle in pointing such out. Tis altogether the sweetest thing to me you ever wrote—tis all honey. "No wish profaned my over whelmed heart,—Blest hour, it was a Luxury to *be*!" I recognise feelings, which I may taste again, if tranquillity have not taken her flight for ever, & I will not believe but I shall be happy very happy again. The next poem to your friend[6] is very beautiful—need I instance the pretty fancy of "the rock's collected tears"—or that **original** line 'pours all its healthful greenness on the soul'—? let it be, since you ask *me,* 'as neigbring fountains each reflect the whole"—tho' that is somewhat harsh—indeed the ending is not so finish'd as the rest, which if you omit in your forth-coming edition, you will do the volume wrong, & the very binding will cry out—. Neither shall you omit the 2 following poems—"The hour when we shall meet again"—is fine fancy tis true, but fancy catering in the Service of the feeling—fetching from her stores most splendid banquets to satisfy her—. Do not, do not omit it—. Your sonnet to the River Otter, excludes those equally beautiful lines, which deserve not to be lost "As the tired savage" &c.[7] & I prefer that copy in your watchman, I plead for its preference—

Another time, I **may** notice more particularly Lloyd's, Southey's, Dermody's Sonnets[8]—I shrink from them now—my teazing lot makes me too confused for a clear judgment of things, too selfish for sympathy—& these ill digested meaning-less remarks I have imposed on myself **as a task,** to **lull** reflection,—as well as to shew you, I did not neglect reading your valuable present. Return my acknowledgements to Lloyd—you two seem to be about **realizing** an Elysium upon earth, & no doubt I shall be happier. Take my best wishes—. Remember me most affectionately to Mrs. **C**—& give little **David Hartley**—God b[l]ess its little heart—a **Kiss for me**—bring him up to know the meaning of his Christian name,[9] & what that name (imposed upon him) will demand of him———. God love you———

C Lamb

I write, for one thing to say, that I shall write no more till you send me word, **where** you are,[10]—for you are so soon to **move**———

My Sister is pretty well, thank God—. **we** think on you very often———

God bless you—continue to be my correspondent, & I will strive to **fancy** that this world is *not* "all barrenness"———[11]

MS: Huntington Library. Pub.: Talfourd (1837), I, 84–86; Talfourd (1848), I, 72–73; Sala, I, 100–103; Purnell, I, 100–103; Fitzgerald, I, 368 and 383–385; Hazlitt, I, 146–148; Ainger (1888), I, 55–56 and 83–85; Ainger (1900), I, 78–81; Macdonald, I, 55–58; Ainger (1904), I, 55–58; Harper, I, facsimile, and II, 85–90; Lucas (1905), VI, 67–69; Lucas (1912), V, 67–69; Lucas (1935), I, 67–69. Address: Samuel T Coleridge/Bristol. Postmark: December 10, 179[6]. That Lamb wrote this letter on December 9 is clear from the next letter. Lucas noted that "this is the last letter to carry the Little Queen Street address" and that the family "soon after moved to 45 Little [sic] Chapel Street, Pentonville" (Lucas [1935], I, 71). The letter, however, carries no address of the Lambs. The first notice of the move is in Letter 28.

1. Consisting of Lloyd's handsome *Poems on the Death of Priscilla Farmer,* of a vanished collection of poems that Lloyd and Coleridge had privately printed on loose sheets but never published (see *Coleridge's Letters,* I, 285–286), and of Coleridge's *Sonnets from Various Authors,* which contains Lamb's "We were two pretty babes, the youngest she," "Was it some sweet device of Faery," "When last I roved these winding wood-walks green," and "O! I could laugh to hear the midnight wind."

2. Lloyd's "My pleasant Home! where erst when sad and faint," line 10, in *Poems on the Death of Priscilla Farmer.* The passage referred to below from *The Task* is VI, 30–49. The lines of William Hayley (1745–1820) to his mother are in his *An Essay on Epic Poetry,* IV, 439–493. The quotation from *The Task* is VI, 42–45.

3. "The Grandame," lines 27 and 28, whose *thys* are restored in *Poems* (1797).

4. Lloyd's "Lines Written on a Friday, the Day in Each Week Formerly Devoted by the Author and His Brothers and Sisters to the Society of Their Grandmother." Lamb following quotes its lines 23–24 and from its line 28. "The Melancholy Man" is also Lloyd's.

5. "Reflections on Having Left a Place of Retirement," which apparently was in part on page 18 of the (vanished) loose sheets. The first three lines, referred to following, are probably 12–14, portions of which are not in the poem as it appears in the *Monthly Magazine,* 2 (October 1796), 732. The last three lines may be those that conclude the poem as it is in *Coleridge's Poetical Works* (1912), I, 106–108. Lamb's next two quotations are from its lines 59 and 41–42.

6. Coleridge's "To a Young Friend [Lloyd] on His Preparing to Domesticate with the Author. *Composed in* 1796." Lamb following quotes from its line 37 and its line 68. Line 71 reads, "As neighbouring fountains image each the whole," which is its last line in *Poems* (1803) but not in *Poems* (1797). "The Hour When We Shall Meet Again. (*Composed during Illness, and in Absence*)" and "Sonnet: To the River Otter" are in *Poems* (1797).

7. "Recollection" (in *The Watchman*), lines 1–10. Its lines 11–16 appear in *Poems* (1797) as "Lines: On an Autumnal Evening," lines 81–86.

8. That is, the one sonnet each by John Codrington Bampfylde (1754–1796), Henry Brooke, or Brooks (1703 or 1706–1783), Thomas Dermody (1775–1802), Thomas Russell (1762–1788), Anna Seward (1747–1809), William Sotheby (1757–1833), and Thomas Warton, the younger (1728–1790); the two sonnets by Charlotte Smith (1749–1806); the three by Bowles; and the four each by Coleridge, Lamb, Lloyd, and Southey—the twenty-eight sonnets in *Sonnets from Various Authors.*

9. The meaning given it by David Hartley (1705–1757), "that great master of Christian Philosophy" (*Coleridge's Letters,* I, 236).

10. The Coleridges were in Bristol until December 31, when they left for Nether Stowey.

11. Laurence Sterne, *A Sentimental Journey through France and Italy,* in the third of the three chapters titled "In the Street, Calais."

17. *C. L. to Coleridge*

December 10, 1796

I had put my letter into the post rather hastily, not expecting to have to acknowledge another from you so soon. This morning's present has made me alive again: my last night's epistle was childishly querulous; but you have put a little life into me, and I will thank you for your remembrance of me, while my sense of it is yet warm; for if I linger a day or two I may use the same phrase of acknowledgment, or similar; but the feeling that dictates it now will be gone. I shall send you a *caput mortuum,* not a *cor vivens.*[1] Thy Watchman's, thy bellman's, verses, I do retort upon thee, thou libellous varlet,—why, you cried the hours yourself, and who made you so proud? But I submit, to show my humility, most implicitly to your dogmas. I reject entirely the copy of verses you reject. With regard to my leaving off versifying, you have said so many pretty things, so many fine compliments, ingeniously decked out in the garb of sincerity, and undoubtedly springing from a present feeling somewhat like sincerity, that you might melt the most un-muse-ical soul,—did you not (now for a Rowland compliment for your profusion of Olivers)[2]—did you not in your very epistle, by the many pretty fancics and profusion of heart displayed in it, dissuade and discourage me from attempting anything after you. At present I have not leisure to make verses, nor anything approaching to a fondness for the exercise. In the ignorant present time,[3] who can answer for the future man? 'At lovers' perjuries Jove laughs'—and poets have sometimes a disingenuous way of forswearing their occupation. This though is not my case. The tender cast of soul, sombred with melancholy and subsiding recollections, is favourable to the Sonnet or the Elegy; but from

> The sainted growing woof,
> The teasing troubles keep aloof.

The music of poesy may charm for a while the importunate teasing cares of life; but the teased and troubled man is not in a disposition to make that music.

You sent me some very sweet lines relative to Burns,[4] but it was at a time when, in my highly agitated and perhaps distorted state of mind, I thought it a duty to read 'em hastily and burn 'em. I burned all my own verses, all my book of extracts from Beaumont and Fletcher and a thousand sources: I burned a little journal of my foolish passion which I had a long time kept:

> Noting ere they past away
> The little lines of yesterday.

I almost burned all your letters,—I did as bad, I lent 'em to a friend to keep out of my brother's sight, should he come and make inquisition into our papers, for, much as he dwelt upon your conversation while you were among us, and delighted to be with you, it has been his fashion ever since to depreciate and cry you down,—you were the cause of my madness—you and your damned foolish sensibility and melancholy—and he lamented with a true brotherly feeling that we ever met, even as the sober citizen, when his son went astray upon the mountains of Parnassus, is said to have 'cursed wit and Poetry and Pope.'[5] I quote wrong, but no matter. These letters I lent to a friend to be out of the way for a season; but I have claimed them in vain, and shall not cease to regret their loss. Your packets, posterior to the date of my misfortunes, commencing with that valuable consolatory epistle, are every day accumulating—they are sacred things with me.

Publish your *Burns* when and how you like, it will be new to me,—my memory of it is very confused, and tainted with unpleasant associations. Burns was the god of my idolatry, as Bowles of yours. I am jealous of your fraternising with Bowles, when I think you relish him more than Burns or my old favourite, Cowper. But you conciliate matters when you talk of the 'divine chit-chat' of the latter: by the expression I see you thoroughly relish him. I love Mrs. Coleridge for her excuses an hundredfold more dearly than if she heaped 'line upon line,'[6] out-Hannah-ing Hannah More, and had rather hear you sing 'Did a very little baby' by your family fire-side, than listen to you when you were repeating one of Bowles's sweetest sonnets in your sweet manner, while we two were indulging sympathy, a solitary luxury, by the fireside at the Salutation. Yet have I no higher ideas of heaven. Your company was one 'cordial in this melancholy vale'[7]—the remembrance of it is a blessing partly, and partly a curse. When

I can abstract myself from things present, I can enjoy it with a freshness of relish; but it more constantly operates to an unfavourable comparison with the uninteresting; converse I always and *only* can partake in. Not a soul loves Bowles here; scarce one has heard of Burns; few but laugh at me for reading my Testament—they talk a language I understand not: I conceal sentiments that would be a puzzle to them. I can only converse with you by letter and with the dead in their books. My sister indeed, is all I can wish in a companion; but our spirits are alike poorly, our reading and knowledge from the self-same sources, our communication with the scenes of the world alike narrow: never having kept separate company, or any 'company' *'together'*—never having read separate books, and few books *together*—what knowledge have we to convey to each other? In our little range of duties and connexions, how few sentiments can take place, without friends, with few books, with a taste for religion rather than a strong religious habit! We need some support, some leading-strings to cheer and direct us. You talk very wisely, and be not sparing of *your advice*. Continue to remember us, and to show us you do remember us: we will take as lively an interest in what concerns you and yours. All I can add to your happiness, will be sympathy. You can add to mine *more;* you can teach me wisdom. I am indeed an unreasonable correspondent; but I was unwilling to let my last night's letter go off without this qualifier: you will perceive by this my mind is easier, and you will rejoice. I do not expect or wish you to write, till you are moved; and of course shall not, till you announce to me that event, think of writing myself. Love to Mrs. Coleridge and David Hartley, and my kind remembrance to Lloyd, if he is with you.

C. Lamb

I will get 'Nature and Art,'[8]—have not seen it yet—nor any of Jeremy Taylor's works.

MS: unrecovered. Text: Lucas (1935), I, 72–74. Also pub.: Talfourd (1837), I, 52–56; Sala, I, 64–68; Purnell, I, 64–68; Fitzgerald, I, 349–353; Hazlitt, I, 149–152; Ainger (1888), I, 52–55; Ainger (1900), I, 73–78; Macdonald, I, 58–62; Ainger (1904), I, 52–55; Harper, II, 90–94; Lucas (1905), VI, 72–74; Lucas (1912), V, 72–74.

1. A "dead head," not a "living heart." Unidentified are the rejected verses attributed to the watchman, or bellman, mentioned following, who customarily left such reminders of his services at the houses on his rounds at Easter. But the verses that form Lamb's "To a Young Lady Going out to India" are a possibility.

2. To a trade a Rowland for an Oliver is to exchange one extravagance for another.

3. *Macbeth,* I, v, 57. Lamb next quotes from *Romeo and Juliet,* II, ii, 92–93, and then a couplet from William Collins' "Ode on the Poetical Character," lines 41–42.

4. "To a Friend Who Had Declared His Intention of Writing No More Poetry," which Coleridge first published "in a Bristol newspaper in aid of a subscription for the family of Robert Burns" (*Coleridge's Poetical Works* [1912], I, 158) and first republished in the second (1800) volume of Southey's *Annual Anthology.* (Lamb's remark about Burns in the next paragraph—"Burns was the god of my idolatry"—Lamb modified in "Imperfect Sympathies" to "In my early life I had a passionate fondness for the poetry of Burns" [*Works,* II, 61].) The next couplet is from Samuel Rogers' *Pleasures of Memory,* II, 262–263. The friend, below, to whom Lamb had entrusted Coleridge's letters has not been identified.

5. Alexander Pope, "Epistle to Dr. Arbuthnot," line 26. Lamb quotes it correctly, but imputes to the character called Arthur what Pope imputed to Cornus.

6. Isaiah 28:10. Lamb applies the expression to the prolixity of the religious writer and minor playwright Hannah More (1745–1833). "'Did a very little babby make a very great noise?'" wrote Mrs. Henry Nelson Coleridge of her father's words, "is the first line of a nursery song, in which Mr. Coleridge recorded some of his experience on this recondite subject" (Coleridge's *Biographia Literaria,* ed. Henry Nelson Coleridge and Sara Coleridge [London: Pickering, 1847], I, 355). The song has not been found.

7. Burns, "The Cotter's Saturday Night," line 78.

8. *Nature and Art* (1796), a romance by the actress, dramatist, and novelist Mrs. Elizabeth Inchbald (1753–1821). Lamb was shortly to become an admirer of Jeremy Taylor (1613–1667), bishop of Down and Connor, administrator of Dromore, and author of *The Rule and Exercises of Holy Living* (1650) and *The Rule and Exercises of Holy Dying* (1651). For some of Taylor's other works see Vol. II, Letter 104, notes.

18. *C. L. to Coleridge*

Monday Morning at Office
London the 2d January 1797

Your success in the higher species of the Ode[1] is such, as bespeaks you born for atchievements of loftier enterprize than to linger in the lowly train of songsters & sonneteers. Sincerely, I think your Ode one of the finest I have read. The opening is in the spirit of sublimest allegory. The idea of the "Skirts of the departing year, seen far onwards, waving on the wind"[2] is one of those noble Hints at which the Reader's imagination is apt to kindle into grand conceptions.— Do the words "impetuous" & "solemnize" harmonize well in the same line? Think & judge. In the 2d strophe, there seems to be too much play of fancy to be consistent with that coninued elevation we are taught to expect from the strain of the foregoing. The parenthised line (by the way I abominate parentheses in this kind of poetry) at the beginng. of 7th page,[3] & indeed all that gradual description of the throes & pangs of nature in childbirth, I do not much like.— & **Those** 4 first lines, I mean "tomb gloom anguish & languish" rise not above mediocrity. In the Epode, your mighty Genius comes again. "I mark'd ambition" &c! Thro' the whole Epode indeed you carry along our souls in a full spring tide of feeling & imaginat: Here is the "Storm of Music" as Cowper[4] expresses it. Would it not be more abrupt "Why does the Northern Conqueress stay" or "where does the Northern Conqueress stay"? this change of measure, rather than the feebler "Ah! Whither." "Foul her life & dark her tomb, mighty army of the dead, dance like deathfires" &c here is genius, here is poetry, rapid, irresistible. The concluding line, is it not a personif: without **use?**— "Nec deus intersit"—except indeed for rhyme sake—. Would the Laws of Strophe & Antistrophe, which, if they are as unchangeable, I suppose are about as wise the Mede & Persian Laws, admit of expunging that line altogether, & changing the preceding one to "And he, poor madman, deemd it quenchd in endless night." *fond* madman or *proud* madman if you will, but *poor* is more contemptuous. If I offer alterations of my own to your poetry, & admit not yours in **mine,** it is upon the principle of a present to a rich man being graciously accepted, & the same present to a poor man being consider'd as in insult—. To return, The Antistrophe that follows is not inferior in grandeur or original: but is I think not faultless v: g: How is Memory ***alone,***[5] when all the etherial multitude are there. Reflect.—Again "storiedst thy sad hours" is harsh, I need not tell you, but you have gained your point in expressing much meaning in few words. "Purple locks & snow white Glories," "mild Arcadians, ever blooming," "seas of milk & ships of amber"—these are things the **muse** talks about, when to borrow H. Walpole's witty phrase, she is not finely-phrenzied, only a little light headed, that's all—. "Purple locks"?—they may manage things differently in fairy land,[6] but your "golden tresses" are to my fancy. The spirit of the Earth is a most happy conceit: and the last line is one of the luckiest I ever heard—*"& stood up beautiful* before the cloudy seat"—I cannot enough admire it. 'Tis somehow picturesque in the very sound. The 2d Antistrophe (what is the meaning of these things?) is fine & faultless (or to vary the alliteration & not diminish the affectation) beautiful & blameless. I only except to the last line as meaningless after the preceding, & useless entirely—besides, why disjoin "nature & the world" here,[7] when you had confounded both in their pregnancy, "the common earth & Nature" recollect, a little before—. And there is a dismal superfluity in the unmeaning vocable "unhurld"—the worse, as it is so evidently a rhyme-fetch. "Death like he dozes" is a prosaic conceit—indeed all that Epode as far as "brother's corse" I most heartily commend to annihilation. The enthusiast of the lyre should not be so feebly, so tediously, delineative of his own feelings; tis not the way to become "Master of our affections."[8] The address to Albion is very agreeable, & concludes even beautifully "Speaks safety to his island child"!—"sworded"—epithet *I* would change for "cruel"—. The immediately succeeding lines are prosaic: "mad" avarice is an unpleasing combination; & the "coward distance yet with kindling pride" is not only reprehensible for the antihetical turn, but as it is a quotation "safe distance" & "coward distance" you have more than once had recourse to before—. And the Lyric muse; in her enthusiasm, should talk the language of her country, something removed from common use, something "recent," unborrowd. The dreams of destruction "soothing her fierce solitude,"[9] are vastly grand & terrific: still you weaken the effect, by that superfluous & easily-conceived parenthesis, that finishes the page. The foregoing image, few minds *could* have conceived; few tongues could have so cloath'd. "Muttring distemper'd triumph" &c is vastly fine. I hate imperfect beginnings & endings. Now your concluding stanza is worthy of so fine an ode. The beginning was awakening & striking; the ending is soothing & solemn.—. Are you serious when you ask, whether you shall admit[10] this ode? it would be strange infatuation to leave out your Chatterton; mere insanity to reject this. Unless you are fearful, that the splendid thing may be a means of "eclipsing many a softer satellite" that twinkles thro' the volume. Neither omit the annex'd little poem—. For my part, detesting alliterations, I should make the 1st line "Away with this fantastic pride of woe"—. Well may you relish Bowles's allegory.[11] I need only tell you, I have read it. & will only add, that I dislike ambition's name *gilded* on his helmet-cap: & that I think, among the more striking personages you notice, you omitted the *most* striking, Remorse! "he saw the trees—the sun—then hied him to his cave again"!!! The 2d stanza of Mania is superfl: the 1st was never exceeded. The 2d is too methodic: for ***her.*** With all its load of beauties, I am more *affected* with the 6 first stanzas of the Elegiac poem written during sickness. Tell me your feelings. If the fraternal sentiment conveyed in the following lines will atone for the total want of anything like merit or genius in it, I desire you will print it next after my other sonnet to my Sister.[12] ⟨the following hasty⟩

⟨**Sonnet**
to my sister⟩

Friend of my earliest years, & childish days,
  My joys, my sorrows, thou with me hast shared,
  Companion dear; & we alike have fared,
Poor pilgrims we, thro' life's unequal ways.
  It were unwisely done, should we refuse
To cheer our path, as featly as we may,
  Our lonely path to cheer, as trav'ellers use
With merry song, quaint tale, or roundelay.
  And we will sometimes talk past troubles o'er.
  Of mercies shewn, & all our sickness heal'd,
    And in his judgments God remembring love:
And we will learn to praise God evermore
  For those "glad tidings of great joy"[13] reveal'd
    By that sooth messenger, sent from above

1797

If you think the epithet "sooth" quaint, substitute "*blest* messenger." I hope you are printing my sonnets, as I directed you—particularly the 2d—"Methinks" &c.[14] with my last-added 6 lines at ye end: & all of 'em as I last made 'em—

This has been a sad long letter of business, with no room in it for what honest Bunyan terms **heart-work.** I have just room left to congratul: you on your removal to Stowey; to wish success to all your projects; to "bid fair peace" be to that house; to send my love & best wishes breath'd warmly after your dear Sara, & her little David Hartley. If Lloyd be with you, bid him write to me: I feel to whom I am obliged, primarily, for 2 very friendly letters I have received already from him—. A dainty sweet book that "Art and Nature" is— —. I am at present re-re-reading Priestly's examinat: of the Scotch Drs:[15] how the Rogue strings 'em up, three together! You have no doubt read that clear, strong, humorous, most entertain'g piece of reasoning. If not, procure it, & be exquisitely amused. I wish I could get more of Priestly's works. Can you recommend me to any more books, easy of access, such as circulating shops afford———

God bless you and yours———

Poor Mary is very unwell with a sorethroat, & a slight species of Scarlet fever. God bless her too—

C.L.

MS: Henry W. and Albert A. Berg Collection, The New York Public Library, Astor, Lenox and Tilden Foundations. Pub.: Talfourd (1837), I, 58 and 59–61; Sala, I, 68–70; Purnell, I, 68–70; Fitzgerald, I, 354–355; Hazlitt, I, 153–155; Ainger (1888), I, 56–57; Ainger (1900), I, 81–82; Macdonald, I, 62–63; Ainger (1904), I, 58–59; Harper, II, 94–100; Lucas (1905), VI, 75–78; Lucas (1912), V, 75–78; Lucas (1935), I, 75–78. Address: S. T. Coleridge/Stowey/near Bridgewater/Somerset.

1. Coleridge's *Ode on the Departing Year,* which appeared in quarto on December 31, 1796, and on the same date but titled "Ode for the Last Day of the Year 1796" in the *Cambridge Intelligencer.* (It is titled "Ode to the Departing Year" in the editions of Coleridge's poems after 1829.)

2. Lines 7–8. The words "impetuous" and "solemnize[d]," below, are in line 12 and were retained.

3. Line 34, which with lines 33 and 35–37 was rewritten for *Poems* (1797) to eliminate the description of Nature in the throes of childbirth. The first four lines of the second strophe, lines 13–16—identified following by the last word in each line—were essentially retained. The quotation from the epode is from line 38.

4. In "Table Talk," line 492. Lamb next suggests changes in the *Ode* for line 40, which was changed to "Ah! wherefore. . . ." He misquotes lines 59–61, questions the use of the personification of Madness in line 73 (which, like lines 64–72, was omitted from *Poems* [1797]), and quotes Horace's *Ars Poetica,* line 191—"Nor let a god intervene."

5. In line 75, which was retained, with line 79, next quoted. The following quotation is from line 81, which was rewritten to eliminate "purple." The next is from Pope's "Song. By a Person of Quality," line 5. The next is from Thomas Otway's *Venice Preserv'd,* V, 369. When Belvidera speaks Otway's line, remarked Horace Walpole in the Postscript to his *The Mysterious Mother,* she is "not being mad, but light-headed." Lamb's "finely-phrenzied" comes from Coleridge's "To the Author of 'The Robbers,' " line 11, which is an echo of *A Midsummer Night's Dream,* V, i, 12.

6. "—They order, said I, this matter better in France—" begins Sterne's *A Sentimental Journey through France and Italy.* The phrase "golden tresses [or locks]," the next letter makes clear, is an alternative that Coleridge offered Lamb to "purple locks." The spirit of the earth is in line 84. The "last line," 85, concludes the first antistrophe.

7. In lines 108 and 109. Coleridge rewrote the second antistrophe after *Poems*

(1803) and then conjoined nature and the world and retained only the first half of its last line, 110. The next quotation refers back to lines 31 and 35, which were revised. The word "unhurl'd," in line 110, was omitted. "Death[-]like he dozes," in line 124, and all before "brother's corse," in line 128, in the second epode were retained.

8. Cf. Shakespeare, Sonnet 20, line 2. The next quotation is from the *Ode,* line 138. The expression "sworded Foeman's," in line 141, was changed to "sworded Warrior's" for *Poems* (1803) and to "proud Invader's" afterward. The figure "mad avarice," in line 143, was retained. The expression "coward distance," in line 144, Coleridge changed to "cowardly distance" and used only in the *Ode.* The phrase "safe distance" he did not use there but did in *The Fall of Robespierre,* II, 97, and in the sonnet "Pitt," line 10.

9. Line 151. The parenthesis, mentioned following, is in lines 151–153 and was revised. The next quotation is from line 157.

10. Into *Poems* (1797). That volume does contain the ode and the monody on Chatterton, but not the poem annexed to the *Ode*—"Addressed to a Young Man of Fortune." The first line of it was never changed. The source of "eclipsing many a softer satellite" has not been identified.

11. "Hope: An Allegorical Sketch." Its description of Ambition is in lines 151–160, of Remorse in 241–250 (line 247 Lamb quotes), and of Mania in 221–240. Lamb is more affected by the opening stanzas of Bowles's "Elegiac Stanzas Written during Sickness at Bath," mentioned below.

12. "If from my lips some angry accents fell," which is in *Poems* (1797). Not there is the sonnet following, published as "Sonnet to a Friend" in the *Monthly Magazine,* 4 (October 1797), 288, and in *Works,* V, 16.

13. Luke 2:10.

14. Which Coleridge did include, with Lamb's sestet. (See Letter 3, note 22, and Letter 7, note 3.) For "heart-work," below, see John Bunyan, *The Pilgrim's Progress,* for example the Pocket Library Edition (1957), pp. 29, 31, and 32. The blessing below that—"bid fair peace"—is from Milton's "Lycidas," line 22.

15. *An Examination of Dr. Reid's Inquiry into the Human Mind on the Principles of Common Sense, Dr. Beattie's Essay on the Nature and Immutability of Truth, and Dr. Oswald's Appeal to Common Sense in Behalf of Religion* (1774), which treats the works specified in its title of the philosophers Thomas Reid (1710–1796) and James Oswald and of the poet James Beattie (1735–1803).

19. *C. L. to Coleridge*

London
Saturday [January 7—
Tuesday, January 10, 1797]

I am completely reconciled to that second strophe,[1] & wave all objection. In spite of the Grecian Lyrists, I persist in thinking your brief personification of Madness useless; reverence forbids me to say, impertinent. Golden locks & snow white glories are as incongruous as your former, & if the great Italian painters, of whom my friend knows about as much as the man in the moon, if these great gentlemen be on your side, I see no harm in retaining the purple—the glories, that *I*[2] have observed to encircle the heads of saints & madonnas, in those old paintings, have been mostly of a dirty drab-color'd yellow—a dull gambogium. Keep your old line: it will excite a confused kind of pleasurable idea in the reader's mind, not clear enough to be call'd a conception, nor just enough, I think, to reduce to painting. It is a rich line, you say; & riches hide a many faults. I maintain, that in the 2d antist: you *do* disjoin Nature & the world, & contrary to your conduct in the 2d strophe. "Nature joins her groans"[3] joins with *whom,* a god's name, but the world or earth in line preceding? but this is being over curious, I acknowledge. Nor *did* I call the *last* line useless, I only objected to "unhur[l'd"]. I cannot be made to like the former part of that 2d Epode; I cannot be made to feel it, as I do the parallel places in Isaiah, Jeremy, & Daniel.[4] Whether it is that in the pr[e]sent case the rhyme impairs the efficacy—or that the circumstances are feigned, & we are conscious of a made up lye in the case, & the narrative is too long winded to preserve the semblance of truth; or that lines 8. 9. 10. 14 in partic: 17 & 18 are mean & unenthusiastic—or that lines 5 to 8[5] in their change of rhyme shew like art—I dont know, but it strikes me as something meant to affect, & failing in its purpose. Remember, my waywardness of feeling is single, & singly stands opposed to all your friends, & what is one among many! This I know, that your quotations from the prophets have never escaped me, & never fail'd to affect me strongly—. I hate that simile,—.—[6] I am glad you have amended that parenthesis in the account of Destruction. I like it well now. only alter that history of child bearing, & all will do well. let the obnoxious Epode remain, to terrify such of your friends, as are willing to be terrified. I think, I would omit the Notes, not as not good per se, but as uncongenial with the dignity of the **Ode.** I need not repeat my wishes to have my little sonnets printed verbatim my last way; In particular, I fear lest you should prefer printing my first sonnet,[7] as you have done more than once, "did the wand of Merlin wave?" it looks so like *Mr* **Merlin** the ingenius successor of the immortal Merlin, now living in good health & spirits, & flourishing in Magical Reputation, in Oxford Street & on my life, one half who read *it,* would understand it so.— Do put 'em forth finally as I have, in various letters, settled it,—for first a man's self is to be pleased, & then his friends,—& of course, the greater number of his friends, if they differ inter se. Thus taste may safely be put to the **vote**—I do long to see our names together—not for vanity's-sake, & naughty pride of heart altogether, for not a living soul, **I know** or am intimate with, will scarce read the book—so I shall gain nothing quoad famam,[8]—& yet there is a little vanity mixes in it, I cannot help denying.—. I am aware of the **unpoetical cast** of the 6 last lines of my last sonnet, & think myself unwarranted in smuggling so tame a thing into the book; only the sentiments of those 6 lines are throughly conginial to me in my state of mind, & I wish to accumulate perpetuating tokens of my affection to poor **Mary**—that it has no originality in its cast, nor anything in the feelings, but what is common & natural to thousands, nor aught properly called poetry, **I see;** stil[l] it will tend to keep present to my mind a view of things which I ought to indulge—. These 6 lines, too have not, to a reader, a connectedness with the foregoing. **omit it if you like—.** What a treasure it is to my poor indolent & unemployed mind, thus to lay hold on a subject to talk about, tho' tis but a sonnet & that of the lowest order. How mournfully inactive I am!—Tis night: good night—

[Sunday evening]

My sister, I thank God, is nigh recover'd. She was seriously ill. **Do,** in your next letter, & that right soon, give me some satisfaction respecting your present situation at Stowey.[9] Is it a farm you have got? & what does your worship know about farming? Coleridge, I want you to write an Epic poem. Nothing short of it can satisfy the vast capacity of true poetic genius. Having one great End to direct all your poetical faculties to, & on which to lay out your hopes, your ambition, will shew you to what you are equal. By the sacred energies of Milton, by the dainty sweet & soothing phantasies of honey tongued Spencer, I adjure you to attempt the Epic—. **Or** do something, more ample, than the writing an occasional brief ode or sonnet; something "to make yourself for ever known,—to make the age to come your own"[10]—but I prate; doubtless, you meditate something. When you are exalted among the **Lords** of Epic fame, I shall recall with pleasure & exultingly, the days of your humility, when you disdaind not to put forth in the same volume with mine, your religious musings, & that other poem from the Joan of Arc, those promising first fruits of high renown to come—. You have learning, you have fancy, you have enthusiasm—you have strength & amplitude of wing enow for flights like those I recommend———

In the vast & unexplored regions of fairyland, there is ground enough unfound & uncultivated; search there, & realize your favorite Susquehanah scheme—.[11] In all our comparisons of taste, I do not know whether I have ever heard your opinion of a poet, very dear to me, the now out of fashion **Cowley**—favor **me** with your judgment of him—& tell me if his prose essays, in particular, as well as no inconsiderable part of his verse, be not delicious. I prefer the graceful rambling of his essays, even to the courtly elegance & ease of Addison—abstracting from this latter's exquisite humour. **Why is not your poem on Burns** in the Monthly magazine? I was much disappointed. I have a pleasurable but confused remembrance of it. When the little volume is printed, send me 3 or 4, at all events not more than 6 copies. & tell me if I put you to any additional expence, by printing with you. I have no thought of the kind, & in that case, must reimburse you—. My epistle is a model of unconnectedness, but I have no partic: subject to write on, & must proportion my scribble in some degree to the increase of postage. It is not quite fair, considering how burdensome your correspondence from different quarters must be, to add to it, with so little shew of reason. I will make an end for this evening. Sunday even:—Farewell—

[Monday evening]

Priestly, whom I sin in almost adoring, speaks of "such a choice of company, as tends to keep up that right bent, & firmness of mind, which a nec[e]ssary intercourse with the world would otherwise warp & relax. Such fellowship is the true ba[lsam] of life, it[s] cement is infinitely more durable than that of the friendships of the world, & it looks for its proper fruit, & complete gratification, to the life beyond the Grave."[12] Is there a possible chance for such an one as me to realize in this world, such friendships? Where am I to look for 'em? what testimonials shall I bring of my being worthy of such friendship? Alas! the great & good go together in separate **Herds,** & leave such as me to lag far far behind in all intellectual, & far more grievous to say, in all moral accomplishments—. Coleridge, I have not one truly elevated character among my acquaintance: not one Christian: not one, but undervalues Christianity—singly what am I to do. Wesley (have you read his life?,[13] was ***he*** not an elevated Character?) Wesley has said, "**Religion** is not a solitary thing." Alas! it necessarily is so with me, or next to solitary. Tis true, you write to me. But correspondence by letter, & personal intimacy, are very widely different. Do, do write to me, & do some good to my mind, already how much "**warped & relaxed**" by the world!— 'Tis the conclusion of another evening—. Goodnight. God have us all in his Keeping—

If you are sufficiently at leisure, oblige me with an account of your plan of life at Stowey—your literary occupations & prospects—in short make me acquainted with every circumstance, which, as relating to you, can be interesting to me. Are you yet a Berkleyan?[14] Make me one. I rejoyce in being, speculatively, a necessarian.—Would to God, I were habitually a practical one. Confirm me in the faith of that great & glorious doctrine, & keep me steady in the contemplation of it. You sometime since exprest an intention you had of finishing some extensive work on the Evidences of Natural & Revealed Religion. Have you let that intention go? Or are you doing any thing towards it? Make to yourself other ten talents: My letter is full of nothingness. I talk of nothing. But I must talk. I love to write to you. I take a pride in it—. It makes me think less meanly of myself. It makes me think myself not totally disconnected from the better part of Mankind. I know, I am too dissatisfied with the beings around me,—but I cannot help occasionally exclaiming "**Woe** is me, that I am constrained to dwell with Mesheck, & to have my habitation among the tents of Kedar"[15]—I know, I am no ways better in practice than my neighbors—but I have a taste for religion, an occasional earnest aspiration after perfection, which they have not. I gain nothing by being with such as myself—we encourage one another in mediocrity—I am always longing to be with men more excellent than myself. All this must sound odd to you, but these are my predominant feelings, when I sit down to write to you, & I should put force upon my mind, were I to reject them. Yet I rejoyce, & feel my privilege with gratitude, when I have been reading some wise book, such as I have just been reading, **Priestly** on Philosophical necessity, in the thought that I enjoy a kind of Communion, a kind of friendship even, with the great & good. Books are to me instead of friends,—I wish they did not resemble the latter in their scarceness.— And how does **little David Hartley?** "Ecquid in antiquam virtutem?"[16]—does his mighty name work wonders yet upon his little frame, & opening mind? I did not distinctly understand you,—you dont mean to make an actual plownman of him?! **Mrs. C—** is no doubt well,—give my kindest respects to her—. Is Lloyd with you yet?— are you intimate with Southey? what poems is he about to publish—he hath a most prolific brain, & is indeed a most sweet poet. But how can you answer all the various mass of interrogation I have put to you in the course of the sheet—. Write back just what you like, only write something, however brief—. I have now nigh finished my page, & got to the **end** of another evening (Monday evening)—& my eyes are heavy & sleepy, & my brain unsuggestive—. I have just heart enough awake to say **Good night once more,** & God love you my dear friend, God love us all—. Mary bears an affectionate remembrance of you———

Charles Lamb

the 10th January 1797

MS: Huntington Library. Pub.: Talfourd (1837), I, 58–59 and 61–68; Sala, I, 76–81; Purnell, I, 76–81; Fitzgerald, I, 361–366; Hazlitt, I, 161–164; Ainger (1888), I, 63–67; Ainger (1900), I, 90–96; Macdonald, I, 64–68; Ainger (1904), I, 65–69; Harper, II, 100–108; Lucas (1905), VI, 80–84; Lucas (1912), V, 79–83; Lucas (1935), I, 83–87. Address: S. T. Coleridge/Stowey/near Bridgewater/Somerset. Postmark: January [1]0, 1797.

1. *Ode on the Departing Year,* lines 13–37.

2. Underscored twice.

3. In line 109.

4. In their sequences of dark dreams and portents of destruction.

5. Lines 118, 119, 120, 124, 127, and 128; and 115–118.

6. Of the soldier on the war field dozing among the heaps of dead, lines 121–128; the simile was retained. The parenthesis, mentioned following, is in lines 151–153. The history of childbearing is in lines 33–37; it was omitted from *Poems* (1797). The notes were revised.

7. "Was it some sweet device of Faery," which is published almost as Lamb wrote it in *Poems* (1797) rather than as Coleridge altered it for *Poems on Various Subjects* and *Sonnets from Various Authors.* Both versions are in *Works,* V, 3 and 277. The quotation following is in Coleridge's version (*Works,* V, 277), lines 4–5. Merlin (*"Mr"* is underscored twice) was John Joseph Merlin (1735–1803), a conjuror and a watch, clock, musical instrument, and an engine maker who was born in Huy, Belgium, resided six years in Paris, came to London in 1760, and amused the public with his inventions at his museum in Princes Street, Hanover Square. Accounts of him are in Arthur Loesser's *Men, Women, and Pianos: A Social History* (New York: Simon and Schuster, 1954), pp. 225–226; the *Gentleman's Magazine,* 73 (May 1803), 485; and the *Annual Register* for 1803, p. 506.

8. "With respect to reputation." Lamb's "last sonnet," referred to below, is in the preceding letter.

9. "We are all remarkably well—" Coleridge wrote John Prior Estlin (1747–1817), a Unitarian minister of Bristol, "& the child grows fat & strong. Our House is better than we expected—there is a comfortable bedroom & sitting room for C. Lloyd, & another for us—a room for Nanny, a kitchen, and outhouse.

Before our door a clear brook runs of very soft water; and in the back yard is a nice *Well* of fine spring water. We have a very pretty garden, and large enough to find us vegetables & employment. And I am already an expert Gardener —& both my Hands can exhibit a callum, as testimonials of their Industry. We have likewise a sweet Orchard; & at the end of it T. Poole has made a gate, which leads into his garden—& from thence either thro' the tan yard into his house, or else thro' his orchard over a fine meadow into the garden of a Mr Cruikshanks [see Letter 28, note 3], an old acquaintance, who married on the same day as I, & has got a little girl a little younger than David Hartley. Mrs Cruikshanks is a sweet little woman, of the same size as my Sara—& they are extremely cordial. T. Poole's Mother behaves to *us,* as a kind & tender Mother— She is very fond indeed of my Wife.—So that, you see, I ought to be happy—& thank God, I am so.——" [*Coleridge's Letters,* I, 301]

10. Abraham Cowley, "The Motto," lines 1–2. "Religious Musings," mentioned below, Coleridge did include in *Poems* (1797). The "poem" from *Joan of Arc,* he did not. See Letter 3, note 2; Letter 14, at the reference to note 7; Letter 21; and Letter 22.

11. For a pantisocracy. (See the Introduction, p. xxxi.) For Coleridge's poem on Burns, referred to below, see Letter 17, note 4.

12. *A Free Discussion of the Doctrines of Materialism, and Philosophical Necessity, in a Correspondence between Dr. Price, and Dr. Priestley,* Dedication. That Lamb remarks later in this letter that he was reading *The Doctrine of Philosophical Necessity, Illustrated* suggests that he was using the second edition (1782) of Priestley's *Disquisitions Relating to Matter and Spirit* (1777), which includes the two former works.

13. Recorded by this time by John Hampson, in *Memoirs of John Wesley. With a Review of His Life and Writings, and a History of Methodism* (1791); Thomas Coke and Henry Moore, in *The Life of the Rev. John Wesley, A.M., Including an Account of the Great Revival of Religion, in Europe and America, of Which He Was the First and Chief Instrument* (1792); and John Whitehead, in *The Life of the Rev. J. Wesley. . . . With the Life of the Rev. C. Wesley, Collected from His Private Journal . . . the Whole Forming a History of Methodism* (1793–1796). Lamb's quotation, following, seems to be a paraphrase of either Coke and Moore, p. 53, or Whitehead (1844 ed.), p. 287. Coleridge came to know the life and teachings of Wesley well enough to add valuable notes to Southey's *Life of Wesley; and the Rise and Progress of Methodism* (1820), which Southey's son, Charles Cuthbert (1819–1888), incorporated into his 1846 edition of the work.

14. Coleridge acknowledged he was a Berkeleian—one who accepts the idealism of George Berkeley (1685–1753), bishop of Cloyne—in his letter to Southey of July 17, 1797. See *Coleridge's Letters,* I, 335.

15. Psalms 120:5.

16. "[Do you arouse him to] anything like ancient virtue?" (*Aeneid,* III, 342–343).

20. *C. L. to Coleridge*

the 16th Jan. 1797

Dear Col.

You have learned by this time, with surprise no doubt, that Lloyd is with me in town. The emotions I felt on his coming so unlooked for are not ill expressed in what follows, & what if you do not object to them as too personal, & to the world obscure, or otherwise wanting in worth, I should wish to make a part of our little volume—[1]

I shall be sorry if that vol. comes out, as it necessarily must do, unless you print those **very** schoolboyish verses I sent you on not getting leave to come down to **Bristol** last summer, I say I shall be sorry, that I have addrest you in nothing, which can appear in our joint volume—

So frequently, so habitually as I you dwell on my thoughts, 'tis some wonder those thoughts came never yet in Contact with a poetical mood—. But you dwell in my heart of hearts,[2] & I love you in all the naked honesty of **prose—.** God bless you, & all your little domestic circle—my tenderest remembrances to your Beloved **Sara,** & a smile & a kiss from me to your dear dear little **David Hartley—.** The verses I refer to above, slightly amended, I have sent (forgetting to ask your leave, tho' indeed I gave them only your initials) to the Month: Mag: where they may possibly appear next month, & where I hope to recognise your **Poem** on Burns.

To Charles Lloyd
an unexpected visitor

Alone, obscure, without a friend,
  A cheerless, solitary thing,
Why seeks my Lloyd the Stranger out?
  What offring can the Stranger bring

of social scenes, home bred delights,
  That him in aught compensate may
For Stowey's pleasant winter nights,
  For loves & friendships far away?

In brief oblivion to forego
  Friends, such as thine, so justly dear,
And be awhile with me content
  To stay, a kindly loiterer, here—

For this a gleam of random joy,
  Hath flush'd my unaccustom'd cheek,

And, with an o'ercharg'd bursting heart,
  I feel the thanks, I cannot speak.

O! sweet are all the Muses' lays,
  And sweet the charm of matin bird—
'Twas long, since these estranged ears
  The **sweeter voice of friend** had heard.

The voice hath spoke: the pleasant sounds
  In memory's ear, in after-time
Shall live, to sometimes rouse a tear,
  And sometimes prompt an honest rhyme.

For when the transient charm is fled,
  And when the little week is oe'r,
To cheerless, friendless solitude
  When I return, as heretofore—

Long, long, within my aching heart
  The grateful sense shall cherish'd be:
I'll think less meanly of myself
  That Lloyd will sometimes think on me.

1797

O. Col: would to God you were in London with us, or we two at Stowey with you all—

Lloyd takes up his abode at the Bull & Mouth Inn,—the Cat & Salutation would have had a charm more forcible for me—. O noctes cœnœque deum:[3] Anglice, Welch rabbits, punch, & poesy.

should you be induced to publish those very schoolboyish verses, print 'em as they will occur, if at all, in Month: Mag: yet I should feel ashamed, that to **you** I wrote nothing better—. But they are too personal & almost trifling—& obscure withal. Some lines of mine to Cowper[4] were in last Month: Mag: they have not body of thought enough to plead for the retaining of 'em—

My Sisters kind love to you all

C Lamb

MS: Huntington Library. Pub.: Talfourd (1848), I, 88–91; Sala, I, 81–83; Purnell, I, 81–83; Fitzgerald, I, 366–367; Hazlitt, I, 165–167; Ainger (1888), I,

67–69; Ainger (1900), I, 96–99; Macdonald, I, 68–70; Ainger (1904), I, 69–71; Harper, II, 108–111; Lucas (1905), VI, 87–88; Lucas (1912), V, 85–87; Lucas (1935), I, 90–91. Address: S. T. Coleridge/Stowey/near Bridgewater/Somerset. Postmark: January 1797.

1. *Poems* (1797), which does contain "To Charles Lloyd. An Unexpected Visitor" (*Works,* V, 11), but not "To Sara and Her Samuel" (see Letter 6), referred to in the next paragraph.

2. *Hamlet,* III, ii, 73.

3. "O nights and feasts of the gods" (Horace, *Satires,* II, vi, 65).

4. See Letter 6. The expression "body of thought," following, was Coleridge's. See Letter 2, the sentence that follows the second poem.

21. *C. L. to Coleridge*

London
Sunday Morning [February 5—
Monday morning, February 6, 1797]

You cannot surely mean to degrade the Joan of Arc into a pot girl;[1] you are not going, I hope, to annex to that most splendid ornament of Southey's poem all this cock & a bull story of Joan the Publican's daughter of Neufchatel, with the lamentable episode of a waggoner, his wife & six children, the texture will be most lamentably disproportionate. The first 40 or 50 lines of these addenda are no doubt in their way admirable too, but many would prefer the Joan of Southey. "on mightiest deeds to brood Of shadowy vastness, such as made my heart throb fast. Anon I paus'd & in a state of half expectance listen'd to the wind."[2] "They wonderd at me, who had known me once a chearful careless damsel." "the eye that of the circling throng & of the visible world unseeing saw the shapes of holy phantasy." I see nothing in your description of the maid equal to these,—there is a fine originality certainly in those lines "for she had lived In this bad world as in a place of tombs And touch'd not the pollutions of the Dead"[3]—but your "fierce vivacity" is a faint copy of the "fierce & terrible benevolence of Southey." Added to this, that it will look like rivalship in you, & extort a comparison with S—I think to your disadvantage. And the lines, consider'd in themselves as an addition to what you had before written, (strains of a far higher mood) are but such as Madam Fancy loves in some of her more familiar moods, at such times as she has met Noll[4] Goldsmith, & walk'd & talk'd with him, calling him old acquaintance. Southey certainly has no pretensions to vie with you in the Sublime of poetry, but he tells a plain tale better than you. I will enumerate some woeful blemishes, some of 'em sad deviations from that simplicity which was your aim. "haild who might be near."[5] (the canvas coverture moving by the bye is laughable) "a woman & 6 children" (by the way why not 9 children, it would have been just half as pathetic again) "Statues of sleep they seemd." "Frost-mangled wretch" & "green putridity." "hail'd him immortal" (rather ludicrous again) "**voiced** a sad & simple tale" (abominable) "unprovenderd" "such his tale" "Ah! suffering to the height of what was suffer'd" "amazements of affright" "the hot sore brain attributes its own hues of ghastliness & torture" (what shocking confusion of ideas). In these delineations of common & natural feelings, in the familiar walks of poetry, you seem to resemble Montauban dancing with Roubigne's tenants "much of his native loftiness remain'd in the execution."[6] I was reading your Religious Musings the other day, & sincerely I think it the noblest poem in the language, next after the Paradise lost, & even that was not made the vehicle of such grand truths. "There is one Mind" &c down to "Almighty's Throne" are without a rival in the whole compass of my poetical reading. "Stands in the sun, & with no partial gaze views all creation." I wish I could have written those lines, I rejoyce that I am able to relish them. The loftier walks of Pindus are your proper region. There you have no compeer, in modern tim[e]s. Leave the lowlands unenvied in possession of Such men as Cowper & Southey. Thus am I pouring balsam in the wounds I may have been inflicting in my poor friend's vanity. In your notice of Southey's new volume[7] you omit to mention the most pleasing of all, the **Miniature** "There were, who form'd high hopes & flattering ones of thee young Robert!" "Spirit of Spenser, was the Wanderer wrong?" Fairfax I have been in quest of a long time. Johnson in his life of Waller gives a most delicious specimen of him, & adds in the true manner of that delicate critic as well as amiable man "it may be presumed that this old version will not be much read after the **elegant** translation of my friend Mr. Hoole!" I endeavor'd, I wish'd to gain some idea of Tasso from this Mr. Hoole, the great boast & ornament of the India house, but soon desisted, I found him more vapid than smallest small beer sun-vinegar'd. Your dream[8] down to that exquisite line "I ca'nt tell half his adventures" is a most happy resemblance of Chaucer. The remainder is so so. The best line I think is "He belong'd I believe to the witch Melancholy." By the way, when will our volume come out? don't delay it, till you have written a new Joan of Arc— —. Send what letters you please by **me,** & in ⟨the way you propose, crossing the £.⟩ any way you choose single or double. The India C*o* is better adapted to answer the cost than the generality of my friend's correspondents—such poor & honest dogs as John Thelwall particularly. I cannot say I know Colson, at least intimately, I once supped with him & **Allen.** I think his manners very pleasing. I will not tell you what I think of Lloyd, for he may by chance come to see this letter, & that thought puts a restraint on me. I cannot think what subject would suit your Epic genius; some philosophical subject, I conjecture, in which shall be blended the Sublime of Poetry & of **Science.** Your proposed Hymns will be a fit preparatory study, whereWith to "discipline your young noviciate soul."[9] I grow dull; I'll go walk myself out of my dullness—

Sunday night

You & Sara are very good to think so kindly & so favorably of poor Mary. I would to God, all did so too. But I very much fear, she must not think of coming home in my father's lifetime. It is very hard upon her. But our circumstances are peculiar, & we must submit to them. God be praised, she is so well as she is. She bears her situation as one who has no right to complain. My poor old Aunt, whom you have seen, the kindest goodest creature to me when I was at school, who used to toddle there to bring me fag,[10] when I school-boy like only despised her for it, & used to be ashamed to see her come & sit herself down on the old coal hole steps as you went into the old grammar school, & opend her apron & brought out her bason, with some nice thing she had caused to be saved for me,—the good old creature is now lying on her death bed,—I cannot bear to think on her deplorable state. To the shock she received on that our **evil** day, from which she never completely recoverd, I impute her illness. She says, poor thing, she is glad she is come home to die with me. I was always her favorite. "No after friendships e'er can raise The endearments of our early days, Nor eer the heart such fondness prove, as when it first began to love."[11] Lloyd has kindly left me for a keep-sake "John

Woolman"—. You have read it, he says, & like it. Will you excuse one short extract? I think, it could not have escaped you. "Small treasure to a resigned mind is sufficient. How happy is it to be content with a little, to live in humility, & feel that in us, which breathes out this language **Abba! Father!"—.** I am almost ashamed to patch up a letter in this miscellaneous sort—but I please myself in the thought, that anything from me will be acceptable to you. I am rather impatient, childishly so, to see our names affixed to the same common volume. Send me **two,** when it does come out. 2 will be enough—or indeed 1—but 2 better—. I have a dim recollection, that when in town you were talking of the **Origin of Evil** as a most prolific subject for a Long Poem—why not adopt it, Coleridge? there would be **room** for imagination. Or the description (from a vision or dream, suppose) of an Utopia in one of the planets, (the Moon for instance)—. Or a five day's dream, which shall illustrate in sensible imagery,

1 2 3
Hartleys 5 motives to conduct—sensation, imagination, ambition,
4 5
sympathy, Theopathy.[12] 1st banquets—music—&c effeminacy—& their insufficiency—. 2*d* "beds of hyacinth & roses, where young Adonis oft reposes"—"fortunate Isles"—the pagan Elysium &c. &c.—antiquity as pleasing to the fancy—poetical pictures—their emptiness madness &c:— 3d warriors—poets—&c some famous yet, more forgotten, their fame or oblivion now alike indifferent pride, vanity &c. &c.— 4th all manner of pitiable storys, in Spencer-like verse—love—friendship relationship &c. &c. 5th hermits—Christ & his apostles—martyrs—heaven—&c. &c. An imagination like yours from these scanity hints may expand into a thousand great Ideas—if indeed you at all comprehend my scheme, which I scarce do myself—

Monday morn— —A London letter 9½.

Look you, Master Poet, I have remorse as well as another man, & my bowels can sound[13] upon occasion. But I must put you to this charge, for I cannot keep back my protest, however ineffectual, against the annexing your latter lines to those former—this putting of new wine in old bottles. This my duty done, will cease from writing till you invent some more reasonable mode of conveyance. Well may the "ragged followers of the nine" set up for flocci-nauci-what-do-you-call-em-**ists—**. And I do not wonder, that in their splendid visions of Utopias in America, they protest against the admission of those *yellow*-complexioned, *copper*-color'd, *white* liver'd Gentlemen, who never proved themselves ***their*** **friends.** Don't you think your verses on a young Ass too trivial a companion for the Religious musings? "scoundrel monarch"[14] alter ***that.*** And the Man of Ross is scarce admissible as it now stands curtailed of its fairer half,— Reclaim its property from the Chatterton, which it does but encumber, & it will be a rich little poem— —. I hope you expunge great part of the old notes in the new edition. That in particular most barefaced unfounded impudent assertion that M*r* Rogers is indebted for his story to Loch Lomo[n]d a Poem by **Bruce!**[15] I have read the latter,—I scarce think you have. Scarce any thing is common to them both. The poor Author of the Pleasures of Memory was sorely hurt, Dyer says, by the accusation of unoriginality. He never saw the **Poem—**. I long to read your Poem on **Burns,—**I retain so indistinct a memory of it. In what shape & **how** does it come into public? As you leave off writing poetry till you finish your hymns, I suppose you print now All you have got by you. You have scarce enough unprinted to make a 2d volume with Lloyd? Tell me all about it—: What is become of Cowper.[16] Lloyd told me of some verses on his mother. If you have them by you, pray send 'em me,—I do so love him! Never mind their merit. May be *I* may like 'em—as your taste & mine do not Always exactly *indentify.*———

Yours
Lamb

the 5th [6th] January [February] 1797

MS: Huntington Library. Pub.: Talfourd (1848), I, 74–83; Sala, I, 70–76; Purnell, I, 70–76; Fitzgerald, I, 355–361; Hazlitt, I, 155–161; Ainger (1888), I, 57–62; Ainger (1900), I, 82–90; Macdonald, I, 70–76; Ainger (1904), I, 59–64; Harper, II, 111–119; Lucas (1905), VI, 89–93; Lucas (1912), V, 87–92; Lucas (1935), I, 92–96. Address: S. T. Coleridge/Stowey/near Bridgewater/Somersetshire.

1. By the transformation of Coleridge's *Joan of Arc* lines into "The Visions of the Maid of Orleans." (See Letter 3, note 2.) After receiving this letter Coleridge wrote Cottle that the "lines which I added to my lines in the 'Joan of Arc,' have been so little approved by Charles Lamb, to whom I sent them, that although I differ from him in opinion, I have not the heart to finish the poem" (*Coleridge's Letters,* I, 309).

2. *Joan of Arc,* I, 480–483. The two quotations next are from I, 468–469, and IV, 64–66.

3. Now in "The Destiny of Nations," lines 176–178. The expression "fierce vivacity," which is in Coleridge's Note Book, fragment 25 (see *Coleridge's Poetical Works* [1912], II, 991), is a "faint copy" of *Joan of Arc,* I, 375. It was altered to "strange vivacity" for "The Destiny of Nations," line 257.

4. Oliver.

5. "The Destiny of Nations," line 203. The description of the coverture, criticized following, is in lines 210 and 251 and was revised. That of the woman and her children is in line 211 and was also revised. For "Statues of sleep . . . " and "Frost-mangled wretch" see lines 212–213 and 218. The expression "green putridity" was omitted. For "hail'd him immortal" and "voiced a sad . . . " see lines 230 and 232. The word "unprovenderd" was omitted. For "such his tale" and "Ah! suffering . . . " see lines 252 and 253. The phrases "amazements of affright" and "the hot sore brain . . . " were omitted.

6. Henry Mackenzie, *Julia de Roubigné,* Letter VI, a book Rosamund reads in *Rosamund Gray* (see Letter 37, note 1), ch. iv (*Works,* I, 8). The lines from "Religious Musings" referred to below are 105–116. Lines 111–112 are praised especially.

7. The first volume of Southey's *Poems* (1797–1799), which Coleridge had noticed not publicly but in his letter to Lamb, who quotes from "On My Own Miniature Picture, Taken at Two Years of Age," lines 16–18 and 34. Lamb then writes of having been in quest of the translation of Tasso's *Gerusalemme Liberata* (see Letter 24, note 4) done in 1600 by Edward Fairfax (1580?–1635). After the comments about and paraphrase from *Lives of the English Poets,* I, 296, Lamb writes that he has "desisted" from the Tasso translation done in 1763 by the translator and small dramatist John Hoole (1727–1803), whose friendship with Johnson dated from about 1761 and whose association with the East India House began with his appointment as a clerk in the accountant general's office in 1744. Hoole was transferred to the auditor's office in 1763, made auditor of Indian accounts in 1770, writer and compiler of Indian correspondence in 1776, clerk to the committee on government troops and stores in 1782, and retired in 1785. William Foster's account of him in *The East India House: Its History and Associations* (London: John Lane, Bodley Head, 1924), pp. 155–164, corrects and expands that in the *DNB.*

8. "The Raven. A Christmas Tale, Told by a School-boy to His Little Brothers and Sisters," whose lines 19 and 8 Lamb quotes. *Poems* (1797) came out on October 28, according to an advertisement in the *Morning Post* cited by Thomas J. Wise in *A Bibliography of the Writings in Prose and Verse of Samuel Taylor Coleridge* (London: Bibliographical Society, 1913), p. 39. John Thelwall (1764–1834), the first of Coleridge's two correspondents mentioned below, started business life as a textile dealer, became a tailor, then an attorney's clerk, and then turned to literature. He published *Poems upon Various Subjects* in 1787 and at about the same time became the editor of the *Biographical and Imperial Magazine.* He also became a supporter of the theorists of the French Revolution, of John Horne Tooke, and of the bootmaker and radical politician Thomas Hardy (1752–1832). In 1794 he, with them, was imprisoned for and acquitted of high treason. Shortly after the appearance of his *Poems Written in Close Confinement in the Tower and Newgate* (1795) he left London to denounce the government from the provinces in "Lectures upon Roman History." In about 1798 he withdrew from politics and took a farm near Brecon, Wales. Soon he began to lecture on elocution. In 1804 or 1805 he returned to London as a teacher of oratory, in 1809 established a speech clinic, and in 1814 published his *Treatment of Cases of Defective Utterance.* He returned to politics in 1818, when he acquired *The*

Champion. (Lamb had contributed to it in 1814, before Thelwall's acquisition, and in 1820, during Thelwall's ownership.) After its failure Thelwall continued to write on elocution and reform until his death. John Colson, or Coulson, the second correspondent, had helped Coleridge with *The Watchman* and would help with *The Friend* (1809–1810). Colson was a lawyer, an acquaintance of Thelwall as well as of Robert Allen, and a member of a Massachusetts family that had settled in Bristol and become close to that of Thomas Poole. See *The Friend,* ed. Barbara Rooke, II, 423.

9. "Religious Musings," line 411.

10. Dialectal for a loach, a kind of fish. Lamb recalled Sarah Lamb's kindnesses in "Christ's Hospital Five and Thirty Years Ago" and perhaps his hateful reactions to them in "Modern Gallantry" (*Works,* II, 13 and 82).

11. John Logan, "Ode on the Death of a Young Lady," lines 33–36. Lloyd's keepsake for Lamb was probably *The Works of John Woolman* (1774–1775), which Lamb urged his readers to memorize in "A Quaker's Meeting" (*Works,* II, 47). Perhaps the keepsake was only Woolman's *Considerations on Pure Wisdom, and Human Policy; on Labour; on Schools; and on the Right Use of the Lord's Outward Gifts* (1768), from which Lamb quotes below. (See *The Works of John Woolman. In Two Parts* [2d ed.; 1775; rpt. Miami: Mnemosyne, 1969], p. 334.) Woolman (1720–1772) was born near Northampton and Rancocas, New Jersey. He became a shopkeeper and tailor in Mount Holly and, in about 1756, an itinerant Quaker minister who wrote and spoke especially against slavery and all other forms of human exploitation. He took his message to England in 1772 and died of smallpox in Yorkshire.

12. In David Hartley's *Observations on Man, His Frame, His Duty, and His Expectations* (1749). The quotation following is from Milton's *Comus,* lines 998–999.

13. "Wherefore my Bowels shall sound like an Harp" (Isaiah 16:11) is the motto of *The Watchman,* No. 2 (March 9, 1796), 33. The quotation following is from Burns's "Second Epistle to J. Lapraik," line 92, and applied here to the pantisocrats. See Letter 2, note 5, for "flocci-nauci. . . ."

14. "To a Young Ass: Its Mother Being Tethered near It," line 36, which was revised for *Poems* (1797). Reclaimed were lines 41–46 from the 1796 version of the "Monody on the Death of Chatterton" for lines 9–14 of the 1797 version of the "Man of Ross," mentioned next.

15. In a note to "Lines: On an Autumnal Evening" in *Poems on Various Subjects,* p. 184, Coleridge erroneously stated that Samuel Rogers had taken the tale of Florio in the *Pleasures of Memory* from "Lochleven," by Michael Bruce (1746–1767). Coleridge apologized for the error in *Poems* (1797), p. 244.

16. Cowper was living with John Johnson (1769–1833), his cousin, guardian, and editor, at East Dereham, Norfolk. Lloyd told Lamb of Cowper's "Lines on the Receipt of My Mother's Picture out of Norfolk."

22. *C. L. to Coleridge*

[Monday,] February 13, 1797

Your poem[1] is altogether admirable—parts of it are even exquisite—in particular your personal account of the Maid far surpasses any thing of the sort in Southey. I perceived all its excellences, on a first reading, as readily as now you have been removing a supposed film from my eyes. I was only struck with [a] certain faulty disproportion in the matter and the *style,* which I still think I perceive, between these lines and the former ones. I had an end in view; I wished to make you reject the poem, only as being discordant with the other; and, in subservience to that end, it was politically done in me to over-pass, and make no mention of merit which, could you think me capable of *overlooking,* might reasonably damn for ever in your judgment all pretensions in me to be critical. There, I will be judged by Lloyd, whether I have not made a very handsome recantation. I was in the case of a man whose friend has asked him his opinion of a certain young lady; the deluded wight gives judgment against her *in toto*—don't like her face, her walk, her manners—finds fault with her eyebrows—can see no wit in her. His friend looks blank; he begins to smell a rat; wind veers about; he acknowledges her good sense, her judgment in dress, a certain simplicity of manners and honesty of heart, something too in her manners which gains upon you after a short acquaintance,—and then her accurate pronounciation of the French language and a pretty uncultivated taste in drawing. The reconciled gentleman smiles applause, squeezes him by the hand, and hopes he will do him the honour of taking a bit of dinner with Mrs. —— and him—a plain family dinner—some day next week. 'For, I suppose, you never heard we were married! I'm glad to see you like my wife, however; you'll come and see her, ha?' Now am I too proud to retract entirely. Yet I do perceive I am in some sort straitened; you are manifestly wedded to this poem, and what fancy has joined let no man separate. I turn me to the Joan of Arc, second book.

The solemn openings of it are with sounds which, Lloyd would say, 'are silence to the mind.'[2] The deep preluding strains are fitted to initiate the mind, with a pleasing awe, into the sublimest mysteries of theory concerning man's nature and his noblest destination—the philosophy of a first cause—of subordinate agents in creation superior to man—the subserviency of Pagan worship and Pagan faith to the introduction of a purer and more perfect religion, which you so elegantly describe as winning with gradual steps her difficult way northward from Bethabra.[3] After all this cometh Joan, a *publican's* daughter, sitting on an ale-house *bench,* and marking the *swingings* of the *signboard,* finding a poor man, his wife and six children, starved to death with cold, and thence roused into a state of mind proper to receive visions emblematical of equality; which what the devil Joan had to do with, I don't know, or indeed with the French and American revolutions; though that needs no pardon, it is executed so nobly. After all, if you perceive no disproportion, all argument is vain: I do not so much object to parts. Again, when you talk of building your fame on these lines in preference to the 'Religious Musings,' I cannot help conceiving of you and of the author of that as two different persons, and I think you a very vain man.

I have been re-reading your letter. Much of it I *could* dispute; but with the latter part of it, in which you compare the two Joans with respect to their predispositions for fanaticism, I *toto corde*[4] coincide; only I think that Southey's strength rather lies in the description of the emotions of the Maid under the weight of inspiration,—these (I see no mighty difference between *her* describing them or *you* describing them), these if you only equal, the previous admirers of his poem, as is natural, will prefer his; if you surpass, prejudice will scarcely allow it, and I scarce think you will surpass, though your specimen at the conclusion (I am in earnest) I think very nigh equals them. And in an account of a fanatic or of a prophet the description of her *emotions* is expected to be most highly finished. By the way, I spoke far too disparagingly of your lines, and, I am ashamed to say, purposely. I should like you to specify or particularise; the story of the 'Tottering Eld,'[5] of 'his eventful years all come and gone,' is too general; why not make him a soldier, or some character, however, in which he has been witness to frequency of 'cruel wrong and strange distress!' I think I should. When I laughed at the 'miserable man crawling from beneath the coverture,' I wonder I did not perceive it was a laugh of horror—such as I have laughed at Dante's picture of the famished Ugolino. Without falsehood, I perceive an hundred beauties in your narrative. Yet I wonder you do not perceive something out-of-the-way, something unsimple and artificial, in the expression, 'voiced a sad tale.'[6] I hate made-dishes at the muses' banquet. I believe I was wrong in most of my other objections. But surely 'hailed him immortal,' adds nothing to the terror of the man's death, which it was your business to heighten, not diminish by a phrase which takes away all terror from it. I like that line, 'They closed their eyes in sleep, nor knew 'twas death.' Indeed, there is scarce a line I do not like. '*Turbid* ecstacy,' is surely not so good as what you *had* written, 'troublous.' Turbid rather suits the muddy kind of inspiration which London porter confers. The versification is, throughout, to my ears unexceptionable, with no disparagement to the measure of the 'Religious Musings,' which is exactly fitted to the thoughts.

You were building your house on a rock, when you rested your fame on that poem. I can scarce bring myself to believe, that I am admitted to a familiar correspondence, and all the licence of friendship, with a man who writes blank verse like Milton. Now, this is delicate flattery, *indirect* flattery. Go on with your 'Maid of Orleans,' and be content to be second to yourself. I shall become a convert to it, when 'tis finished.

This afternoon I attend the funeral of my poor old aunt, who died on Thursday.[7] I own I am thankful that the good creature has ended all her days of suffering and infirmity. She was to me the 'cherisher of infancy,' and one must fall on these occasions into reflections which it would be commonplace to enumerate, concerning death, 'of chance and change, and fate in human life.' Good God, who could have foreseen all this but four months back! I had reckoned, in particular, on my aunt's living many years; she was a very hearty old woman. But she was a mere skeleton before she died, looked more like a corpse that had lain weeks in the grave, than one fresh dead. 'Truly the light is sweet, and a pleasant thing it is for the eyes to behold the sun; but let a man live many days and rejoice in them all, yet let him remember the days of darkness, for they shall be many.'[8] Coleridge, why are we to live on after all the strength and beauty of existence are gone, when all the life of life is fled, as poor Burns expresses it? Tell Lloyd I have had thoughts of turning Quaker, and have been reading, or am rather just beginning to read, a most capital book, good thoughts in good language, William Penn's 'No Cross, no Crown;'[9] I like it immensely. Unluckily I went to one of his meetings, tell him, in St. John Street, yesterday, and saw a man under all the agitations and workings of a fanatic, who believed himself under the influence of some 'inevitable presence.' This cured me of Quakerism; I love it in the books of Penn and Woolman, but I detest the vanity of a man thinking he speaks by the Spirit, when what he says an ordinary man might say without all that quaking and trembling. In the midst of his inspiration—and the effects of it were most noisy—was handed into the midst of the meeting a most terrible blackguard Wapping sailor; the poor man, I believe, had rather have been in the hottest part of an engagement, for the congregation of broad-brims, together with the ravings of the prophet, were too much for his gravity, though I saw even he had delicacy enough not to laugh out. And the inspired gentleman, though his manner was so supernatural, yet neither talked nor professed to talk anything more than good sober sense, common morality, with now and then a declaration of not speaking from himself. Among other things, looking back to his childhood and early youth, he told the meeting what a graceless young dog he had been, that in his youth he had a good share of wit: reader, if thou hadst seen the gentleman, thou wouldst have sworn that it must indeed have been many years ago, for his rueful physiognomy would have scared away the playful goddess from the meeting, where he presided, for ever. A wit! a wit! what could he mean? Lloyd, it minded me of Falkland in the 'Rivals,' 'Am I full of wit and humour? No, indeed you are not. Am I the life and soul of every company I come into? No, it cannot be said you are.'[10] That hard-faced gentleman, a wit! Why, Nature wrote on his fanatic forehead fifty years ago, 'Wit never comes, that comes to all.' I should be as scandalised at a *bon mot* issuing from his oracle-looking mouth, as to see Cato go down a country-dance. God love you all. You are very good to submit to be pleased with reading my nothings. 'Tis the privilege of friendship to talk nonsense, and to have her nonsense respected.—

Yours ever,
C. Lamb

MS: unrecovered. Text: Lucas (1935), I, 98–102. Also pub.: Talfourd (1837), I, 69–76; Sala, I, 83–89; Purnell, I, 83–89; Fitzgerald, I, 368–374; Hazlitt, I, 167–171; Ainger (1888), I, 69–73; Ainger (1900), I, 99–105; Macdonald, I, 76–81; Ainger (1904), I, 71–75; Harper, II, 119–126; Lucas (1905), VI, 95–98; Lucas (1912), V, 94–98.

1. "The Visions of the Maid of Orleans."

2. "Dirge, Occasioned by an Infant's Death," line 8, in Lloyd's *Poems on Various Subjects*. The poem is called "Lines on the Death of an Infant," and the quotation is in its line 4 in Coleridge's *Poems* (1797).

3. Now in "The Destiny of Nations," lines 124–125.

4. "Whole-heartedly."

5. Now in "The Destiny of Nations," line 157. The three quotations following are from lines 161, 156, and 207. The passage on Ugolino is in the *Inferno*, Canto 33.

6. See the preceding letter, note 5, regarding this and the next quotation. See "The Destiny of Nations," lines 246 and 272, for the two quotations after those.

7. February 9, when Lamb wrote "Written on the Day of My Aunt's Funeral"

(*Works,* V, 19–20). The first of the two quotations below, from Lloyd's "My pleasant Home! where erst when sad and faint," line 13, is also in *Rosamund Gray,* ch. vii (*Works,* I, 16). The second quotation is from Milton's *Paradise Regained,* IV, 265.

8. Ecclesiastes 11:7–8. Burns's "Lament for James, Earl of Glencairn," line 46, (misquoted below) reads, "For a' the life of life is dead." Its lines 75–80 are in *Rosamund Gray,* ch. vii (*Works,* I, 20).

9. Penn's defense of Quakerism, published in 1669. Lamb, whose interest in the Quakers may have begun as a result of the influence of his father or the Lloyds (and was certainly sustained by the Lloyds, Hester Savory [see Letter 87, note 5], and his later correspondent the poet Bernard Barton), attended the Peel Meeting House in St. John's Street, Clerkenwell. He retold the story, told below, of the Wapping sailor in "A Quaker's Meeting" (*Works,* II, 48). The phrase "inevitable presence" is from a passage now in "The Destiny of Nations," line 271.

10. An approximation of Sheridan's *The Rivals,* II, i, 187–194. The truism on wit, following, Lamb adapted from Milton's on hope in *Paradise Lost,* I, 66–67.

23. *C. L. to Coleridge*

April 7, 1797

Your last letter was dated the 10th February; in it you promised to write again the next day. At least, I did not expect so long, so unfriend-like, a silence. There was a time, Col., when a remissness of this sort in a dear friend would have lain very heavy on my mind, but latterly I have been too familiar with neglect to feel much from the semblance of it. Yet, to suspect one's self overlooked and in the way to oblivion, is a feeling rather humbling; perhaps, as tending to self-mortification, not unfavourable to the spiritual state. Still, as you meant to confer no benefit on the soul of your friend, you do not stand quite clear from the imputation of unkindliness (a word by which I mean the diminutive of unkindness). Lloyd tells me he has been very ill, and was on the point of leaving you.[1] I addressed a letter to him at Birmingham: perhaps he got it not, and is still with you. I hope his ill-health has not prevented his attending to a request I made in it, that he would write again very soon to let me know how he was. I hope to God poor Lloyd is not very bad, or in a very bad way. Pray satisfy me about these things. And then David Hartley was unwell; and how is the small philosopher, the minute philosopher?[2] and David's mother? Coleridge, I am not trifling, nor are these matter-of-fact questions only. You are all very dear and precious to me; do what you will, Col., you may hurt me and vex me by your silence, but you cannot estrange my heart from you all. I cannot scatter friendship[s] like chuck-farthings, nor let them drop from mine hand like hour-glass sand. I have but two or three people in the world to whom I am more than indifferent, and I can't afford to whistle them off to the winds.[3]

By the way, Lloyd may have told you about my sister. I told him. If not, I have taken her out of her confinement, and taken a room for her at Hackney, and spend my Sundays, holidays, &c., with her. She boards herself. In one little half year's illness, and in such an illness of such a nature and of such consequences! to get her out into the world again, with a prospect of her never being so ill again—this is to be ranked not among the common blessings of Providence. May that merciful God make tender my heart, and make me as thankful, as in my distress I was earnest, in my prayers. Congratulate me on an ever-present and never-alienable friend like her. And do, do insert, if you have not *lost,* my dedication.[4] It will have lost half its value by coming so late. If you really are going on with that volume, I shall be enabled in a day or two to send you a short poem to insert. Now, do answer this. Friendship, and acts of friendship, should be reciprocal, and free as the air; a friend should never be reduced to beg an alms of his fellow. Yet I will beg an alms; I entreat you to write, and tell me all about poor Lloyd, and all of you. God love and preserve you all.

C. Lamb

MS: unrecovered. Text: Lucas (1935), I, 102–103. Also pub.: Talfourd (1837), I, 77–78; Sala, I, 89–91; Purnell, I, 89–91; Fitzgerald, I, 374–376; Hazlitt, I, 172–174; Ainger (1888), I, 73–75; Ainger (1900), I, 106–108; Macdonald, I, 81–83; Ainger (1904), I, 75–77; Harper, II, 126–128; Lucas (1905), VI, 99–100; Lucas (1912), V, 98–99.

1. See Letter 10, note 4.
2. After Bishop George Berkeley's *Alciphron, or the Minute Philosopher.*
3. *Othello,* III, iii, 262.
4. See Letter 13. The Dedication is also in *Works,* V, 283.

24. *C. L. to Coleridge*

London
the 15th April 1797

A Vision of Repentance[1]

I saw a famous fountain in my dream,
Where shady pathways to a Valley led;

A weeping willow lay upon that stream,
  And all around the fountain brink were spread
Wide branching trees, with dark green leaf rich clad,
Forming a doubtful twilight desolate & sad.

The place was such, that whoso enter'd in
  Disrobed was of every earthly thought,
And strait became as one that knew not sin,
  Or to the world's first innocence was brought.
Enseem'd it now, he stood on holy ground,
In sweet & tender melancholy wrapt around.

A most strange calm stole oer my soothed sprite:
  Long time I stood, & longer had I staid,
When lo! I saw, saw by the sweet moon light,
  Which came in silence o'er that silent shade,
Where near the fountain **Something** like **Despair**
Made of that weeping willow garlands for her hair

And eke with painful fingers she inwove
  Many an uncouth stem of savage thorn—
"The willow-garland—*that* was for her **Love,"**
  "And *these* her bleeding temples would adorn."
With sighs her heart nigh burst—salt tears fast fell,
As mournfully she bended oer that sacred well.

To whom when I addrest myself to speak,
  She lifted up her eyes, & nothing said,
The delicate red came mantling oer her cheek,
  And, gathering up her loose attire, she fled
To the dark covert of that woody shade,
And in her goings seem'd a timid gentle maid.

Revolving in my mind what this should mean,
  And why that lonely Lady plained so;
Perplex'd in thought at that mysterious scene,
  And doubting if 'twere best to stay or go,
I cast mine Eyes in wistful gaze around;
When from the shades came slow a small & plaintive Sound.

    "Psyche* am I, who love to dwell
    In these brown shades, this woody dell,

Where never busy mortal came,
Till now, to pry upon my shame."

"At thy feet what thou dost see
The Waters of Repentance be,
Which, night & day, I must augment
With tears,[2] like a true Penitent,
If haply so my day of Grace
Be not yet past—& this lone place,
Oershadowy, dark, excludeth hence
All thoughts but grief & penitence."

"Why dost thou weep, thou gentle maid
And wherefore in this barren shade
Thy hidden thoughts with sorrow feed?
Can thing so fair repentance need?"[†]

"O! I have done a deed of shame,
And tainted is my virgin fame,
And stain'd the beauteous maiden white,[‡]
In which my bridal robes were dight."

"And who the promised spouse declare,
And what those bridal garments were?"[§]

"Severe & saintly righteousness
Composed the clear white bridal dress:
Jesus, the Son of Heaven's high Ring
Bought with his blood the marriage ring"

"A wretched sinful Creature I
Deem'd lightly of that sacred tye,
Gave to a treachrous World my heart,
And plaid the foolish wanton's part."

"Soon to these murky shades I came
To hide from the Sun's light my shame—
And still I haunt this woody dell
And bathe me in that healing well,
Whose waters clear have influence
From sin's foul stains the Soul to cleanse;

And, night & day, I them augment
With tears, like a true Penitent,
Until, due expiation made,
And fit atonement fully paid,
The Lord & Bridegroom me present
Where in sweet strains of high concent,
God's throne before, the Seraphim
Shall chant th' extatic marriage hymn."

"Now Christ restore thee soon"||—I said,
And thenceforth all my dream was fled———

The above you will please to print immediately before the blank verse fragments—tell me if you like it—. I fear the latter half is unequal to the former, in parts of which I think you will discover a delicacy of pencilling not quite **Un**-spencer like—. The latter half aims at the *measure,* but has failed to attain the *poetry,* of Milton in his Comus, & Fletcher in that exquisite thing ycleped the Faitful shepherdess,[3] where they both use 8 syllable lines—. But this latter half was finish'd in great haste, & as a task, not from that impulse which affects the name of inspiration———

By the way I have lit upon Fairfax's Godfrey of Bullen[4] for half a crown. Rejoyce with me.

Poor dear Lloyd, I had a letter from him yesterday—his state of mind is truly alarming—he has, by his own confession, kept a letter of mine **unopen'd 3 weeks!** afraid, he says, to open it, lest I should speak upbraidingly to him. & yet this very letter of mine was in answer to one, wherein he informed me, that an alarming illness had alone prevented him from writing—. You will pray with me, I know, for his recovery— for Surely, Coleridge, a ⟨delicacy⟩ exquisiteness of feeling like this must border on derangement. But I love him more & more,— & will not give up the hope of his speedy recovery, as he tells me he is under Dr Darwin's regimen———

God bless us all, and shield us from insanity, which is "the sorest malady of all"———[5]

My kind love to your wife and child

C Lamb

Pray write now.— —— ——

* The **Soul**

† the *lines* mean to mark Italics—to mark the change of persons in the dialogue—

‡ Jeremy Taylor speaks of the Soul "staining the whiteness of her *baptismal* robes." [So, almost, in *The Rule and Exercises of Holy Living,* ch. iv, ad sect. 5, 9, 10, "A Prayer to be said upon our Birth-day, or day of Baptism."—Ed.]

§ Italics again

‖ Italics again

MS: William Luther Lewis Collection, Mary Couts Burnett Library, Texas Christian University, Fort Worth, Texas. Pub.: Talfourd (1848), I, 91–92; Sala, I, 91–92; Purnell, I, 91–92; Fitzgerald, I, 376–377; Hazlitt, I, 175–176; Ainger (1888), I, 75–76; Ainger (1900), I, 108–109; Macdonald, I, 83–84; Ainger (1904), I, 77–78; Harper, II, 128–132; Lucas (1905), VI, 101–103; Lucas (1912), V, 100–102; Lucas (1935), 104–107. Address: S. T. Coleridge/Stowey/near Bridgewater/Somersetshire. Postmark: [April] 15 [1797].

1. The poem is in *Poems* (1797) and *Works,* V, 12–13.
2. *As You Like It,* II, i, 43.
3. John Fletcher, *The Faithful Shepherdess.*
4. *Godfrey of Bulloigne, or the Recoverie of Jerusalem, Done into English Heroicall Verse,* Edward Fairfax's translation of Tasso's *Gerusalemme Liberata.* See Letter 21, note 7.
5. Lamb, "To the Poet Cowper," line 2.

25. *C. L. to Coleridge*

Monday Night, June 13 [12], 1797

I stared with wild wonderment to see thy well-known hand again. It revived many a pleasing recollection of an epistolary intercourse, of late strangely suspended, once the pride of my life. Before I even opened thy letter, I figured to myself a sort of complacency which my little hoard at home would feel at receiving the new-comer into the little drawer where I keep my treasures of this kind. You have done well in writing to me. The little room (was it not a little one?) at the Salutation was already in the way of becoming a fading idea! it had begun to be classed in my memory with those 'wanderings with a fair hair'd maid,'[1] in the recollection of which I feel I have no property. You press me, very kindly do you press me, to come to Stowey; obstacles, strong as death, prevent me at present; maybe I shall be able to come before the year is out;[2] believe me, I will come as soon as I can, but I dread naming a probable time. It depends on fifty things, besides the expense, which is not nothing. Lloyd wants me to come and see him; but, besides that you have a prior claim on me, I should not feel myself so much at home with him, till he gets a house of his own. As to Richardson, caprice may grant what caprice only refused, and it is no more hardship, rightly considered, to be dependent on him for pleasure, than to lie at the mercy of the rain and sunshine for the enjoyment of a holiday: in either case we are not to look for a suspension of the laws of nature. 'Grill will be Grill.' Vide Spenser.[3]

I could not but smile at the compromise you make with me for printing Lloyd's poems first; but there is in nature, I fear, too many tendencies to envy and jealousy not to justify you in your apology. Yet, if any one is welcome to pre-eminence from me, it is Lloyd, for he would be the last to desire it. So pray, let his name *uniformly* precede mine, for it would be treating me like a child to suppose it could give me pain. Yet, alas! I am not insusceptible of the bad passions. Thank God, I have the ingenuousness to be ashamed of them. I am dearly fond of Charles Lloyd; he is all goodness, and I have too much of the world in my composition to feel myself thoroughly deserving of his friendship.

Lloyd tells me that Sheridan put you upon writing your tragedy.[4] I hope you are only Coleridgeizing when you talk of finishing it in a few days. Shakspeare was a more modest man; but you best know your own power.

Of my last poem you speak slightingly; surely the longer stanzas were pretty tolerable; at least there was one good line in it,

> Thick-shaded trees, with dark green leaf rich clad.[5]

To adopt your own expression, I call this a 'rich' line, a fine full line. And some others I thought even beautiful. Believe me, my little gentleman will feel some repugnance at riding behind in the basket;[6] though, I confess, in pretty good company. Your picture of idiocy, with the sugar-loaf head, is exquisite; but are you not too severe upon our more favoured brethren in fatuity? Lloyd tells me how ill your wife and child have been. I rejoice that they are better. My kindest remembrances and those of my sister. I send you a trifling letter; but you have only to think that I have been skimming the superficies of my mind, and found it only froth. Now, do write again; you cannot believe how I long and love always to hear about you.

Yours, most affectionately,
Charles Lamb

MS: unrecovered. Text: Lucas (1935), I, 107–109. Also pub.: Talfourd (1837), I, 78–81; Sala, I, 93–95; Purnell, I, 93–95; Fitzgerald, I, 378–380; Hazlitt, I, 177–179; Ainger (1888), I, 76–78; Ainger (1900), I, 109–111; Macdonald, I, 84–86; Ainger (1904), I, 78–79; Harper, II, 132–134; Lucas (1905), VI, 103–105; Lucas (1912), V, 103–104.

1. "Was it some sweet device of Faery," line 3.
2. He went in July. For Richardson, below, see Letter 5, note 8.
3. *The Faerie Queene,* II, xii, 782: "Let Gryll be Gryll, and have his hoggish minde." The next sentence refers to Coleridge's having written Cottle on March 10 to print Lamb's poems before Lloyd's in *Poems* (1797), but having directed Cottle on March 15, without explaining his change of mind, to reverse the order.
4. "Osorio. A Tragedy," which Coleridge had begun in March after hearing that Richard Brinsley Sheridan, who had a share in and had managed Drury Lane since 1776, wanted him to write a tragedy for it. Coleridge sent the manuscript to him on October 14 through William Linley (1771–1835), Sheridan's brother-in-law, who by December 2 had notified Coleridge of its rejection on the grounds of obscurity in its last three acts. Coleridge reworked it intermittently during the next thirteen years and saw it first performed, successfully, as *Remorse. A Tragedy, in Five Acts,* at Drury Lane on January 23, 1813. He published it with that title in the same year. Lamb wrote its Prologue, which is republished in *Works,* V, 125–126. *Osorio. A Tragedy. As Originally Written in 1797 . . .,* ed. Richard Herne Shepherd, was published in 1873.
5. An alteration of "A Vision of Repentance," line 5.
6. The Supplement to *Poems* (1797). Coleridge's picture of idiocy—

> Stood in the sun, rocking his sugar-loaf Head,
> And staring at a bough from Morn to Sunset
> *See-saw'd* his voice in inarticulate Noises

—which was apparently in the letter Lamb is answering and is in Coleridge's to Poole of October 5, 1801 (*Coleridge's Letters,* II, 764), reappears revised in *Remorse,* II, i, 187–191.

26. *C. L. to Coleridge*

Saturday, June 24, 1797

Did you seize the grand opportunity of seeing Kosciusko[1] while he was at Bristol? I never saw a hero; I wonder how they look. I have been reading a most curious romance-like work, called the 'Life of John Buncle, Esq.' 'Tis very interesting, and an extraordinary compound of all manner of subjects, from the depth of the ludicrous to the heights of sublime religious truth. There is much abstruse science in it above my cut and an infinite fund of pleasantry. John Buncle is a famous fine man, formed in nature's most eccentric hour. I am ashamed of what I write. But I have no topic to talk of. I see nobody, and sit, and read or walk, alone, and hear nothing. I am quite lost to conversation from disuse; and out of the sphere of my little family, who, I am thankful, are dearer and dearer to me every day, I see no face that brightens up at my approach. My friends are at a distance; worldly hopes are at a low ebb with me, and unworldly thoughts are not yet familiarised to me, though I occasionally indulge in them. Still I feel a calm not unlike content. I fear it is sometimes more akin to physical stupidity than to a heaven-flowing serenity and peace. What right have I to obtrude all this upon you? what is such a letter to you? and if I come to Stowey, what conversation can I furnish to compensate my friend for those stores of knowledge and of fancy, those delightful treasures of wisdom, which I know he will open to me? But it is better to give than to receive; and I was a very patient hearer and docile scholar in our winter evening meetings at Mr. May's;[2] was I not, Col.? What I have owed to thee, my heart can ne'er forget.

God love you and yours.

C. L.

MS: unrecovered. Text, headed without stated reason "(*Possibly only a fragment*)": Lucas (1935), I, 109–110. Also pub.: Talfourd (1837), I, 81–83; Sala, I, 95–96; Purnell, I, 95–96; Fitzgerald, I, 380–381; Hazlitt, I, 179–180; Ainger (1888), I, 78–79; Ainger (1900), I, 111–113; Macdonald, I, 86–87; Ainger (1904), I, 79; Harper, II, 134–136; Lucas (1905), VI, 106; Lucas (1912), V, 105–106.

1. The Polish soldier and statesman Tadeusz Andrzej Bonawentura Kosciuszko (1746–1817) during the Polish insurrection against final partition had been taken prisoner by the Russians on October 10, 1794, and released from confinement in St. Petersburg on December 19, 1796. He visited Bristol from June 13 to 19, 1797, while touring England (and America) before settling, in 1798, at Berville, near Paris. Coleridge was with the Wordsworths at Racedown Lodge at the time and seems not to have left them. Thomas Amory (1691?–1788), an eccentric writer of Irish descent who was acquainted with Swift, wrote *The Life of John Buncle, Esq.* (1756–1766), mentioned below, which Amory based in part on his own life.

2. At The Salutation and Cat. Lamb concludes his paragraph with Bowles's "Oxford Revisited," line 14.

27. *C. L. to Coleridge*

Thursday [June 29, 1797]

I discern a possibility of my paying you a visit **next week.** May I, can I, shall I come so soon? Have you *room* for me, *leisure* for me, & are you all pretty well? Tell me all this honestly—immediately.

And by what ***day*** coach could I come soonest, & nearest to Stowey?

A few months hence may suit you better: certainly me as well . . If so, say so.

I long, I yearn, with all the longings of a child do I desire to see you, to come among you—to see the young philosopher to thank Sara for her last year's invitation in person—to read your tragedy—to read over together our little book—to breathe fresh air—to revive in me vivid images of "Salutation scenery."[1] There is a sort of sacrilege in my letting such ideas slip out of my mind & memory— —

Still, that Richardson remaineth—a thorn in the Side of Hope, when she would lean towards Stowey—

Here I will leave off, for I dislike to fill up this paper, which involves a question so connected with my heart & soul, with meaner matter, or subjects to me less interesting. I can talk as I can think nothing else

Ch. Lamb

Thursday the 29th Inst

MS: Huntington Library. Pub.: Talfourd (1848), I, 93–94; Sala, I, 92–93; Purnell, I, 92–93; Fitzgerald, I, 377–378; Hazlitt, I, 177; Ainger (1888), I, 76; Ainger (1900), I, 113; Macdonald, I, 87; Ainger (1904), I, 80–81; Harper, II, 136–137; Lucas (1905), VI, 107; Lucas (1912), V, 106–107; Lucas (1935), I, 111. Address: S. T. Coleridge/Stowey/near Bridgewater/Somerset. Postmark: June 29 [1797]. This letter, like Letter 26, Lucas headed "(*Possibly only a fragment*)," but it is not.

1. Conjecturally, a phrase from Coleridge's letter.

PART II

Letters 28–68

45 and 36 Chapel Street, Pentonville

July 19 or 26, 1797—May 17, 1800

28. *C. L. to Coleridge*

Wednesday Evening
[July 19 or 26, 1797]

I am scarcely yet so reconciled to the loss of you, or so subsided into my wonted uniformity of feeling, as to sit calmly down to think of you and write to you. But I reason myself into the belief that those few and pleasant holidays shall not have been spent in vain. I feel improvement in the recollection of many a casual conversation. The names of Tom Poole, of Wordsworth and his good sister, with thine and Sara's, are become 'familiar in my mouth as household words.'[1] You would make me very happy, if you think W. has no objection, by transcribing for me that inscription of his. I have some scattered sentences ever floating on my memory, teasing me that I cannot remember more of it. You may believe I will make no improper use of it. Believe me I can think now of many subjects on which I had planned gaining information from you; but I forgot my 'treasure's worth'[2] while I possessed it. Your leg is now become to me a matter of much more importance—and many a little thing, which when I was present with you seemed scarce to *indent* my notice, now presses painfully on my remembrance. Is the Patriot come yet? Are Wordsworth and his sister gone yet? I was looking out for John Thelwall all the way from Bridgewater, and had I met him, I think it would have moved almost me to tears. You will oblige me too by sending me my great-coat, which I left behind in the oblivious state the mind is thrown into at parting—is it not ridiculous that I sometimes envy that great-coat lingering so cunningly behind?—at present I have none—so send it me by a Stowey waggon, if there be such a thing, directing for C. L., No. 45, Chapel-Street, Pentonville, near London. But above all, *that Inscription!*—it will recall to me the tones of all your voices—and with them many a remembered kindness to one who could and can repay you all only by the silence of a grateful heart. I could not talk much, while I was with you, but my silence was not sullenness, nor I hope from any bad motive; but, in truth, disuse has made me awkward at it. I know I behaved myself, particularly at Tom Poole's and at Cruikshank's,[3] most like a sulky child; but company and converse are strange to me. It was kind in you all to endure me as you did.

Are you and your dear Sara—to me also very dear, because very kind—agreed yet about the management of little Hartley? and how go on the little rogue's teeth? I will see White to-morrow, and he shall send you information on that matter;[4] but as perhaps I can do it as well after talking with him, I will keep this letter open.

My love and thanks to you and all of you.

C. L.

MS: unrecovered. Text: Lucas (1935), I, 111–112. Also pub.: Talfourd (1837), I, 140–142; Sala, I, 106–108; Purnell, I, 106–108; Fitzgerald, I, 388–390; Hazlitt, I, 238–239; Ainger (1888), I, 79–80; Ainger (1900), I, 114–115; Macdonald, I, 88–89; Ainger (1904), I, 81–82; Harper, II, 137–139; Lucas (1905), VI, 108–109; Lucas (1912), V, 107–108. If the date ca. July 17 is correct for the letter to Southey in which Coleridge remarked, "Charles Lamb has been with me for a week—he left me Friday morning" (*Coleridge's Letters,* I, 334), then Lamb must have visited Nether Stowey from July 7 to 14, written this letter on one of the two dates assigned to it, and moved to his new address between July 14 and 26.

1. *Henry V,* IV, iii, 52. Wordsworth's "inscription," mentioned below, may be "Lines Left upon a Seat in a Yew-tree."

2. Cowper, *The Task,* VI, 50. In his next sentence Lamb refers to Mrs. Coleridge's having spilled a pan of boiling milk on her husband's foot on June 30. During his confinement, which extended through Lamb's visit, Coleridge wrote and addressed to Lamb "This Lime-tree Bower My Prison." The "Patriot" is John Thelwall, who arrived on July 17. Coleridge had brought the Wordsworths back on June 28 from Racedown Lodge and installed them, probably on the day Lamb left (see *Wordsworths' Letters,* I, 190), in Alfoxden House, three miles west of Nether Stowey.

3. John Cruikshank, or Cruickshank (bapt. 1773), a son of William (d. 1802) of Enmore, Bridgwater. Cruikshank entered the Middle Temple in 1793, was married to Anna Buclé, or Budé, in 1795, and settled at Nether Stowey. There he probably assisted his father in managing the estates of John Perceval, third Earl of Egmont (1738–1822). Cruikshank's dream, in 1797, of a skeleton ship became one of the motifs in "The Rime of the Ancient Mariner." See Letter 19, note 9, and *Wordsworths' Letters,* I, 211.

4. Unidentified.

29. *C. L. to Coleridge*

[Thursday, August 24, 1797]

Poor Charles Lloyd came to me about a fortnight ago. He took the opportunity of Mr Hawkes[1] coming to London, & I think at his request, to come with him—. It seemed to me, & he acknowledged it, that he had come to gain a little time & a little peace, before he made up his mind. He was a good deal perplexed what to do—wishing earnestly that he had never entered into engagements which he felt himself unable to fulfill, but which on Sophia's account he could not bring himself to relinquish— — —. I could give him little advice or comfort, & feeling my own inability painfully, eagerly snatched at a proposal he made me to go to Southey's with him for a day or two. He then meant to return with me, who could stay only one night. While there, he at one time thought of going to consult you, but changed his intention & stayed behind with Southey, & wrote an explicit letter to Sophia. I came away on the Tuesday, & on the Saturday following, *last Saturday,* receiv'd a letter dated Bath, in which he said he was on his way to Birmingham. That Southey was accompanying him,—& that he went for the purpose of persuading Sophia to a Scotch marriage— — —

I greatly feared, that she would never consent to this, from what Lloyd had told me of her character. But waited most anxiously the result. Since then I have had not one letter—. For God's sake, if you get any intelligence of or from Chas Lloyd, communicate it, for I am much alarmed—

C Lamb

I wrote to Burnett[2] what I write now to you,—was it from him you heard or elsewhere?— — —

He[3] said if he *had* come to you, he could never have brought himself to leave you. In all his distress he was sweetly & exemplarily calm and master of himself,—& seemed perfectly free from his disorder———

How do you all do?

MS: Mr. W. Hugh Peal, Leesburg, Va. Pub.: Harper, II, 140–141; Lucas (1905), VI, 110–111; Lucas (1912), V, 109–110; Lucas (1935), I, 113–114. Address: S. T. Coleridge/Stowey/near Bridgewater/Somerset. Postmark: August 24, 1797.

1. Thomas Hawkes of Moseley, near Birmingham, a friend of Lloyd and Coleridge who, according to an unpublished note of Mrs. Coleridge (see *Coleridge's Letters,* I, 235), first brought the two men together in 1796. Lloyd was trying to make up his mind about becoming married to Sophia Pemberton. De Quincey, who was at this time with the Southeys at Burton, Hampshire, wrote in his *Autobiography* (*De Quincey's Writings,* II, 389) that Southey had agreed to help with an elopement, since the parents of Miss Pemberton objected to the match. But she would consent neither to that nor apparently to a Scotch marriage, mentioned below, one simply by mutual declaration before witnesses. Lamb was at Burton on August 14 and 15.

2. The miscellaneous writer George Burnett (1776–1811). He was the son of a farmer at Huntspill, Somersetshire, studied the classics as a boy under a neighboring clergyman, and in 1793 was matriculated at Balliol College, Oxford, intending to prepare for the church. There he met Southey and Coleridge, became a pantisocrat, and had his religious beliefs undermined. He left Oxford in 1795 or 1796, entered the dissenting college at Manchester, and left it to become a student of medicine at the University of Edinburgh. In 1798 he became a Unitarian minister at Yarmouth, Norfolk, where he tutored Southey's younger brother Henry Herbert (1783–1865), later a successful London physician. In 1801 Burnett worked as a clerk for the statistician John Rickman (see Letter 86, note 4), helping to compute the first census returns for Great Britain. In 1802 Burnett succeeded George Dyer as a conversationalist and tutor in the family of Lord Stanhope. During that period Burnett was also employed by Richard, later Sir Richard, Phillips (1767–1840), an author, a publisher of schoolbooks, and the founder, in 1792, of the Leicester *Herald* and, in 1796, of the *Monthly Magazine.* Phillips employed him as a contributor to *Universal History, Ancient and Modern; from the Earliest Periods to the General Peace of 1801* (25 vols.; 1802–1804), which William Fordyce Mavor (1758–1837) was preparing. Burnett soon decided to become a naval surgeon, gained some gratuitous hospital experience through the influence of Southey and Rickman, but transferred his interest to the army and in 1803 joined a militia regiment as an assistant surgeon. In less than a year he left the army and went to Poland as a tutor to the children of a Count Zamoyska, or Zamovski. Burnett returned to London in 1805. He settled for a time into steady literary work and in 1807 published *View of the Present State of Poland* (a series of letters he had written for the *Monthly Magazine*) and *Specimens of English Prose-writers, from the Earliest Times to the Close of the Seventeenth Century, with Sketches Biographical and Literary.* He published a two-volume edition of Milton's prose works in 1809. In 1810 he applied for but failed to obtain an assistant librarianship at the London Institution. In early March 1811 he died in Marylebone, "wretchedly in a workhouse" (*H. C. R. on Books and Writers,* I, 24). The best account of him is Orlo Williams' "A Study in Failure," *Blackwood's Edinburgh Magazine,* 189 (1911), 324–333. Lamb's letter to him has not been recovered.

3. Lloyd.

30. *C. L. to Coleridge*

[Wednesday, September ?20, 1797]

Written a twelvemonth after the Events.*

Alas! how am I chang'd! where be the tears,
The sobs, and forc'd suspensions of the breath,
And all the dull desertions of the heart,
With which I hung o'er my dear mother's corse?
Where be the blest subsidings of the storm
Within, the sweet resignedness of hope
Drawn heavenward, and strength of filial love,

In which I bow'd me to my Father's will?
My God, and my Redeemer, keep not thou
My heart in brute & sensual thanklessness
Seal'd up, oblivious ever of that dear grace,
And health restor'd to my long-loved Friend,[1]
Long lov'd & worthy known. Thou didst not keep
Her soul in death. O keep not now, my Lord,
Thy servants in far worse, in spiritual death,
And darkness blacker than those feared shadows
O' the Valley, all must tread. Lend us thy balms,
Thou dear Physician of the sin sick soul,
And heal our cleansed bosoms of the wounds,
With which the world hath pierc'd us thro' & thro'!
Give us new flesh, new birth. Elect of Heaven
May we become, in thine Election sure
Contain'd, & to one purpose stedfast drawn,
Our Souls' Salvation—.

Thou and I, dear friend,[†]
With filial recognition sweet, shall know
One day the face of our dear mother in heaven,
And her remember'd looks of love shall greet
With answering looks of love, her placid smiles
Meet with a smile as placid, and her hand
With drops of fondness wet, nor **fear repulse.—**

Be witness for me, **Lord,** I do not ask
Those days of vanity to return again,
(Nor fitting me to ask, nor thee to give)
Vain loves, & "wandrings with a fair haird maid,"[2]
(Child of the dust, as I am) who so long
My foolish heart steep'd in Idolatry
And creature-loves.— Forgive it, Oh my **Maker,**
If, in a mood of grief, I sin almost
In sometimes brooding on the days of long past,
(And from the grave of time wishing them back)
Days of a mother's fondness t[o] her child,
Her little one—. Oh where be now those sports,
And infant playgames? Where the joyous troops

of children, and the haunts I did so love?
O my companions,‡ O ye loved names
of friend, or playmate dear, gone are ye now,
Gone divers ways; to honor & credit some,
And some, I fear, to ignominy & shame.
I only am left, with unavailing grief
One Parent dead to mourn, & see one live
of all life's joys bereft, & desolate:———
Am left, with a few friends, & one[3] above
The rest, found faithful in a length of years,
Contented as I may, to bear me on
T' the not unpeaceful Evening of a Day
Made black by morning storms.———

The following[4] I wrote when I had returned from C Lloyd leaving him behind at Burton with Southey—— — ———

To understand some of it, you must remember that at that time he was very much perplexed in Mind—

A stranger and alone I past those scenes
We past so late together; & my heart
Felt something like desertion, as I look'd
Around me, & the pleasant voice of friend
Was absent, & the cordial look was there
No more, to smile on me. I thought on Lloyd,
All he had been to me! And now I go
Again to mingle with a world impure,
With men who make a mock of holy things,
Mistaken, & of man's best hope think scorn.—
The World does much to warp the heart of Man,
And I may sometimes join its ideot laugh———
Of this I now complain not.— Deal with me,
Omniscient father, as thou judgest best;
And in *thy* season tender§ thou my heart——
I pray not for myself. I pray for him
Whose sole is sore perplex'd. Shine thou on him,
Father of lights, & in the difficult paths
Make plain his way before him: his own thoughts
May he not think, his own ends not pursue;

So shall he best perform thy will on earth.
Greatest & Best, thy will be **ever ours!**

The former of these Poems I wrote with unusual celerity tother morning at office—. I expect you to like it better than any thing of mine. Lloyd does, & I do myself—— —— ———

You use Lloyd very ill—never writing to him.[5] I tell you again that his is not a mind with which you should play tricks. He dese[r]ves more tenderness from you———

For myself, I must spoil a little passage of Beaumont & Fletcher to adapt it to my feelings—

I am Prouder
That I was once your friend, tho' now forgot,
Than to have had another true to me———[6]

If you dont write to me now,—as I told Lloyd, I shall get angry, & call you hard names, Manchineel, & I dont know what else— —. I wish you would send me my Great coat—the snow & the rain season is at hand & I have but a wretched old coat, once my fathers, to keep 'em off— —& that is transitory— —

When time drives flocks from field to fold,[7]
When ways grow foul and blood gets cold—

I shall remember where I left my coat—meek Emblem wilt thou be, old Winter, of a friend's neglect—Cold, cold, cold,———

C L

Remembrances where remembrance is due—.

*Friday next, Coleridge, is the day on which my mother died—

†this is almost literal—f[rom a] letter of my sister's,— —less than a year ago——— [Lamb refers to the entire stanza.—Ed.]

‡alluding to some of my old play **fellows** being literally **on the town!**—and some otherwise wretched—

§soften

MS: Huntington Library. Pub.: Talfourd (1848), I, 95–98; Sala, I, 97–100; Purnell, I, 97–100; Fitzgerald, I, 382–383; Hazlitt, I, 181–183; Ainger (1888), I, 81–83; Ainger (1900), I, 116–119; Macdonald, I, 89–92; Ainger (1904), I, 83–85; Harper, I, facsimile, and II, 141–144; Lucas (1905), VI, 111–113; Lucas (1912), V, 110–112; Lucas (1935), I, 115–117. Address: S. T. Coleridge/Stowey near Bridgewater/Somerset. Postmark: [September] 1797. The date is estimated from Lamb's first gloss. The first poem is in *Works,* V, 20–22.

1. Mary.

2. "Was it some sweet device of Faery," line 3. Cf. this stanza with the central section of the last paragraph of Letter 13.

3. Possibly Coleridge, as Lucas suggested (*Works,* V, 293), but the structure of the poem suggests Mary.

4. Titled "To a Friend" in the *Monthly Magazine,* 4 (October 1797), 288, and "To Charles Lloyd" in *Blank Verse* (see Letter 10, note 4) and *Works,* V, 19.

5. Coleridge had sent Lloyd a letter (which is unrecovered), probably in July, enclosing a copy of "This Lime-tree Bower My Prison." See *The Poetical Works of Samuel Taylor Coleridge,* ed. James Dykes Campbell (London: Macmillan, 1893), p. 591.

6. *The Maid's Tragedy,* II, i, 124–126. The passage is included, uncorrupted, in *Specimens of English Dramatic Poets* (*Works,* IV, 284). Coleridge used "Manchineel," below, in the dedicatory poem of *Poems* (1797), "To the Rev. George Coleridge of Ottery St. Mary, Devon. *With Some Poems,*" line 26.

7. Sir Walter Ralegh, "The Nymph's Reply to the Shepherd," line 5. The next line is an adaptation of *Love's Labour's Lost,* V, ii, 916.

31. *C. L. to Marmaduke Thompson*

[January 1798]

I spent an evening about a week ago with Lloyd. White, and a miscellaneous company was there. Lloyd had been playing on a pianoforte till my feelings were wrought too high not to require Vent. I left em suddenly & rushed into ye Temple, where I was born, you know—& in ye state of mind that followed [I composed these] stanzas. They pretend to little like Metre, but they will pourtray ye Disorder I was in.[1]

[The Old Familiar Faces

Where are they gone, the old familiar faces?

I had a mother, but she died, and left me,
Died prematurely in a day of horrors—
All, all are gone, the old familiar faces.

I have had playmates, I have had companions,
In my days of childhood, in my joyful school-days—
All, all are gone, the old familiar faces.

I have been laughing, I have been carousing,
Drinking late, sitting late, with my bosom cronies—
All, all are gone, the old familiar faces.

I loved a love once, fairest among women.
Closed are her doors on me, I must not see her—
All, all are gone, the old familiar faces.

I have a friend, a kinder friend has no man.
Like an ingrate, I left my friend abruptly;
Left him, to muse on the old familiar faces.

Ghost-like, I paced round the haunts of my childhood.
Earth seem'd a desert I was bound to traverse,
Seeking to find the old familiar faces.

Friend of my bosom, thou more than a brother!
Why wert not thou born in my father's dwelling?
So might we talk of the old familiar faces.

For some they have died, and some they have left me,
And some are taken from me; all are departed;
All, all are gone, the old familiar faces.

January, 1798.]

MS: unrecovered. Text, of Lamb's introductory remarks: Lucas (1935), I, 121; of the poem: Lucas (1905), VI, 116–117. This letter is my reconstruction of the one Lamb had evidently sent to Thompson. (See the Introduction, p. xxxii.) According to Lucas (1935), I, 121, Thompson transcribed its prose portion opposite the poem (republished revised in *Works,* V, 23–24) in the copy of Lloyd and Lamb's *Blank Verse* that Lamb had presented to him.

1. The principal cause of the disorder, one gathers from "Written on Christmas Day, 1797" (*Works,* V, 22–23), was probably the relapse that Mary had suffered, necessitating her return from lodgings at Hackney to stricter confinement. A secondary cause may have been the increasing deterioration of their father. The allusions in lines 11, 14, 20, and 24 of the poem are probably to Ann Simmons, Lloyd, Coleridge, and especially Mary.

32. *C. L. to Coleridge*

[January 28, 1798]

You have writ me Many kind letters, and I have answered none of them—. I do'nt deserve your attentions—an unnatural indifference has been creeping on me, since my last misfortunes, or I should have seized the first opening of a correspondence with *you*—to you I owe much, under God—in my brief acquaintance with you in London your conversations won me to the better cause, and rescued me from the polluting spirit of the world—. I might have been a worthless character without you—as it is, I do possess a certain improveable portion of devotional feelings—tho' when I view myself in the light of divine truth, and not according to the common measures of human judgment, I am altogether corrupt & sinful—this is no cant—I am very sincere— — — —

These last afflictions, Coleridge, have failed to soften and bend my will—they found me unprepared—my former calamities produced in me a spirit of humility, and a spirit of prayer—. I thought, they had sufficiently disciplined me—but the event ought to humble me—if God's judgments now fail to take away from me the heart of stone, what more grievous trials ought I not to expect!— —. I have been very querulous—impatient under the rod—full of little jealousies & heart-burnings— —. I had well nigh quarrelled with Charles Lloyd—& for no other reason, I believe, than that the good creature did all he could to make me happy— —. the truth is, I thought he tried to force my mind from its natural & proper bent, he continually wished me to be from home, he was drawing me *from* the consideration of my poor dear Mary's situation, rather than assisting me to gain a proper view of it, with religious consolations—. I wanted to be left to the tendency of my own mind in a solitary state, which in times past, I knew, had led to quietness & a patient bearing of the yoke—he was hurt, that I was not more constantly with him—but he was living with **White**, a man to whom I had never been accustomed to impart my ***dearest feelings*—**tho' from long habits of friendliness, & many a social & good quality, I loved him very much—. I met company there sometimes— ——indiscriminate company, any society almost, when I am in affliction, is sorely painful to me—. I seem to breathe more freely, to thin[k] more collectedly, to feel more properly & calmly, when alone—all these things the good creature did with the kindest intentions in the world—but they produced in me nothing but soreness and discontent—. I became, as he complained, "jaundiced" towards him—. . but he has forgiven me—and his smile, I hope, will draw all such humours from me—. I am recovering, God be praised for it, a healthiness of mind—something like calmness—but I want more religion—. I am jealous of human helps & leaning-places.

I rejoyce in your good fortunes— —may God at the last **settle** you—you have had many & painful trials— — —humanly speaking, they are going to end—.— —but we should rather pray, that disclipline may attend us thro' the whole of our lives . . . . . a careless and a dissolute spirit has advanced upon *me* with large strides—pray God, that my present afflictions may be sanctified to me—. Mary is recovering . . . . but I see no opening yet of a situation for her—your invitation went to my very heart—but you have a power of exciting interest, [o]f leading all hearts captive,[1] too forcible [to] admit of Mary's being with you—. I consider her as perpetually on the brink of madness—. I think, you would almost make her dance within an inch of the precipice—she must be with duller fancies, & cooler intellects . . . . I know a young man of this description, who has suited her these twenty years, & may live to do so still—if we are one day restor'd to each other—. In answer to your suggestions of occupation for me, I must say that I do not think my capacity altogether suited for disquitions of that kind . . . . I have read little, I have a very weak memory & retain little of what I read, am unused to compositions in which any methodizing is required— ———but I thank you sincerely for the hint, and shall receive it as far as I am able—that is, endeavor to engage my mind in some constant & innocent pursuit— — — ——. I know my capacities better than you do———

Accept my kindest love———& believe me

Yours as ever
C L

MS: Huntington Library. Pub.: Talfourd (1848), I, 103–106; Sala, I, 103–106; Purnell, I, 103–106; Fitzgerald, I, 385–388; Hazlitt, I, 185–186; Ainger (1888), I, 85–87; Ainger (1900), I, 119–122; Macdonald, I, 92–95; Ainger (1904), I, 85–87; Harper, II, 144–148; Lucas (1905), VI, 114–116; Lucas (1912), V, 113–115; Lucas (1935), I, 118–120. Address: S. T. Coleridge/at the Reverend Mr. Rowe's/Shrewsbury/Shropshire. Postmark: January 28, 1798. Coleridge was in Shrewsbury as a result of an invitation he had received in December from its Unitarian congregation to take the place of its minister, John Rowe, who was resigning to join John Prior Estlin in Bristol. At about the same time, Coleridge received a letter from Josiah (1769–1843) and Thomas (1771–1805) Wedgwood, sons of the potter Josiah (1730–1795), containing a draft for £100 to free him from the need of such engagements. Coleridge first accepted but then refused the draft and on January 13 arrived in Shrewsbury ready to serve the congregation. On the sixteenth he received an offer from the Wedgwoods of a lifetime annuity of £150. That he did accept, left town on the thirtieth, and was home on February 9.

1. Cf. *Paradise Regained,* II, 221–222.

33. *C. L. to Coleridge*

[The Lloyds', Birmingham
Ca. May 23—June 6,]1798

Theses Quædam Theologicæ.

1. Whether God loves a lying Angel better than a true Man?

2. Whether the Archangel Uriel *could* affirm an untruth? & if he *could* whether he *would*?

3. Whether Honesty be an angelic virtue? or not rather to be reckoned among those qualities which the Schoolmen term *Virtutes minus splendidæ, et terræ et hominis participes?*[1]

4. Whether the higher order of Seraphim Illuminati ever sneer?

5. Whether pure Intelligences can love?

6. Whether the Seraphim Ardentes do not manifest their virtues by the way of vision & theory? & whether practice be not a sub-celestial & merely human virtue?

7. Whether the Vision Beatific be anything more or less than a perpetual representment to each individual Angel of his own present attainments & future capabilities, somehow in the manner of mortal looking-glasses, reflecting a perpetual complacency & self-satisfaction?

8 & last. Whether an immortal & amenable soul may not come to be damned at last, & the man never suspect it beforehand?

Learned Sir, my Friend,

Presuming on our long habits of friendship, & emboldened further by your late liberal permission to avail myself of your correspondence, in case I want any knowledge, (which I intend to do when I have no Encyclopædia, or Lady's Magazine at hand to refer to in any matter of science,) I now submit to your enquiries the above Theological Propositions, to be by you defended, or oppugned, or both, in the Schools of Germany, whither I am told you are departing, to the utter dissatisfaction of your native Devonshire, & regret of universal England; but to my own individual consolation, if thro the channel of your wished return, Learned Sir, my Friend, may be transmitted to this our Island, from those famous Theological Wits of Leipsic &

Gottingen, any rays of illumination, in vain to be derived from the home growth of our English Halls and Colleges. Finally, wishing Learned Sir, that you may see Schiller, & swing in a wood[2] (*vide* Poems), & sit upon a Tun, & eat fat hams of Westphalia,

I remain
Your friend and docile Pupil to instruct
Charles Lamb

To S. T. Coleridge

MS: Buffalo and Erie County Public Library, Buffalo, N.Y. Pub.: Sala, I, 108–109; Purnell, I, 108–109; Fitzgerald, I, 390–391; Hazlitt, I, 190–191; Macdonald, I, 95–96; Ainger (1904), I, 380; Harper, II, 148–150; Lucas (1905), VI, 117–118; Lucas (1912), V, 116–117; Lucas (1935), I, 123–124. The place and approximate date of composition of this letter are with reasonable certainty established by Lloyd's statement in a letter to Cottle dated June 7 from Birmingham—"Lamb quitted me yesterday, after a fortnight's visit"—and Coleridge's statement on presenting this letter of Lamb's to Cottle—"These young visionaries will do each other no good" (Joseph Cottle, *Early Recollections, Chiefly Relating to the Late Samuel Taylor Coleridge, during His Long Residence in Bristol* [London: Longman, Rees and Co. and Hamilton Adams and Co., 1837], I, 304 and 301). Between Letter 32 and this letter passed letters between Lamb and Coleridge that would, were they extant, probably tell more than can now be told of Coleridge's troubles with Lloyd and Southey that led to the one interruption in the lifelong friendship of Coleridge and Lamb. The estrangement may have begun when Lloyd took his problems with Sophia Pemberton to Lamb and Southey rather than to Coleridge. Coleridge did not help matters when, possibly from a feeling of being slighted, he published "Sonnets Attempted in the Manner of Contemporary Writers." (See Letter 10, note 4.) Its effect, whatever its cause, moved Southey to charge Coleridge with ridiculing him in the sonnet "To Simplicity" and drove Lloyd to request Coleridge, through Cottle, not to include his poems in a contemplated but never prepared second edition of *Poems* (1797). Coleridge may have felt slighted again because Lamb and Lloyd had been working independently of him, not only on *Rosamund Gray* and *Edmund Oliver* but also together on *Blank Verse*. Furthermore, *Edmund Oliver* (see again Letter 10, note 4), when Cottle brought it out in April 1798, understandably offended Coleridge. Finally, Lloyd passed on to Lamb, Southey, and Dorothy Wordsworth Coleridge's confidential comments about them. Lloyd was a "sad Tattler" who came close to alienating Coleridge from Lamb or Lamb from Coleridge. Lamb came to realize that and expressed himself so in a letter to Coleridge of January 10, 1820. But at this time Lamb sided with Lloyd. After Lloyd informed Coleridge, through Dorothy Wordsworth, of Lamb's sympathies and that Lamb no longer intended to write to Coleridge, Coleridge in early May wrote to Lamb (see *Coleridge's Letters,* I, 403–405) blaming Lamb's misplaced allegiance on Lamb's lack of wisdom and on Lloyd's diabolical mind. When Lamb read the censure and heard, presumably from Lloyd, of Coleridge's further remark—"poor Lamb . . . if he wants any *knowledge,* he may apply to me" (quoted in Letter 34)—Lamb responded (perhaps, as is conjectured in Lucas [1935], I, 124, having Aquinas' *Summa theologiae* and Pope and John Arbuthnot's *Memoirs of Martinus Scriblerus* in mind) with this letter containing the "Certain Theological Propositions." Lamb suspended his correspondence with Coleridge for almost two years. The affair may have quickened in Coleridge the desire to leave England for the

intellectual climate of Germany. He persuaded the Wordsworths to accompany him, and they and his friend John Chester of Nether Stowey, who wished to go along to study German agriculture, sailed from Yarmouth on September 16, 1798.

1. "Capacities less brilliant and sharing in earth and man."

2. Coleridge, "To the Author of 'The Robbers,'" line 12.

34. *C. L. to Robert Southey*

Saturday 28 July 98

I am ashamed that I have not thanked you before this for the Joan of Arc,[1] but I did not know your address, and it did not occur to me to write thro' Cottle. The poem delighted me, and the notes amused me, but methinks she of Neufchatel, in the print, holds her sword too "like a **Dancer.**" I sent your *notice* to Phillips, particularly requesting an immediate insertion, but I suppose it came too late. I am sometimes curious to know what progress you make in that same Calendar,[2] whether you insert the nine worthies and Whittington, what you do or how you can manage when two **saints** meet & quarrel for precedency; Martlemas & Candlemas & Christmas are glorious themes for a writer, like you, Antiquity-bitten, smit with the Love of Boar's heads[3] & rosemary, but how you can ennoble the 1st of April I know not,—by the way, I had a thing to say, but a certain false modesty has hitherto prevented me, perhaps I can best communicate my wish by a hint,—my birthday is on the 10th of February, new Stile, but if it interferes with any remarkable Event, why, rather than my country should lose her fame, I care not if I put my nativity back eleven days—.[4] Fine family patronage for your Calendar, if that old Lady of prolific memory were living, who lies (or lyes) in some church in London, (saints forgive me, but I have forgot *what* church) attesting that enormous legend of as many children as days in the year; I marvel her impudence did not grasp at a Leap year. 365 dedications, and all in a family—you might spit, in spirit, on the oneness of Mecœnas[5] patronage. . . . . .—. . . . .———

Samuel Taylor Coleridge, to the eternal regret of his native Devonshire, emigrates to Westphalia—"poor Lamb" (these were his last words) "if he wants any *knowledge,* he may apply to me"— —in ordinary cases, I thank'd him, I have an Encyclopædia at hand, but on such an occasion as going over to a German University, I could not refrain from sending him the following propositions, to be by him defended or oppugn'd (or both) at Leipsic or Goetingen. . . . .— — — — — — ———

Theses quædam Theologicæ—

1

Whether God loves a lying angel better than a true man?———

2

Whether the arch angel **Uriel** *could* knowingly affirm an untruth, and whether, if he *could,* he *would*?

3

Whether honesty be an angelic virtue, or not rather belonging to that class of qualities, which the schoolmen term "virtutes minus splendidæ, et hominis & terræ nimis participes"?———[6]

4

Whether the Seraphim ardentes do not manifest their goodness by the way of vision & theory? & whether **practice** be not a sub-celestial & merely human virtue?

5

Whether the higher order of Seraphim Illuminati ever ***sneer?***

6

Whether pure Intelligencies can ***love;*** or whether they can love anything besides pure Intellect?

7

Whether the Beatific Vision be any thing more or less, than a perpetual representment to each individual Angel of his own present attainments, and future capabilities, something in the manner of mortal lookinglasses?

8

Whether an **"immortal & amenable Soul"** may not come to be damn'd at last, & the man never suspect it beforehand?

Samuel Taylor hath not deign'd an answer—was it impertinent in me to avail myself of that offer'd source of knowledge? . . .

Lloyd is return'd to town from Ipswich, where he has been with his Brother—.[7] he has brought home 3 acts of a play, which I have not yet seen— —the scene for the most part laid in a Brothel, O tempora O mores!— but as friend Coleridge said, when he was talking bawdy to Miss . . . . , "to the **Pure** all things are pure"— ———

Wishing Madoc may be born into the world with as splendid promise as the second birth, or purification, of the Maid of Neufchatel,— — —I remain

yours sincerely—
C Lamb

I hope Edith[8] is better, my kindest remembrancs to her. . . . . — —. . . .

You have a good deal of trifling to forgive in this Letter

Love and respects to Co[ttle]—

MS: The Pierpont Morgan Library, New York. Pub.: Talfourd (1837), I, 95–98; Sala, I, 172–175; Purnell, I, 172–175; Fitzgerald, II, 26–28; Hazlitt, I, 192–194; Ainger (1888), I, 87–89; Ainger (1900), I, 122–126; Macdonald, I, 98–100; Ainger (1904), I, 87–90; Harper, II, 154–157; Lucas (1905), VI, 121–123; Lucas (1912), V, 120–122; Lucas (1935), I, 125–127. Address: Mr. Cottle/Bookseller/High Street/Bristol/for Robert Southey. Southey had been living since June at Westbury, two miles outside Bristol.

1. A second edition of *Joan of Arc,* which Cottle had published this year. The print, referred to below, Southey apparently sent separately, for the 1798 edition of the poem is not illustrated. The quotation is from *Antony and Cleopatra,* III, xi, 36. Phillips is Richard Phillips of the *Monthly Magazine.* See Letter 29, note 2.

2. "Poetical Almanac" was Southey's original title for what became *The Annual Anthology* (2 vols.; 1799–1800). The Nine Worthies are the Jews Joshua, David, and Judas Maccabaeus; the Gentiles Hector, Alexander, and Julius Caesar; and the Christians Arthur, Charlemagne, and Godfrey of Bouillon. Whittington is presumably Richard Whittington (d. 1423), the lord mayor of London celebrated for his cat. None of those figures appears in *The Annual Anthology.*

3. Perhaps old England generally, as evoked through Shakespeare's and Falstaff's tavern. The rosemary is the shrub of remembrance and evocative of *Hamlet,* IV, v, 175–176.

4. The difference between the Gregorian, or New Style, and the Julian, or Old Style, calendars. The legend to which the old lady of prolific memory, referred to following, could have attested is that of a beggar woman with twin children who asked the childless Margaret, Countess of Henneberg and wife of Hermann II of Henneberg, for alms. When questioned about her children, the beggar woman told her that they were legitimate and born at one birth. The countess refused to

believe her and drove her away. The beggar woman cursed the countess and implored God to cause her to bear at one birth as many children as there are days in the year. On Good Friday, March 26, 1277, the countess gave birth to 365 children. The boys were called John, and the girls Elizabeth. They were baptized by Guido, bishop of Utrecht, and died with their mother on the day of their birth. At Loosduinen, near The Hague, is a church monument commemorating the legend. Called the "Monument of the Woman," it portrays an earl, a lady, and her many children. In the church are the basins in which the children were baptized and a tomb on which the legend is inscribed. Not known is why the legend is connected with the historical Margaret, who died in fact on Good Friday 1277. The story is retold by John Evelyn in his *Diary* (see the edition of E. S. de Beer [Oxford: Clarendon Press, 1955], II, 55–56) and by James Howell (1594?–1666), an intimate of Ben Jonson, in *Epistolæ Ho-Elianæ or the Familiar Letters of James Howell* (1655), Sect. II, Letter 13 (April 10, 1623).

5. Gaius Cilnius Maecenas (ca. 74–8 B.C.), Roman statesman and friend and patron of Virgil and Horace, among others.

6. "Capacities less brilliant and sharing *too much* [my italics] in man and earth." (Cf. the similar passage in the third proposition in the preceding letter.) The quotation in the eighth proposition, below, is from the eighth proposition in the preceding letter, but now emphasized.

7. Robert (1778–1811), the third of the Lloyd brothers. From 1794 or 1795 to 1798 he was an apprentice in the drapery establishment of Day and Green in Saffron Walden, Essex. In 1799 he became a partner, through the generosity of his father, in the Birmingham bookselling firm that thereafter was known as Knott and Lloyd. In 1804 he was married to Hannah Hart, a Quakeress, a daughter of Francis, a Nottingham banker. Lamb wrote "Memoir of Robert Lloyd" (*Works,* I, 132–133) for the *Gentleman's Magazine,* 81 (November 1811), 484–485, and sent the manuscript to Charles. Charles sent a transcription to Robert's widow with the words, "Such is the beautiful and appropriate account sent to the 'Gentleman's Magazine,' by dear Charles Lamb, who, if I lov'd him for nothing else, I should now love for the affecting interest that he has taken in the memory of my dearest Brother and Friend" (*Lamb and the Lloyds,* p. 169). Charles Lloyd neither produced nor published his play. The Latin following translates, "O the times; O the customs!" and is in Cicero's "In Catilinam," I, 1 and 2; "In Virrem," II, 4, 25, and 26; "Pro rege Deiotaro," XI, 31; and "Ad pontifices," LIII, 137. Coleridge's auditor (to whom he quoted Titus 1:15) was probably Dorothy Wordsworth.

8. Mrs. Southey, the former Edith Fricker. See the Introduction, p. xxxv.

35. *C. L. to Robert Lloyd*

[Early to mid-August 1798]

My dear Robert,

I am a good deal occupied with a calamity near home, but not so much as to prevent my thinking about you with the warmest affection—you are among my very dearest friends—. I know you will feel deeply, when you hear that my poor sister is unwell again,——one of her old disorders, but I trust it will hold no longer than her former illnesses have done—. do not imagine, Robert, that I sink under this misfortune,—I have been season'd to such events, and think I could bear any thing tolerably well— ——. my own health is left me, and my good spirits, & I have some duties to perform—these duties shall be *my object*—. I wish, Robert, *you* could find an object, I know the painfulness of vacuity, all its achings, & inexplicable longings—. I wish to God I could recommend any plan to you—stock your mind well with religious knowledge; discipline it to wait with patience for duties, that may be your lot in life; prepare yourself not to expect too much out of yourself; *read* & *think*— —— ——. . . this is all common place advice, I know—. I know too, that it is easy to give advice, which in like circumstances we might not follow ourselves—. **You** must depend upon yourself—. there will come a time, when you will wonder you were not more content.— I know you will excuse my saying any more———

Be assur'd of my kindest warmest affection—

C Lamb

MS: The Philip H. & A. S. W. Rosenbach Foundation, Philadelphia. Pub.: Ainger (1900), I, 131–132; Macdonald, I, 97–98; Ainger (1904), I, 94; Harper, II, 153–154; Lucas (1935), I, 128. Address: R Lloyd/Day & Green's/Saffron Waldon/Essex. The date is estimated from the next letter.

36. *C. L. to Robert Lloyd*

[August 13 or 23, 1798]

My dear Robert,

Mary is better, and I trust that she will yet be restored to me, I am in good spirits, so do not be anxious about me:— I hope you get reconciled to your situation. The worst in it is that you have no *friend* to talk to—but wait in patience, and you will in good time make friends. The having a friend is not indispensibly necessary to virtue or happiness—religion removes those barriers of sentiment which partition us from the disinterested love of our brethren—. we are commanded to love our enemies, to do good to those that hate us; how much more is it our duty then to cultivate a forbearance and complacence towards those who only differ from us in dispositions and ways of thinking—. there is always, without very unusual care there must always be, something of **self** in friendship, we love our friend because he is like ourselves, can consequences altogether unmix'd and pure be reasonably expected from such a source—do not even the publicans & sinners the same?——— Say, that you love a friend for his moral qualities,—is it not rather because those qualities resemble what you fancy your own?— . — this then is not without danger. . . . The only true cement of a valuable friendship, the only thing that even makes it not sinful, is when two friends propose to become mutually of benefit to each other in a moral or religious way—but even this friendship is perpetually liable to the mixture of something not pure—we love our friend, because he is *ours*—so we do our money, our wit, our knowledge, our virtue, and whereever this sense of **appropriation and property enters,** so much is to be subtracted from the value of that friendship or that virtue. Our duties are to do good expecting nothing again, to bear with contrary dispositions, to be candid and forgiving, not to crave and long after a communication of sentiment and feeling, but rather to avoid dwelling upon those feelings, however good, because they are our own—a man may be intemperate & selfish, who indulges in *good feelings,* for the mere pleasure they give him. I do not wish to deter you from making a friend, a true friend, and such a friendship where the parties are not blind to each others faults, is very useful and valuable. I perceive a tendency in you to this error, Robert. I know you have chosen to take up an high opinion of my moral worth, but I say it before God, and I do not lie, you are mistaken in me. I could not bear to lay open all my failings to you, for the sentiment of shame would be too pungent. Let this be as an example to you— —. Robert, friends fall off, friends mistake us, they change, they grow unlike us, they go away, they die, but God is everlasting & uncapable of change, and to him we may look with chearful, unpresumptuous **hope,** while we discharge the duties of **life** in situations more untowardly than yours. You complain of the impossibility of improving yourself, but be assurd that the opportunity of improvement lies more in the mind than the situation—. humble yourself before God, cast out the selfish principle, wait in patience, do good in every way you can to all sorts of people, never be easy to neglect a duty tho' a small one, praise God for all, & see his hand in all things, & he will in time raise you up *many friends*—or be himself in stead an unchanging friend—. God bless you.

C Lamb

MS: Dartmouth College Library, Hanover, N.H. Pub.: Ainger (1900), I, 132–134; Macdonald, I, 100–102; Ainger (1904), I, 94–96; Harper, I, facsimile, and II, 157–159; Lucas (1935), I, 129–130. Address: R Lloyd/Day & Green's/Saffron Waldon/Essex. Postmark: August [1(3) or 2]3, 1798.

37. *C. L. to Southey*

October 18, 1798

Dear Southey,

I have at last been so fortunate as to pick up Wither's Emblems[1] for you, that 'old book and quaint,' as the brief author of *Ros Gray* hath it—it is in most detestable state of preservation, and the cuts are of a fainter impression than I have seen. Some child, the curse of antiquaries and bane of bibliopolical rarities, hath been dabbling in some of them with its paint and dirty fingers, and in particular hath a little sullied the author's own portraiture, which I think valuable, as the poem that accompanies it is no common one; this last excepted, the Emblems are far inferior to old Quarles. I once told you otherwise, but I had not then read old Q. with attention. I have pickt up too another copy of Quarles for ninepence!!! O tempora! O lectores![2] so that if you have lost or parted with your own copy, say so, and I can furnish you; for you prize these things more than I do. You will be amused, I think, with honest Wither's 'Supersedeas to all them whose custom it is, without any deserving, to importune authors to give unto them their books.' I am sorry 'tis imperfect, as the Lottery board[3] annexed to it also is. Methinks you might modernize and elegantize this supersedeas, and place it in front of your Joan of Arc, as a gentle hint to Messrs. Park, &c.

One of the happiest emblems and comicalest cuts is the owl and little chirpers, page 63.

Wishing you all amusement, which your true emblem-fancier can scarce fail to find in even bad emblems, I remain your Caterer to command,

C. Lamb

Love and respects to Edith. I hope she is well. How does your Calendar prosper?

MS: unrecovered. Text: Lucas (1935), I, 130–131. Also pub.: Talfourd (1837), I, 114–115; Sala, I, 175–176; Purnell, I, 175–176; Fitzgerald, II, 29–

30; Hazlitt, I, 194–195; Ainger (1888), I, 90; Ainger (1900), I, 126–127; Macdonald, I, 102–103; Ainger (1904), I, 90–91; Harper, II, 159–161; Lucas (1905), VI, 124–125; Lucas (1912), V, 123–124.

1. George Wither's *A Collection of Emblemes, Ancient and Moderne* (1635). The quotation, following, is from *Rosamund Gray,* ch. i (*Works,* I, 2). *A Tale of Rosamund Gray and Old Blind Margaret* (its full title) had been published earlier in the year in Birmingham and by Lee and Hurst in London.

2. "O the times! O the readers!" See Letter 34, note 7.

3. "A Direction, Shewing How They Who Are so *Disposed, Shall Find out Their* Chance, *in the* Lotteries *Aforegoing.*" It and the "Supersedeas . . . " are in *A Collection of Emblemes.* The reference at the end of the paragraph is to the engraver, antiquary, and bibliographer Thomas Park (1759–1834) and others devoted to such pursuits. The cut of the owl and chirpers is reproduced in Lucas (1905), VI, facing p. 124.

38. *C. L. to Southey*

Monday [October 29, 1798]

I thank you heartily for the Eclogue[1]—it pleased me mightily, being so full of picture-work & circumstances. I find no fault in it, unless perhaps that Joanna's ruin is a catastrophe too trite, and this is not the first or second time you have cloth'd your indignation in verse in a tale of ruined Innocence.— The Old Lady, spinning in the Sun, I hope would not disdain to claim some kindred with old Margaret—. I could almost wish you to vary some circumstances in the conclusion. A Gentleman seducer has so often been described in prose & verse—what, if you had accomplish'd Joanna's ruin by the clumsy arts & rustic gifts of some country fellow— ? — I am thinking, I believe, of the Song "An old woman cloathed in grey, Whose daughter was charming & young, and she was deluded away By Roger's false flattering tongue."[2] A Roger-Lothario would be a novel character, I think you might paint him very well—. You may think this a very silly suggestion, & so indeed it is, but in good truth nothing else but the first words of that foolish Balad put me upon scribbling my Rosamund. But I thank you heartily for the poem. Not having any thing of my own to send you in return, tho' to tell truth I am at work upon something,[3] which If I were to cut away & garble, perhaps I might send you an extract or two that might not displease you—but I will not do that, and whether it will come to anything I know not, for I am as slow as a Fleming painter, when I compose any thing.—. I will crave leave to put down a few lines of old Christopher Marlow's— —I take them from his tragedy the Jew of Malta.—[4] The Jew is a famous character, **quite out of nature,** but, when we consider the terrible **Idea** our simple ancestors had of a **Jew,** not more to be discommended for a certain discolouring (I think Addison calls it) than the witches & fairies of Marlow's mighty successor—. the scene is betwixt Barabas, the Jew, & Ithamore, a Turkish captive, expos'd to sale for a slave—

Barabas. As for myself, I walk abroad a nights,
a precious rascal { And kill sick people groaning under walls:
Sometimes I go about, & poison wells; }
And now & then, to cherish Christian thieves,
I am content to lose some of my crowns,
That I may, walking in my gallery,
See 'em go pinion'd along by my door.
Being young I studied physic, & began
To practise first upon the Italian:
There I enrich'd the priests with burials,
And always kept the sexton's arms in ure
With digging graves, & ringing dead men's knells:
And, after that, was I an engineer,
And in the wars twixt France & Germany,
Under pretence of serving Charles the fifth,
Slew friend & enemy with my stratagems.
Then, after that was I an **Usurer,**
And with extorting, cozening, forfeiting,
And tricks belonging unto brokery,
I fill'd the jails with bankrupts in a year;
And with young orphans planted hospitals;
And every moon made some or other mad;
And now & then one hang himself for grief,
Pinning upon his breast a long great scroll,
How I with interest had tormented him.

(Now hear Ithamore, the other gentle nature)

Ithamore Faith, master, and I have spent my time
In setting Christian villages on fire,
Chaining of Eunuchs, binding galley slaves.
One time I was an hostler in an inn,
And in the night time secretly would I steal

To travellers' chambers, & there cut their throats:
Once at Jerusalem, where the pilgrims kneel'd,
comical dog { I strewed powder on the marble stones,
And therewithal their knees would rankle so,
That I have laugh'd a good to see the cripples
Go limping home to Christendom on stilts

Barabas. Why, this is something = ———

there is a mixture of the ludicrous & the terrible in these lines, brimful of genius and antique invention, that at first reminded me of your old description of Cruelty in Hell[5]—which was in the true Hogarthian style.— — — I need not tell *you*, that Marlow was author of that pretty Madrigal "Come live with me & be my love"—and of the Tragedy of Edward 2d, in which are *certain lines* unequal'd in our English tongue—. Honest Walton mentions the said madrigal under the denomination of "certain smooth verses made long since by Marlow"—[6]

I am glad you have put me on the scent after Old Quarles, if I do not put up those Eclogues, and that shortly, say I am no true nosed hound—

I have had a letter from Lloyd;[7] the young metaphysician of Caius is well—and is busy recanting the new heresy, metaphysics,—for the old dogma, **Greek**— ———

his Brother Robert, the flower of their family, has left his ugly situation in Saffron Waldon—

my sister, I thank you, is quite well—she had a slight attack the other day, which frighten'd me a good deal, but it went off unaccountably—

love & respects to Edith—

Yours sincerely
C Lamb

MS: Mr. David Satinoff, Hale, Cheshire. Pub.: Talfourd (1837), I, 108–112; Sala, I, 176–179; Purnell, I, 176–179; Fitzgerald, II, 30–32; Hazlitt, I, 195–198; Ainger (1888), I, 90–93; Ainger (1900), I, 127–131; Macdonald, I, 103–105; Ainger (1904), I, 91–93; Harper, II, 161–164; Lucas (1905), VI, 125–127; Lucas (1912), V, 124–127; Lucas (1935), I, 131–134. Address: Robert Southey/ Mr Cottle's/Bookseller/High Street/Bristol. Postmark: October 29, 1798.

1. A manuscript of Southey's "The Ruined Cottage." Its story of the destruction of the happy state of Joanna and her widowed grandmother and the death of the grandmother consequent to the seduction of Joanna is similar to that of

Rosamund Gray. **The description of the old lady spinning in the sun, mentioned below, is in lines 49–51.**

2. "The *Worcestershire* Wedding, or Joy after Sorrow," lines 1–4. It is in *A Collection of Old Ballads. Collected from the Best and Most Ancient Copies* (3 vols.; London: F. Roberts, 1723–1725), II, 230. Although Lamb remarks below that the first words of the folk ballad put him upon writing *Rosamund Gray* and though he has Matravis, the seducer in the novel, sing it at the end (*Works,* I, 30), it is supposed that Lamb took his title from Charles Lloyd's "Rosamund Gray," which is included in Lloyd's *Poems on Various Subjects.*

3. A work first called "Pride's Cure," but in November 1801 changed to *John Woodvil.* G. and J. Robinson of London published it in 1802, with the title *John Woodvil: A Tragedy. To Which Are Added, Fragments of Burton, the Author of the Anatomy of Melancholy.* Its components are in *Works,* V, 131–176, 26–29, and 296–297; and I, 31–36 and 394–396.

4. Christopher Marlowe, *The Jew of Malta,* II, iii, 178–202 and 206–217. The allusion to Joseph Addison, below, is probably to either the first section of "Of the Christian Religion" or to *The Spectator,* No. 495, but in neither is there the word "discolouring." In a note to the excerpts from *The Rich Jew of Malta* (Lamb's title for Marlowe's play) in *Specimens of English Dramatic Poets* (*Works,* IV, 26), Lamb wrote, "It is curious to see a superstition wearing out. The idea of a Jew (which our pious ancestors contemplated with such horror) has nothing in it now revolting. We have tamed the claws of the beast, pared its nails, and now we take it to our arms, fondle it, write plays to flatter it: it is visited by princes, affects a taste, patronises the arts, and is the only liberal and gentlemanlike thing in Christendom." Marlowe's successor, below, was Shakespeare.

5. In *Joan of Arc* (1796), IX, 621–630. Lamb had also commented on the description in Letter 3, near the reference to note 5. Next mentioned are "The Passionate Shepherd to His Love" (Lamb quotes its first line) and *Edward II.*

6. *The Compleat Angler,* ch. ii.

7. Charles, who had been admitted to Caius College, Cambridge, on August 31.

39. *C. L. to Southey*

[Saturday, November 3, 1798]

I have read you[r] Eclogue[1] **repeatedly,** and cannot call it bald or without interest, the cast of it & the design are completely original, and may set people upon thinking, it is as poetical as the subject requires, which asks no poetry; but it is defective in pathos:— The woman's own story is the tamest part of it—I should like you to remold that—it too much resembles the young maid's history, both had been in service. Even the omission would not injure the Poem; after the words "growing wants"[2] you might, not unconnectedly, introduce "look at that little chub" down to "welcome one"—. And decidedly I would have you end it somehow thus "Give them at least this evening a good meal (gives her money) Now fare thee well: hereafter you have taught me to give sad meaning to the village bells" &c—which would leave a stronger impression, (as well as more pleasingly recall the beginning of the Eclogue) than the present common place reference to a better world, which the woman "must have heard at church"—.[3] I should like you too a good deal to enlarge the most striking part, as it might have been, of the poem—"**Is it Idleness**"? &c— —that affords a good field for dwelling on sickness & inabilities & old age— —. And you might also a good deal enrich the piece with a picture of a country wedding—the woman might very well, in a transient fit of oblivion, dwell upon the ceremony and circumstances of her own nuptials 6 years ago, the smugness of the bridegroom, the feastings, the cheap merriment, the welcomings & the secret envyings of the maidens—then dropping all this recur to her present **Lot**———. I do not know that I can suggest any thing else, or that I have suggested any thing new or material—. I shall be very glad to see some more poetry, tho' I fear your trouble in transcribing will be greater than the service my remark may do them.—

Yours affectionately
C Lamb

I cut my letter short, because I am call'd off to business—

MS: Berg Collection, New York Public Library. Pub.: Talfourd (1837), I, 106–108; Sala, I, 179–181; Purnell, I, 179–181; Fitzgerald, II, 33–35; Hazlitt, I, 198–199; Ainger (1888), I, 93–95; Ainger (1900), I, 137–139; Macdonald, I, 106–107; Ainger (1904), I, 98–99; Harper, II, 164–166; Lucas (1905), VI, 128; Lucas (1912), V, 127–128; Lucas (1935), I, 134–135. Address: Robert Southey/ Mr Cottle's/Bookseller/High Street/Bristol. Postmark: November 3, 1798.

1. "The Wedding." It tells of the hopelessness of married life in poverty by means of the dreary responses of a woman so poor she has often wished her children dead to the questions of a sanguine traveler about what seems to him the happy event of a wedding between a cheerful servant girl and an industrious laborer.

2. Line 102. The expressions "look at that little chub" and "welcome one" are not in the published version of the poem. But Southey did end it somewhat as Lamb would have him do so, with "You have taught me / To give sad meaning to the village bells," which recalls its opening, "I pray you, wherefore are the village bells / Ringing so merrily?"

3. Line 50. The next quotation is from line 97. Lamb's suggested enrichments are not in the poem.

40. *C. L. to Southey*

[Thursday,] November 8, 1798

I do not know that I much prefer this Eclogue[1] to the last; both are inferior to the former.

And when he came to shake me by the hand,
And spake as kindly to me as he used,
I hardly knew his voice—

is the only passage that affected me.

Servants speak, and their language ought to be plain, and not much raised above the common, else I should find fault with the bathos of this passage:

And when I heard the bell strike out,
I thought (what?) that I had never heard it toll
So dismally before.

I like the destruction of the martens' old nests hugely, having just such a circumstance in my memory. I should be very glad to see your remaining Eclogue, if not too much trouble, as you give me reason to expect it will be the second best.

I perfectly accord with your opinion of Old Wither. Quarles is a wittier writer, but Wither lays more hold of the heart. Quarles thinks of his audience when he lectures; Wither soliloquises in company with a full heart. What wretched stuff are the 'Divine Fancies'[2] of Quarles! Religion appears to him no longer valuable than it furnishes matter for quibbles and riddles; he turns God's grace into wantonness. Wither is like an old friend, whose warm-heartedness and estimable qualities make us wish he possessed more genius, but at the same time make us willing to dispense with that want. I always love W., and sometimes admire Q. Still that portrait poem[3] is a fine one; and the extract from 'The Shepherds' Hunting' places him in a starry height far above Quarles. If you wrote that review in 'Crit. Rev.,' I am sorry you are so sparing of praise to the 'Ancient Marinere;'—so far from calling it, as you do, with some wit, but more severity, 'A Dutch Attempt,' &c., I call it a right English attempt, and a successful one, to dethrone German sublimity. You have selected a passage fertile in unmeaning miracles, but have passed by fifty passages as miraculous as the miracles they celebrate. I never so deeply felt the pathetic as in that part,

A spring of love gush'd from my heart,
And I bless'd them unaware—

It stung me into high pleasure through sufferings. Lloyd does not like it; his head is too metaphysical, and your taste too correct; at least I must allege something against you both, to excuse my own dotage—

> So lonely 'twas, that God himself
> Scarce seemèd there to be!—&c., &c.

But you allow some elaborate beauties—you should have extracted 'em. 'The Ancient Marinere' plays more tricks with the mind than that last poem, which is yet one of the finest written. But I am getting too dogmatical; and before I degenerate into abuse, I will conclude with assuring you that I am

Sincerely yours,
C. Lamb

I am going to meet Lloyd at Ware on Saturday, to return on Sunday. Have you any commands or commendations to the metaphysician? I shall be very happy if you will dine or spend any time with me in your way through the great ugly city; but I know you have other ties upon you in these parts.

Love and respects to Edith, and friendly remembrances to Cottle.

MS: unrecovered. Text: Lucas (1935), I, 135–137. Also pub.: Talfourd (1837), I, 112–114; Sala, I, 181–182; Purnell, I, 181–182; Fitzgerald, II, 35–36; Hazlitt, I, 199–200; Ainger (1888), I, 95–96; Ainger (1900), I, 139–141; Macdonald, I, 107–109; Ainger (1904), I, 100–101; Harper, II, 167–168; Lucas (1905), VI, 129–130; Lucas (1912), V, 128–130.

1. Southey's "The Last of the Family," which Lamb may prefer to "The Wedding" and finds inferior to "The Ruined Cottage." "The Last of the Family" has James and Gregory, the old servants of young Master Edward and his parents, reminisce about the goodness of him and their noble ancestors while awaiting the funeral cortege bearing Edward's corpse. Lamb first quotes lines 83–85, then 10–12, and then praises the destruction of the martins' nest described in 48–50.

2. Possibly quoted from Southey's letter.

3. Wither's "The Author's Meditation upon Sight of His Picture," in *A Collection of Emblemes*. Wither's *The Shepherd's Hunting* (1615), praised following, is a continuation of *The Shepherd's Pipe* (1614), by William Browne (1591–1643?). Southey did write the review in the *Critical Review*, 24 (October 1798), 197–204, of *Lyrical Ballads*, which had come out on about September 15. "The Rime of the Ancient Mariner," he states, "appears to us perfectly original in style as well as in story. Many of the stanzas are laboriously beautiful; but in connection they are absurd or unintelligible" (p. 200). At that point Southey invites his readers to "exercise their ingenuity in attempting to unriddle" lines 309–330 and concludes that the poem "is a Dutch attempt at German sublimity" (p. 201), on which genius had been employed to little purpose. In his letter of December 17, 1798, to his close friend the politician Charles Watkin Williams Wynn (1775–1850), Southey called the poem "nonsense" (*New Southey Letters,* I, 177). Lamb singles out for comment its lines 284–285 and 599–600. He judges as among "the finest ever written" the last poem in the volume, Wordsworth's "Lines Written a

Few Miles above Tintern Abbey." It is strange that Lamb says nothing about a fine notice in the same number of the *Critical Review,* pp. 232–234, of his and Lloyd's *Blank Verse* (see Letter 10, note 4), which John and Arthur Arch of 23 Gracechurch Street, London, had issued earlier in the year.

41. *C. L. to Robert Lloyd*

London
the 13th Novr. 1798

Now tis Robert's turn— — —.

My dear Robert,

one passage in your Letter a little displeas'd me.— The rest was nothing but kindness, which Roberts' letters are ever brimful of— —. You say that "this World to you seems drain'd of all its **sweets!**"— — At first I had hoped you only meant to insinuate the high price of Sugar! but I am afraid you meant more—. O Robert, I do'nt know what you call sweet,— — Honey & the honey comb, roses & violets, are yet in the earth. The sun & moon yet reign in Heaven, & the lesser lights keep up their pretty twinklings— —meats & drinks, sweet sights & sweet smells, a country walk, spring & autumn, follies & repe[ntan]ce, quarrels & reconcilements, have all a sweetness by turns—. . . good humor & good nature, friends at home that love you, & friends abroad that miss you, you possess all these things, & more innumerable, & these are all sweet things— — — —. You may extract honey from every thing; do not go a gathering after gall—. the bees are wiser in their generation than the race of sonnet writers & complainers, Bowless & Charlotte Smiths,[1] & all that tribe, who can see no joys but what are past, and fill peoples' heads with notions of the Unsatisfying nature of Earthly comforts—. I assure you I find this world a very pretty place— —. my kind love to all your Sisters & to Thomas—he never writes to me . . & tell Susanna I forgive her.

C Lamb

MS: Huntington Library. Pub.: Ainger (1900), I, 141–142; Macdonald, I, 109; Ainger (1904), I, 101–102; Harper, I, facsimile, and II, 169–170; Lucas (1935), I, 138. Address: Robert Lloyd/Charles Lloyd's/Birmingham. Postmark:

November 13, 1798. The openings of this and the next letter indicate they followed an unrecovered one from Lamb to Robert's eldest sister, Priscilla (1781–1815), who during the Christmas holidays in 1798 would become engaged and in 1804 be married to Wordsworth's brother Christopher (1774–1846). He was Charles Lloyd's tutor in Greek during Lloyd's first term at Caius College. From 1820 to 1841 he was master of Trinity College, Cambridge.

1. The poet and novelist Charlotte Smith. (See Letter 16, note 8.) Mentioned below are Robert's brother Thomas (1779–1811), who became a Birmingham merchant, and perhaps Susannah Whitehead, who in 1805 became Thomas' wife. She was the daughter of John, a banker of Barford, Warwickshire.

42. *C. L. to Robert Lloyd*

Novr. 20th 98

As the little copy of verses I sent gave Priscilla & Robert some pleasure, I now send them another little tale,[1] which is all I can send, for my stock will be exhausted— . . . .

Tis a tale of Witchcraft, told by an old Steward in the family to Margaret, the ward of Sir Walter Woodvil. *Who* Sir Walter is you may come to know bye & bye, when I have finish'd a Poem, from which this & the other are Extracts, and all the extracts I can make without mutilating.— — — —— —— ———

Old Steward.
One summer night Sir Walter, as it chanc'd,
Was pacing to and fro in the avenue
That westward fronts our house,
Among those aged oaks said to have been planted
Three hundred years ago
By a neighb'ring Prior of the Woodvil name;
But so it was,
Being o'er task'd in thought he heeded not
The importune suit of one that stood by the gate,
And begg'd an alms.
Some say, he shov'd her rudely from the gate
With angry chiding; but I can never think,
(Sir Walter's nature hath a sweetness in it,)
That he could treat a woman, an old woman,
With such discourtesy,
For old she was who begg'd an alms of him.
Well, he refus'd her,

(Whether for importunity I know not,
Or that she came between his meditations,)
But better had he met a Lion in the Streets,[2]
Than this old woman that night,
For she was one who practis'd the black arts,
And serv'd the Devil, being since burnt for witchcraft.
She look'd at him like one that meant to blast him;
And with a frightful noise,
('Twas partly like a woman's voice,
And partly like the hissing of a snake,)
She nothing spake but this: Sir Walter told the words.
A mischief, mischief, mischief,
And a nine times killing curse,
By day & by night, to the caitive wight,
Who shakes the poor, like snakes, from his door,
And shuts up the womb of his purse:
And a mischief, mischief, mischief,
And a nine fold with'ring curse,—
For that shall come to thee, that will undo thee,
Both all that thou fear'st & worse—
These words four times repeated, she departed,
Leaving Sir Walter like a man, beneath
Whose feet a scaffolding had suddenly **fall'n!**

Margaret. A terrible curse!

Old Steward. O Lady! such bad things are told of that old woman,
You would be loth to hear them!
As, namely, that the milk she gave was sour,
And the babe, who suck'd her, shrivell'd like a
mandrake!*[3]
And things besides, with a bigger horror in them,
Almost, I think, unlawful to be told!

Margaret. Then I must never hear them. But proceed,
And say what follow'd on the witche's curse.

Old Steward. Nothing immediate; but some nine months after
Young Stepen Woodvil suddenly fell sick,
And none could tell what ail'd him; for he lay,
And pin'd, & pin'd, till all his hair came off,

And he, that was full flesh'd, became as thin
As a two month's babe that has been starv'd in the
nursing.
And sure, I think,
He bore his illness like a little child,
With such rare sweetness, & dumb melancholy,
He strove to clothe his agony in smiles,
Which he would force up in his poor pale cheeks,
Like ill-tim'd guests that had no proper dwelling there.
And, when they ask'd him his complaint, he laid
His hand upon his heart to shew the place,
Where Susan came to him a nights, he said,
And prick'd him with a pin.
And thereupon Sir Walter call'd to mind
The beggar witch who stood in the gateway,
And begg'd an alms.

Margaret. And so he died?

Old Steward. Tis thought so.

Margaret. But did the witch confess?

Old Steward. All this, & more at her death.

Margaret. I do not love to credit tales of magic.
Heavn's music, which is Order, seems unstrung,
And this brave world,
Creation's beauteous workmanship, unbeautify'd,
Disorder'd, marr'd, where such strange things are acted.

*a *mandrake* is a root resembling the human form, as sometimes a carrot does, & the old superstitution is, that when the mandrake is torn out of the earth a dreadful shriek is heard, which makes all who hear it go mad.— Tis a fatal poison besides—

I will here conclude my tiny portion of Prose with hoping you may like the story, and my kind remembrances to all— —

C Lamb

Write soon, Robert.

MS: Huntington Library. Pub.: Ainger (1900), I, 142–145; Macdonald, I, 110–112; Ainger (1904), I, 102–104; Harper, II, 170; Lucas (1935), I, 139–140. Address: Robert Lloyd/Charles Lloyd's/Birmingham. Postmark: November 20, 1798.

1. Later omitted from *John Woodvil.* Lamb published the tale separately, titled "The Witch: A Dramatic Sketch of the Seventeenth Century," in *Works* (1818). It is in *Works,* V, 177–179.

2. Proverbs 26:13.

3. The context of Lamb's gloss requires its retention at the end of the tale.

43. *C. L. to Southey*

[November 20, 1798]

The following is a second Extract from my Tragedy, *that is to be,*—tis narrated by An old Steward to Margaret, Orphan Ward of Sir Walter Woodvil, ... This, and the Dying Lover[1] I gave you, are the only Extracts I can give without mutilation—. I expect you to like the old woman's **curse**———

Old Steward.
One summer night Sir Walter, as it chanc'd,
Was pacing to & fro in the avenue
That westward fronts our house,
Among those aged oaks said to have been planted
Three hundred years ago
By a neighbring Prior of the Woodvil name.
But so it was;
Being overtask'd in thought he heeded not
The importune suit of one who stood by the gate,
And beg'd an alms.
Some say, he shov'd her rudely from the gate
With angry chiding, but I can never think,
(Sir Walter's nature hath a sweetness in it,)
That he could use a woman, an old woman,
With such discourtesy,
For old she was who beg'd an alms of him.
Well, he refus'd her,
Whether for importunity I know not,
Or that she came between his meditations.
But better had he met a Lion in the streets,
Than this old woman that night
For she was **one** who practis'd the black arts,

And serv'd the devil, being since burn'd for witchcraft
She look'd at him like one that meant to blast him,
And with a frightful noise,
(Twas partly like a woman's voice,
And partly like the hissing of a snake)
She nothing said but this; Sir Walter told the words.

A mischief, mischief, mischief,
And a nine times killing curse,
By day & by night, to the caitive wight,
Who shakes the poor like snakes from his door,
And shuts up the womb of his Purse.
And a mischief, mischief, mischief,
And a ninefold withering curse,
For that shall come to thee, that will undo thee,
Both all that thou fearst & worse.—

These words four times repeated, she departed,
Leaving Sir Walter like a man, beneath
Whose feet a scaffolding had suddenly faln!
So he describ'd it.

Margaret— A terrible curse—

Old Steward. O Lady, such bad things are told of that old woman;
As namely that the milk she gave was sour,
And the babe who suck'd her shrivel'd like a
mandrak[e]
And things besides, with a bigger horror in them,
Almost I think unlawful to be told!

Marg. Then I must never hear them. But proceed
And say what follow'd on the witche's curse.—

Stew. Nothing immediate, but some 9 months after
Young Stephen Woodvil suddenly fell sick,
And none could tell what ail'd him: for he lay,
And pind, & pind, till all his ⟨flesh⟩ hair came off,
And he, that was full flesh'd, became as thin
As a 2 month's babe that hath been starv'd in the
nursing.
And sure I think,
He bore his illness like a little child,
With such rare sweetness of dumb melancholy

He strove to clothe his agony in Smiles,
Which he would force up in his poor pale cheeks,
Like ill tim'd guests that had no proper business
there—
And when they ask'd him his complaint, he laid
His hand upon his heart to shew the place,
Where Susan came to him a nights, he said,
And prick'd him with a pin.—
And hereupon Sir Walter call'd to mind
The Beggar witch that stood in the gateway,
And begg'd an alms.—

Mar. I do not love to credit Tales of magic.
Heavn's music, which is **order,** seems unstrung;
And this brave world,
Creation's beauteous workmanship, unbeautified,
Disorder'd, marr'd, where such strange things are
acted.

This is the Extract I brag'd of, as superior to that I sent you from **Marlow,**[2]—perhaps you will smile— —but I should like your remarks on the above, as you are deeper **witch-read** than I—

Yours Ever
C Lamb

MS: Berg Collection, New York Public Library. Pub.: Sala, I, 196–198; Purnell, I, 196–198; Fitzgerald, II, 50; Hazlitt, I, 219–221; Ainger (1888), I, 107; Ainger (1900), I, 160–161; Macdonald, I, 110; Ainger (1904), I, 115; Harper, II, 171–173; Lucas (1905), VI, 132–133; Lucas (1912), V, 132–133; Lucas (1935), I, 156–157. Address: Rob. Southey/Mr. Cottles/Bookseller/High Street/Bristol. Postmark: November 20, 1798.

1. Apparently sent after Letter 38 (October 29) in a letter that is unrecovered. Lamb later omitted from *John Woodvil* the "Dying Lover" and published it separately, titled "Fragment in Dialogue," in *Recreations in Agriculture, Natural History, Arts and Miscellaneous Literature,* 4 (November 1800), 237–238. It is titled "Dramatic Fragment" in *Works,* V, 79–80.

2. In Letter 38.

44. *C. L. to Southey*

[November 28, 1798]

I can have no objection to your printing "Mystery of God"[1] with my name, and all due acknowledgments for the honor and favor of the communication; indeed tis a poem that can dishonor no name.

Now that is in the true strain of modern modesto-vanitas. . . But for the sonnet, I heartily wish it, as I thought it was, dead and forgotten,—if the exact circumstances under which I wrote could be known or told, it would be an interesting sonnet, but to an indifferent & stranger reader it must appear a very bald thing, certainly inadmissible in a compilation. I wish you could affix a different name to the volume, there is a contemptible book, a wretched assortment of vapid feelings,[2] entituled *Pratt's gleanings,* which hath damnd and impropriated the Title for ever,—pray think of some other. The gentleman is better known, (better had he remain'd unknown) by an **ode** to **Benevolence,** written & spoken for & at the Annual dinner of the **Humane Society,** who walk in procession once a year, with all the objects of their charity before them, to return God thanks for giving them such benevolent hearts,— — — ———

I like Bishop Bruno,[3] but not so abundantly as your Witch Balad, which is an exquisite thing of its kind. . . . . I shew'd my Witch & Dying Lover to Dyer last night, but George could not comprehend how that could be poetry, which did not go upon ten feet, as George & his predecessors had taught it to do; so George read me some lectures of the distinguishing qualities of the Ode, the Epigram, & the Epic, & went home to illustrate his doctrine by correcting a proof sheet of his own Lyrics . . George writes odes where the rhimes, like fashionable man & wife, keep a comfortable distance of 6 or 8 lines apart, & calls that observing the **Laws** of **verse—.** George tells you, before he recites, that you must listen with great attention, or you'll miss the rhymes—I did so, and found them pretty Exact—. George speaking of the **Dead Ossian** exclaimeth, "Dark are the Poet's eyes"—.[4] I humbly represented to him that his own Eyes were dark, & many a living Bard's beside—& recommended **"Clos'd** are the Poet's eyes"—. But that would not do—I found there was an antithesis between the darkness of his Eyes, & the splendor of his Genius—& I acquiesced. . — — — — — ———

Lloyd does not come to London till Christmas—. A Letter will find him at **Caius',** as usual—. Your recipe[5] for a Turk's poison is invaluable and truly Marlowish— — — — ———

Lloyd objects to "shutting up the womb of his purse" in my curse, (which for a Christian witch in a Christian country is not too mild I hope)— —do you object?— I think there is a strangeness in the idea, as well as "shaking the poor like snakes from his door," which suits the speaker—. Witches illustrate, as fine Ladies do, from their own familiar objects, & snakes & shutting up of wombs is in their way. I dont know that this last charge has been before brot. against 'em, nor either the sour milk or the mandrake **Babe**— —but I affirm these be things a **Witch** would do if she could—. My Tragedy will be a medley (or I intend it to be a medley) of laughter & tears, prose & verse & in some places rhime, songs, wit, pathos, humour, & if possible sublimity,—at least, tis not a fault in my intention, if it does not comprehend most of these discordant atoms,— Heaven send thy dance not the dance of **Death!**———[6]

I hear that the Two Noble Englishmen have parted no sooner than they set foot on german Earth, but I have not heard the reason——— Possibly to give Moralists an handle to exclaim "Ah! me! what things are perfect?"— I think I shall adopt your emendation in the Dying Lover, tho' I do not myself feel the objection against **"Silent Prayer"**—[7]

My Taylor has brought me home a [ne]w coat Lappel'd with a **Velvet** collar. **He** assures me every body wears velvet collars now— — Some are born fashionable, some achieve fashion, & others, like your humble servant, have fashion thrust upon them—.[8] The rogue has been making inroads hitherto by modest degrees, foisting upon me an additional Button, recommending **gayters,** but to come upon me thus **full tide of Luxury,** neither becomes him as a Taylor or the ninth of a man—. My meek gentleman was robbd the other day, coming with his wife and family in a one horse **shay** from Hampstead, the villains rifled him of four guineas, some shillings & halfpence, and a bundle of customers measures, which they swore were bank notes; they did not shoat him, & when they rode off he addrest them with profound gratitude, making a congee, "Gentlemen I wish you good night, and we are very much obliged to you that you have not used us **ill**—." And this is the **Cuckow,** that has had the audacity to foist upon me **ten buttons** on a side, and a black velvet Collar—. A damn'd **ninth** of a scoundrel!—

Yours sincerely
C Lamb

Love and respects to Edith—
I hope she is well— — —

When you write to Lloyd, he wishes his Jacobin correspondents to address him as *Mr*[9] C. Ll.

MS: Robert H. Taylor Collection, Princeton, N.J. Pub.: Talfourd (1837), I, 93–94, 103, 106, and 116–117; Talfourd (1848), I, 100–101; Sala, I, 182–186; Purnell, I, 182–186; Fitzgerald, II, 36–40; Hazlitt, I, 202–204; Ainger (1888), I, 96–99; Ainger (1900), I, 145–149; Macdonald, I, 112–115; Ainger (1904), I, 104–107; Harper, II, 173–176; Lucas (1905), VI, 134–136; Lucas (1912), V, 134–136; Lucas (1935), I, 140–142. Address: Robert Southey/Joseph Cottle's/ Bookseller/High Street/Bristol. Postmark: November 28, 1798.

1. Retitled "Living without God in the World" (*Works,* V, 17–18) for the first (1799) volume of *The Annual Anthology.* The Latin in the following sentence translates, "vanity without moderation." The sonnet has not been identified.

2. A canceled line follows. *Gleanings* (1795–1799), whose title Southey thought to use for *The Annual Anthology,* was compiled by the author of *Triumph of Benevolence* (1786), Samuel Jackson Pratt (1749–1814).

3. Southey's poem "Bishop Bruno" describes the events surrounding the accidental death of St. Bruno of Würzburg (1005?–1045). Lamb does not like it so well as "The Old Woman of Berkeley. A Ballad, Showing How an Old Woman Rode Double, and Who Rode before Her."

4. Dyer's "Ode XVI. Addressed to Dr. Robert Anderson, of Heriot's-green, Edinburgh, after a Visit Paid Him by the Author, and Various Pedestrian Excursions in Scotland," line 9, in Dyer's *Poems* (1801), p. 89.

5. Which seems to have existed only in Southey's letter. Lamb next misquotes from his own "Witch," lines 33 and 32 in the versions of the poem given in the two preceding letters (lines 29 and 28 in *Works,* V, 178), and refers to the sour milk and mandrake babe in lines 44 and 45, which are not in the published poem.

6. Cf. Coleridge's "Ode on the Departing Year," line 59. Coleridge and Wordsworth (Lamb's sarcastic epithet for them, below, is an echo of John Fletcher's *The Two Noble Kinsmen*) had parted amicably after sharing twelve days in Hamburg. Coleridge and Chester left on September 30, first for the house of a Pastor Unruke in Ratzeburg, where Coleridge learned colloquial German, and later for Göttingen, where on February 16, 1799, he was matriculated in *studia humaniora* at the university to continue his study of the language and its literature. The Wordsworths left Hamburg on October 3, 1798, first for Brunswick and Goslar, then in late February 1799 for Nordhausen, where, as in the previous regions, they were disappointed in their attempts to gain enough mastery of the language to supplement their money by translating and where Wordsworth devoted much of his time to his poetry. They rejoined Coleridge in Göttingen for a day, about April 20, en route to England. They reached Yarmouth on perhaps May 1. By May 13 they were settled on a farm at Sockburn, Durham, with Thomas Hutchinson (1773–1849), since 1888 its owner, and his sisters Sara (1775–1835) and Mary (1770–1859). With the former Coleridge would fall in love, and to the latter Wordsworth, in 1802, would be married. Coleridge and Chester left Göttingen on June 24 for a walking tour with friends through the Harz mountains before sailing for home. They were at Nether Stowey by July 29.

7. Retained in "Dramatic Fragment," line 11.

8. *Twelfth Night,* II, v, 145–146; III, iv, 41–45; and V, i, 370–372. Lamb has altered the lines for his own purpose. "Nine tailors make a man" is the proverb that Lamb calls on below. I thank Marion Kaplan for identifying it for me.

9. Underscored twice. Lamb is alluding to the attacks against himself, Coleridge, Southey, Lloyd, and other proponents of Theophilanthropy, first in the

(unsigned) satirical poem "New Morality," in the *Anti-Jacobin, or Weekly Examiner,* 2 (July 9, 1798), esp. p. 636; then in the cartoon by the caricaturist James Gillray (1757–1815) in the *Anti-Jacobin Review and Magazine,* 1 (July 1798), facing p. 114; and then by "Fabricus" in "The Anarchists.—An Ode," in the *Anti-Jacobin Review and Magazine,* 1 (September 1798), esp. p. 366. A last stroke against Coleridge alone is in a footnote to the reappearance of "New Morality" in *The Beauties of the Anti-Jacobin; or, Weekly Examiner* (1799), p. 306, where its (anonymous) editor accuses him of nonattendance at chapel while at Cambridge, of hypocrisy while he was speaking to a soldier in a park, and of desertion for leaving his family for Germany. Coleridge considered suing for libel, but changed his mind. Lloyd took the affair so seriously that he wrote the pamphlet *Letter to the Anti-Jacobin Reviewers* (1799), in which he defended "Mr. Charles Lamb." The statesman George Canning (1770–1827), who co-founded the *Anti-Jacobin* with the author George Ellis (1753–1815), was the principal writer of "New Morality." Ellis and the diplomatist John Hookham Frere (1769–1846) contributed to it. For additional information and the Gillray cartoon see esp. Burton R. Pollin's "Charles Lamb and Charles Lloyd as Jacobins and Anti-Jacobins," *Studies in Romanticism,* 12 (Summer 1973), 633–647. Another good recent study of the subject, Mrs. Winifred F. Courtney's "Lamb, Gillray, and the Ghost of Edmund Burke," is expected to appear shortly in the *CLSB.*

45. *C. L. to Southey*

[December 27, 1798]

dear Southey,

Your friend John May has formerly made kind offers to Lloyd of serving me in the India house by the interest of his friend Sir Francis Baring—.[1] It is not likely that I shall ever put his goodness to the test on my own account, for my prospects are very comfortable—. But I know a man, a young man, whom he could serve thro' the same channel, and I think would be dispos'd to serve, if he were acquainted with his case—. This poor fellow (whom I know just enough of, to vouch for his strict integrity & worth) has lost two or three employments from illness, which he cannot regain; he was once insane, and from the distressful uncertainty of his Livelihood, has reason to apprehend a return of that malady—he has been for some time dependant on a woman, whose Lodger he formerly was, but who can ill afford to maintain him, and I know that on Christmas night last he actually walkd about the streets all night, rather than accept of her Bed which she offer'd him, and offerd herself to sleep in the kitchen, and that in consequence of that severe cold he is labouring under a bilious disorder, besides a depression of spirits which incapacitates him from exertion when he most needs it—. For God's sake, Southey, if it does not go against you to ask favors, do it now,—ask it as for me—but do not do a violence to your feelings, because he does not know of this application, and will suffer no disappointment— —

What I meant to say was this—there are in the India house what are called ***Extra Clerks,*** not on the Establishment, like me, but employed in **Extra** business, by-jobs,—these get about £50 a year, or rather more, but never rise,—a Director can put in at any time a young man in this office, and it is by no means considerd so great a favor as making an establish'd Clerk— —. He would think himself as rich as an Emperor, if he could get such a certain situation, and be relieved from these disquietudes which I do fear may one day bring back his distemper— —. You know John May better than I do, but I know enough to believe that he is a good man—he did make me that offer I have mentiond, but you will perceive that such an offer cannot authorize me in applying for another Person— —

But I cannot help writing to you on the subject, for the young man is perpetually before my eyes, and I should feel it a crime not to strain all my petty interest to do him service, tho' I put my own delicacy to the question by so doing—. I have made one other unsuccessful attempt already—

At all events I will thank you to write, for I am tormented with anxiety—

I suppose you have somehow heard, that poor Mary Dollin[2] has poisoned herself, after some interviews with John Reid, the ci-devant Alphonso of her days of hope

C Lamb

how is Edith?

MS: Yale University Library, New Haven, Conn. Pub.: Talfourd (1837), I, 99–101; Sala, I, 186–187; Purnell, I, 186–187; Fitzgerald, II, 40–41; Hazlitt, I, 204–205; Ainger (1888), I, 99–100; Ainger (1900), I, 149–151; Macdonald, I, 115–117; Ainger (1904), I, 107–108; Harper, II, 177–179; Lucas (1905), VI, 137–138; Lucas (1912), V, 137–138; Lucas (1935), I, 144–145. The date assigned, which is also penciled at the end of the holograph letter, is that shown as Lamb's by all previous editors. They presumably took it from a postmark or an endorsement on the (now missing) address leaf. Southey acknowledged receipt of the letter in his letter postmarked December 1798 to John May (1775–1856) of London and Richmond, once a pupil of Coleridge's brother George, probably at Newcome's Academy in Hackney. Southey had met May in Portugal in 1796. He was a wine merchant, like his father and grandfather, with the London firm Stert

and May. From 1827, following the collapse of his family's fortunes, he was the manager of a bank in Bristol. See *New Southey Letters,* esp. I, 178, and II, 495–496.

1. Sir Francis Baring (1740–1810), the founder with his brother John of the financial house Baring Brothers & Co., was an M.P. from 1784 to 1790 and from 1794 to 1806. Sir Francis became a director of the East India Company in 1779 and was its chairman from 1792 to 1793. The name of the young man whom Lamb seeks to help, and who soon revealed himself as "a thorough and compleat rascal" (*New Southey Letters,* I, 192), is not known.

2. Possibly a special acquaintance of Charles Lloyd, for in his letter to Thomas Manning dated from Leicester January 6, 1799, Lloyd exclaims that Southey writes to him "as if he were commencing ideot . . . , that he had 'day dreams' of marrying me to Miss Dollin—and why forsooth?—because the poor girl had passions and fell on Lambs knees" (*Lloyd-Manning Letters,* p. 20). He mentions John Reid (mentioned below) in the same letter, but only as the son of a respectable woman of Leicester to whom Lloyd felt indebted for her hospitality. The allusion in Reid as "the ci-devant Alphonso of her days of hope" could be (given Southey's interest in Portugal and Spain) to Alphonso I (1094–1185), king of Portugal. Of the many Portuguese and Spanish kings of that name, he is the one revered, by the Portuguese for his character and as the founder of their country.

46. *C. L. to Southey*

January 21, 1799

I am requested by Lloyd to excuse his not replying to a kind letter received from you. He is at present situated in most distressful family perplexities, which I am not at liberty to explain; but they are such as to demand all the strength of his mind, and quite exclude any attention to foreign objects. His brother Robert (the flower of his family) hath eloped from the persecutions of his father, and has taken shelter with me. What the issue of his adventure will be, I know not. He hath the sweetness of an angel in his heart, combined with admirable firmness of purpose: an uncultivated, but very original, and, I think, superior genius. But this step of his is but a small part of their family troubles.[1]

I am to blame for not writing to you before on *my own account;* but I know you can dispense with the expressions of gratitude, or I should have thanked you before for all May's kindness. He has liberally supplied the person I spoke to you of with money, and had procured him a situation just after himself had lighted upon a similar one and engaged too far to recede. But May's kindness was the same, and my thanks to you and him are the same. May went about on this business as if it had been his own. But you knew John May before this: so I will be silent.

I shall be very glad to hear from you when convenient. I do not know how your Calendar and other affairs thrive; but, above all, I have not heard a great while of your 'Madoc'—the *opus magnum.* I would willingly send you something to give a value to this letter; but I have only one slight passage to send you, scarce worth the sending, which I want to edge in somewhere into my play, which, by the way, hath not received the addition of ten lines, besides, since I saw you. A father, old Walter Woodvil (the witch's **Protégé**) relates this of his son John, who 'fought in adverse armies,'[2] being a royalist, and his father a parliamentary man:—

I saw him in the day of Worcester fight,
Whither he came at twice seven years,
Under the discipline of the Lord Falkland
(His uncle by the mother's side,
Who gave his youthful politics a bent
Quite *from* the principles of his father's house;)
There did I see this valiant Lamb of Mars,
This sprig of honour, this unbearded John,
This veteran in green years, this sprout, this Woodvil,
(With dreadless ease guiding a fire-hot steed,
Which seem'd to scorn the manage of a boy),
Prick forth with such a *mirth* into the field,
To mingle rivalship and acts of war
Even with the sinewy masters of the art,—
You would have thought the work of blood had been
A play-game merely, and the rabid Mars
Had put his harmful hostile nature off,
To instruct raw youth in images of war,
And practice of the unedged players' foils.
The rough fanatic and blood-practised soldiery,
Seeing such hope and virtue in the boy,
Disclosed their ranks to let him pass unhurt,
Checking their swords' uncivil injuries,
As loth to mar that curious workmanship
Of Valour's beauty pourtray'd in his face.

Lloyd objects to 'pourtrayed in his face,'—do you? I like the line.

I shall clap this in somewhere. I think there is a spirit through the lines; perhaps the 7th, 8th, and 9th owe their origin to Shakspeare, though no image is borrowed.

He says in 'Henry the Fourth'—[3]

> This infant Hotspur,
> Mars in swathing clothes.

But pray did Lord Falkland die before Worcester fight? In that case I must make bold to unclify some other nobleman.

Kind love and respects to Edith.

C. Lamb

MS: unrecovered. Text: Lucas (1935), I, 145–147. Also pub.: Talfourd (1837), I, 125–127; Sala, I, 187–190; Purnell, I, 187–190; Fitzgerald, II, 41–44; Hazlitt, I, 210–212; Ainger (1888), I, 100–102; Ainger (1900), I, 151–153; Macdonald, I, 117–119; Ainger (1904), I, 108–110; Harper, II, 179–181; Lucas (1905), VI, 139–140; Lucas (1912), V, 139–140.

1. Brought on by the senior Charles Lloyd. Distressed by money problems, he had become so unreasonable with Priscilla, because of her desire to accept Christopher Wordsworth's proposal of marriage, that she had been taken seriously ill. He had become so unreasonable with Robert, because of his wish to discontinue attending the meetings of the Quakers, that Robert had come to Lamb. But by February 5 Mr. Lloyd consented to his daughter's betrothal and on February 20 welcomed back his son.

2. Neither this phrase nor the passage following is in the published version of *John Woodvil.* But see *Works,* V, 361, for the placement of the passage in the manuscript copy of the play that Lamb later sent to Manning.

3. *I Henry IV,* III, ii, 112–113. Lucius Cary, second Viscount Falkland (1610?–1643), was killed in the fight at Newbury eight years before the battle at Worcester on September 3, 1651. In the manuscript copy referred to in note 2 Lamb accordingly changed the battle to Naseby (1645) and the nobleman to Anthony Ashley Cooper, first Baron Ashley and first Earl of Shaftesbury (1621–1683).

47. *C. L. to Southey*

[January 23, 1799]

Dr[1] Southey,

Lloyd will now be able to give you an account of himself, so to him I leave you for satisfaction. Great part of his troubles are lightend by the partial recovery of his sister, who had been alarmingly ill, with similar diseases to his own—. The other part of the family troubles sleeps for the present, but I fear will awake at some future time to *confound* and *disunite*. He will probably tell you all about it.— Robert still continues here with me, his father has proposed nothing, but would willingly lure him back with fair professions. But Robert is endowed with a wise fortitude; and in this business has acted quite from himself, and wisely acted. His parent must compound in the End.— — ——— I like reducing parents to a sense of undutifulness. I like confounding the relations of life— — — — —. Pray let me see you, when you come to town, and contrive to give me some of your company. . . I thank you heartily for your intended presents, but do by no means see the necessity you are under of burthening yourself thereby.— You have read old Wither's *supersedeas* to small purpose—. You object to my pauses being at the end of my lines, I do not know any great difficulty I should find in diversifying or changing my blank verse, but I go upon the model of Shakspere in my play, and endeavour after a colloquial ease & spirit something like him, ... I could as easily imitate Milton's versification, but my ear & feeling would reject it, or any approaches to it, in the *drama*— —. I do not know whether to be glad or sorry that Witches have been detected aforetimes in shutting up of wombs, I certainly invented that conceit, and its coincidence with fact is incidental, for I never heard it— —

I have not seen those verses on Col. Despard.[2] I do not read any newspapers—are they short, to copy without much trouble—? I should like to see them— —

I just send you a few rhymes from my play—the only rhymes in it— —. a forest-liver giving an account of his amusements—

"What sports have you in the forest?—"
Not many,—some few,—as thus,
To see the Sun to bed, and see him rise,
Like some hot amourist with glowing eyes,
Bursting the lazy bands of sleep that bound him,
With all his fires and travelling glories round him.
Sometimes the moon on soft night-clouds to rest,
Like Beauty nestling in a young man's breast,
And all the winking stars, her handmaids, keep
Admiring silence, while those Lovers sleep:
Sometimes, outstretchd in very idleness;
Nought doing, saying little, thinking less,

To view the leaves, thin dancers upon air,
Go eddying round; and small birds, how they fare,
When mother Autumn fills their beaks with corn,
Filch'd from the careless Amalthea's horn;[3]
And how the woods Berries & Worms provide,
Without their **pains,** when Earth hath nought beside
To answer their small wants:
To **View** the graceful deer come trooping by,
Then pause, and gaze, then turn they know not why,
Like bashful younkers in society.
To mark the structure of a plant or tree;
And all fair things of earth, how fair they be!

&c. &c[4]

I love to anticipate charges of unoriginality; the first line is almost Shakesperes;—

"To have my love to bed & to arise"

midsummer nights dream

I think there is a sweetness in the versification not unlike some rhymes in that Exquisite play—and the Last line but three is yours

an Eye
"That met the gaze, or turn'd it knew not why"

Rosamunds Epistle

I shall anticipate all my play & have nothing to shew you—

An idea for Leviathan

Commentators on **Job** have been puzzled to find out a meaning for Leviathan,[5]—tis a whale, say some, a crocodile, say others, in my simple conjecture Leviathan is neither more nor less than the Lord Mayor of London for the time being— — —

Rosamund sells well in london, maugre the non-reviewal of it— —

I sincerely wish you better health, & better health to Edith—kind remembrance to her.

C Lamb

If you come to town by ash wensday, you will certainly see Lloyd here[6]— —I expect him by that time—

my sister Mary was never in better health or spirits than now—

MS: Hornby Library, City of Liverpool, Libraries Department. Pub.: Talfourd (1837), I, 104–105; Sala, I, 198–200; Purnell, I, 198–200; Fitzgerald, II, 50–52; Hazlitt, I, 217–219; Ainger (1888), I, 107–109; Ainger (1900), I, 161–163; Macdonald, I, 124–126; Ainger (1904), I, 115–117; Harper, II, 181–184; Lucas (1905), VI, 141–142; Lucas (1912), V, 141–143; Lucas (1935), I, 147–149. Address: Robert Southey/Joseph Cottle's/Bookseller/High Street/Bristol. Postmark: January 23, 1799.

1. For "Dear."

2. Edward Marcus Despard (1751–1803) had served as a lieutenant in the colonial service in Jamaica in 1772, as commandant of the island of Rattan (on the Spanish main) in 1781, and as superintendent of the king's affairs in Yucatan from 1784 to 1790. He was suspended from the last post by Home Secretary William Wyndham Grenville, Baron Grenville (1759–1834), on charges so questionable that they were later dropped, but imprisoned from 1798 to 1800 because of his claims for compensation. In 1802 he engaged in a plot to overthrow the government, was arrested and found guilty of high treason, and with six fellow conspirators was executed at Newington. (I also have not seen, or identified, the verses on him.) Southey remained sufficiently interested in him to write of him and his conspiracy in *Letters from England: By Don Manuel Alvarez Espriella* (1807), esp. Letter 61. The quoted passage following is Simon's speech near the end of the second act of *John Woodvil* (*Works,* V, 153). Hazlitt related in *The Spirit of the Age* (*Hazlitt's Works,* XI, 182–183) that Godwin was so impressed by its beauty "and with a consciousness of having seen it before, that he was uneasy till he could recollect where, and after hunting in vain for it in Ben Jonson, Beaumont and Fletcher, and other not unlikely places, sent to Mr. Lamb to know if he could help him to the author."

3. The horn of the divine goat whose milk nourished the infant Zeus on Crete. Zeus afterward endowed it to be the horn of plenty, or cornucopia. In some traditions Amalthea is the goat, and in others she is the nymph who provided Zeus with the goat's milk.

4. Underscored twice. The quotations below are from *A Midsummer Night's Dream,* III, i, 171, and Southey's "Rosamund to Henry. Written after She Had Taken the Veil," lines 67–68. The poem seems to be only in Lovell and Southey's *Poems: Containing The Retrospect, Odes, Elegies, Sonnets, &c.*

5. In Job 41.

6. Southey planned to come to London, but sickness kept him in Westbury. Charles Lloyd arrived at Lamb's on February 5 and left with Robert for Birmingham on February 19. See *New Southey Letters,* I, 180, and *Lloyd-Manning Letters,* pp. 25–27.

48. *C. L. to Southey*

[March 15, 1799]

Dear Southey,

I have receivd your little volume,[1] for which I thank you, tho' I do not entirely approve of this sort of intercourse, where the presents are all on one side— —. I have read the last Eclogue again with great pleasure—. It hath gained considerably by abridgement, and now I think it wants nothing but enlargement—you will call this one of

Tyrant Procrustes' criticisms, to cut and pull so to his own standard; but the old Lady is so great a favorite with me, I want to **hear** more of her, and of Joanna you have given us still less.— But the picture of the rustics leaning over the bridge, & the old Lady travelling abroad on summer evening to see her garden waterd,[2] are images so new & true, that I decidedly prefer this ruin'd cottage to any poem in the book. Indeed I think it the only one that will bear comparison with your Hymn to the Penates in a former vol.— I compare dissimilar things, as one would a rose & a star for the pleasure they give us, or as a child soon learns to chuse betwe[e]n a cake & a rattle. For dissimilars have mostly some points of comparison—. The next best poem I think is the 1st Eclogue,[3] tis very complete, and abounding in little pictures, &—realities.— The remainder Eclogues, excepting only the "funeral" I do not greatly admire— —. I miss *one,* which had at least as good a title to publication as the Witch or the Sailor's mother— —. You call'd it the Last of the family—. The Old woman of Berkley comes next, in some humours I would give it the preference above any—. But who the devil is Mathew of Westminster? You are as familiar with these antiquated monastics, as Swedenbourg, or, as his followers affect to call him, the **Baron,** with his Invisibles— —. . But you have raised a very comic effect out of the true narrative of Mathew of Westminster. Tis surprising with how little addition you have been able to convert, with so little alteration, his incidents meant for terror into circumstances & food for the spleen. . The Parody[4] is *not* so successful, it has one famous line indeed, which conveys the finest death bed image I ever met with, "The Doctor whisperd the nurse, **And the Surgeon knew what he said."**— —but the offering the Bribe three times bears not the slightest analogy or proportion to the fiendish **noises 3 times heard!—. .— —**

In Jaspar, the circumstance of the **Great Light**[5] is very affecting. . But I had heard you mention it before— — —.

The Rose is the only insipid piece in the volume, it hath neither thorns nor sweetness.— And besides sets all chronology & probability at defiance— — —

Cousin Margaret,[6] you know, I like— —the allusions to the Pilgrim's progress are particularly happy, & harmonize **tacitly** & delicately with old cousins & **aunts**—to familiar faces we do associate familiar scenes & accustom'd objects— —but what hath Apollidon &

his sea nymphs to do in these affairs? Apollyon I could have born, tho he stands for the devil, but who is Apollidon?— — I think you **are** too apt to conclude **faintly**, with some cold moral, as in the end of the Poem calld **"the Victory"**—"Be thou her comforter, who art the widow's **friend**"[7]—a single common place line of comfort, which bears no proportion in weight or number to the many lines which describe suffering— —. This is to convert Religion into mediocre feelings, which should burn & glow & tremble.—. A Moral should be wrought into the body and soul, the matter and tendency, of a Poem, not taggd to the end, like "A God send the good ship into harbour" at the conclusion of our bills of Lading. . . — — The finishing of the "Sailor"[8] is also imperfect. Any dissenting minister may say & do as much—

These remarks, I know, are crude & unwrought, but I do not lay claim to much accurate thinking—I never judge system-wise of things, but fasten upon particulars— — —. After all, there is a great deal in the book, that I must for **time** leave *unmentiond*, to deserve my thanks for its own sake, as well as for the friendly remembrance implied in the gift—. I again return you my thanks—

Pray present my Love to Edith—

C L

have you been in town?— I calld twice at Longman's[9] for the travels, but fancy you forgot to give the Order, you said you had or would for a Copy for me—

MS: Robert H. Taylor Collection. Pub.: Talfourd (1837), I, 130–133; Sala, I, 190–192; Purnell, I, 190–192; Fitzgerald, II, 44–46; Hazlitt, I, 212–214; Ainger (1888), I, 102–104; Ainger (1900), I, 154–156; Macdonald, I, 119–121; Ainger (1904), I, 110–112; Harper, II, 184–187; Lucas (1905), VI, 143–145; Lucas (1912), V, 143–145; Lucas (1935), I, 150–152. Address: Robert Southey/ Mr. Cottle's/Bookseller, High Street/Bristol. Postmark: March 15, 1799.

1. The second (1799) volume of Southey's *Poems* (1797–1799). Its last eclogue, praised below, is "The Ruined Cottage."

2. In "The Ruined Cottage," lines 71–75 and 54–63. The "Hymn to the Penates," referred to below, is in the first (1797) volume of Southey's *Poems*.

3. "The Old Mansion House." The remainder of the "English Eclogues" are "The Grandmother's Tale," "The Funeral" (later retitled "The Alderman's Funeral"), "The Sailor's Mother," and "The Witch." Not in the volume is "The Last of the Family." In later editions of Southey's poems it is among the "English Eclogues." "The Old Woman of Berkeley . . ." is, in *Poems* (1797–1799), preceded by a Latin quotation from Matthew Westminster, the name assigned to the unknown writers from the abbeys of St. Albans and Westminster who compiled the chronicle *Flores historiarum* (1567). Lamb next mentions Emanuel Swedenborg (1688–1772), the Swedish scientist, philosopher, and mystic.

4. "The Surgeon's Warning," from which Lamb below quotes lines 1–2. He criticizes the three offerings of the bribe, in 93–100, 109–120, and 125–140, as disproportionate to the description in 135–136—"And they could not stand the sound in his hand / For he made the guineas chink."

5. "Jaspar," lines 157–164. Lamb's strictures, in the next paragraph, on "The Rose," which retells the story from the fourteenth-century work *The Travels of Sir John Mandeville* of the miraculous creation of the white and red roses as an answer to a condemned woman's prayer, probably hurt the feelings of Southey. For he had addressed the poem to his wife.

6. Called "Metrical Letter Written from London" in *Poems* and "To Margaret Hill. Written from London, 1798" later. Its allusions to *The Pilgrim's Progress* are in lines 16–17 and 59–63. Apollidon (who remains unidentified) is in 43–46. Apollyon figures in Christian demonology. His name, from the Greek *Abaddon,* means "the destroyer." In Revelation 9:11 he is called "the angel of the bottomless pit."

7. "The Victory," lines 45–46. Southey slightly changed the lines later to " . . . be thou, / Who art the widow's friend, her comforter!"

8. "The Sailor Who Had Served in the Slave Trade."

9. The publishing firm whose principals at this time were Thomas Norton Longman (1771–1842) and Owen Rees (1770–1837). Lamb had probably called for Mandeville's *Travels.*

49. *C. L. to Southey*

March 20, 1799

I am hugely pleased with your 'Spider,' 'your old freemason,'[1] as you call him. The three first stanzas are delicious; they seem to me a compound of Burns and Old Quarles, those kind of home-strokes, where more is felt than strikes the ear; a terseness, a jocular pathos, which makes one feel in laughter. The measure, too, is novel and pleasing. I could almost wonder Rob. Burns in his lifetime never stumbled upon it. The fourth stanza is less striking, as being less original. The fifth falls off. It has no felicity of phrase, no old-fashioned phrase or feeling.

Young hopes, and love's delightful dreams,[2]

savour neither of Burns nor Quarles; they seem more like shreds of many a modern sentimental sonnet. The last stanza hath nothing striking in it, if I except the two concluding lines, which are Burns all over. I wish, if you concur with me, these things could be looked to. I am sure this is a kind of writing, which comes tenfold better recommended to the heart, comes there more like a neighbour or familiar, than thousands of Hamuels and Zillahs and Madelons.[3] I beg you will send me the 'Holly-tree,' if it at all resemble this, for it must please me. I have never seen it. I love this sort of poems, that open a new intercourse with the most despised of the animal and insect race. I think this vein may be further opened; Peter Pindar hath very prettily apostrophised a fly; Burns hath his mouse and his louse; Coleridge, less successfully, hath made overtures of intimacy to a jackass, therein only following at unresembling distance Sterne and greater Cervantes. Besides these, I know of no other examples of breaking down the partition between us and our 'poor earth-born companions.'[4] It is sometimes revolting to be put in a track of feeling by other people, not one's own immediate thoughts, else I would persuade you, if I could (I am in earnest), to commence a series of these animal poems, which might have a tendency to rescue some poor creatures from the antipathy of mankind. Some thoughts come across me;—for instance—to a rat, to a toad, to a cockchafer, to a mole—People bake moles alive by a slow oven-fire to cure consumption. Rats are, indeed, the most despised and contemptible parts of God's earth. I killed a rat the other day by punching him to pieces, and feel a weight of blood upon me to this hour. Toads you know are made to fly,[5] and tumble down and crush all to pieces. Cockchafers are old sport; then again to a worm, with an apostrophe to anglers, those patient tyrants, meek inflictors of pangs intolerable, cool devils; to an owl; to all snakes, with an apology for their poison; to a cat in boots or bladders. Your own fancy, if it takes a fancy to these hints, will suggest many more. A series of such poems, suppose them accompanied with plates descriptive of animal torments, cooks roasting lobsters, fishmongers crimping skates, &c., &c., would take excessively. I will willingly enter into a partnership in the plan with you: I think my heart and soul would go with it too—at least, give it a thought. My plan is but this minute come into my head; but it strikes me instantaneously as something new, good and useful, full of pleasure and full of moral. If old Quarles and Wither could live again, we would invite them into our firm. Burns hath done his part. I the other day threw off an extempore epitaph on Ensign Peacock[6] of the 3rd Regt. of the Royal East India Volunteers, who like other boys in this scarlet tainted age was ambitious of playing at soldiers, but dying in the first flash of his valour was at the particular instance of his relations buried with military honours! like any veteran scarr'd or chopt from Blenheim or Ramilies. (He was buried in sash and gorget.)

Marmor Loquitur

Here lies a Volunteer so fine,
Who died of a decline,
As you or I may do one day;
Reader, think of this, I pray;
And I humbly hope you'll drop a tear
For my poor Royal Volunteer.
He was as brave as brave could be,
Nobody was so brave as he;
He would have died in Honor's bed,
Only he died at home instead.
Well may the Royal Regiment swear,
They never had such a Volunteer.
But whatsoever they may say,
Death is a man that will have his way:
Tho' he was but an ensign in this world of pain;
In the next we hope he'll be a captain.
And without meaning to make any reflection on his mentals,
He begg'd to be buried in regimentals.

Sed hæ sunt lamentabiles nugæ[7]—But 'tis as good as some epitaphs you and I have read together in Christ-Church-yard.

Poor Sam. Le Grice! I am afraid the world, and the camp, and the university, have spoilt him among them. 'Tis certain he had at one time a strong capacity of turning out something better. I knew him, and that not long since, when he had a most warm heart. I am ashamed of the indifference I have sometimes felt towards him. I think the devil is in one's heart. I am under obligations to that man for the warmest friendship and heartiest sympathy, even for an agony of sympathy exprest both by word and deed, and tears for me, when I was in my greatest distress. But I have forgot that! as, I fear, he has nigh forgot the awful scenes which were before his eyes when he served the office of a comforter to me. No service was too mean or troublesome for him to perform. I can't think what but the devil, 'that old spider,'[8] could have suck'd my heart so dry of its sense of all gratitude. If he does come in your way, Southey, fail not to tell him that I retain a most affectionate remembrance of his old friendliness, and an earnest wish to resume our intercourse. In this I am serious. I cannot recommend him to your society, because I am afraid whether he be quite worthy of it. But I have no right to dismiss him from *my* regard. He was at one time, and in the worst of times, my own familiar friend, and great comfort to me then. I have known him to play at cards with my father, meal-times excepted, literally all day long, in long days too, to save me from being teased by the old man, when I was not able to bear it.

God bless him for it, and God bless you, Southey.

C. L.

MS: unavailable; purchased by Bernard Quaritch, Ltd., from Sotheby's on October 27, 1959. Text: Lucas (1935), I, 152–155. Also pub.: Talfourd (1837), I, 101–103 and 127–130; Sala, I, 192–195; Purnell, I, 192–195; Fitzgerald, II, 46–49; Hazlitt, I, 214–216; Ainger (1888), I, 104–107; Ainger (1900), I, 157–160; Macdonald, I, 121–124; Ainger (1904), I, 112–115; Harper, II, 187–192; Lucas (1905), VI, 145–147, and VII, 965; Lucas (1912), V, 145–148. Postmark, from a description of the letter in the *CLSB* of January 1960: March 20, 1799. The description includes this statement: "Some three lines of this letter have been crossed through and the deleted words have never been published. This celebrated letter has not been published from the original since it was printed by W. C. Hazlitt."

1. "To a Spider," line 13.

2. "To a Spider," line 35. The concluding lines, which Lamb praises below, read, "Thy bowels thou dost spin, / I spin my brains."

3. Hamuel and Zillah are characters in "The Rose." Madelon is in the third book of Southey's "The Vision of the Maid of Orleans." It (including the first and second books) forms the ninth book of *Joan of Arc* and is in the second volume of *Poems* (1797–1799). "The Holly Tree" has no insects. It and "To a Spider," the latter of which Lamb saw in manuscript, first appeared in the first (1799) volume of *The Annual Anthology*. Except for "To a Bee," Southey wrote no other poems on the lower animals and thus did not continue in the vein opened by the pseudonymous Peter Pindar, the satirist John Wolcot (1738–1819), in "To a Fly" and "The Lousiad"; Burns in "To a Mouse" and "To a Louse"; Coleridge in "To a Young Ass"; Sterne in *Tristram Shandy,* Vol. VII, ch. xxxii, and *A Sentimental Journey through France and Italy,* the chapter titled "The Dead Ass. Nampont"; and Cervantes, by means of Dapple, in *Don Quixote.*

4. Burns, "To a Mouse," line 11.

5. By filliping them: a toad is placed on the end of a stick balanced across a rock, and the other end is struck with a beetle, or mallet. (See, for example, *II Henry IV,* I, ii, 228.) A Mrs. Coe, who as a girl had known Lamb at Widford, told Lucas that "he could rarely, if ever, be tempted to join the anglers. Affixing the worm was too much for him. 'Barbarous, barbarous,' he used to say" (Lucas [1935], I, 155).

6. Probably a fiction, attractive for his name, contrived from the facts that the third regiment of the Royal East India Volunteers was formed of men from the company's warehouses and that there had been employed in the Botolph Wharf warehouse from 1780 to 1797 a Joseph, or Josiah, Peacock (d. 1803?), who had been retired on pension in 1797 because of infirmities and old age. Lamb never

published the poem, whose title translates as "The Marble Speaks," and it is not in *Works*. Blenheim, Germany, was where John Churchill, first Duke of Marlborough (1650–1722), defeated the French in August 1704. Ramillies, Belgium, was where he defeated them in May 1706.

7. "But these are deplorable trifles." It is not known what Le Grice, below, had done.

8. Cf. "To a Spider," line 13.

50. *C. L. to Robert Lloyd*

[St. George's Day, April 23, 1799]

My dear Robert,

I acknowledge I have been sadly remiss of late. If I descend to any excuse, (and all excuses, that come short of a direct denial of a charge are poor creatures at best,) it must be taken from my state of mind for some time past, which has been stupid rather and unfilled with any object, than occupied, as you may imagine with, any favorite idea to the exclusion of friend Robert.— You, who are subject to all the varieties of the mind will give me credit in this.—

I am sadly sorry that you are relapsing into your old complaining strain. I wish I could adapt my consolations to your disease, but alas I have none to offer which your own mind, and the suggestions of books, cannot better supply. Are you the first whose situation hath not been exactly squar'd to his ideas? or rather, will you find me that man, who does not complain of the one thing wanting?—that thing obtained, another wish will start up, while this eternal craving of the mind[1] keeps up its eternal hunger, no feast that my palate knows of will satisfy that hunger, till we come to drink the new wine (whatever it be) in the kingdom of the father.— —See what trifles disquiet us—. You are Unhappy because your Parents expect you to attend meetings—I dont know much of quaker's meetings, but I believe I may moderately reckon them to take up the space of six hours in the week.— Six hours to please your parents—and that time not absolutely lost—your mind remains, you may think, and plan, remember, and foresee, and do all human acts of mind sitting as well as walking—you are quiet at meeting, one likes to be so sometimes—you may advantageously crowd your day's devotions into that space—nothing you see or hear there can be unfavorable to it—you are for that time at least exempt from the counting house, and your parents cannot chide you there—surely at so small an expence you cannot grudge to observe the 5th Commandment—. I decidedly consider your refusal as a breach of that God-descended precept— —. Honour & observe thy parents in all lawful things—. Silent worship cannot be *Un*lawful—there is no Idolatry, no invocation of saints, no bowing before the consecrated wafer in all this—nothing which a wise man would refuse, or a good man fear to do—. What is it? Sitting a few hours in a week with certain Good people, who call *that* worship—you subscribe to no articles—if your mind wanders, it is no crime in you, who do not give credit to these infusions of the spirit—they sit in a **temple,** you sit as in a **room** adjoining—only do not disturb their pious work with gabbling, nor your own necessary peace with heart burnings at your not-ill-meaning parents, nor a silly contempt of the work which is going on before you. . I know that if my parents were to live again, I would do more things to please them, than merely sitting still six hours in a week— — —. Perhaps I enlarge too much on this affair, but indeed your objection seems to me ridiculous, and involving in it a principle of frivolous & vexatious **resistance**— — —— ——

You have often borne with my freedoms, bear with me once more in this—. If I did not love you, I should not trouble myself whether you went to meeting or not—whether you conformd or not to the will of your father— — —

I am now called off to dinner before **one** oClock, being a holyday we dine early, for Mary and me to have a long walk afterwards— ———

my kindest remembrance to Charles
God give him all joy and quiet——[2]
Mary sends her **Love**

C L

MS: Huntington Library. Pub.: Ainger (1900), I, 134–137; Macdonald, I, 139–141; Ainger (1904), I, 96–98; Harper, II, 224–227; Lucas (1935), I, 158–159. Address: Robert Lloyd/Ch Lloyd's/Birmingham. Postmark: April 23 [1799]. It seems as reasonable to assume now as it seemed to Lucas (see Lucas [1935], I, 155) that, immediately after the death this month and burial on the thirteenth of their father, Lamb took Mary from confinement and they began their life together anew in new lodgings at 36 Chapel Street. But notice of the address does not occur until Coleridge gives it in his letters of early March 1800. See *Coleridge's Letters,* I, 579.

1. Cf. George Crabbe, *The Library,* line 102.

2. In his marriage to Sophia Pemberton. The ceremony took place on the next day in Birmingham.

51. *C. L. to Robert Lloyd*

[September or October 1799]

My dear Robert,

I suppose by this time you have returned from Worcester with Uncle Nehemiah.[1] You neglected to inform me whether Charles is yet at Birm. . I have heard here, that he is returned to Cambridge—. Give him a gentle tap on the shoulder to remind him how truly acceptable a letter from him would be—. I have nothing to write about.—

Thomson[2] remains with me. He is pe[r]petually getting into mental vagaries. He is in **Love!** and tosses and tumbles about in his bed, like a man in a barrel of spikes. He is more sociable; but I am heartily sick of his domesticating with me; he wants so many sympathies of mine, and I want his, that we are daily declining into *civility*. . I shall be truly glad when he is gone. . I find tis a dangerous experiment to grow too familiar. Some natures cannot bear it without converting into indifference—I know but one Being that I could ever consent to live perpetually with, and that is Robert. .[3] But Robert must go whether prudence and paternal regulations indicate a way—. I shall not soon forget you—do not fear that— —nor grow cool towards Robert—my not writing is no proof of these disloyalties— — —. Perhaps I am unwell, or vexed, or spleend, or something, when I should otherwise write—

Assure Charles of my unalterable affection—. And present my warmest wishes for his & Sophia's happiness. . How goes on Priscilla? I am much pleased with his Poems in the Anthology—.[4] **One** in Particular—. The other is a kind & no doubt just tribute to Robert & Olivia—but I incline to opinion that these domestic addresses should not always be made public. I have, I know, more than once exposed my own secretest feelings of that nature, but I am sorry that I did— —. Nine out of ten readers laugh at them—. When a man dies leaving the name of a great Author behind him, any unpublish'd relicks which let one into his domestic retirements are greedily gathered up, which in his life time, and before his fame had ripened, would by many be considered as impertinent—. But if Robert & his sister were gratifyd with seeing their brother's heart in Print, let the rest of the world go hang.

They may prefer the remaining trumpery of the Anthology. . All I mean to say is, I think I perceive an indelicacy in thus exposing one's virtuous feelings to criticism—. But of delicacy Charles is at least as true a judge as myself———

Pray request him to let me somehow have a sight of his novel.[5] I declined offering it here for sale for good reasons as I thought—being unknown to Booksellers, & not made for making bargains. . But for that reason I am not to be punished with not seeing the book—

I shall count it a kindness if Chas. will send me the manuscript, which shall certainly be returned—[. . .]

MS: Huntington Library. Pub.: Ainger (1900), I, 163–165; Macdonald, I, 126–128; Ainger (1904), I, 117–118; Harper, II, 192–194; Lucas (1935), I, 159–161. The second leaf of the folio on which this letter is written has, with the exception of about two lines at its top, been torn away. With it went the address and postmark. See notes 1 and 4 for the dating.

1. Nehemiah Lloyd (1746–1801), the bachelor brother of the senior Charles Lloyd. Lucas stated in *Lamb and the Lloyds,* p. 101, that Robert visited Nehemiah Lloyd in September.

2. Marmaduke Thompson.

3. Priscilla Lloyd believed living with Lamb would not be good for Robert. Lamb, she advised Robert in June 1799, "would not I think by any means be a person to take up your abode with. He is too much like yourself—he would encourage those feelings which it certainly is your duty to suppress. Your station in life—the duties which are pointed out by that rank in society which you are destined to fulfil—differ widely from his" (*Lamb and the Lloyds,* p. 99).

4. Southey's *Annual Anthology.* The first volume came out on about September 6 (see *New Southey Letters,* I, 199) and contains Charles Lloyd's "To a Young Man," "Sonnet X. To a Wood Pigeon," "Sonnet XI. To the Sabbath," and "Lines to a Brother and Sister." Olivia Lloyd (1783–1854), the sister addressed in the last poem and mentioned below, was in 1808 married to Paul Moon James (1780–1854). He was a Quaker, a banker of Birmingham and Manchester, and the editor of *Poems and Letters* (1811) of William Isaac Roberts (1787?–1806) of Bristol. James was the author of *Poems* (1821). For further particulars see Ruth I. Aldrich, "Paul Moon James, Quaker Banker and Poet," in the *CLSB* of April 1974.

5. *Isabel,* which Charles Lloyd had completed by May 28, revised and had privately printed at Ulverston in 1809 but quickly ordered suppressed, and had published in London in 1820. See the *Lloyd-Manning Letters,* p. 35, and *Lamb and the Lloyds,* pp. 245–247.

52. *C. L. to Southey*

October 31, 1799

Dear Southey,

I have but just got your letter,[1] being returned from Herts, where I have passed a few red-letter days with much pleasure. I would describe the county to you, as you have done by Devonshire, but alas! I am a poor pen at that same. I could tell you of an old house with a tapestry bed-room, the 'judgment of Solomon' composing one pannel, and 'Actæon spying Diana naked' the other. I could tell of an old marble hall, with Hogarth's prints and the Roman Cæsars in marble hung round. I could tell of a *wilderness,* and of a village church, and where the bones of my honoured grandam lie; but there are feelings which refuse to be translated, sulky aborigines, which will not be naturalized in another soil. Of this nature are old family faces and scenes of infancy.

I have given your address, and the books you want, to the Arches;[2] they will send them as soon as they can get them, but they do not seem quite familiar to their names. I have seen Gebor! Gebor aptly so denominated from Geborish, *quasi* Gibberish. But Gebor hath some lucid intervals. I remember darkly one beautiful simile veiled in uncouth phrases about the youngest daughter of the Ark. I shall have nothing to communicate, I fear, to the Anthology.[3] You shall have some fragments of my play, if you desire them, but I think I would rather print it whole. Have you seen it, or shall I lend you a copy? I want your opinion of it.

I must get to business, so farewell. My kind remembrances to Edith.

C. Lamb

MS: unrecovered. Text: Lucas (1935), I, 161–162. Also pub.: Talfourd (1837), I, 134–135; Sala, I, 200–201; Purnell, I, 200–201; Fitzgerald, II, 52–53; Hazlitt, I, 222–223; Ainger (1888), I, 109; Ainger (1900), I, 165–166; Macdonald, I, 128–129; Ainger (1904), I, 118–119; Harper, II, 194–195; Lucas (1905), VI, 149–150; Lucas (1912), V, 149–150.

1. Unrecovered, but Southey's descriptions to others of his visit to Devonshire are in *Southey's Correspondence,* II, 22–24, and *New Southey Letters,* I, 197–200. Lamb had passed a few days at Blakesware and its environs in Widford and writes here of the adornments and sights he would write of again in "Dream-children; a Reverie" and "Blakesmoor in H——shire" (*Works,* II, 102 and 154–157).

2. John and Arthur Arch, the publishers of *Blank Verse.* (See Letter 40, note 3.) Gebor, mentioned below, is Walter Savage Landor's *Gebir* (1798), whose simile at VII, 248–256, Lamb but darkly remembers. He quotes an exclamation of its character Charoba in "The Old Margate Hoy" (*Works,* II, 181).

3. Its second (1800) volume, in which Lamb is not represented. His only contribution to its first volume is "Living without God in the World." (See Letter 44, note 1.) It is clear from the next two sentences that Lamb has now completed at least a first draft of "Pride's Cure," or *John Woodvil.*

53. *C. L. to Thomas Manning*

[Mid-]Decemr 99

Dear Manning,

the particular kindness, even up to a degree of attachment, which I have experienced from you, seems to claim some distinct acknowledgment on my part. I could not content myself with a bare remembrance to you, conveyed in some letter to Lloyd— — — ———

Will it be agreeable to you, if I occasionally recruit your memory of me, which must else soon fade, if you consider the brief intercourse we have had? I am not likely to prove a troublesome correspondent. My scribbling days are past. I shall have no sentiments to communicate, but as they spring up from some living and worthy occasion. . .—

I look forwards with great pleasure to the performance of your promise, that we should meet in London early in the ensuing year—. The century must needs commence auspiciously for me, that brings with it Manning's friendship, as an earnest of its after gifts.— — ———

I should have written before, but for a troublesome inflammation in one of my eyes, brought on by night travelling with the coach windows sometimes up—

What more I have to say shall be reserved for a letter to Lloyd.— I must not prove tedious to you in my first outside, lest I should affright you by my ill judg'd loquacity.

I am
Yours most sincerely
C Lamb

MS: Huntington Library. Pub.: Talfourd (1837), I, 135–136; Sala, I, 327–328; Purnell, I, 327–328; Fitzgerald, II, 161–162; Hazlitt, I, 224; Ainger (1888), I, 111–112; Ainger (1900), I, 169–170; Macdonald, I, 129–130; Ainger (1904), I, 121; Harper, II, 195–196; Lucas (1905), VI, 151; Lucas (1912), V, 151; Lucas (1935), I, 164. Address: Mr. T. Manning/Cambridge. A statement of Mr. Lloyd in his letter from London of December 5 to his sons Robert and Thomas that he had called at the East India House with his daughters Priscilla and Rachel (details about her are unknown) to see Lamb but was told he had left for Cambridge, and the December 15 date on Manning's reply to this letter of Lamb's, reasonably establish that Charles Lloyd had introduced Lamb and Manning at Cambridge in the first week of December and that Lamb wrote this first letter to Manning in the week following. (See *Lamb and the Lloyds,* p. 105, and the *Manning-Lamb Letters,* pp. 21–22.) Manning (1772–1840), Lloyd's mathematics tutor at the university, was to become the first European scholar of Chinese and the first Englishman to enter Lhasa, Tibet. He was born in the parish of Broome, Norfolk, the second son of William (1733?–1810), rector successively of Broome and Diss, and his wife, Elizabeth (1748?–1782), the only child of William Adams, rector of Rollesby, Norfolk. Manning attended Bury School in Bury St. Edmunds for one year, was withdrawn because of ill health and tutored at home by his father, and in 1790 was admitted to Gonville and Caius College, Cambridge, where he distinguished himself in mathematics but was denied a degree for refusing to submit to examinations and to subscribe to the required oaths. He nevertheless remained at Cambridge, giving private lessons in mathematics in his rooms above a Mr. Crisp's barber shop at 3 St. Mary's Passage, writing *An Introduction to Arithmetic and Algebra* (2 vols.; 1796–1798), and beginning his study of Chinese. During the next few years the language so captivated him that he left for London in November 1801—only a month after the signing of the peace preliminaries that permitted travel into France and led in March 1802 to the Treaty of Amiens—and in January 1802 crossed to Paris to study it into 1805 under a Dr. Hagar and through the resources of the Bibliothèque Nationale. He was one of the many Englishmen detained in France as a result of the rupture of the peace with England in May 1803. But because of their regard for him and his intention now to travel to China, the authorities allowed him his liberty. By 1805 Napoleon, at the request of Talleyrand, granted him his passport. Manning returned to England to spend time with his family and friends until November 1805. Then he went to London to increase his knowledge of medicine at Westminster Hospital. In May 1806 he sailed on board the *Thames* for China under the patronage of the East India Company and settled at the company's factory in Canton. There he remained, except for an excursion in 1808 into Cochin China, until 1810. He then moved to Calcutta, whence he set out as a doctor, with a single Chinese servant, for Lhasa in September 1811. He reached Lhasa in December, left in April 1812, and was back in Calcutta in June. A few months later he was back in Canton. In 1816 he became attached to the embassy of William Pitt Amherst, later Earl Amherst of Arracan (1773–1857), as a secretary and an interpreter at the court of Peking. When the embassy failed in its mission to secure improved trade agreements with China and upset the Chinese government by refusing to follow protocol, Manning's plans for further explorations of the country were doomed. Manning returned with the embassy party to Canton and departed with it on the *Alceste* for England. The ship was wrecked in the Java Sea near Sunda on February 17, 1817, and its passengers taken on the *Caesar* from Batavia to St. Helena. There Manning interviewed Napoleon in June. Manning reached England on July 25 and went to live on a farm at Redbourn, Hertfordshire. He visited Italy from 1827 to 1829. When he returned he retired, first to Bexley and then to a property called the Orange Grove, near Dartford, Kent. In 1838 he lost the use of his right hand, removed to Bath for medical attention, and died there of a second paralytic stroke. Although he published nothing on China or her language, he assisted other scholars and left a collection of books on China said to have been the most extensive in Europe at the time. It is preserved by the Royal Asiatic Society. His journal was edited by the geographer and historical writer Sir Clements Robert Markham (1830–1916) from a fair copy made by Manning's sister and is in Markham's *Narratives of the Mission of George Bogle to Tibet, and of the Journey of Thomas Manning to Lhasa* [*1811–1812*] . . . *with Notes, an Introduction and Lives of Mr. Bogle and Mr. Manning* (London: Trübner, 1876), pp. 213–294. For additional information on Manning see the *DNB;* Barry E. O'Meara's *Napoleon in Exile; or, a Voice from St. Helena* (2 vols.; New York: Peter Eckler, n.d.), II, 43–46; Edith

Christina Johnson's *Lamb Always Elia* (London: Methuen, 1935), pp. 39–75; and Morchard Bishop's "Lamb's Mr. M.: The First Englishman in Lhasa," *Cornhill Magazine,* No. 1046 (Winter 1965–1966), 96–112. Manning's brothers and sister are named in my Vol. III, Lamb's letter to Manning of January 2, 1810, notes.

54. *C. L. to Robert Lloyd*

[Tuesday, December 17, 1799]

Dear Rab—

Thy presents will be most acceptable, whenever they come, both for thy sake, and for the liquor, which is a beverage I most admire—. Wine makes me hot, and brandy makes me drunk, but porter warms without intoxication; and elevates, yet not too much above the point of tranquillity,— But I hope Robert will come himself, before the tap is out.— He may be assured, that his good honest company is the most valuable present, after all, he can make us.— These cold nights crave something, beside Porter;—good English mirth & heart's ease.— Rob. must contrive to pass some of his Christmas with us, or at least drink in the century with a welcome.— ———

I have not seen your father or Priscilla since.[1] Your father was in one of his best humours, (I have seldom seen him in one not good,)— and after dinner, while we were sitting comfortably before the parlour fire, after our wine, he beckoned me suddenly out of the room. I, expecting some secrets, followed him, but it was only to go & sit with him in the old forsaken compting house, which he declared to be the pleasantest spot in the house to him, and told me how much business used to be done there in former days.—Your father whimsically mixes the good man and the man of business in his manners, but he is not less a good man for being a man of business.— He has conceived great hopes of thy one day uniting both characters, & I joyfully expect the same.— — ——

I hope to see Priscilla, for the first time, some day the end of this week, but think it at least dubious, as she stays in town but one day, I think your father said. .— ——

I wonder Rob. could think, I should take his presents in evil part.— I am sure from him they are the genuine result of a sincere friendship, not immediately knowing, how better to express itself. . . I shall enjoy them with tenfold gust, as being his presents.— At the same time, I must remind him, that such expressions, if too thickly repeated, would be in danger of proving oppressive.—

I am not fond of presents all on one side,— & Rob. knows I have little to present to him, except the assurances of an undiminish'd & an undiminishable friendship. . Rob. will take as a hint, what his friend does not mean as an affront— —. I hope our friendship will stand firm, without the help of scaffolding.— At the same time I am determined to enjoy Robert's present, and to drink his health in his own porter, and I hope he will be able to partake with us.— Bread & cheese and a hearty sympathy may prove no bad supplement to Robert's good old English beverage———

Charles has not written to me since I saw him.— I trust he goes on as comfortably as I witness'd— —. No husband & wife can be happier, than Sophia & your Brother appear to be in each other's company.— Robert must marry next—I look to see him get the start of Wordsworth & Priscilla, whom yet I wish to see united—

farewell dearest Rab—

C L

Mary joins with me in remembrances to Robert, and in expectation of the coming beverage— — —

Do you think you shall be able to come?— ———

MS: Huntington Library. Pub.: Macdonald, I, 130–131; Harper, II, 197–199; Lucas (1935), I, 165–166. Address: Robt. Lloyd/Charles Lloyd's/Birmingham. Postmark: December 17, 1799.

1. Apparently since Lamb had returned their call and was entertained in the London quarters of Mr. Lloyd's bank.

55. *C. L. to Manning*

Saturday the 28th Decr [1799]

Dear Manning,

having suspended my correspondence a decent interval, as knowing that even good things may be taken to satiety, a wish cannot but recur to learn whether you be still well and happy. Do all things continue in the state I left them in Cambridge.———

Do your night parties still flourish? & do you continue to bewilder your company, with your thousand faces, running down thro' all the Keys of Ideotism, (like Lloyd over his perpetual harpsichord,) from the smile and the glimmer of half-sense, and quarter-sense, to the grin and the hanging lip of Betty Foy's own Johnny. ?—[1] And does the face-dissolving curfew sound at twelve?—

How unlike the great originals were your petty terrors in the Post-[s]cript, not fearful enough to make a fairy shudder, or a lilliputian fine lady, eight months full of child, miscarry.———

Yet one of them which had more beast than the rest, I thought faintly resembled *one* of your brutifications. .— ———

But, seriously, I long to see your own honest Manning-face again—I did not mean a pun,—your *man's* face, you will be apt to say, I know your wicked will to pun—. I cannot—now—write to Lloyd and you too, so you must convey as much interesting intelligence as this may contain, or be thought to contain, to him and Sophia, with my dearest love and remembrances.———

By the bye, I think you and Sophia both incorrect with regard to the *title* of the *play*—.[2] Allowing your objection (which is not necessary, as Pride may be, and is in real life often, cured by misfortunes not directly originating from its own acts, as Jeremy Taylor will tell you a naughty desire is sometimes sent to cure it,—I know you read these *practical divines*) but allowing your objection,—does not the betraying of his father's secret directly spring from pride?— from the pride of wine, and a full heart, and a proud overstepping of the ordinary rules of morality, and contempt of the prejudices of mankind, which are not to bind superior souls—"as *trust* in *the matter* of *secrets,* all *ties* of *blood,* &c &c. keeping *of promises,* the feeble mind's religion, binding our *morning knowledge* to the performance of what *last nights' ignorance* spake"[3]—does he not prate, that ***"Great Spirits"*** must do more than die for their friend—does not the pride of wine incite him to display some evidence of friendship, which its own *irregularity* shall make great?———

This I know, that I meant his punishment not alone to be a cure for his daily & habitual *pride,* but the direct consequence, and appropriate punishment, of a particular act of pride.— — —

If you do not understand it so, it is my fault in not explaining my meaning———

I have not seen Coleridge since,[4] and scarcely expect to see him—perhaps he has been at Cambridge— ———

Is Mr. Lloyd at Cambridge?— he talk'd uncertainly of going.— —
I dined with him in town, and breakfasted with him and Priscilla,—

who, you may tell Charles, has promised to come & see me, when she returns from Clapham

I will write to Charles on monday—. need I turn over, to blot a fresh clean half sheet, Merely to say, what I hope you are sure of without my repeating it, that I would have you consider me, dear Manning,——

Your sincere friend—
C Lamb

What is your *proper address?*

MS: Huntington Library. Pub.: Talfourd (1837), I, 136–139; Sala, I, 325–327; Purnell, I, 325–327; Fitzgerald, II, 159–161; Hazlitt, I, 224–226; Ainger (1888), I, 110–111; Ainger (1900), I, 167–169; Macdonald, I, 132–133; Ainger (1904), I, 119–121; Harper, II, 199–201; Lucas (1905), VI, 152–153, and VII, 965; Lucas (1912), V, 152–153; Lucas (1935), I, 166–168. Address: Mr. Thomas Manning/near St Mary's church/Cambridge. Postmark: December 28, 1799.

1. In Wordsworth's "The Idiot Boy." The reference in the next paragraph is to the assortment of "Night-mares, Hobgoblins, & Spectres" that Manning had sketched in his letter of the fifteenth. See the *Manning-Lamb Letters,* p. 22, and the facsimile tipped in between pp. 22 and 23.

2. Lamb's "Pride's Cure," of which Sophia Lloyd had observed, wrote Manning, that the "Folly, whose consequences humble the Pride & ambition of John's heart, does not originate in the workings of *those* passions, but from an underpart in his character, & as it were accidentally, viz from the ebullitions of a drunken mind & from a rash confidence" (*Manning-Lamb Letters,* p. 22). Taylor's observation to which Lamb refers below is in *The Rule and Exercises of Holy Living,* ch. ii, sect. 4, "Acts or Offices of Humility," nos. 6 and 9; and sect. 6, "Of Contentedness in All Estates and Accidents," no. 2.

3. Lamb is writing generally of the third act of his play. For this quotation and the next see *Works,* V, 161 and 160.

4. Since when is not known, but it seems from the next letter that it was before Coleridge moved to London. While visiting Wordsworth and the Lake District, Coleridge had received and shortly afterward accepted a proposal from Daniel Stuart (1766–1846), from 1795 to 1803 proprietor with his brother Peter (fl. 1788–1805) of the *Morning Post* and from 1796 to 1822 proprietor with Peter Street of *The Courier,* to go to London and write political articles for the *Morning Post.* Coleridge arrived on November 27 and by December 19 was established with his wife and son in rooms at 21 Buckingham Street, the Strand. What drew Priscilla Lloyd to Clapham, below, I cannot say.

56. *C. L. to Charles Lloyd, the younger*

[December 30, 1799]

dear Lloyd,

I make it my particular request, that you will immediately transmit me your copy of my Play.— I promise religiously to restore it some time again. I want it particularly, as I am liable every day to be called upon for a copy.— Sophia will pack it up, I know, if you ask her.———

I have presented my copy to Kemble.—[1] I left it at his house yesterday morning, before he was up, with no other introduction but an anonymous note, requesting his opinion; but having taken the precaution to write my name and address in a blank leaf, was surprized in the evening with a Letter from Kemble, in very handsome terms declining to determine upon it, as not being in his province, but offering "with great pleasure to put my play into the hands of the Proprietors of Drury Lane Theatre, and hoping that it may succeed with them to Mr. Lamb's wishes."— this from a perfect stranger, who never saw me, and the very day in which I had so awkwardly and improperly obtruded it upon him, was most handsome and gentleman-like,—and, I confess has revived in me some antiquated pretensions———

It is evident he has read it with some approbation, of a voluntary offer to present it for me— — —so, you will see the necessity of my having another copy fairly written in the house, which I have not, only a rough draught.— — I will certainly some day replace yours— — —but pray send it directly———

I purpose calling upon Kemble, whom I have not yet seen, tomorrow morning—I am not very sanguine, but the profits of acting plays are so large now adays, that a very shadow of a hope ought to make me glad.— direct it to India house—

I have just learned, that Coleridge has taken lodgings with his family in the Adelphi—.[2] But I have seen nothing of him— —

Pray present my love to Sophia, and bid Manning write, when you send my parcel— —

And respects to your father, if he is in Cam—

Yours truly
C L

MS: By permission of the Harvard College Library, Cambridge, Mass. Pub.: Lucas (1935), I, 162–163. Address: Mr. Ch. Lloyd Junr/Mr. Styles's Jesus Lane/ Cambridge. Postmark: December 30, 1799.

1. The actor John Philip Kemble (1757–1823), who managed Drury Lane from 1788 to 1796 and from 1800 to 1802. Almost a year passed (see Letter 86, at the

reference to note 10) before Lamb learned, upon inquiry to Kemble, that the manuscript of "Pride's Cure" had been lost and that he would have to submit a second copy.

2. A district south of the Strand that includes Buckingham Street.

57. *C. L. to Coleridge*

[Thursday, January 23, 1800]

Dear Coleridge,

Now I write, I cannot miss this opportunity of acknowledging the obligations myself, and the readers in general of that luminous paper, the 'Morning Post,' are under to you for the very novel and exquisite manner in which you combined political with grammatical science, in your yesterday's dissertation on Mr. Wyndham's unhappy composition. It must have been the death-blow to that ministry. I expect Pitt and Grenville to resign. More especially the delicate and Cottrellian[1] grace with which you officiated, with a ferula for a white wand, as gentleman usher to the word 'also,' which it seems did not know its place.

I expect Manning of Cambridge in town to-night—will you fulfil your promise of meeting him at my house? He is a man of a thousand. Give me a line to say what day, whether Saturday, Sunday, Monday, &c., and if Sara and the Philosopher[2] can come. I am afraid if I did not at intervals call upon you, I should *never see you*. But I forget, the affairs of the nation engross your time and your mind.

Farewell.

C. L.

MS: unrecovered. Text: Lucas (1935), I, 168–169. Also pub.: Talfourd (1837), I, 143–144; Sala, I, 111–112; Purnell, I, 111–112; Fitzgerald, I, 393–394; Hazlitt, I, 226–227; Ainger (1888), I, 113; Ainger (1900), I, 171–172; Macdonald, I, 134; Ainger (1904), I, 122; Harper, II, 202; Lucas (1905), VI, 154; Lucas (1912), V, 154. The date is fixed by the reference to Coleridge's contribution to the *Morning Post* of January 22 criticizing a note signed and dated "Grenville, Downing-street, Jan. 4, 1800," in the *Morning Post* of January 7 replying to Napoleon's offer of peace. (A letter signed and dated "A Friend of Lord Grenville, Pall Mall, Jan. 13," in the *Morning Post* of January 16 identifies the note as by Secretary of War William Windham [1750–1810] and explains that William Wyndham Grenville, Baron Grenville [see Letter 47, note 2] "only signed it in his official capacity.")

1. After Sir Charles (1612?–1701), Sir Charles Lodowick (1654–1710), and Sir Clement (d. 1758) Cotterell, who with the exception of the period 1650–1659 were masters of the ceremonies from 1641 to 1758. According to Lucas (1935), I, 169, the Cotterells' tenure extended (through another member of the family) to

1808. With the word "also," below, Lamb alludes to this passage in Coleridge's *Morning Post* article of January 22, one critical of the grammar in the note to which he responded: " 'The *same* system, to the prevalence of which France justly ascribes all her present miseries, is that which has *also* involved the rest of Europe in a long and destructive warfare, of a nature long since unknown *to* the practice of civilized nations.' Here the connective word 'also' should have followed the word 'Europe.' As it at present stands, the sentence implies that France, miserable as she may be, has, however, not been involved in a warfare" (quoted from Samuel Taylor Coleridge, *Essays on His Own Times: Forming a Second Series of The Friend,* ed. Sara Coleridge [London: Pickering, 1850], I, 262).

2. The Coleridges' son, David Hartley. It is apparent from Sophia Lloyd's letter to Manning in London of January 26 (*Lloyd-Manning Letters,* esp. p. 41) that Coleridge and Manning did meet at this time and that the former "dazzled" the latter.

58. *C. L. to Manning*

Saturday [February 8, 1800]

Lloyd's Letter to Miss Hays[1] I look upon to be a most curious specimen of the apologetic style. . . How a man could write such a letter to a woman, and dream that there was in it any tendency to sooth or conciliate, from no analogous operations in my own wrong Brain can I explain.— — "Mary Hays, I said that I believed that you were in love with me."— "I had heard several times repeated, that you had loved both Godwin and Friend, moreover I had heard several times repeated, that all your first novel was but a transcript of letters sent by yourself to the latter Gentleman. I have been told this so often, that it seems to my mind like a general report. I have heard it in all places." "Dr. Reid[2] & I were laughing in the wantonness in which our sex too often indulges at the consequence of your theories, & I most wickedly &c.". .— (In God's name, how came he & the Dr. so graciously familiar, just after he had discover'd the Dr's. complete worthlessness & wickedness?—) "I most *wickedly* exprest myself as if I thought you would in conduct demonstrate all that you proposed in speculation! I did not say this Grossly."— (Wheugh! Wheugh! what a delicate invention, how to call a woman a whore, and not be indictable in the Spiritual courts!—) "In the confounding medley of ordinary conversation, I have interwoven my abhorrence of your principles with a glanced contempt for your personal character." . . . But "in spite of all these inconsistencies I am your friend, & for the future, if we maintain our intercourse, will prove to you by conduct, how severely I condemn the past."— — C Lloyd must have a damned "spite to inconsistencies," if he can reconcile this language to the ordinary meaning of the term *apology.*— — ——

Now, Manning, seriously what do you think of this Letter?[3] does it appear that Coleridge has added one jot to what Miss Hays might fairly represent from Lloyd's own confession.?— You doubt, whether Southey ever exprest himself so stongly on this subject. I suppose you refer to Coleridge's account of him. I can tell you, that Southey did express himself in very harsh terms of Lloyd's conduct, when he was last in town. He came fresh from Miss Hays, who had given him all the story, as I find she tells every body! and told Southey that she despised Lloyd. I am not sure, that Southey was not in a humour, after this representation to say all that Coleridge declared he did say.— Particularly, if he saw this Letter, which I believe he did.— Now, do not imagine, that Col. has prejudiced my mind in this *at all.*— the truth is, I write from my own single judgment, and when I shewed the Letter to Coleridge, he read it in silence, or only once muttered the word "indelicate."— But I should not have been easy in concealing my true sentiment from you. My whole moral sense is up in arms against the Letter. To my apprehension, it is shockingly & nauseously indelicate, and I perceive an aggravation or multiplication of the Indelicacy, in Lloyd's getting his sister **Olivia** to transcribe it. An ignorant Quaker girl, I mean ignorant in the best sense, who ought not to know, that such a thing was possible or in rerum naturæ, that a woman should **court** a man. . . And a dear sister, who least of all should apprehend such an **omen!** realiz'd in her o[wn][4] Brother. Manning, do not misapprehend me, I would not say so much to Lloyd's own self, for this plain reason, that I shou[ld not] b[e] able to convince him, and I would no[t cause] unnecessary pain. Yet as much of this, as y[our] discretion & tenderness will give leave, you have my full leave to shew him.— — But I could not let you remain ignorant of so big a part of my nature, as now rises up against this ill judged Letter, particularly as I am doubtful, whether you may not see it in a quite different light.—. So much for Lloyd's amours with Mary Hays, which would not form an unentertaining romance. From this time, they are no concern of mine. I will sum up the controversy in the words of Coleridge, all he has since said to me, "Miss Hays has acted **like** a fool, & Charles Lloyd not very wisely."— ——

I cannot but smile at Lloyd's beginning to find out, that Col. can tell lyes. He brings a serious charg[e] against him, that he told Caldwell,[5] he had no engagements with the Newspapers! As long as Lloyd or I have known Col. so long have we known him in the daily & hourly habit of quizzing the world by lyes most unaccountable & most disinterested **fictions.**—. With a correct knowledge of these inaccuracies on both sides, I am still desirous of keeping on kind terms with Lloyd, and I am to sup with Coleridge to night—. Godwin[6] will be there, whom I am rather curious to see—& Col. to partake with me of Manning's Bounty tomorrow.—. By the way, I am anxious to get specimens of all English Turkeys.— Pray, send me at your Leisure separate specimens from every County in Great Britain, including Wales, as I hate nationalities—. The **Irish** Turkeys I will let alone, till the **union** is determined.— To sum up my inferences from the above facts, I am determined to live a merry Life in the midst of Sinners. I try to consider all men as such, and to pitch my expectations from human nature as low as possible. In this view, all unexpected virtues are God-sends & beautiful exceptions. Only let **Young Love** beware, when he sets out in his progress thro' life, how he forms erroneous conceptions of finding all **Saints!**— — To conclude, the Blessing of St. Peter's master rest upon you & all honest anglers.—

C Lamb

The Turkey is just come——the Largest I ever saw—

Coleridge has conceived a most high (Quere[7] if just) opinion of you, most illustrious Archimedes: . . .

Philosopher Godwin! dines with me on your Turkey this day. = I expect the roof to fall and crush the Atheist. I have been drunk two nights running at Coleridge's—how my Head burns!—— ——

MS: Huntington Library. Pub.: Harper, I, facsimile, and II, 205–209; Lucas (1935), I, 170–172. Address: Mr. Thos. Manning/Mr Crisp's/Cambridge. Postmark: February 8, 1800.

1. Mary Hays (1760–1843) was the author of *Letters and Essays* (1793), *Memoirs of Emma Courtney* (1796), *The Victim of Prejudice* (1799), and *Female Biography, or Memoirs of Illustrious and Celebrated Women* (1803). It is to the second of those that Lamb refers below. Since 1793 she had been the friend of Godwin, Frend, and Dyer, with all three of whom she at various times imagined herself in love. Between 1797 and 1800 Dyer introduced her to Coleridge, Lamb, Charles Lloyd, Southey, and the attorney, journalist, and diarist Henry Crabb Robinson (1775–1867). (The fullest accounts of her are in *The Love Letters of Mary Hays* [*1779–1780*], ed. A. F. Wedd [London: Methuen, 1925]; M. Ray Adams, *Studies in the Literary Backgrounds of English Radicalism* [see Letter

1, note 2], pp. 83–103; and Joyce M. S. Tompkins, "Mary Hays, Philosophess," in *The Polite Marriage* [Cambridge: Cambridge University Press, 1938].) Southey, in a letter to his wife of May 15, 1799, clarifies the greater part of this letter by explaining that Miss Hays had gone out one evening in depressed spirits with Charles Lloyd and Stephen Weever Browne, the author of *The Duties of Christian Ministers* (1819), a friend of Southey's since 1798. Browne so wearied her with his constant talk that when he left them at her lodgings she broke down before Lloyd. Lloyd consoled her then and in a letter the next day. Shortly afterward Lloyd broadcast the story that Miss Hays was in love with him, had sent Browne away to be alone with him, and had burst into tears when he would not understand her. The story got back to Miss Hays, who wrote to Lloyd of his vanity. Lloyd answered "by confessing that he had traduced her character—and apologizing most humbly for it, alledging [sic] that her principles were so very bad that he had suspected her conduct—yet saying that no one who knew her could doubt her excellence unless he were a fool or a villain. Of course," Southey added, "she thinks him either the one or the other" (*New Southey Letters,* I, 188). Coleridge wrote Southey on January 25, 1800: "Miss Hays I have seen. Charles Lloyd's conduct has been atrocious beyond what you stated—. Lamb himself confessed to me, that during the time in which he [Lloyd] kept up his ranting sentimental Correspondence with Miss Hays, he frequently read her Letters in company, as a subject for *laughter*—& then sate down & answered them quite a la Rosseau!" (*Coleridge's Letters,* I, 563).

2. John Reid (1776–1822), a London physician and the author of *Essays on Insanity* (1816) and *Essays on Hypochondriasis and Other Nervous Affections* (1821). His second wife, to whom he was married in 1821, was Elizabeth Jesser Sturch Reid (1794?–1866), the cofounder of Queen's College and, in 1849, Bedford College, University of London. Reid, Robinson recorded in 1799, "who delighted in sarcasm, and had quarrelled with Charles Lloyd, resented Lloyd's satirical attack on Miss Hays in his *Edmund Oliver* by a very bitter review [unidentified] in the *Analytical Review*" (*H. C. R. on Books and Writers,* I, 5).

3. Manning thought Miss Hays largely culpable and on February 9 answered Lamb's question in part: "There is a certain degree of blame attaches itself to this business. Let us divide it into 10 thousand parts & give one part to Lld—He will then have his share to the full. That is my opinion. What business has Miss H. to go about exhibiting a private correspondence of this kind?—L. does not go round to his friends & acquaintances babbling forth her follies—he never *did,* & he never *does.*— If he did employ his sister to transcribe the letter, we ought to consider who Olivia is—not a tattling pert minx, but a good girl, that would copy the letter at her Brother's request, & think no more about the matter. As to Southey's implication in the business—it is sufficient to state Southey now corresponds with L. as a friend—whoever deems Southey a man of character & integrity is satisfied by this that he does not consider L. as a guilty man—however erroneous & faulty he *may have* judged his conduct—& this, whatever sentences S. may have uttered. You know, Lamb, from the expressions I used at your house, my conviction of Lds integrity, & my respect for his character" (*Manning-Lamb Letters,* pp. 27–28).

4. Some of the locutions in brackets here and below, whose originals have been torn from the paper, are supplied from Lucas (1935), I, 171.

5. George Caldwell (1773?–1848), the son of Charles, a Liverpool merchant, had been the friend of Coleridge since their days at Jesus College, Cambridge. From there Caldwell received his B.A. in 1795 and his M.A. in 1798 and there served as a fellow from 1796 to 1817. In 1817 he was ordained a deacon and a priest and was married to Harriet, a daughter of William Abdy, sixth baronet (d. 1803), and the former Mary Gordon (d. 1829). Coleridge's alleged lie to him "turned out to be all a mistake" (*Manning-Lamb Letters,* p. 33).

6. Lamb was now to meet Godwin, who still considered himself an atheist, though Coleridge later this year would make him a theist. Godwin had published, among other works, *An Enquiry concerning the Principles of Political Justice, and Its Influence on General Virtue and Happiness* (1793), *The Adventures of Caleb Williams, or Things as They Are* (1794), and *Memoirs of the Author of a Vindication of the Rights of Woman* (1798). In 1797 he had been married to Mary Wollstonecraft (b. 1759). She died in the year of their marriage as a result of the birth of their daughter, later Mary Wollstonecraft Shelley (d. 1851).

7. "Complain." Archimedes (287?–212 B.C.), Lamb's name for Manning following, was the illustrious Greek mathematician.

59. *C. L. to Manning*

[February 18, 1800]

dear Manning,

Olivia ***is***[1] **a good girl; & if** you turn to my Letter you will find, that this very plea you set up to vindicate Lloyd, I had made use of as a reason why he should never have employ'd Olivia to make a copy of such a **Letter! A Letter** I could not have sent to my **Enemy's Bitch,** if she had thought proper to seek me in the way of **marriage.—.—** But you see it in one view, I in another—. Rest you merry in your opinion! . . Opinion is a species of Property, and tho' I am always desirous to share with my friend to a certain extent, I shall ever like to keep some tenets, & some property, properly my own.— — — Some day, Manning, when we meet, substituting Corydon & fair Amaryllis,[2] for Ch Lloyd & Mary Hayes, we will dis[c]uss together this question of moral feeling, "In what cases & how far **Sincerity** is a **Virtue."**— I do not mean **Truth,** a good Olivia-Like Creature, God bless her, who meaning no offence is always ready to give an **answer** When she is asked why she did so & so, but a certain forward talking half **Brother** of hers, **Sincerity,** that amphibious Gentleman, who is so ready to perk up his obnoxious sentiments **unasked** into your notice, as Midas would his ears[3] into your face uncalled for.—

But I despair of doing any thing by a Letter in the way of explaining or coming to explanations—

A good wish, or a pun, or a piece of secret history, may be well enough that way convey'd—nay it has been known, that intelligence of a **Turkey** hath been convey'd by that medium, without much ambiguity— — ———

Godwin I am a good deal pleased with—. He is a well behaved

decent man, nothing very brilliant about him or imposing as you may suppose; quite another Guess sort of Gentleman from what your Anti Jacobins Christians imagine him—. I was well pleased to find he has neither horns nor claws, quite a tame creature I assure you. A middle-sized man both in stature & in understanding—whereas from his **noisy** fame, you would expect to find a **Briareus** Centimanus[4] or a Tityus tall enough to **pull** Jupiter from his Heavens! I begin to think you Atheists not quite so tall a species!

Coleridge enquires after you pretty often. . I wish to be the Pandar[5] to bring you together again once before I day. . When we die, you & I must part, the sheep you know take the right hand signpost, & the goats the Left— —. Stript of its allegory, you must know the sheep are *I,* and the apostles, and the martyrs, & the Popes, & Bishop Taylor, and Bishop Horsley & Coleridge &c &c—the goats are the **Atheists** & adulterers & fornicators & dumb dogs & Godwin & M. . . . .g & that Thyestœan crew—yaw! how my saintship sickens at the idea— — — — —

You shall have my play, and the **Falstaff's Letters** in a day or two.—

I will write to **Ll——** by this day's **Post—**

Pray, is it a part of your sincerity to shew my Letters to Lloyd.?[6] for, really, Gentlemen ought to explain their **virtues** upon a 1st acquaintance to prevent mistakes?—

God bless you, Manning—. Take my trifling *as trifling*— —. And believe me seriously and deeply your well wisher and friend

C L

MS: Huntington Library. Pub.: Talfourd (1837), I, 149–150; Talfourd (1848), I, 112; Sala, I, 333–335; Purnell, I, 333–335; Fitzgerald, II, 167–169; Hazlitt, I, 234–235; Ainger (1888), I, 118–119; Ainger (1900), I, 172–174; Macdonald, I, 135–136; Ainger (1904), I, 123–124; Harper, II, 203–205; Lucas (1905), VI, 155–156; Lucas (1912), V, 155–156; Lucas (1935), I, 174–175. Address: Mr. Thomas Manning/Mr Crisp's/St. Mary's Church/Cambridge. Postmark: February 18, 1800.

1. Underscored twice. "Enemy's Bitch," below, is an embellishment of *King Lear,* IV, vii, 35.

2. Traditional pastoral names. Corydon is in Milton's "L'Allegro," line 83, and Amaryllis is in "Lycidas," line 68.

3. Which Apollo turned into those of an ass when Midas ruled against him in his musical contest with Pan.

4. One of the hundred-armed giant defenders of Zeus. Tityus, following, another giant, spanned nine acres when stretched out on a plain. Manning objected (*Manning-Lamb Letters,* p. 32) to Lamb's calling him an atheist.

5. In Chaucer and Shakespeare he is Pandarus, the procurer of Criseide, or Cressida, for Troilus. The word "day" at the end of the sentence is an error for "die," and "die" in the next sentence is written over "day." See Matthew 25:31–46 for the parable of the sheep and the goats. Samuel Horsley (1733–1806) is mentioned in this context because he was a mathematician and had been engaged in a controversy, in his case with Priestley from 1783 to 1790 over the Incarnation. "Thyestœan crew" refers to the seduction by Thyestes of the wife of Atreus, his brother, who in revenge killed the sons of Thyestes and served them to him at a banquet.

6. "No," Manning answered on March 9. "I shewed *that former* letter of yours to him, *because* anything, that might, per se, appear harsh, is corrected by the statement of the reason why you could not write so freely to him on that subject; yea better corrected & qualified than any extract wou'd have been by comments of *mine*. Your last letter [this one] I did not shew him, altho it concerned himself—I thought he would neither see the beauty of, nor be *exactly* pleased with the sentence (which upon my soul I think exquisite) 'A letter I would not have sent to my Enemy's Bitch, if she had thought proper to seek me in the way of marriage.'—I expect you to see, from this example, without my saying anything further, that you may write most freely to me" (*Manning-Lamb Letters,* pp. 31–32).

60. *C. L. to Manning*

[March 1, 1800]

I hope by this time you are prepared to say, the Falstaff's Letters are a bundle of the sharpest, queerest, profoundest humours, of any these juice-drained latter times have spawned.— I should have advertiz'd you, that the meaning is frequently hard to be got at; and so are the future Guineas, that now lie ripening & aurifying in the womb of some undiscoverd Potosi;[1] but dig, dig, dig, dig, Manning. . . . . . .———

I set to, with an unconquerable propulsion to write, with a lamentable want of what to write. My private goings on are orderly as the movements of the spheres, and stale as their music to angel's ears. Public affairs—except as they touch upon me, & so turn into private—I cannot whip my mind up to feel any interest in.— — I grieve indeed that War and Nature & Mr. Pitt that hangs up in Lloyd's best parlour, should have conspired to call up three necessaries, simple commoners as our fathers knew them, into the upper house of Luxuries— —. Bread, and Beer, and Coals,[2] Manning.— But as to France and Frenchman, And the Abbe Sieyes & his constitutions, I cannot make these present times present to me. I read histories of the past, and I live in them; altho' to abstract senses they are far less momentous, than the noises which keep Europe awake. I am reading Burnet's Own

Times.—[3] Did you ever read that garrulous, pleasant history? He tells his story like an old man, past political service, bragging to his sons, on winter evenings, of the part he took in public transactions, when "his old cap was new." Full of scandal, which all true history is. No palliatives, but all the stark wickedness, that actually gives the momentum to national actors. Quite the prattle of age & out lived importance. Truth & sincerity staring out upon you perpetually in alto relievo.— Himself a party man, he makes you a party man. None of the Damned Philosophical Humeian indifference, so cold & unnatural & unhuman. None of the damned Gibbonian fine writing so fine & composite. None of Mr. Robertson's periods with three members. None of Mr. Roscoe's sage remarks, all so apposite & coming in so clever, lest the reader should have had the trouble of drawing an inference.[4] Burnet's good old prattle I can bring present to my mind; I can make the revolution present to me—. the French Revolution, by a converse perversity in my nature, I fling as far *from* me.——

To quit this damned subject, and to relieve you from two or three dismal yawns, which I hear in spirit, I here conclude my more than commonly obtuse letter; dull, up to the dullness of a Dutch commentator on Shakspere—

My love to Lloyd and to Sophia

C L

MS: Huntington Library. Pub.: Talfourd (1837), I, 189–192; Sala, I, 339–341; Purnell, I, 339–341; Fitzgerald, II, 173–175; Hazlitt, I, 227–228; Ainger (1888), I, 114–115; Ainger (1900), I, 174–176; Macdonald, I, 136–138; Ainger (1904), I, 124–125; Harper, II, 210–211; Lucas (1905), VI, 157–158; Lucas (1912), V, 158–159; Lucas (1935), I, 176–177. Address: Mr. Thomas Manning/ Mr Crisp's/near St. Mary's church/Cambridge. Postmark: March 1, 1800.

1. Potosí, a city and department of Bolivia. It was a rich silver mining center at the time Lamb was writing. For "orderly as the movements of the spheres," below, see Sir Thomas Browne, *Religio Medici,* Part 2.

2. Lamb echoes the cries of "Bread, Peace, and No Pitt" that the populace had shouted at George III while he was on his way to an open Parliament in October 1795. By the time of this letter, because of the war with France and the actions of Pitt as prime minister and chancellor of the exchequer in making the land tax perpetual and introducing an income tax, England was threatened with financial panic. Abbé Emmanuel-Joseph Sieyès (1748–1836), following, was one of the chief theorists of the French Revolution, a member of the Directory since 1799, and the creator of a draft of a constitution that he believed perfect and thus the perfect replacement for that of 1795. Napoleon, believing otherwise, completely remodeled it.

3. Bishop Gilbert Burnet (1643–1715), *History of His Own Times* (1723–1734). The quotation below is from the ballad by Martin Parker (d. 1656?), "Time's

Alteration; or, the Old Man's Rehearsal, What Brave Days He Knew, a Great While Agone, When His Old Cap Was New." It is in *The British Anthology,* V: *The Jonson Anthology: 1617–1637 A.D.,* ed. Edward Arber (London: Henry Frowde, 1899), 226–229.

4. In "Detached Thoughts on Books and Reading" (*Works,* II, 172) Lamb reckoned the works of David Hume, Edward Gibbon, and William Robertson (1721–1793) among "*books which are no books—biblia a-biblia.*" Lamb did not include those of William Roscoe (1753–1831), whose principal work is a *Life of Lorenzo de' Medici* (1796).

61. *C. L. to Mrs. Charles Lloyd, the elder*

E. I. H.

Wednesday Morng [March 12, 1800]

C Lamb's respects to Mrs. Lloyd, and will comply with her kind invitation for *Friday*[1] morning———

C L. has just received a very long letter from Robert, whom he had hoped to have seen with Mrs. Ll——

MS: Hoose Library, University of Southern California, Los Angeles, Calif. Pub.: Lucas (1935), I, 177. The next letter establishes the date of this one.

1. Underscored twice.

62. *C. L. to Manning*

[March 17, 1800]

Dear Manning,

I am living in a continuous feast.[1] Coleridge has been with me now for nigh threee weeks, and the more I see of him in the quotidian undress and relaxation of his mind, the more cause I see to love him and believe him a *very* **good** *man,* and all those foolish impressions to the contrary fly off like morning slumbers—. He is engaged in Translations, which I hope will keep him this month to come. .—

He is uncommonly kind & friendly to me—. He ferrets me day and night to *do something.* He tends me, amidst all his own worrying and heart oppressing occupations, as a gardiner tends his young *tulip*—. Marry come up, what a pretty similitude, & how like your humble servant! !— He has lugg'd me to the brink of engaging to a Newspaper, & has suggested to me for a 1st plan the forgery of a supposed

Manuscript of **Burton** the Anatomist of Melancholy[2]—I have even written the introductory **Letter**—and if I can pick up a few guineas this way, I feel they will be most *refreshing*—bread being so dear—. If I go on with it, I will apprize you of it, as you may like to see **my** things! ! and the *Tulip;* of all flowers, loves to be admired most.——

Pray pardon me, if my Letters do not come very thick.— I am so taken up with one thing or other that I cannot pick out (I will not say time but) *fitting times* to write to you——

My dear Love to Lloyd and Sophia, and pray split this thin letter into 3 parts, and present them with the *two biggest* in my name——

They are my oldest friends,[3] but ever the new friend driveth out the old, as the Balad sings——— ! ——

God **bless** you all three—. I would hear from Ll. if I could

C L

flour has just fallen nine shilling a sack! we shall be all too **rich**——

Tell Charles, I have seen his Mama, and am almost fallen in love with ***her,*** since I may'nt with Olivia,—she is so fine & graceful a complete **Matron-Lady-Quaker**———

She has given me two little Books. Olivia grows a charming girl—full of feeling. .

and *thinner* than she **was**——. But I have not time to fall in ***Love***

Mary presents her *general compliments.* She keeps in fine health!

Huzza Boys! and down with the **Atheists**— —

MS: Huntington Library. Pub.: Talfourd (1837), I, 144–146; Sala, I, 341–342; Purnell, I, 341–342; Fitzgerald, II, 175–176; Hazlitt, I, 228–229; Ainger (1888), I, 115–116; Ainger (1900), I, 176–178; Macdonald, I, 138–139; Ainger (1904), I, 126–127; Harper, II, 212–213; Lucas (1905), VI, 159; Lucas (1912), V, 159–160; Lucas (1935), I, 178–179. Address: Mr. Thos. Manning/Mr. Crisp's/opposite Saint Mary's/Cambridge. Postmark: March 17, 1800.

1. Proverbs 15:15. On the evening of March 2 Coleridge, who had quit his work for Daniel Stuart on the *Morning Post* so that he might proceed with his translations of Schiller's *The Piccolomini; or, the First Part of Wallenstein* and *The Death of Wallenstein* (both 1800), had seen his wife and son off for a visit to friends in Gloucestershire and Bristol and by the next day had moved in with the Lambs. He remained until about April 5. By the tenth he was with the Wordsworths at Dove Cottage, Grasmere, near Ambleside, Westmorland, their home since December 20, 1799. He left there on May 4, stopped at Bristol and London, and then with his family tried to resettle at Nether Stowey.

2. Stuart rejected Lamb's forgery, and Lamb published it in the *John Woodvil* volume as "Curious Fragments, Extracted from a Common-place Book, Which

Belonged to Robert Burton, the Famous Author of *The Anatomy of Melancholy.*" He separated from the volume Extract III, the poem originally called "A Conceipt of Diabolical Possession" and retitled "Hypochondriacus" (after *The Anatomy,* "The Argument of the Frontispiece," line 33), and separated from the conclusion of Extract IV the poem called "A Ballad: Noting the Difference of Rich and Poor, in the Ways of a Rich Noble's Palace and a Poor Workhouse" when he republished them in *Works* (1818). See Letters 65 and 71 and *Works,* I, 31–36 and 394–396; and V, 27–29 and 296–297.

3. Coleridge, Southey, White, and others were older. The ballad, called upon following, has not been identified. *Macmillan's Book of Proverbs, Maxims, and Famous Phrases* (1965) suggests that it may be imaginary, and the observation on friends thus original with Lamb, by attributing the entire saying, including "as the Balad sings," to this letter.

63. *C. L. to Manning*

[April 5, 1800]

C L's Moral Sense presents her Com'pts to Doctor Manning, is very thankful for his medical advice,[1] but is happy to add that her disorder has died of it self.——

Dr. Manning,

Coleridge has left us, to go into the North, on a visit to his God, Wordsworth.— With him have flown all my splendid prospects of Engagement with the Morning Post, all my visionary guineas, the deceitful wages of **Unborn Scandal——**. In truth, I wonder you took it up so seriously. . All my intention was but to make a little sport with such public & fair Game as Mr Pitt, Mr. Wilberforce,[2] Mrs. Fitzherbert, the Devil &c. Gentry, dipt in Styx all over, whom no Paper Javelin-lings can touch—. To have made free with these cattle, where was the Harm;—twould have been but giving apolish to Lamp black, not nigrifying a negro primarily—. .———

After all, I cannot but regret my Involuntary **Virtue.** Damn Virtue, that's thrust upon us. . It behaves itself with such constraint, till conscience opens the window, & lets out the **Goose—**

I had struck off two imitations of Burton, quite abstracted from any modern allusions, which was my intent only to lug in from time to time to make 'em Popular.— — — ——— Stuart has got these, with an introductory Letter,[3] but not hearing from him, I have ceased from my labors, but I write to him to day to get a final answer. . I am afraid they wont do for a Paper. Burton is a scarce Gentleman, not much known, Else I had done 'em pretty well. .— — — I have also hit off a few Lines in the Name of Burton, being a conceit of diabolic possession—Burton was a man often assaild by deeps't melancholy, & at other times much given to laughing, jesting, as is the way with melancholy men— —

I will send them you—they were almost extempore, & no great things, but you will indulge them.——

Rob. Lloyd is come to town.— **He** is a good fellow, with the best heart, but his feelings are Shockingly ***un*sane—**

Priscilla meditates going to see Pizarro[4] at Drury lane to night, (from her uncles) under cover of coming to dine with me—heu! tempora! heu! Mores!—

I have barely time to finish, as I expect her & Robin every minute

yours as usual

C L

MS: Huntington Library. Pub.: Talfourd (1837), I, 146–148; Sala, I, 347–348; Purnell, I, 347–348; Fitzgerald, II, 181–182; Hazlitt, I, 262–263; Ainger (1888), I, 139–140; Ainger (1900), I, 212–213; Macdonald, I, 169–170; Ainger (1904), I, 151–152; Harper, II, 214–215; Lucas (1905), VI, 160–161; Lucas (1912), V, 161–162; Lucas (1935), I, 179–180. Address: Mr. Thos. Manning/ Diss/Norfolk. Postmark: April 5, 1800.

1. In an unrecovered letter, but probably regarding the "gap in our correspondence" (*Manning-Lamb Letters,* p. 33) about which Manning expressed concern in his letter of March 17.

2. William Wilberforce (1759–1833), an intimate of Pitt, a leader of Parliament, and a philanthropist. Maria Anne Fitzherbert (1756–1837), a daughter of Walter Smythe, was first the wife of Edward Weld of Lulworth Castle, then of Thomas Fitzherbert of Swynnerton, and then of George, Prince of Wales, later George IV. She was married to him in 1785 and for years lived with him though the Royal Marriage Act and the Act of Settlement made the marriage illegal because of her Roman Catholicism and his minority.

3. Unrecovered. The letter mentioned following, if Lamb did write it, is also unrecovered.

4. Sheridan's tragedy *Pizarro.* Priscilla Lloyd's uncle is presumably Nehemiah Lloyd. The Latin translates, "what times! what Customs!" (see Letter 34, note 7).

64. *C. L. to Coleridge*

[April ca. 5–10, 1800]

Dr. Coler.—

I have just receivd your first sheet,[1] & will punctually obey you—. We are all well, and *chearful, according to your desire.* . I have open'd a parcel, inclosing a letter from Pool. The Letter I send. The parcel, I will detain, till further orders. It contains M. S. in your hand writing.— I have sent you 1 letter from Southey 2 from Mrs. C.—1 to day from Bristol besides Pool's: I am aware of the Expence, but what am I to do. I do not know what are of consequence and what not— — —. This Poem[2] incurs no postage, as it serves for my Letter & all—

C Lamb

MS: Victoria University Library, Toronto. Unpublished. The date of the letter seems implied by its content, indicating that Coleridge had either not yet reached the Wordsworths or not had time to inform his correspondents that he had.

1. Of Coleridge's translation of Schiller's *The Piccolomini.* "To morrow morning," Coleridge wrote of the work to Josiah Wedgwood on April 21, "I send off the last sheet of my irksome & soul-wearying Labor" (*Coleridge's Letters,* I, 586–587). Pool, below, is Thomas Poole.

2. A fragment, by neither Coleridge nor Lamb, on the verso of the scrap on which Lamb wrote this letter.

65. *C. L. to Manning*

[Mid-April? 1800]

I dont know whether you ever dipt into Burton's Anatomy. His manner is to shroud and carry off his feelings under a cloud of learned words. He has written but one Poem, which is prefix'd to his Anatomy, and called The Abstract of Melancholy.[1] Most likely you have seen it. It is in the last edition of the Elegant Extracts.— It begins "When I go musing all alone, Thinking of divers things foredone."— So that I have collected my imitation rather from his prose Book, than any Poetry. . I call it

A conceipt of Diabolical Possession—

By myself walking,
To myself talking,
While as I ruminate
On my untoward fate,
Scarcely seem I
Alone sufficiently;
Black thoughts continually
Crouding my privacy,

They come unbidden,
Like foes at a wedding,
Thrusting their faces
In better guests' places,
Peevish and mallcontent,[2]
Clownish impertinents,
Dashing the merriments;—
So in like fashion
Dim Cogitations
Follow and haunt me,
Striving to daunt me,
In my heart festering,
In my ears whispering,
"Thy friends are treacherous,
  Thy foes are dangerous,
  Thy dreams ominous"

Fierce Anthropophagi,
Spectra, Diaboli,
What scared Saint Anthony,[3]
Shapes undefined,
With my fears twined,
Hobgoblins, Lemures,
Dreams of Antipodes,
Night riding Incubi,
Troubling the fantasy,
All dire illusion,
Causing confusion,
Figments heretical,
Scrŭples fantastical,
Doubts diabolical,[4]
Abaddon vexeth me,
Mahu* perplexeth me,
Lucifer teareth me,— — —

Jesu Mariæ,
libera nos ab his tentationibus,
orat, împlorat, R. Burton Peccator.———

To this I will add a little Song,[5] which I paraphras'd for Coleridge from Schiller.— —— —— (which by the bye, is better than Schiller's balad a huge deal)[5]

The clouds are blackning, the storms threatning,
And ever the forest maketh a moan,
Billows are breaking, the Damsel's heart aching,
Thus by herself she singeth alone,
Weeping right plenteously.
"The world is empty, the heart is dead surely,
"In this world plainly all seemeth amiss,
"To thy breast, Holy One, take now thy Little one,
"I have had earnest of all earth's bliss,
"Living right lovingly——"

The manner in both is so antique, that I should despair of many folks liking them. . ———

You may *perhaps* never have met with Percy's Relicks of ancient English Poetry;[6] if you have, and are acquainted with the following Poem, no harm is done;—if not, I send you a treat;—that's all.———

It is in Scotch, and a very old Balad, I anglicise it as I write it, for my own convenience.———

Edward, Edward.—

[I change my mind, I will give it you in its own old Scottish shape. . The rimes else will be lost———][7]

Why does your Brand[†] so drop with bluid,
Edward, Edward?
Why does your Brand so drop with Bluid?
And why so sad gang ye, O?—

O! I have kill'd my hawk so gude,
Mother, Mother:
O! I have kill'd my hawk so gude,
And I had no more but he, O!

Your hawk's bluid was never so red,
Edward, Edward.
Your hawk's bluid was never so red;
My dear son, I tell thee, O!

O! I have kill'd my red-roan-steed,
Mother, Mother,
O! I have kill'd my red-roan steed,
That erst was so fair and free, O!

Your steed was auld, & ye ha' got more,
Edward, Edward;
Your steed was auld, & ye ha' got more,
Some other dule ye drie, O.[8]

O! I have kill'd my Father dear,
Mother, mother;—
O! I have kill'd my father dear,
Alas! & woe is me, O!—

And whatten penance will ye do for that,
Edward, Edward?
And whatten penance will ye do for that?
My dear son, now tell me, O!

I'll set my feet in yonder Boat,
Mother, mother,
I'll set my feet in yonder Boat,
And I'll far over the sea, O!

[And quhat wul ze do wi' zour towirs and zour ha',[9]
Edward, Edward?
And quhat wul ze do wi' zour towirs and zour ha',
That ware sae fair to see, O?

Ile let thame stand til they doun fa',
Mither, mither:
Ile let thame stand til they doun fa',
For here nevir mair maun I bee, O.

And quhat wul ze leive to zour bairns and zour wife,
Edward, Edward:
And quhat wul ze leive to zour bairns and zour wife,
Quhan ze gang ovir the sea, O?

The warldis room, let thame beg throw life,]

Mother, mother,
The world's room. Let 'em beg thro' life,
For them never more will I see, O!

And what will ye leave to your own mother dear?
Edward, Edward
And what will ye leave to your own mother dear?
My dear son, now tell me, O!

The curse of hell frae[10] me shall ye bear,
Mother, mother:
The curse of Hell frae me shall ye bear,
Sic counsels ye gave me, O!
! ! ! ! ! ! ! ! ! ! ! ! ! ! ! !

By which I mean to say, that **Edward, Edward** is the very **first** dramatic poem in the English Language.—. If you deny that, I'll make you eat your words.———

C Lamb

*the name of a Great Devil.—
†Sword

MS: Huntington Library. Pub.: Harper, I, facsimile, and II, 215–219; Lucas (1935), I, 180–184. A portion of the letter that has been torn away includes the address and postmark, but its date is suggested by the fourth and fifth paragraphs of Letter 63. Manning's letters of March 17 to August 10 have not been recovered.

1. "The Author's Abstract of Melancholy," from which Lamb, below, quotes lines 1–2. I have not located an edition of Knox's *Elegant Extracts* that contains it. About the publication of Lamb's poem see Letter 62, note 2.

2. A canceled line follows.

3. St. Anthony of Egypt (250–356?), who experienced the temptations of the devil in terrifying animal forms while living in a tomb in the Libyan Desert outside Comus and in his next habitation, an abandoned fort and vault on the plateau of Mount Pispir in the desert of Arabia.

4. Two canceled lines follow. For Abaddon see Letter 48, note 6. The Latin at the end translates, "Jesus of Mary, free us from these temptations, R. Burton, Sinner, prays, implores.—"

5. Thekla's song, which Lamb paraphrased from Coleridge's prose translation for *The Piccolomini* and Coleridge published, altered, in a note to II, vi, 33. Lamb restored his own wording and titled the poem "Ballad from the German" in the *John Woodvil* volume. See *Works,* V, 27 and 295–296, and *Coleridge's Poetical Works* (1912), II, 653.

6. Thomas Percy (1729–1811), *Reliques of Ancient English Poetry* (1765).

7. Lamb's brackets.

8. "Some other sorrow you endure, O."

9. This line and the next twelve lines, supplied from the version of the ballad in *Reliques* to replace those torn away, reveal the extent to which Lamb did Anglicize. Quhat/quhan: what/when; ha'/fa': hall/fall; maun: must.
10. From; sic: such.

66. *C. L. to Coleridge*

Land of Shadows
Shadow-month [April]
the 16th or 17th, 1800

I send you, in this parcel, my play, which I beg you to present in my name, with my respect and love, to Wordsworth and his sister. You blame us for giving your direction to Miss Wesley;[1] the woman has been ten times after us about it, and we gave it her at last, under the idea that no further harm would ensue, but she would *once* write to you, and you would bite your lips and forget to answer it, and so it would end. You read us a dismal homily upon 'Realities.' We know, quite as well as you do, what are shadows and what are realities. You, for instance, when you are over your fourth or fifth jorum, chirping about old school occurrences, are the best of realities. Shadows are cold, thin things, that have no warmth or grasp in them. Miss Wesley and her friend, and a tribe of authoresses that come after you here daily, and, in defect of you, hive and cluster upon us, are the shadows. You encouraged that mopsey, Miss Wesley, to dance after you, in the hope of having her nonsense put into a nonsensical Anthology. We have pretty well shaken her off, by that simple expedient of referring her to you; but there are more burrs in the wind. I came home t'other day from business, hungry as a hunter, to dinner, with nothing, I am sure, of *the author but hunger* about me, and whom found I closeted with Mary but a friend of this Miss Wesley, one Miss Benje, or Benjey—[2] I don't know how she spells her name. I just came in time enough, I believe, luckily to prevent them from exchanging vows of eternal friendship. It seems she is one of your authoresses, that you first foster, and then upbraid us with. But I forgive you. 'The rogue has given me potions to make me love him.'[3] Well; go she would not, nor step a step over our threshold, till we had promised to come and drink tea with her next night. I had never seen her before, and could not tell who the devil it was that was so familiar. We went, however, not to be impolite.

Her lodgings are up two pairs of stairs in East Street. Tea and coffee, and macaroons—a kind of cake I much love. We sat down. Presently Miss Benje broke the silence, by declaring herself quite of a different opinion from D'Israeli,[4] who supposes the differences of human intellect to be the mere effect of organization. She begged to know my opinion. I attempted to carry it off with a pun upon organ; but that went off very flat. She immediately conceived a very low opinion of my metaphysics; and, turning round to Mary, put some question to her in French,—possibly having heard that neither Mary nor I understood French. The explanation that took place occasioned some embarrassment and much wondering. She then fell into an insulting conversation about the comparative genius and merits of all modern languages, and concluded with asserting that the Saxon was esteemed the purest dialect in Germany. From thence she passed into the subject of poetry; where I, who had hitherto sat mute and a hearer only, humbly hoped I might now put in a word to some advantage, seeing that it was my own trade in a manner. But I was stopped by a round assertion, that no good poetry had appeared since Dr. Johnson's time. It seems the Doctor has suppressed many hopeful geniuses that way by the severity of his critical strictures in his 'Lives of the Poets.' I here ventured to question the fact, and was beginning to appeal to *names,* but I was assured 'it was certainly the case.' Then we discussed Miss More's book on education,[5] which I had never read. It seems Dr. Gregory, another of Miss Benjey's friends, has found fault with one of Miss More's metaphors. Miss More has been at some pains to vindicate herself—in the opinion of Miss Benjey, not without success. It seems the Doctor is invariably against the use of broken or mixed metaphor, which he reprobates against the authority of Shakspeare himself. We next discussed the question, whether Pope was a poet? I find Dr. Gregory is of opinion he was not, though Miss Seward[6] does not at all concur with him in this. We then sat upon the comparative merits of the ten translations of 'Pizarro,' and Miss Benjey or Benje advised Mary to take two of them home; she thought it might afford her some pleasure to compare them *verbatim;* which we declined. It being now nine o'clock, wine and macaroons were again served round, and we parted, with a promise to go again next week, and meet the Miss Porters,[7] who, it seems, have heard much of Mr. Coleridge, and wish to meet *us,* because we are *his* friends. I have been preparing for the occasion. I crowd cotton in my ears. I read all the reviews and magazines of the past month against the dreadful meeting, and I hope by these means to cut a tolerable second-rate figure.

Pray let us have no more complaints about shadows. We are in a fair way, *through you,* to surfeit sick upon them.

Our loves and respects to your host and hostess. Our dearest love to Coleridge.

Take no thought about your proof-sheets; they shall be done as if Woodfall[8] himself did them. Pray send us word of Mrs. Coleridge and little David Hartley, your little reality.

Farewell, dear Substance. Take no umbrage at any thing I have written.

C. Lamb, *Umbra*

Coleridge, I find loose among your papers a copy of '*Christabel.*' It wants about thirty lines; you will very much oblige me by sending me the beginning as far as that line,—

> And the spring comes slowly up this way;

and the intermediate lines between—

> The lady leaps up suddenly,
> The lovely Lady Christabel;

and the lines,—

> She folded her arms beneath her cloak,
> And stole to the other side of the oak.[9]

The trouble to you *will be small,* and the benefit to us *very great!* A pretty antithesis! A figure in speech I much applaud.

Godwin has called upon us. He spent one evening here. Was very friendly. Kept us up till midnight. Drank punch, and talked about you. He seems, above all men, mortified at your going away. Suppose you were to write to that good-natured heathen—'or is he a *shadow?*' If I do not *write,* impute it to the long postage, of which you have so much cause to complain. I have scribbled over a *queer letter,* as I find by perusal; but it means no mischief.

I am, and will be, yours ever, in sober sadness,

C. L.

Write your *German* as plain as sunshine, for that must correct itself.

You know I am homo unius linguæ:[10] in English, illiterate, a dunce, a ninny.

MS: unrecovered. Text: Lucas (1935), I, 184–187. Also pub.: Talfourd (1837), I, 155–161; Sala, I, 128–132; Purnell, I, 128–132; Fitzgerald, I, 410–414; Hazlitt, I, 230–233; Ainger (1888), I, 159–162; Ainger (1900), II, 12–17; Macdonald, I, 142–146; Ainger (1904), I, 171–174; Harper, II, 219–224; Lucas (1905), VI, 161–164; Lucas (1912), V, 162–165. The month in which Lamb wrote has been determined from his first sentence and the information given in Letter 62, note 1.

1. Sarah Wesley (1760–1828), the surviving daughter of the divine and hymn writer Charles (1707–1788) and the former Sarah Gwynne (1726?–1822). Miss Wesley was the niece of John Wesley, the evangelist and leader of Methodism. Her writing seems never to have been published.

2. Elizabeth Ogilvy Benger (1778–1827), an acquaintance of Anna Letitia Barbauld, Elizabeth Inchbald, Mme de Staël (Anne Louise Germaine Necker, Baronne de Staël-Holstein [1766–1817]), the poet Thomas Campbell (1777–1844), Henry Crabb Robinson, and the painter Robert Smirke (1752–1845). She used reproductions of Smirke's engravings to illustrate her poem *On the Slave Trade* (1809). She wrote two novels and wrote biographies of the dramatist John Tobin (see Letter 90, note 3), Anne Boleyn, Mary Queen of Scots, and Elizabeth of Bohemia. She translated a volume of the letters of the German poet Friedrich Gottlieb Klopstock (1724–1803).

3. *I Henry IV,* II, ii, 18–19.

4. Isaac D'Israeli (1766–1848), the father of Benjamin Disraeli, was the author of *Curiosities of Literature* (1791) and like works, novels, *Commentaries on the Life and Reign of Charles I* (1828–1830), and *Genius of Judaism* (1833).

5. Hannah More, *Strictures on the Modern System of Female Education* (1799). Dr. Gregory, following, is probably George (1754–1804), who was made Doctor of Divinity at Edinburgh in 1792. For some years he edited the *New Annual Register,* which Dr. Andrew Kippis (1725–1795) founded and conducted with others, and in 1795 succeeded Kippis as editor of the *Biographia Britannica,* 2d ed. In 1806 Gregory became prebendary of St. Paul's. His *Life of T. Chatterton* (first published in *Biographia Britannica,* IV, 573–619, and separately in 1789) Walpole brought to the attention of Miss More in a letter of about September 10, 1789. (See W. S. Lewis, ed., *The Yale Edition of Horace Walpole's Correspondence,* XXXI [New Haven: Yale University Press, 1961], 326.) Among Gregory's other works are *Essays Historical and Moral* (1783 and 1788), *An History of the Christian Church* (1790 and 1795), *The Elements of Polite Education, Carefully Selected from the Letters of Lord Chesterfield* (1800 and 1807), *Letters on Literature, Taste, and Composition* (1808), and *A Dictionary of the Arts and Sciences* (1808).

6. Anna Seward (1747–1809), known as the Swan of Lichfield. She was the friend of Dr. Johnson and James Boswell and some in their circle; of Thomas Day (1748–1789), the author of *Sandford and Merton;* of Dr. Erasmus Darwin, a memoir of whose life she published in 1804; and of Sir Walter Scott, to whom she bequeathed her literary works. Scott edited her poetical works and published them with a memoir and extracts from her correspondence in 1810. The "ten translations of 'Pizarro,'" below, refers to the reworkings in English of August Friedrich Ferdinand von Kotzebue's *Die Spanier in Peru, oder: Rolla's Tod* (1795). There are for the time three theatrical adaptations—*Pizarro* (1799), by Sheridan; *Pizarro in Peru; or, the Death of Rolla* (1800), by the American playwright William Dunlap (1766–1839); and *Pizarro; a Tragedy in Five Acts:*

Differing Widely from All Other Pizarro's in Respect of Characters, Sentiments, Language, Incidents, and Catastrophe (1800), by "A North-Briton"—a blank-verse *Pizarro* (1799), by the Reverend Mr. Matthew West; and six literal translations—*Rolla; or the Peruvian Hero* (2d ed.; 1799), by Matthew Gregory Lewis (1775–1818); *The Spaniards in Peru; or the Death of Rolla* (1799), by the author and linguist Anna, or Anne, Plumptre (1760–1818); *Pizarro or, the Death of Rolla,* by the dramatist Benjamin Thompson (1776?–1816), in his *The German Theatre* (1800–1801), Vol. I; *Pizarro in Peru; or, the Death of Rolla* (2d ed.; 1799), by Thomas Dutton; *Pizarro, or the Death of Rolla* [1799], by Richard Heron; and *Pizarro; or the Spaniards in Peru* (1800), by Charles Smith. For additional information and later reworkings see Myron Matlaw, "English Versions of *Die Spanier in Peru,*" *Modern Language Quarterly,* 16 (1955), 63–67.

7. Jane (1776–1850), who wrote the novels *Thaddeus of Warsaw* (1803) and *The Scottish Chiefs* (1810) and a few plays, and Anna Maria (1780–1832), the author of *Artless Tales* (1795), *The Hungarian Brothers* (1807), and other works of fiction. They were sisters of the painter and traveler Robert Ker Porter (1777–1842).

8. George (1767–1844), the son and partner of the printer and journalist Henry Sampson Woodfall (1739–1805), was the printer of Coleridge's translations of *Wallenstein.* Both father and son earned high reputations as meticulous craftsmen and for their knowledge of "Junius" and their publications of his letters.

9. "Christabel," I, 22, 37–38, and 55–56. Coleridge did not publish the poem, which remained incomplete, until 1816. Then he released it in *Christabel; Kubla Khan, a Vision; The Pains of Sleep.*

10. "A man of one language."

67. *C. L. to Coleridge*

Monday [May 12, 1800]

My dear Coleridge,

I dont know why I write except from the propensity misery has to tell her griefs.— Hetty[1] died on Friday night, about 11 o Clock, after 8 days illness. . Mary in consequence of fatigue and anxiety is fallen ill again, and I was obliged to remove her yesterday.— I am left alone in a house with nothing but Hetty's dead body to keep me company. . . . Tomorrow I bury her, and then I shall be quite alone, with nothing but a cat, to remind me that the house has been full of living beings like myself.— My heart is quite sunk, and I dont know where to look for relief—. Mary will get better again, but her constantly being liable to such relapses is dreadful,—nor is it the least of our Evils, that her case & all our story is so well known around us. . We are in a manner *marked.*— Excuse my troubling you, but I have nobody by me to speak to me.

I slept out last night, not being able to endure the change and the stillness.—— But I did not sleep well, and I must come back to my own bed—I am going to try to get a friend to come & be with me tomorrow—

I am completely shipwreck'd.— My head is quite bad. . . . I almost wish that Mary were dead. . .[2]

God bless you
Love to Sara & Hartly
C Lamb

MS: Mr. W. Hugh Peal. Pub.: Talfourd (1848), I, 85–86; Sala, I, 112–113; Purnell, I, 112–113; Fitzgerald, I, 394–395; Hazlitt, I, 236; Ainger (1888), I, 116–117; Ainger (1900), I, 178–179; Macdonald, I, 141–142; Ainger (1904), I, 127; Harper, II, 227–228; Lucas (1905), VI, 166–167; Lucas (1912), V, 167–168; Lucas (1935), I, 188. Address: Mr Coleridge/No. 10 Stokes Croft/Bristol. Postmark: May 12, 1800.

1. The Lambs' aged servant.

2. "My poor Lamb!" Coleridge wrote from Nether Stowey on the twenty-first to Godwin, "—how cruelly afflictions crowd upon him! I am glad, that you think of him as I think—he has an affectionate heart, a mind sui generis, his taste acts so as to appear like the unmechanic simplicity of an Instinct—in brief, he is worth an hundred men of *mere* Talents. Conversation with the latter tribe is like the use of leaden Bells—one warms by *exercise*—Lamb every now & then *eradiates,* & the beam, tho' single & fine as a hair, yet is rich with colours, & I both see & feel it" (*Coleridge's Letters,* I, 588).

68. *C. L. to Manning*

[James White's, London
May 17, 1800]

Dear Manning,

I am quite out of spirits, and feel as if I should never recover them. But why should not this pass away?— I am foolish, but judge of me by my situation— —. Our servant is dead, and my sister is ill— —so ill as to make a removal to a place of confinement absolutely necessary— —. I have been left *alone* in a house, where but 10 days since living Beings were, &—Noises of life were heard. I have made the experiment & find I cannot bear it any longer—. Last night I went to sleep at White's, with whom I am to be till I can find a settlement—. I have given up my house, and must look out for lodgings. .— I expect Mary will get better, before many weeks are gone—but at present I feel my daily & hourly prop has fallen from me. . I totter and stagger with weakness, for nobody can supply her place to me—. White has *all kindness,* but not *sympathy*— —. R Lloyd, my only correspondent, you except, is a good Being, but a weak one. . I know not where to look but to you,— If you will suffer me to weary your shoulders with part of my Burthen———

I shall write again to let you know how I go on. . Meantime, a letter from you would be a considerable **relief** to me. . Believe my

"yours most sincy."

C L

MS: Huntington Library. Pub.: Ainger (1900), I, 179–180; Ainger (1904), I, 128; Harper, II, 228–229; Lucas (1935), I, 189. Address: Mr. T. Manning/ Mr Crisp's/Opposite St. Mary's/Cambridge. Postmark: May 17, 1800.

PART III

Letters 69–102

27 Southampton Buildings, Chancery Lane, Holborn

May 20, 1800—February 27? 1801

69. *C. L. to Manning*

[May 20, 1800]

dear Manning,

I feel myself unable to thank you sufficiently for your kind Letter. It was doubly acceptable to me both for the choice poetry and the kind honest prose which it contained. It was just such a Letter as I should have expected from Manning.— ———

I am in much better spirits than when I wrote last. I have had a very eligible offer to Lodge with a friend[1] in Town. He will have rooms to let at Midsummer, by which time I hope my sister will be well enough to join me. . It is a great object to me to live in town, where we shall be much more *private*;[2] and to quit a house & a neighborhood where poor Mary's disorder, so frequently recurring, has made us a sort of marked people. . We can be no where private except in the midst of London—. We shall be in a family where we visit very frequently. . . . Only my Landlord and I have not yet come to a conclusion. He has a partner to consult.— I am still on the tremble. For I do not know where we could go into Lodgings, that would not be in many respects highly exceptionable. Only God send Mary well again, and I hope all will be well.— The prospect, such as it is, has made me quite happy—. I have just time to tell you of it, as I know it will give you pleasure. . . Farewell. .

C Lamb

MS: Huntington Library. Pub.: Talfourd (1848), I, 107–108; Sala, I, 335–336; Purnell, I, 335–336; Fitzgerald, II, 169–170; Hazlitt, I, 241; Ainger (1888), I, 117–118; Ainger (1900), I, 180–181; Macdonald, I, 146; Ainger (1904), I, 128–129; Harper, II, 229–230; Lucas (1905), VI, 167; Lucas (1912), V, 168; Lucas (1935), I, 189–190. Address: Mr. Manning/Mr Crisp's/near St. Mary's/ Cambridge. Postmark: May 20, 1800.

1. John Mathew Gutch. (See the Introduction, pp. xxxvi–xxxvii.) I have assumed, without confidence but on the basis of the third sentence in Letter 71 and the first paragraph in Letter 75, that Lamb is now with Gutch at 27 Southampton Buildings, though perhaps not in what would by midsummer become Lamb and Mary's own rooms at that address.

2. Underscored twice.

70. *C. L. to Manning*

[Ware Road, Hertfordshire]
Sunday [June 1, 1800]

Dear Manning,

I am a Letter in your Debt, but I am scarcely rich enough (in spirits) to pay you—. I am writing at an Inn on the Ware road, in the neighborhood of which I am going to pass two days, being whitsuntide—. Excuse the pen, tis the best I can get— —. Poor Mary is very bad yet. I went yesterday hoping I should see her getting well, then I might have gone into the country more chearful, but I could not get to see her. This has been a sad.[1] damp. Indeed I never in my life have been more wretched than I was all day yesterday. I am glad I am going away from business for a little while, for my head has been hot & ill—. I shall be very much alone, where I am going, which always revives me. I hope you will accept of this worthless memento, which I merely send as a token, that I am in your Debt. . I will write upon my return, on Thursday at farthest. . I return on Wednesday. .

God bless you

I was afraid you would think me forgetful & that made me scribble this jumble. .

MS: Wordsworth Collection, Cornell University Library, Ithaca, N.Y. Pub.: Harper, II, 230–231; Lucas (1905), VI, 168; Lucas (1912), V, 169; Lucas (1935), I, 190.

1. Perhaps an abbreviation for "saddening."

71. *C. L. to Manning*

Sunday [June 8, 1800]

Dear Manning,

I have been passing three or four quiet days in Hertfordshire which have done my spirits a world of good. On my return I found my sister perfectly recover'd. She is to join me next Sunday.— So soon hath this terrifying tempest passed over. I am ashamed I ever troubled you with the story.—

I am sitting in minutely expectation of a friend's coming to Tea.—
I will hastily transcribe a little Poem,[1] which I wrote for Burton—

The Case plainly stated between

a rich noble's Palace & a poor Workhouse—

The Argument

In a costly palace Youth meets respect.
In a wretched Workhouse Age finds neglect.

Evidenced thus

1

In a costly palace Youth goes clad in gold;
In a wretched workhouse Age's limbs are cold,
There they sit, the old men, by a shivering fire,
Still close & closer cow'ring, warmth is their desire.

2

In a costly palace when the brave gallants dine,
They have store of good venison with old Canary wine,
With singing and music to heighten the Cheer;
Coarse bits with grudging are the Pauper's best fare.

3

In a costly palace Youth is still carest
By a train of Attendants which laugh at my young Lord's jest,
In a wretched workhouse the contrary prevails,
When Age begins to prattle, no man hark'neth to his tales.

4

In a costly palace if the child with a pin
Do but chance to prick a finger, strait the Doctor is call'd in;
In a wretched workhouse men are left to perish
For want of proper cordials which their old age might cheri[sh.]

5

In a costly palace Youth enjoys his Lust;
In a wretched workhouse Age, in corners thrust,[2]
Thinks upon the former days when he was well to do,
Had children to stand by him, both friends & kinsmen too.

6

In a costly palace Youth his temples hides
With a new devised Peruke that reaches to his sides;
In a wretched workhouse Age's crown is bare,
With a few thin locks just to fence out the cold air.

7

In peace as in war tis our young gallants' pride
To walk each one in the streets with a rapier at his side,
That none to do them injury may have pretence;
Wretched Age in Poverty must brook offence—

The Consequence—

Wanton Youth is ofttimes haught & swelling found,
When Age for very shame goes stooping to the ground—

You see I have followed the old Writers, whose way was to take the *Extremes* of *either State* & make a *fair*[3] *Comparison*—

I wish you to like it,—I think it my *cheff du ver*—how do ye spell it?

C L

MS: Huntington Library. Pub.: Harper, I, facsimile; Lucas (1935), I, 191–192. In the latter the postscript to the letter and the gloss to the poem are Lucas' private notations, accidentally printed, regarding the letter in Harper ("*B*[*ibliophile*] *Ed.*") and the poem in Thomas Hutchinson, ed., *The Works in Prose and Verse of Charles and Mary Lamb,* (2 vols.; Oxford: Henry Frowde [1908]).

1. "A Ballad: Noting the Difference of Rich and Poor, in the Ways of a Rich Noble's Place and a Poor Workhouse." See Letter 62, note 2, about its publication. See also Letter 76, note 8.

2. *As You Like It,* II, iii, 42.

3. Underscored twice. The French for which Lamb reaches below is *chef-d'oeuvre.*

72. *C. L. to John Mathew Gutch*

Saturday [July 1800]

Dear Gutch,

Anderson[1] is not come home, and I am almost afraid to tell you what has happen'd, lest it should seem to have happend by my fault in not writing for you home sooner.—

This morning Henry, the eldest lad was missing, we supposd he was only gone out on a morning's stroll, and that he would return, but he did not return and we discovered that he had opened your desk before he went and I suppose taken all the money he could find, for on diligent search I could find none, and on opening your Letter to Anderson, which I thought necessary to get at the Key I learn that you had a good deal of money there.—

Several people have been here after you to day, and the boys seem quite frightened, and do not know what to do. In particular, one Gentleman[2] wants to have some writings finished by Tuesday—. For Gods sake set out by the first coach. Mary has been crying all day about it, and I am now just going to some law stationer in the neighborhood, that the eldest boy has recommended, to get him to come and be in the house for a day or so, to manage. I cannot think what detains Anderson. His sister[3] is quite frightend about him—. I am very sorry I did not write yesterday, but Henry persuaded me to wait till he could ascertain when some job must be done (at the furthest) for Mr. Foulkes, and as nothing had occurrd besides I did not like to disturb your pleasures. I now see my error, and shall be heartily ashamed to see you.

A Bite ! ! !

Anderson is come home, and the wheels of thy business are going on *as ever*

The boy is honest, and I am thy friend.—

And how does the coach maker's daughter.— Thou art her Phaeton, her Gig, and her Sociable.— Commend me to Rob.—

C Lamb

MS: Mr. W. Hugh Peal. Pub.: Ainger (1900), I, 206–207; Ainger (1904), I, 146–147; Harper, II, 231–233; Lucas (1905), VI, 169; Lucas (1912), V, 170–171; Lucas (1935), I, 195–196. Address: [. . .]'s/[. . .] Street/[Birming]ham. Watermark: 1800. The date is derived from Letters 74 and 75. Gutch was in Birmingham seeing Mary Wheeley (see the Introduction, p. xxxvi) and Robert, at least, of the Lloyds.

1. Gutch's partner. Henry, below, is apparently an office boy.
2. Perhaps (the unidentified) Mr. Foulkes, below.
3. Unidentified.

73. *C. L. to Manning*

[East India House]
Monday morning [July 1800]

I have just got your *scrap*—Pray tell me if you consider *this* as just payment for *value received.* If not, to work again, my pen. I am just now engaged in the addition of 900 pages, continent of twenty sums a piece—O the drudgery to which your great geniuses are exposed—But Jupiter wore a Bull's hide,[1] and Apollo kept Admetus's swine, each for his goddess.— Mine is Pecunia, Blessing on her golden Looks.—

Pray write. [. . .]

MS: unrecovered. Text: Lucas (1935), I, 197. Address, from Betram Dobell, "Some Unpublished Letters of Charles Lamb," *The Athenaeum,* No. 4097 (May 5, 1906), 546: Mr. Thos. Manning,/Mr. Crisp's/near St. Mary's/Cambridge.

1. When he carried off Europa. Having been pressed into the service of Admetus by Jupiter for shooting his arrows at the Cyclopes, Apollo pastured the flocks of Admetus and helped him win Alcestis. Both Lucas and Dobell note that the last portion of the letter has been torn away.

74. *C. L. to Robert Lloyd*

[July 22, 1800]

Dear Robert

My mind has been so barren and idle of late, that I have done nothing. I have received many a summons from you, and have repeatedly sat down to write, and broke off from despair of sending you any thing worthy your acceptance. I have had such a deadness about me. Man delights not me nor woman neither.[1] I impute it in part or altogether to the stupefying effect which continued fine weather has upon me. I want some rains or even snow & intense cold winter nights to bind me to my habitation, and make me value it as a **home**—a sacred character which it has not attained with me hitherto. I cannot read or write when the sun shines. I can only walk. .— — —. . . .
. . . .— — — — —

I must tell you, that since I wrote last I have been two days at **Oxford** on a visit (long put off) to Gutch's family (my Landlord). I was much gratifyed with the Colleges & Libraries and what else of Oxford I could see in so short a time. In the All Soul's Library is a fine head of Bishop Taylor, which was one great inducement to my Oxford **Visit.** In the Bodleian are many Portraits of illustrious Dead, the only Species of painting I value at a farthing. But an indubitable good Portrait of a great man is worth a pilgrimage to go & see.—. Gutch's family is a very fine one, consisting of well grown sons & daughters, and all likely & well favor'd. What is called a **Happy** family—that is, according to my interpretation, a **numerous** assemblage of young men & women, all fond of each other to a certain degree, & all happy together, but where the very number forbids any two of them to get close enough to each other to share secrets & ***be friends.*** That close intercourse can only exist, (commonly, I think) in a family of two or three—I do not envy large families. The fraternal affection by diffusion & multi-participation is ordinarily thin & weak—. They dont get near enough to each other.——.———

I expected to have had an account of Sophia's being brought to bed before this time.[2] But I remain in confidence that you will send me the earliest news. I hope it will be happy—

(Coleridge is settled at Keswick, so that the probability is that he will be once again united [w]ith your Brother. . Such men as he and Wordsworth would exclude solitude in the Hebrides or Thule.)—

Pray have you seen the New Edition of Burns including his posthumous works?—[3] I want very much to get a sight of it, but cannot afford to buy it. My Oxford Journey, though very moderate, having pared away all supperfluities—

Will you accept of this short Letter, accompanid with professions of deepest regard for you?

Yours unalterably
C Lamb

MS: Huntington Library. Pub.: Ainger (1900), I, 182–184; Macdonald, I, 147–149; Ainger (1904), I, 130–131; Harper, II, 234–236; Lucas (1935), I, 194–195. Address: Robert Lloyd/C Lloyd's/Birmingham. Postmark: July 22, 1800.

1. *Hamlet,* II, ii, 309.

2. The Charles Lloyds' son Charles Grosvenor was born at Olton Green on July 31. The Coleridges had moved toward but did not settle at Greta Hall, Keswick, Cumberland, until July 24.

3. Edited by the Scottish physician James Currie (1756–1805), *The Works of Robert Burns; with an Account of His Life, and a Criticism on His Writings. To*

Which Are Prefixed, Some Observations on the Character and Condition of the Scottish Peasantry **(4 vols.; 1800).**

75. *C. L. to Coleridge*

[July 28, 1800]

Dear Coleridge,

Soon after I wrote to you last,[1] an offer was made me by **Gutch** (you must remember him at Christ's—you saw *him* slightly one day with Thomson at our house)—to come and lodge with him at his house in Southampton Buildings Chancery Lane. .— This was a very comfortable offer to me, the rooms being at a reasonable rent, and including the use of an old servant, besides being infinitely preferable to ordinary Lodgings—*in our case,* as you must perceive. As Gutch knew all our story, and the perpetual liability to a recurrence in my sister's disorder, probably to the end of her life, I certainly think the offer very generous & very friendly. . I have got three rooms (including servant) under £34 a Year.— — Here I soon found myself at home; and here in six weeks after Mary was well enough to join me. So we are once more settled. . .— I am afraid we are not placed out of the reach of future interruptions. . But I am determined to take what snatches of pleasure, we can, between the acts of our distressful drama . . . .——

I have past two days at Oxford on a visit, which I have long put off, to Gutch's family.— The sight of the Bodleian Library and above all a fine Bust of Bishop *Taylor* at All Soul's, were particularly gratifying to me. . Unluckily it was not a family, where I could take Mary with me, and I am afraid there is something of dishonesty in any pleasures I take without *her*.[2] She never goes anywhere.—

I do not know what I can add to this Letter.— I hope you are better by this time—. And I desire to be affectionately remember'd to Sara and Hartley.— — I expected before this to have had tidings of another little philosopher. .[3] Lloyd's wife is on the point of favoring the world. . .

Have you seen the new edition of **Burns**— —his posthumous works & letters. ? I have only been able to procure the 1st vol. which contains his life = very confusedly and badly written, & interspersed—with dull pathological & *medical* discussions.— It is written by a Dr. **Currie.** do you know the well meaning Doctor. . Alas! ne sutor ultra crepidam[4]—

or as some readings have it **ne** sutor ultra ***Crepitum,*** which I thus English—**Let not a *Suitor*** presume to fart above once in the presence of his mistress.—.— — —

I hope to hear again from you very soon

Godwin is gone to Ireland on a visit to Grattan. .[5] Before he went I past much time with him, and he has shew'd me particular attentions. . N. B. A thing I much like!

Your Books are all safe.— Only I have not thought it necessary to fetch away your last batch, which I understand are at Johnson's[6] the Bookseller; who has got quite as much room, & will take as much care of them, as myself—and you can send for them immediately from him— ——

I wish you would advert to a Letter I sent you at Grassmere about Christabel &— ***comply*** *with my request contained therein—*

Love to all friends round Skiddaw

C Lamb

MS: Huntington Library. Pub.: Talfourd (1848), I, 108–110; Sala, I, 109–111; Purnell, I, 109–111; Fitzgerald, I, 391–393; Hazlitt, I, 242–243; Ainger (1888), I, 134–135; Ainger (1900), I, 204–206; Macdonald, I, 149–150; Ainger (1904), I, 145–146; Harper, II, 236–238; Lucas (1905), VI, 170–171; Lucas (1912), V, 171–172; Lucas (1935), I, 192–194. Address: Mr Coleridge/Greta Hall/Keswick/Cumberland. Postmark: [July] 28, 1800.

1. Presumably in Letter 67. Referred to after Gutch is Marmaduke Thompson.
2. Two canceled lines follow.
3. Derwent Coleridge (d. 1883) was not born until September 14.
4. "Let the cobbler stick to his last." Similar sayings predate the elder Pliny (23–79). Lamb could have taken his language verbatim from Burton's *The Anatomy of Melancholy,* "Democritus Junior to the Reader."
5. The statesman Henry Grattan (1746–1820), whom Godwin saw while visiting Dublin at the invitation of John Philpot Curran (1750–1817), judge, parliamentarian, orator. See *Godwin,* I, 363–374, and II, 4–6.
6. Joseph Johnson (1738–1809), of 72 St. Paul's Churchyard, had met and befriended Coleridge shortly before Coleridge left for Germany in 1798 and had published the quarto volume of his *Fears in Solitude, Written in 1798, during the Alarm of an Invasion. To Which Are Added, France, and Ode; and Frost at Midnight* (1798). Lamb below directs Coleridge to Letter 66.

76. *C. L. to Coleridge*

Wednesday night, August 6, 1800

Dear Coleridge,

I have taken to-day, and delivered to Longman and Co., *Imprimis:* your books, viz., three ponderous German dictionaries, one volume (I can find no more) of German and French ditto, sundry other German books unbound, as you left them, Percy's Ancient Poetry, and one volume of Anderson's Poets.[1] I specify them, that you may not lose any. *Secundo:* a dressing-gown (value, fivepence), in which you used to sit and look like a conjuror, when you were translating 'Wallenstein.' A case of two razors and a shaving-box and strap. This it has cost me a severe struggle to part with. They are in a brown-paper parcel, which also contains sundry papers and poems, sermons, *some few Epic* Poems,—one about Cain and Abel,[2] which came from Poole, &c., &c., and also your tragedy; with one or two small German books, and that drama in which Got-fader performs. *Tertio:* a small oblong box containing *all your letters,* collected from all your waste papers, and which fill the said little box. All other waste papers, which I judged worth sending, are in the paper parcel aforesaid. But you will find *all* your letters in the box by themselves. Thus have I discharged my conscience and my lumber-room of all your property, save and except a folio entitled Tyrrell's Bibliotheca Politica,[3] which you used to learn your politics out of when you wrote for the Post, *mutatis mutandis, i.e.,* applying past inferences to modern *data.* I retain that, because I am sensible I am very deficient in the politics myself; and I have torn up—don't be angry, waste paper has risen forty per cent., and I can't afford to buy it—all Buonaparte's Letters,[4] Arthur Young's Treatise on Corn, and one or two more light-armed infantry, which I thought better suited the flippancy of London discussion than the dignity of Keswick thinking. Mary says you will be in a damned passion about them when you come to miss them; but you must study philosophy. Read Albertus Magnus[5] de Chartis Amissis five times over after phlebotomising,—'tis Burton's recipe—and then be angry with an absent friend if you can. I have just heard that Mrs. Lloyd is delivered of a fine boy, and mother and boy are doing well. Fie on sluggards, what is thy Sara doing? Sara is obscure. Am I to understand by her letter, that she sends a *kiss* to Eliza Buckingham?[6] Pray tell your wife that a note of interrogation on the superscription of a letter is highly ungrammatical—she proposes writing my name *Lamb?* Lambe is quite enough. I have had the Anthology, and like only one thing in it, *Lewti;* but of that the last stanza is detestable, the rest most exquisite!—the epithet *enviable* would dash the finest poem. For God's sake (I never was more serious), don't make me ridiculous any more by terming me gentle-hearted in print,[7] or do it in better verses. It did well enough five years ago when

I came to see you, and was moral coxcomb enough at the time you wrote the lines, to feed upon such epithets; but, besides that, the meaning of gentle is equivocal at best, and almost always means poor-spirited, the very quality of gentleness is abhorrent to such vile trumpetings. My *sentiment* is long since vanished. I hope my *virtues* have done *sucking*. I can scarce think but you meant it in joke. I hope you did, for I should be ashamed to think that you could think to gratify me by such praise, fit only to be a cordial to some green-sick sonneteer.

I have hit off the following[8] in imitation of old English poetry, which, I imagine, I am a dab at.

[The Case plainly stated between
a rich noble's Palace & a poor Workhouse—

The Argument

In a costly palace Youth meets respect.
In a wretched Workhouse Age finds neglect.

Evidenced thus

1

In a costly palace Youth goes clad in gold;
In a wretched workhouse Age's limbs are cold,
There they sit, the old men, by a shivering fire,
Still close & closer cow'ring, warmth is their desire.

2

In a costly palace when the brave gallants dine,
They have store of good venison with old Canary wine,
With singing and music to heighten the Cheer;
Course bits with grudging are the Pauper's best fare.

3

In a costly palace Youth is still carest
By a train of Attendants which laugh at my young Lord's jest,
In a wretched workhouse the contrary prevails,
When Age begins to prattle, no man hark'neth to his tales.

4

In a costly palace if the child with a pin
Do but chance to prick a finger, strait the Doctor is call'd in;
In a wretched workhouse men are left to perish
For want of proper cordials which their old age might cheri[sh.]

5

In a costly palace Youth enjoys his Lust;
In a wretched workhouse Age, in corners thrust,
Thinks upon the former days when he was well to do,
Had children to stand by him, both friends & kinsmen too.

6

In a costly palace Youth his temples hides
With a new devised Peruke that reaches to his sides;
In a wretched workhouse Age's crown is bare,
With a few thin locks just to fence out the cold air.

7

In peace as in war tis our young gallants' pride
To walk each one in the streets with a rapier at his side,
That none to do them injury may have pretence;
Wretched Age in Poverty must brook offense—

The Consequence—

Wanton Youth is ofttimes haught & swelling found,
When Age for very shame goes stooping to the ground—]

The measure is unmeasureable; but it most resembles that beautiful ballad of the 'Old and Young Courtier'; and in its feature of taking the extremes of two situations for just parallel, it resembles the old poetry certainly. If I could but stretch out the circumstances to twelve more verses, *i.e.,* if I had as much genius as the writer of that old song, I think it would be excellent. It was to follow an imitation of Burton in prose, which you have not seen. But fate 'and wisest Stewart' say No.[9]

I can send you 200 pens and six quires of paper *immediately,* if they will answer the carriage by coach. It would be foolish to pack 'em up *cum multis libris et cæteris,*[10]—they would all spoil. I only wait your commands to coach them. I would pay five-and-forty thousand carriages to read W.'s tragedy, of which I have heard so much and seen so little—only what I saw at Stowey. Pray give me an order in writing on Longman for 'Lyrical Ballads.' I have the first volume, and, truth to tell, six shillings is a broad shot. I cram all I can in, to save a multiplying of letters—those pretty comets with swingeing tails.

I'll just crowd in God bless you!

C. Lamb

MS: unrecovered. Text: Lucas (1935), I, 197–199. Also pub.: Talfourd (1837), I, 151–155; Sala, I, 114–117; Purnell, I, 114–117; Fitzgerald, I, 396–399; Hazlitt, I, 244–246; Ainger (1888), I, 120–122; Ainger (1900), I, 184–188; Macdonald, I, 151–153; Ainger (1904), I, 131–133; Harper, II, 238–242; Lucas (1905), VI, 171–173; Lucas (1912), V, 173–175.

1. Robert Anderson (1750–1830), ed., *A Complete Edition of the Poets of Great Britain* (13 vols.; 1792–1795).

2. Coleridge's prose poem "The Wanderings of Cain," which Coleridge did not publish until 1828, though the verses in its Prefatory Note he published beforehand in *Aids to Reflection* (1825). His tragedy is "Osorio." The drama may be Hans Sachs's *Ein spiel mit 11 personen, wie Gott, der Herr, Adam unnd Eva ihre kinder segnet* [1553?], in which Adam, in the second line of his fourth speech, addresses *Gott* as *du himlischer vatter.*

3. *Bibliotheca Politica: Or, an Enquiry into the Ancient Constitution of the English Government* . . . comprises fourteen dialogues (the first thirteen published during the period 1692–1694, the fourteenth in 1702, and the whole in folio in 1718) by the historical writer James Tyrrell (1642–1718).

4. From the letters Coleridge intended to but never did construct an essay on the character of Napoleon. The *British Museum General Catalogue of Printed Books,* LXXVII, 721–722, lists ten editions of or works containing Napoleon's letters published through 1800. The treatise by the agriculturist Arthur Young (1741–1820) is *The Expediency of a Free Exportation of Corn at This Time* (1770).

5. Albertus Magnus (1206?–1280), the scholastic philosopher and bishop of Ratisbone whom Burton did mention in *The Anatomy,* Part. 3, sect. 3, mem. 2, subs. 1, but not for the purpose Lamb gives. The "Chartis Amissis" has not been identified.

6. Perhaps, as is conjectured in Lucas (1935), I, 199, a servant at the Coleridges' recent Buckingham Street residence. "Lambe," below, looks back to the satirists of the *Anti-Jacobin* (see Letter 44, note 9), who so misspelled Lamb's name. But occasionally Mrs. Coleridge and Wordsworth took advantage of the franking privileges of the East India House by so addressing to Lamb at his office their letters meant for Coleridge. Lamb, thus alerted, would see that Coleridge received them. Line 69 of Coleridge's "Lewti, or the Circassian Love-chaunt" in the second (1800) volume of *The Annual Anthology* contains the epithet "enviable," below, which Coleridge eliminated before he republished the poem in *Sibylline Leaves* (1817).

7. As Coleridge did in "This Lime-tree Bower My Prison. A Poem Addressed to Charles Lamb, of the India House, London" (composed three, not five, years before), lines 28, 68, and 75, when he published it in the second volume of *The*

Annual Anthology. See Letter 79, second paragraph, for another outburst against the epithet "gentle-hearted Charles."

8. "A Ballad: Noting the Difference of Rich and Poor, in the Ways of a Rich Noble's Palace and a Poor Workhouse," which must have come in the holograph letter at about where I have inserted it here, transcribed from Letter 71. Its published version carries the notation (*Works,* V, 28) "To the tune of the 'Old and Young Courtier,'" a ballad in Percy's *Reliques of Ancient English Poetry.*

9. An adaptation of Milton's "On the Morning of Christ's Nativity," line 149. By "Stewart" Lamb means Daniel Stuart.

10. "With many books and other things." Wordsworth's tragedy (mentioned following), *The Borderers,* was not published until 1842. Longman did not issue the second edition of *Lyrical Ballads* until late January 1801, though it is dated 1800. By the first volume Lamb means the first edition, which consists of almost the same poems as the first volume of the second edition. The second volume of the second edition, which he would like to be able to buy separately, consists of new poems.

77. *C. L. to Manning*

[August 9, 1800]

Dear Manning,

I suppose you have heard of Sophia Lloyd's good fortune, and paid the customary compliments to the Parents. Heaven keep the new born Infant from star blasting and moon blasting, from **Epilepsy,** marasmus & the **Devil!** may he live to see many days, and they good ones; some friends, & they *pretty regular correspondents*! with as much **Wit** & Wisdom as will eat their bread & cheese together under a poor roof without quarrelling! as much goodness as will earn Heaven if there be such a place, & deserve it if there be not, but, rather than go to bed Solitary, would truckle with the meanest **Succubus** on her Bed of Brimstone.—here I must leave off, my Benedictory Powers failing me. I could ***curse*** the sheet full; so much stronger is **Corruption** than **Grace** in the **Natural** man!

And now, when shall I catch a glimpse of your honest face to face countenance again? Your fine *dogmatical, sceptical,* face by punch-Light?— **O! One** glimpse of the human face, & shake of the human hand, is better than whole reams of this cold thin correspondence—yea of more worth than all the **Letters,** that have sweated the fingers of Sensibility, from Madame Sevigne[1] & Balzac (observe my **Larning!**) to Sterne and Shenstone.———

Coleridge is settled with his Wife (with a child in her Guts) and the young philosopher at **Keswick** with the Wordsworths. . They have contriv'd to spawn a new volume of **Lyrical** Balads, which is to see the Light in about a month, & causes no little excitement in the ***Literary World.*** **George Dyer** too—that goodnatur'd Heathen—is more than 9 months' gone with his Twin volumes of Ode, pastoral, sonnet, Elegy, Spenserian, Horation, akensidish, & Masonic,[2] **verse—.** Clio prosper the Birth—it will be twelve shillings out of somebody's pocket— —. I find he means to exclude **"Personal Satire"**—so it appears by his truly original advertisements—. well, God put it into the hearts of the English Gentry to come in shoals & subscribe to his Poems—for **He** never put a kinder heart into flesh of man than George Dyer's!—

Now farewell—for dinner is at hand, & yearning guts do chide.[3]

C L

MS: Huntington Library. Pub.: Talfourd (1837), I, 179–180; Sala, I, 342–343; Purnell, I, 342–343; Fitzgerald, II, 176–177; Hazlitt, I, 246–247; Ainger (1888), I, 127–128; Ainger (1900), I, 194–195; Macdonald, I, 153–154; Ainger (1904), I, 138–139; Harper, II, 242–243; Lucas (1905), VI, 175; Lucas (1912), V, 176; Lucas (1935), I, 200–201. Address: Mr Manning/Mr Crisp's/opposite St. Mary's/Cambridge. Postmark: August 9, 1800.

1. Marie de Rabutin-Chantal, Marquise de Sévigné (1626–1696), was famed for her letters, as was Jean Louis Guez de Balzac (1594–1654) for his.

2. After William Mason (1724–1797), the friend, imitator, biographer, and literary executor of Thomas Gray. Clio, the Muse of history, virtually aborted the birth of Dyer's *Poems* (1800). For in December (see Letter 96) Dyer discovered an error in his prefatory argument that led him to suppress the work. Only a title page and a Preface of sixty-five pages were printed. In that Preface, pp. lix–lx, and in the Advertisement to *Poems* (1801) he remarked about an intended second volume of poetry and a third, of criticism. He in fact wrote, beyond *Poems* (1801), the two-volume *Poems and Critical Essays* (1802) and the two-volume *Poetics: Or a Series of Poems, and of Disquisitions on Poetry* (1812). The British Museum holds copies of *Poems* (1800) and *Poems* (1801), which are bound together and contain manuscript notes by Lamb and Coleridge.

3. Cf. *Troilus and Cressida,* V, i, 18.

78. *C. L. to Manning*

[August 11, 1800]

My dear **fellow,** (N. B. mighty familiar of late!)

for me to come to Cambridge now is one of G–d Almighty's Impossibilities; metaphysicians tell us Even He can work nothing which implys a contradiction. I can explain this by telling you that I am engaged to do **double Duty** (this hot weather!) for a man who has taken advantage of this very weather to go & cool himself in **"green retreats"**[1] all the month of August.—

But for You to come to **London** in stead!—— muse upon it, revolve it, cast it about in your mind—. I have a Bed at your command—. You shall drink Rum, Brandy, Gin, Aquavitæ, Usquebagh, or Whiskey a nights— —& for the after-dinner-Trick I have 8 Bottles of genuine Port which mathematically divided gives 1 1/7 for every day you stay, provided you stay a **week.** Hear John Milton sing,

"Let Euclid rest & Archimedes pause."

21st Sonnet—[2]

& elswhere,

What neat repast shall feast us, light* & choice,
Of Attic Taste, with wine,† whence we may rise
To hear the Lute well touch'd, or artful voice
Warble immortal notes* & *Tuscan air?

Indeed the Poets **are** full of this pleasing Morality—
veni Cito, Domine Manning!—[3]

N B. I **lives** at No. *27* Southampton Buildings Holborn——. Think upon it

C Lamb

Excuse the Paper.— *it is all I have*—[4]

**We* Poets! generally give *light* dinners:
†no doubt the Poet here alludes to **Port** wine—38/– the dozen

MS: Huntington Library. Pub.: Talfourd (1837), I, 163–164; Sala, I, 344; Purnell, I, 344; Fitzgerald, II, 178; Hazlitt, I, 247–248; Ainger (1888), I, 128; Ainger (1900), I, 195–196; Macdonald, I, 154–155; Ainger (1904), I, 139; Harper, II, 244–245; Lucas (1905), VI, 176; Lucas (1912), V, 177–178; Lucas (1935), I, 202. Address: Mr Manning/Mr Crisp's/near Saint Mary's/Cambridge. Postmark: August 11, 1800.

1. Pope's "Windsor Forest," line 1, and "Summer. The Second Pastoral, or Alexis," line 72; and Cowper's "Retirement," line 571.
2. Line 7. The next quotation is from Sonnet 20, lines 9–12.
3. "Come Quickly, Lord Manning!—"
4. Underscored twice.

79. *C. L. to Coleridge*

Thursdy 14 Aug. [1800]

Read on, & you'll come to the ***Pens.***———

My head is playing all the tunes in the world, ringing such peals! it has just finished the "merry Xt. Church Bells"[1] and absolutely is beginning "Turn again Whittington." Buz, buz, buz, bum, bum, bum, wheeze, wheeze, wheeze, feu, feu, feu, tinky, tinky tinky, *craunch.* I shall certainly come to be damned at last. I have been getting drunk two days running. I find my moral sense in the last stage of a consumption, my religion burning as blue and faint as the tops of evening bricks.[2] Hell gapes, and the Devils great guts cry "cupboard" for me. In the midst of this infernal larum, Conscience (and be damn'd to her) barking & yelping as loud as any of them, I have sat down to read over again your **Satire** upon **me**[3] in the Anthology—. And I think I do begin to spy out something like beauty & design in it. I perfectly accede to all your alterations, and only desire that you had cut deeper, when your hand was in. In the next edition of the Anthology, (which Phoebus[4] avert, and those nine other wandering maids also!) please to blot out *gentle hearted*, and substitute drunken dog, ragged-head, seld-shaven, odd-ey'd, stuttering, or any other epithet which truly and properly belongs to the Gentleman in question. And for Charles read Tom, or Bob, or Richard, *for more delicacy.*— **Damn** you, I was beginning to forgive you, & believe in earnest that the lugging in of my Proper name was purely unintentional on your part, when looking back for further conviction, stares me in the face Charles Lamb **of the *India House. Now*** I am convinced it was all done in **Malice,** heaped, sack-upon-sack, congregated, studied Malice. **You Dog!**— you[r] 141st Page[5] shall not save you. I own I was just ready to acknowledge that there is a something **not** unlike good poetry in that Page, if you had not run into the unintelligible abstraction-fit about the manner of the Deity's making Spirits perceive his presence. God, nor created thing alive, can receive any honor from such thin, shew-box, attributes. . By the bye, where did you pick up that scandalous piece of private history about the Angel & the Duchess of Devonshire?[6] If it is a fiction of your own, why truly tis a very modest one *for you.* Now I do affirm, that **Lewti** is a very beautiful Poem. I *was* in earnest when I praised it. It describes a silly species of one not the wisest of passions. *Therefore* it cannot deeply affect a disenthralled mind. . But such imagery, such novelty, such delicacy, & such versification, never got into an **Anthology** before. I am only sorry that the cause of all the passionate complaint is not greater, than the trifling circumstance of Lewti being out of temper one day; . . . . . **In sober truth,** I cannot see any great merit in the little dialogue called **Blenheim.**[7] It is rather novel & pretty, but the thought is very obvious, and children's poor prattle a thing of easy imitation. Pauper vult videri et *est.* Gualberto certainly has considerable originality, but sadly wants finishing. It is, as it is, one of the very best in the Book. Next to **Lewti** I like the **Raven,** which has a good deal of humour. I was pleas'd to see it again, for you once sent it me, & I have lost the Letter which containd it. . . Now I am on the subject of **Anthologies,** I must say I am sorry the Old Pastoral way is fallen into disrepute. The Gentry, which now endite **Sonnets** are certainly the legitimate descendants of the ancient **Shepherds.** The same simpering face of description, the old family face, is visibly continued in the line. Some of their ancestors' labours are yet to be found in Allan Ramsay's, & Jacob Tonson's,[8] *Miscellanies.* But miscellanies decaying, & the old Pastoral Way dying of mere want, their Successors (driven from their paternal acres) now adays settle & hive upon magazines, anthologies. This **Race** of **men** are uncommonly addicted to Superstition. Some of them are Idolaters & worship the **Moon.** Others deify qualities, as Love, friendship, sensibility; or bare accidents, as solitude.— Grief, & Melancholy have their respective altars & temples among them, as the Heathens builded theirs to Mors, Febris, Pallororis.[9] They all agree in ascribing a peculiar sanctity to the number **fourteen.** One of their own Legislators affirmeth, that whatever exceeds that number "**encroacheth** upon the province of the Elegy"—vice versa whatever "**Cometh** short of that number **abutteth** upon the premises of the Epigram. ." I have been able to discover but few ***Images*** in their Temples, which like the Caves of Delphos[10] of old are famous for giving ***Echoes.*** They impute a religious importance to the letter **O,** whether because by its roundness it is thought to typify the **Moon,** their principal Goddess, or for its analogies to their own Labours all ending where they begun, **Or** for whatever other high & mystical reference, I have never been able to discover, but I observe they never begin their invocations to their Gods without it = except indeed one insignificant sect among them, who use the Doric **A,** pronounced like **ah!** broad, instead. These boast to have restored the old Dorian mood—

Now I am on the subject of **Poetry,** I must announce to **you,** who doubtless in your remote part of the Island have no[t] heard Tidings of so great a blessing, that **George Dyer** hath prepared **two** ponderous volumes, full of **Poetry & Criticism**—they impend over the Town, and are threaten'd to fall in the winter. The first **Volume** contains **every sort of Poetry, except Personal Satire** (which George in his truly [orig]inal prospectus renounceth for ever, [wh]imsically foisting the intention in between [t]he price of his Book & the proposed number of subscribers—if I can I will get you a copy of his *handbill*)—he has tried his *vein* in every species besides, the Spenserian, Thompsonian, Masonic, & akensidish more especially. The 2d vol. is all **Criticism,** wherein he demonstrates to the entire satisfaction of the literary world, in a way that must silence all reply for ever, that the Pastoral was introduced by Theocritus & polished by Virgil & Pope—that Gray & Mason (who always hunt in couple's in Georges brain) have a good deal of poetical fire and true lyric genius; that **Cowley** was ruined by **excess of wit**[11] (a warning to all moderns)—that Charles Lloyd, Charles Lamb, and Wm. Wordsworth in later days have struck the true chords of **Poesy;**— — — **O George, George,** with a head uniformly wrong & a heart uniformly right, that I had power and might equal to my wishes, then would I call the Gentry of thy native Island, and they should come in troops, flocking at the sound of thy Prospectus-Trumpet, and crowding who shall be first to stand in thy List of Subscribers.— I can only put twelve shillings into thy pocket (which I will answer for them will not stick there long) out of a pocket almost as bare as thine. .—Is it not a pity so much **fine** writing should be erased—[12] but to tell truth I began to scent that I was getting into that sort of style which Longinus & Dionysuis Halicarn. aptly call the **Affected—.** But I am suffering from the combined effect of two days drunkenness, & at such times it is not very easy to think or express in a natural series.— — **The only** useful **Object** of this **Letter** is to apprize you that on **Saturday** I shall transmit the **Pens**[13] by the same coach I sen[t] the Parcel. So enquire them out. You had better write to Godwin *here,* directing your letter to be forwarded to him. I dont know his address. You know your letter must at any rate come to London first.———

C L

MS: Huntington Library. Pub.: Talfourd (1837), I, 230–233; Talfourd (1848), I, 101–102; Sala, I, 117–121; Purnell, I, 117–121; Fitzgerald, I, 399–403; Hazlitt, I, 248–252; Ainger (1888), I, 129–132; Ainger (1900), I, 196–201; Macdonald, I, 155–159; Ainger (1904), I, 140–143; Harper, I, facsimile, and II, 242–250; Lucas (1905), VI, 177–180; Lucas (1912), V, 178–181; Lucas (1935), I, 203–206. Address: Mr. Coleridge/Greta Hall/Keswick/Cumberland. Postmark: August 18[00].

1. "The Merry Christ Church Bells," in *A Choice Collection of 180 Loyal Songs* (3d ed., London: n.p., 1685; 4th ed., London: Richard Butt, 1694). "Turn Again Wittington" is in many collections, among them *Wit and Mirth: Or Pills to Purge Melancholy; Being a Collection of the Best Merry Ballads and Songs, Old and New* (2d and 3d eds.; London: John Young, 1707 and 1712).

2. Briquettes. To cry "cupboard," following, is to crave food.

3. "This Lime-tree Bower My Prison. A Poem Addressed to Charles Lamb, of the India House, London," in the second (1800) volume of Southey's *Annual Anthology.* Lamb's comments resume the discussion in Letter 76, near the reference to note 7.

4. Apollo, here as the leader of the Muses, the nine "wandering maids."

5. Page 141 and part of page 142 contain the second stanza of "This Lime-tree Bower My Prison," lines 20–43. The objectionable abstraction, referred to below, is in lines 32–43.

6. In "Ode to Georgiana, Duchess of Devonshire, on the Twenty-fourth Stanza in Her 'Passage over Mount Gothard,'" a poem that praises the measure of the poem in the *Morning Chronicle* and the *Morning Post* of December 20 and 21, 1799, by Georgiana Cavendish, Duchess of Devonshire (1756–1806). Coleridge concludes she was granted her stately language by means of a momentary glance from the "Angel of the Earth" (line 68). "Lewti," praised following, which Lamb qualifiedly praised in Letter 76, near the reference to note 6, is a lover's complaint asking for the return and constancy of his mistress.

7. Southey's "The Battle of Blenheim," in which old Kaspar tells his grandchildren of the encounter and hints at the horrors of war. The Latin, below—*est* is underscored twice—translates, "[Cinna] wishes to appear poor and poor he *is*" (Martial's *Epigrams,* VIII, 19). The subject of Southey's "St. Gualberto" is the Vallambrosan St. John Gualbert (995?–1073). For Lamb's earlier commendation of Coleridge's "The Raven" see Letter 21, at the reference to note 8.

8. Six canceled lines follow. Allan Ramsay (1686–1758) published *The Tea-table Miscellany* from 1724 to 1727. Jacob Tonson (1656?–1736) published *Miscellany Poems* from 1684 to 1709.

9. Roman deifications of death, sickness or torment, and fear. The legislator, below, is possibly Dyer.

10. Meant are probably the perpendicular and crannied cliffs called the Phaedriades, which bound three sides of the valley in which Delphi is situated. Frederik Poulsen, in his *Delphi,* tr. G. C. Richards (London: Glydendal [1920]), pp. 38–40, described them and pointed out that Justin, in his *Historiae,* XXIV, 6, wrote "of the echo they gave, whether of the human voice or the sound of the trumpet: it was such as made its listener turn pale and wonder."

11. "We are not of opinion with those critics who condemn Cowley for excess of wit," Lamb stated in "Odes and Addresses to Great People" (*Works,* I, 285).

12. Six canceled lines precede. Although usually attributed to Longinus, *On the Sublime,* to whose chapters 5, 10–12, 22, or 39 Lamb may allude below, has from time to time been ascribed to the historian and rhetorician Dionysius Halicarnassensis (fl. 27 B.C.–A.D. 14).

13. Pens were also transmitted in 1804. See *Coleridge's Letters,* II, 1090.

80. *C. L. to Manning*

[Thursday, August 21, 1800]

Dear Manning,

I am going to ask a favor of you, and am at a loss how to do it in the most delicate manner. For this purpose I have been look[ing] into Pliny's Letters, who is noted to have had the best Grace in begging, of all the ancients, (I read him in the elegant translation of Mr. Melmoth)— —.[1] But not finding any case there exactly similar with mine, I am constrained to beg in my own barbarian way—. To come to the point then, & hasten into the middle of things—**have you a Copy** of your Algebra to give away?—. . I do not ask it for myself. I have too much reverence for the Black Arts ever to approach thy Circle, illustrious Trismegist! .[2] But that worthy man, and excellen[t] Poet **George Dyer** made me a visit yesternight on purpose to borrow **one,** supposing, rationally enough I must say, that you had made me a present of one before this—the omission of which I take to have proceeded only from Negligence, but it is a fault— —. I could lend him no assistance—you must know he is just now diverted from the pursuit of the **Bell Letters**[3] by a paradox which he has heard his friend **Friend** (that learned mathematician) maintain, that the negative quantities of Mathematicians were meræ nugæ, things scarcely in rerum naturæ, and smacking too much of mystery for Gentlemen of Mr. Friend's clear Unitarian Capacity— —. However, the dispute once set a going, has seizd violently on Georges Pericranic, and it is necessary for his health that he should speedily come to a resolution of his doubts—. He goes about teazing his friends with his new mathematics—. He even frantically talks of purchasing **Manning's** Algebra, which shews him far gone, for to my knowledge he has not been master of seven shillings a good time. George's Pockets &. . . .'s[4] brains are two things in nature which do not abhor a vacuum. . .

Now if you could step in, in this trembling suspense of his reason, and he should find on **Saturday** morning, lying for him at the **Porter's Lodge Clifford's Inn**—his safest address—M'gs Algebra with a neat manuscription in the blank leaf running thus **"From the Author! ."**—it might save his wits, and restore the unhappy Author to those studies of Poetry & Criticism, which are at present suspended to the infinite regret of the whole Literary World—. N. B. . dirty books, smear'd leaves, & dog's ears, will be rather a recommendation than otherwise. N. B. . he must have the book as soon as possible, or nothing can withhold him from madly purchasing the Book on **Tick**—. . Then, shall we see him sweetly restored to the chair of Longinus—to dictate in smooth & modest phrase the Laws of Verse.—To prove that Theocritus first introduced the Pastoral & Virgil & Pope brought it to its perfection—that Gray & Mason (who always hunt in couples in George's brain) have shewn a great deal of poetical fire in their lyric Poetry—that Aristotle's rules are not to be servilely followed, which George has shewn to have imposed great shackles upon modern Genius— —. His Poems I find are to consist of two vol's—reasonable octavo—& a third book will exclusively contain Criticisms, in which he asserts he has gone *pretty deeply* into the laws of blank verse & rhime—epic poetry, dramatic & pastoral ditto—all which is to come out before Xmas.— But above all he has *touched* most *deeply* upon the Drama—comparing the English with the modern German Stage, their merits & defects—. Apprehending that his ***studies*** (not to mention his ***Turn,*** which I take to be chiefly towards the Lyrical Poetry) hardly qualifyd him for these disquisitions, I modestly enquired what Plays he had read. I found by George's reply, that he *had* read Shaksperere, but that was a good while since: he calls him a great but irregular genius, which I think to be an original & just remark. .[5] (Beaumont & Fletcher, Massinger, Ben Jonson, Shirley, Mar[lowe,] Ford, & the worthies of Dodsleys collection he confessd he had rea[d] none of them, but profest an *intention* of looking thro them a[ll,] so as to be able to *touch* upon them in his book—)—. So Shakspere, Otway, & I believe Rowe, to whom he was natura[lly] directed by Johnson's Lives, & these not read lately, are to stand him in stead of a general knowledge of the subject—. God bless his dear absurd head—— ——

By the Bye, did I not write you a Letter, with something about an invitation in it?—but let that pass. I suppose it is not **agreeable**— — —— ——

N. B. it would not be amiss if you were to accompany your *present* with a dissertation on Negative quantities—

C L

MS: Huntington Library. Pub.: Talfourd (1848), I, 119–123; Sala, I, 330–333; Purnell, I, 330–333; Fitzgerald, II, 164–167; Hazlitt, I, 257–259; Ainger (1888), I, 123–125; Ainger (1900), I, 188–191; Macdonald, I, 159–161; Ainger (1904), I, 134–136; Harper, II, 253–256; Lucas (1905), VI, 180–182; Lucas (1912), V, 182–184; Lucas (1935), I, 207–208. Address: Mr Manning/Mr Crisp's/near St. Mary's/Cambridge. Postmark: August 21, 1800.

1. William Melmoth, the younger (1710–1799), was an author and a commissioner of bankrupts as well as a translator. His translation of the *Letters of Pliny the Younger* was published in 1746 and, in second and third editions, in 1747 and 1748.

2. Trismegistus, an appellation of the Greek Hermes, was identified in late classical times with the Egyptian Thoth, the patron deity of knowledge, the scribe of the gods, and the inventor of writing, numbers, and geometry.

3. Perhaps a pun, allowing for Lamb's habitually bad French, on John Bell (1745–1831) as the publisher of *Bell's British Poets* (1777–1782) and of editions of Shakespeare and works on the British theater. Dyer's friend is William Frend. The first Latin phrase in the sentence translates, "sheer nonsense."

4. Probably Lamb's. The saying "Nature abhors a vacuum," employed by Lamb following, is generally considered proverbial. For another appearance of it see Johnson's letter to Boswell of June 20, 1771, in Boswell's *Life of Samuel Johnson*.

5. See Dyer's *Poetics: Or a Series of Poems, and of Disquisitions on Poetry,* II, 19–21, for an expatiation on Shakespeare. Lamb below refers to *Select Collection of Old Plays* (1744), by the poet, dramatist, and bookseller Robert Dodsley (1703–1764).

81. *C. L. to Manning*

[Saturday, August 23, 1800]

George Dyer is an Archimedes, and an Archimagus,[1] and a Tycho Brahe, and a Copernicus, and thou art the darling of the nine, and midwife to their wandring babe also! We take **Tea** with that learned Poet & Critic on Tuesday night at half past five, in his neat Library, the repast will be light and Attic, with Criticism—if thou couldst contrive to wheel up thy dear carcase on the **Monday,** and after dining with us on **Tripe,** Calves' kidneys, or whatever else the Cornucopia of St. Clare[2] may be willing to pour out on the occasion, might we not adjourn together to the **Heathen's?**—thou with thy Black Backs and I with some innocent volume of the Bell Letters, Shenstone or the

Like— —it would make him wash his old flannel gown, (that has not been washed to my knowledg since it has been *his*—O the long Time!)—with **Tears** of joy—. Thou shouldst settle his Scruples, and unravel his cobwebs, & spunge off the sad stuff that weighs upon his dear wounded Pia Mater—thou shouldst restore light to his Eyes and him to His friends and the Public. . Parnassus should shower her civic crowns upon thee for saving the wits of a Citizen— —

I thought I saw a lucid Interval in George the other night—he broke in upon my studies just at Tea time, and brought with him a Dr. Anderson,[3] an old Gentleman who ties his breeches knees with packthread & boasts that he has been disappointed by Ministers—the Dr. wanted to see *me,* for I being a Poet, he thought I might furnish him with a copy of verses to suit his Agriculteral Magazine—. The Dr. in the course of the conversation mentioned a Poem called the **Epigoniad** by one Wilkie, an Epic Poem in which there is not one tolerable good Line all thro, but every incident & speech borrowed from **Homer.**— George had been sitting inattentive seemingly to what was going on—hatching of negative quantities—when suddenly the name of his old friend **Homer** stung his pericranics. . and jumping up, he beggd to know where he could meet with Wilkie's works— "it was a curious fact that there should be such an Epic Poem and he not know of it, and he *must* get a copy of it, as he was going to touch pretty deeply upon the subject of the **Epic**—and he was sure there must be somethings good in a Poem of **1400 Lines**"— —. I was pleased with this transient return of his reason, and recurrence to his old ways of thinking—it gave me great hopes of a recovery, which nothing but your **Books** can completely ensure—

Pray come on Monday, if you ***Can*** and stay your **own time**—. I have a good large room with two beds in it, in the handsomest of which thou shalt repose a nights, and dream of Spheroides—

I hope you will understand by the Nonsense of this Letter, that I am *not* melancholy at the thoughts of thy coming—I thought it necessary to add this, because you love ***precision***—. Take notice, that our stay at Dyers will not exceed eight oClock, after which our pursuits will be our own. But indeed I think a **Little** recreation among the **Bell Letters & Poetry** will do you some service in the interval of severer studies——. I hope we shall fully discuss with George Dyer what I have never yet heard done to my satisfaction, the reason of

Dr Johnson's Malevolen[t] Strictures on the higher species of the **Ode**— ——[4]

MS: Huntington Library. Pub.: Talfourd (1848), I, 124–126; Sala, I, 328–330; Purnell, I, 328–330; Fitzgerald, II, 162–164; Hazlitt, I, 259–261; Ainger (1888), I, 125–127; Ainger (1900), I, 191–193; Macdonald, I, 161–163; Ainger (1904), I, 136–138; Harper, II, 250–252; Lucas (1905), VI, 186–187; Lucas (1912), V, 188–189; Lucas (1935), I, 212–214. Address: Mr Manning/Mr Crisp's/near St. Mary's/Cambridge. Postmark: August 23, 1800.

1. The high priest of the hereditary caste of Magi of ancient Media and Persia, who regulated the rites of the Zoroastrians and were celebrated as astrologers and enchanters. The principal work of the Danish astronomer Tycho Brahe (1546–1601) is the *Astronomiæ instauratæ progymnasmata,* which Johannes Kepler edited and published in two volumes during the period 1602–1603.

2. Clara of Assisi (1194–1253), foundress of the order of Franciscan nuns known as the Poor Clares because of its strict adherence to St. Francis' primitive concept of poverty. "Black Backs," below, seems an allusion either to Manning's *Introduction to Arithmetic and Algebra* or to the mathematical books from Manning's library generally, all mysterious to Lamb.

3. James Anderson (1739–1808), a manager of farms in the vicinities of Edinburgh and Aberdeen and the author of such works on agriculture and political economy as *Essays Relating to Agriculture and Rural Affairs* (1777), *An Account of the Present State of the Hebrides* (1785), *Observations on Slavery* (1789), and *A General View of the Agriculture and Rural Economy of the County of Aberdeen* (1794). He received the LL.D. from the University of Aberdeen in 1780; moved to Edinburgh in 1783, where from 1790 to 1794 he issued the weekly *Bee;* and removed to Isleworth, Middlesex, in 1797, where from 1799 to 1801 he conducted the monthly *Recreations in Agriculture, Natural History, Arts and Miscellaneous Literature,* in which both Dyer and Lamb are represented. Anderson was attracted to Lamb because, as John M. Turnbull pointed out in "Earliest Disinterested Recognition of Charles Lamb as Poet," *Notes and Queries,* 195 (February 18, 1950), 79, Anderson had been so impressed by Lamb's "Living without God in the World" that he quoted its lines 8–14 in *Recreations,* 2 (December 1799), 354. His meeting Lamb led to his publishing in *Recreations,* 4 (November 1800), 236–238, the extracts from *John Woodvil* titled for their serial appearance "Fragment in Dialogue," "The General Lover," and "Description of a Forest Life." The last two are Simon's longer speeches in *John Woodvil,* II, ii (*Works,* V, 152 and 153). (About the first see Letter 43, note 1. About "Living without God in the World" see Letter 44, note 1.) William Wilkie (1721–1772), below, received his education at the University of Edinburgh. He became minister of Ratho in 1756 and professor of natural philosophy at St. Andrews in 1759. After the publication in 1757 of the *Epigoniad,* an epic in nine books based on the fourth book of the *Iliad* and using the heroic couplets of Pope, Wilkie became known as the Scottish Homer.

4. Johnson's strictures, particularly of Gray, are in *Lives of the English Poets,* III, 434–442, and in Boswell's *Life of Samuel Johnson,* the year 1780, "Langton's Collectanea."

82. *C. L. to Coleridge*

[August 26, 1800]

How do you like this little Epigram?—[1] It is not my writing, nor had I any finger in it—if you concur with me in thinking it very elegant and very original, I shall be tempted to name the author to you. I will just hint that it is almost *or* quite a first attempt—

Helen repentant too late.—

1

High-born Helen!
Round your dwelling
These twenty years I've pac'd in vain;
Haughty Beauty,
Your Lover's duty
Has been to glory in his pain.

2

High-born Helen!
Proudly telling
Stories of your cold disdain,
I starve, I die:—
Now you comply,
And I no longer can complain.

3

These twenty years
I've liv'd on tears,
Dwelling for ever on a frown;
On sighs I've fed,
Your scorn my bread:
I perish now you kind are grown!

4

Can I, who loved
My Beloved

But for the "scorn was in her eye,"[2]
Can I be moved
For my Beloved,
When she returns me "sigh for sigh"?

5

In stately pride,
By my bedside
High-born Helen's portrait's hung,
Deaf to my praise;
My mournful lays
Are nightly to the portrait sung.

6

To that I weep,
Nor ever sleep,
Complaining all night long to her!
Helen grown old,
No longer cold,
Said **"You to all men I prefer.—"**

Godwin returned from Wicklow[3] the week before last. Tho' he did not reach home till the Tuesday after,—he has been rambling in Wales.— He might much better have spent that time with you.— But you see your invitation would have come too late. He greatly regrets the occasion he mist of visiting you, but he intends to revisit Ireland in the next summer, and then he will certainly take **Keswick in** his way— ——. I dined with the **Heathen** on Sunday— ———

—By the bye, I have a sort of recollection that some body, I think *you,* promis'd me a sight of Wordsworth's Tragedy.—[4] I should be very glad of it just now, for I have got Manning with me and should like to read it *with him*. . But this I confess is a refinement—. Under any circumstances, alone, in Cold Bath Prison, or in the Desart Island, just when Prospero & his crew had set off, with Caliban in a cage, to Milan, it would be a treat to me to read that play. .— Manning has read it, so has Lloyd, and all Lloyd's family—but I could not get him to betray his trust by giving *me* a sight of it—. Lloyd is sadly deficient in some of those virtuous vices.— — — I have just lit upon a most beautiful fiction of hell punishments,[5] by the author of Hurlothrumbo a mad farce—the inventor imagines that in Hell there is a great caldron of hot water, in which a man can scarce hold his finger, and an immense **sieve** over it into which the probationary souls are put,

> **And all the *little* Souls**
> **Pop through the riddle-holes!——**

Mary's Love to Ms Coleridge———
mine to all—
N B—I pays no Postage———

George Dyer is the only literary character I am happily acquainted with. The oftener I see him, the more deeply I admire him. He is goodness itself.— If I could but calculate the precise date of his death, I would write a novel on purpose to make George the **Hero.** I could hit him off to a hair—. George brought a Doctor Anderson to see me—the Dr. is a very pleasant old man, a great genius for agriculture, one that ties his breeches knees with Packthread & boa[s]ts of having had disappointments from ministers—. The Doctor happen'd to mention an **Epic Poem** by one Wilkie call'd the Epigoniad in which he assur'd us there is not one tolerable line from beginning to end, but all the characters incidents &c.—verbally copied from *Homer*—. George, who had been sitting quite inattentive to the Doctor's criticism, no sooner heard the sound of Homer strike his pericranicks, than up he gets and declares he must see that Poem immediately—where was it to be had?— an Epic Poem of 800 Lines, and he not hear of it—there must be some things good in it—and it was necessary he should see it—for he had touched pretty deeply upon that subject in his criticisms on the Epic—. . George has touched pretty deeply upon the Lyric I find.—. . he has also prepard a dissertation on the Drama and the comparison of the English & German theatres.— As I rather doubted his competency to do the latter, knowing that his peculiar ***turn*** lies in the Lyric species of composition, I questiond George what English Plays he had read. I found that he *had* read Shakspere (whom he calls an original but irregular genius) but it was a good while ago. . and he has dipt into Rowe & Otway, I suppose having found their names in Johnsons Lives at full length—and upon this slender ground he has undertaken the task—. He never seemd even to have heard of fletcher, ford, marlow, massinger, and the

Worthies of Dodsleys collection—but he is to read **all** these—to prepare him for bringing out his paralell in the winter.— I find he is also determind to vindicate Poetry from the shackles which Aristotel & some others have imposed upon it; which is very good natured of him, & very necessary just now!— **Now** I am *touching* so *deeply* upon Poetry, Can I forget that I have just received from Cottle a magnificent copy of his Guinea Alfred.[6] Four & twenty Books to read in the dogdays. I got as far as the Mad monk the first day & fainted. Mr Cottles genius strongly points him to the *Pastoral,* but his inclinations divert him perpetually from his calling—. He imitates Southey, as Rowe did Shakespeare with his Good morrow to ye good master Lieut— instead of *a* man, *a* woman, *a* daughter, he constantly writes one, a man, one, a woman, one, his daughter—instead of *the* King, *the hero;* he constantly writes **he,** the King, **he,** the hero. . **Two flowers** of rhetoric palpably from the Joan.— But Mr Cottle soars a higher pitch, and when he *is* original it is in a most original way indeed——. His terrific scenes are indefatigable. Serpents, asps, spiders, ghosts, dead bodies, stair cases **made of no thing** with Adder's tongues for bannisters—. My God! what a brain **he** must have—he puts as many plums in his pudding as my Grandmother used to do & then his emerging from Hell's horrors into *Light,* and treading on pure flats of this earth for 23 books together—!—

C L

MS: Huntington Library. Pub.: Talfourd (1837), I, 161–162; Talfourd (1848), I, 116–119; Sala, I, 122–125; Purnell, I, 122–125; Fitzgerald, I, 404–407; Hazlitt, I, 254–256; Ainger (1888), I, 135–138; Ainger (1900), I, 207–212; Macdonald, I, 165–169; Ainger (1904), I, 147–150; Harper, II, 257–262; Lucas (1905), VI, 183–185; Lucas (1912), V, 184–187; Lucas (1935), I, 209–212. Address: Mr. Coleridge/Greta Hall/Keswick/Cumberland. Postmark: August 26, 1800.

1. By Mary Lamb, in sisterly ridicule of Lamb's fondness for a portrait in Blakesware of one of the Plumer women. Lamb published it in the volume with *John Woodvil* and incorporated it in "Blakesmoor in H——shire" (*Works,* V, 26, and II, 408–409).

2. Cf. *As You Like It,* iii, 50; *Much Ado about Nothing,* III, i, 51; and *Richard III,* I, iv, 31. The next quotation is from Thomas Moore's "'Tis the Last Rose of Summer," line 8.

3. In Ireland.

4. *The Borderers.* Coldbath Fields Prison (mentioned below), located on the Farringdon Road until it was demolished in 1877, had a reputation for severity. Its name appears in Coleridge and Southey's "The Devil's Thoughts," line 34, and "The Devil's Walk," line 71. Imagined next is the island after, as it were, the last act of *The Tempest.*

5. Probably *Harmony in Uproar* (n.d.), the only published work I have not been able to examine by Samuel Johnson (1691–1773), a Manchester dancing master and the author of *Hurlothrumbo* (1729), *The Mad Lovers, or the Beauties of the Poets* (1732), *A Vision of Heaven* (1738), *Court and Country: A Paraphrase upon Milton* [1780?], and five unpublished dramatic pieces.

6. Joseph Cottle's *Alfred; an Epic Poem, in Twenty-four Books* (1800), whose mad-monk scene is at II, 214–330. Lamb, below, has Cottle imitating *Joan of Arc* as Nicholas Rowe in *Lady Jane Gray,* V, i, 31, imitated *Othello,* III, i, 41.

83. *C. L. to Manning*

[September 22, 1800]

Dear Manning

You needed not imagine any apology necessary. Your fine hare and fine birds (which just now are dangling by our kitchen blaze) discourse most eloquent music in your justification. You just nick'd my palate. For, with all due decorum & leave may it be spoken, my worship hath taken physic for his body to day, and being low and puling requireth to be pampered. Foh! how beautiful and strong those buttered onions come to my nose. For you must know we extract a divine spirit of Gravy from those materials, which duly compounded with a consistence of bread & cream (y'clept bread sauce) each to each giving double grace, do mutually illustrate and set off (as skilful gold-foils to rare jewels) Your partridge, pheasant, woodcock, snipe, teal, widgeon, and the other lesser daughters of the **Ark.** . . My friendship, struggling with my Carnal & **fleshly** prudence (which suggests that a bird a man is the proper allotment in such cases) yearneth sometimes to have thee here to pick a wing or so. I question if your Norfolk sauces match our London culinarie.— — —

George Dyer has introduced me to the Table of an agreeable old Gent. Dr. Anderson, who gives hot legs of mutton and grape pies at his sylvan Lodge at Isleworth—where in the middle of a street he has **shot** up a wall most preposterously before his small Dwelling, which with the circumstance of his taking severa[l] panes of glass out of bedroom windows (for air) causeth his neighbours to speculate strangely on the state of the good man's Pericranics. Plainly, he lives under the reputation of being deranged. George does not mind this circumstance; he rather likes him the better for it. . The Doctor in his pursuits joins agricultural to poetical science, and has set George's brains mad about the old Scotch Writers, Barbour,[1] Douglas's Eneid, Blind Harry &c. .— We returned home in a return Post chaise (having dind with the Doctor) and George kept wondering & wondering for eight or nine turnpike miles What was the Name & striving to recollect the name of a Poet anterior to Barbour—. I beggd to know what was remaining of his works. "There is nothing *extant* of his works, Sir, but by all accounts he seems to have been a **fine genius"!**— This fine genius, without any thing to shew for it, or any Title beyond George's courtesy, without even a name, and Barbour, & Douglas, & blind Harry **Now** are the predominant sounds in Georges pia mater, and their buzzings exclude Politics, Criticism, and Algebra, the Late Lords of that illustrious Lumber room—. Mark, he has never read any of these Bucks, but is impatient till he reads them *all* at the Dr's. suggestion— —

Poor Dyer—his friends should be careful what Sparks they let fall into such inflammable matter——

Could I have my will of the heathen, I would lock him up from all access of new ideas, I would exclude all critics that would not swear me first (upon their Virgil) that they would feed him with nothing but the old, safe, familiar Notions & Sounds (the rightful aborigines of his Brain) Gray, Akenside, & Mason— —. In these Sounds reiterated as often as possible there could be nothing painful, nothing distracting—

God bless me, here are the **Birds,** smoking hot——

all that is gross and unspiritual in me rises at the sight— —

Avant friendship! and all memory of absent friends

C Lamb

MS: Huntington Library. Pub.: Talfourd (1848), I, 113–116; Sala, I, 345–347; Purnell, I, 345–347; Fitzgerald, II, 179–181; Hazlitt, I, 252–253; Ainger (1888), I, 132–134; Ainger (1900), I, 201–204; Macdonald, I, 163–165; Ainger (1904), I, 143–145; Harper, II, 262–264; Lucas (1905), VI, 188–189; Lucas (1912), V, 190–191; Lucas (1935), I, 214–216. Address: Mr Thos. Manning/Diss/Norfolk. Postmark: September 22, 1800.

1. John Barbour (1316?–1395), archdeacon of Aberdeen, the author of *Brus* (1571). The *Aeneid* of Gawin, or Gavin, Douglas (1474?–1522), archbishop of St. Andrews and bishop of Dunkeld, appeared in 1553. Blind Harry, or Hary, or Henry the Minstrel (fl. 1470–1492), wrote *The Actis and Deidis of the Illustere and Vailzeand Campioun Schir William Wallace, Knicht of Ellerslie* (1508?; 1st complete ed., 1570).

84. *C. L. to Coleridge*

[October 9, 1800]

I suppose you have heard of the death of Amos Cottle.[1] I paid a solemn visit of condolence to his brother, accompany'd with George Dyer of burlesque memory. I went, trembling to see poor Cottle so immediately upon the event. He was in black. And his younger brother was also in black. Every thing wore an aspect, suitable to the respect due to the freshly dead.— For sometime after our entrance, nobody spake. Till George modestly put in a question, whether Alfred was likely to sell. This was Lethe to Cottle, and his poor face, wet with tears, and his kind Eye brightend up in a moment. Now I felt it was my cue to speak. I had to thank him for a present of a magnificent Copy, and had promised to send him my remarks—the least thing I could do—. So I ventured to suggest, that I perceived a considerable improvement he had made [in] his first book, since the state in which he first read it to me. Joseph, who till now had sat with his knees cowering in by the fire place, wheeled about, and with great difficulty of body shifted the same round to the Corner of a table where I was sitting, and first stationing One thigh over the other, which is his sedentary mood, and placidly fixing his benevolent face right against mine, waited my observations. At that moment it came strongly into my mind, that I had got **Uncle Toby**[2] before me he looked so kind and so **good.** I could not say an unkind thing of **Alfred.** So I set my memory to work to recollect what was the name of Alfred's Queen, and with some adroitness recalled the well known sound to Cottle's ears of **Alswitha.**— At that moment I could perceive that Cottle had forgot his brother was so lately become a blessed spirit. In the language of Mathematicians the Author was as **9** the brother as **1.** I felt my cue, and strong pity working at the root, I went to work, and beslabberd Alfred with most unqualify'd praise =[3] or only qualifying my praise by the occasional politic interposition of an exception taken against trivial faults, slips, & human imperfections, which by removing the appearance of insincerity did but in truth heighten the relish. .— Perhaps I might have spared that refinement, for Joseph was in a humour **to hope** and believe **all things.**— What I said was beautifully suppor[ted], corroborated & confirmed by the stupidity of his brother on my left hand, and by George on my right, who has an utter incapacity of comprehending that there can be any thing **bad** in Poetry. **All** Poems are *good* Poems to George. All men are *fine Geniuses.*— **So,** what with my actual memory, of which I made the most, and Cottle's own helping me out, for I *really* had forgotten a good deal of Alfred, I made a shift to discuss the most essential parts, entirely to the satisfaction of its Author, who repeatedly declared that he loved nothing better than **candid** criticism. . .— — Was I a Candied Greyhound[4] **now** for all this? . or did I do right? I believe I did. The effect was luscious to my Conscience. For all the rest of the evening **Amos** was no more heard of, till George revived the subject by enquiring whether some account should not be drawn up by the friends of the deceased to be inserted in Phillips monthly Obituary, adding that Amos was estimable both for his head & heart, and would have made a fine Poet, if he had lived.[5] T[o] the expediency of this measure Cottle fully assented, but could not help adding, that he always thought that the qualities of his brother's heart exceeded those of his head. I believe his brother, when living, had formed precisely the same idea of him.— And I apprehend the world will assent to both judgments. . I rather guess that the Brothers were poetical rivals. I judged so, when I saw them together. .— **Poor Cottle,** I must leave him, after his short dream, to muse again upon his poor brother, for whom I a[m] sure in secret he will yet shed many a tear.

C L

Now send me in return some Greta news.——

MS: Huntington Library. Pub.: Sala, I, 125–127; Purnell, I, 125–127; Fitzgerald, I, 407–409; Hazlitt, I, 263–264; Ainger (1888), I, 140–142; Ainger (1900), I, 214–216; Macdonald, I, 170–172; Ainger (1904), I, 152–154; Harper, II, 264–267; Lucas (1935), I, 216–217. Address: Mr Coleridge/Greta Hall/ Keswick/Cumberland. Postmark: October 9, 1800.

1. Amos Simon Cottle (b. 1768?), the brother of Joseph and Robert (1780?–1858), the latter of whom was also a Bristol printer. Amos received his B.A. in 1799 from Magdalene College, Cambridge, where he translated *Icelandic Poetry, or the Edda of Saemund* (1797) and wrote the occasional verse that Joseph included in his own *Malvern Hills* (1798). Amos afterward became Dyer's neighbor in Clifford's Inn, where on September 28 he died. His obituary, to which Lamb later refers, is in Richard Phillips' *Monthly Magazine,* 10 (November 1, 1800), 368.

2. Of *Tristram Shandy.*

3. A canceled line follows.
4. Cf. *I Henry IV*, I, iii, 251–252.
5. A canceled line follows.

85. *C. L. to Manning*

[October 16, 1800]

Dear Manning,

Had you written one week before you did, I certainly should have obeyed your injunction; you should have seen **me** before my letter. I will explain to you my situation.— There are **six** of us in one department. Two of us (within these four days) are confined with severe fevers.— And two more, who belong to the Tower Militia, expect to have marching orders on friday. **Now Six** are absolutely necessary. I have already asked & obtained two young hands to supply the loss of the *Fever*ites.— And with the other prospect before me, **You** may believe I cannot decently ask Leave of Absence for myself. . All I can promise (and I do promise, with the sincerity of *Saint* Peter, and the contrition of *Sinner* Peter if I fail) that I will come *the very first spare week*,[1] and go no where till I have been at Camb.— No matter if you are in a state of **Pupilage** when I come. For I can employ myself in Camb. very pleasantly in the mornings——. Are there not Libraries, Halls, Colleges, Books, Pictures, Statues?—

I wish to **God You** had made London in your Way. There is an exhibition quite uncommon in Europe, which could not have escaped *your genius*.— A **Live Rattle Snake 10 feet in Length**, and of the thickness of a big **Leg.** I went to see it last night by candlelight. We were ushered into a room very little bigger than ours at Pentonville. A Man and woman & four boys live in this room, joint Tenants with **9 Snakes**, most of them Such, as no remedy has been discoverd for their bite. We walked into the middle, which is formed by a half moon of wired Boxes, all mansions of ***Snakes***.— Whip snakes, Thunder snakes, Pig nose snakes, American **Vipers**, and *this monster*.— He lies curled up in folds, and immediately a stranger enters (for he is used to the family, & sees them play at cards) he set up a rattle like a watchman's in London or near as loud, and reared up a head, from the midst of these folds, like a **Toad**, and shook his head, and shewed every sign a snake can show of irritation.— I had the foolish curiosity to strike the wires with my finger, and the devil flew at me, with his Toad-mouth wide open,—the inside of his mouth is quite white. I had got my finger away, nor could he well have bit me with his damn'd big mouth, which would have been certain death in five minutes. But it frightend me so much, that I did not recover my voice for a minute's space. I forgot in my fear that he was secured. You would have forgot too, for tis incredible how such a monster can be confined in small gauzy-looking wires.— I dream'd of snakes in the night—. I wish to heaven you sould see it. He absolutely swelled with passion to the bigness of a large **thigh—.** I could not retreat, without impinging on another box, and just behind a little Devil not an inch from my back had got his nose out with some difficulty and pain quite thro' the bars! He was soon taught better manners———. All the Snakes were curious & objects of Terror. But this Monster, like Aarons serpent,[2] swallowed up the impression of the rest—. He opened his damned mouth, when he made at me, as wide as his head was broad.— I hollood out quite loud—. And felt pains all over my body with the fright———

I have had the felicity of hearing **George Dyer read out** one book of the **Farmer's Boy.**[3] I thought it rather childish. No doubt, there is originality in it (which in your self taught geniuses is a most rare quality, they generally getting hold of some bad models, in a scarsity of books, & forming their taste on *them*) but no *selection. All* is described.—

Mind I have only heard **read one book.—**

Yours sincerily
Philo-snake
C L

MS: Huntington Library. Pub.: Talfourd (1837), I, 176–179; Sala, I, 348–350; Purnell, I, 348–350; Fitzgerald, II, 182–184; Hazlitt, I, 268–269; Ainger (1888), I, 143–145; Ainger (1900), I, 218–221; Macdonald, I, 174–176; Ainger (1904), I, 155–157; Harper, II, 269–271; Lucas (1905), VI, 189–191; Lucas (1912), V, 192–193; Lucas (1935), I, 218–219. Address: Mr Manning/Mr Crisp's/near St. Mary's/Cambridge. Postmark: October 16, 1800.

1. That beginning Monday, January 5, 1801.

2. In Exodus 4, esp. verse 12.

3. *The Farmer's Boy,* by Robert Bloomfield (1766–1823), was published this year and met with considerable success. Bloomfield would increase his reputation as a poet with *Rural Tales* (1802), *Good Tidings, or News from the Farm* (1804), *Wild Flowers* (1806), and *Banks of the Wye* (1811). He was born to

George Bloomfield (d. 1767) and his wife in Honington, Suffolk. In 1781 he was sent to London from the farm of William Austin, his mother's brother-in-law of Sapiston, to begin work under his own brother George (d. 1831) as an apprentice shoemaker. Bloomfield continued in the trade until 1802. Then he became successively an undersealer in the seal office, a manufacturer of aeolian harps, and a bookseller. In 1814 he retired to Shefford, Bedfordshire, where he died, leaving a widow with four children in the terrible poverty from which he had never escaped. The miscellaneous writer and book collector George Daniel (1789–1864) told in his *Recollections of Charles Lamb* (1927; rpt. Folcroft, Pa.: Folcroft Press, 1969), p. 32, that in 1823 he and Lamb dined with Bloomfield in Islington.

86. *C. L. to Manning*

[November 3, 1800]

Ecquid meditatur Archimedes?[1] What is Euclid doing? what hath happened to learned Trismegist?—doth he take it in ill part, that his Humble friend did not comply with his courteous invitation?— Let it suffice, I **could not come—.** Are Impossibilities nothing?—be they abstractions of the intellect?—or not (rather) most Sharp & mortifying realities? **nuts** in the **will's** mouth too hard for her to crack?—brick & stone walls in her way which she can by no means eat thro'?—sore lets, impedimenta viarum, no-thoroughfares?—**racemi** nimium **alte** pendentes?[2]—is the phrase classic? I allude to the **Grapes in Æsop,** which cost the fox a strain, and gained the world an aphorism— —. Oberse[3] the superscription of this letter. In adapting the *size* of the letters which constitute *your* name & Mr. *Crisp's* name respectively, I had an eye to your different stations in life. Tis truly curious and must be soothing to an *aristocrat*——. I wonder it has never been hit on before my time. .—

I have made an acquisition latterly of a *pleasant hand,* one Rickman,[4] to whom I was introduced by George Dyer! ! ! **Not** the most flattering auspices under which one man can be introduced to another—. George brings all sorts of people together, setting up a sort of Agrarian Law or common property in matter of society—. But for once he has done me a great pleasure, while he was only pursuing a principle, As Ignes fatui *may* light you home.— This Rickman lives in our Buildings immediately opposite our house—the finest fellow to **drop** in a nights about nine or ten oClock, cold bread & cheese time, just in the ***wishing*** time of the night,[5] when you *wish* for somebody to come in, without a distinct idea of a probable anybody—. Just in the Nick, neither too early to be tedious, nor too late to sit a reasonable time—. He is a most pleasant hand;—a fine *rattling* fellow, has gone through Life laughing at solemn apes; himself hugely literate, oppressively full of information in all stuff of conversation from matter of fact to Zenophon[6] and Plato—can talk Greek with Porson, politics with Thelwall, conjecture with George Dyer, nonsense with me, & any thing with anybody—. A great farmer: ⟨Editor of an⟩ somewhat concerned in an agriculteral magazine—. Reads no Poetry but **Shakspeare** = Very intimate with Southey, but ⟨never reads[?]⟩ does not always [read (?)][7] his poetry—relishes George Dyer—thoroughly penetrates into the ridiculous wherever found—understands the *first time* (a great desideratum in common minds) you need never twice speak to him. Does not want **explanations,** translations, limitations, as Professor Godwin does when you make an assertion. *Up* to any thing. *Down* to every thing. Whatever *sapit hominem.*—[8] A perfect ***man***— —. **All** this farrago, which must perplex you to read, and has put me to a little trouble to ***select***! ! Only proves how impossible it is to describe a ***pleasant hand*—.** You must see Rickman to know him, for he is a **Species** in one. A new Class. An exotic, any slip of which I am proud to put in my garden-pot—. The clearest headed fellow. Fullest of matter with least verbosity—. If there be any allay[9] in my fortune to have met with such a man, it is that he commonly **divides** his time between town & country, having some foolish family tyes at Christ[chur]ch, by which means he can only gladden our London Hemisphere with ***returns*** of Light—. He is now going for 6 weeks—— ——

At last I have written to Kemble to know the event of my **Play,** which was presented last Christmas— —.[10] As I suspected came an answer back, that the Copy was lost & could not be found, no hint that any body had to this day ever looked into it—with a courteous (reasonable!) **request** of another Copy (if I had one by me) and a promise of a definitive answer in a **week.** I could not resist so facile & moderate demand, so scribbled out another, omitting Sundry things, such as the witch story, about half of the forest scene (which is too leisurely—for *story*)—& transposing that damn'd soliloq[u]y about England getting drunk, which like its reciter, stupidly stood **alone,** nothing prevenient or antevenient.— And cleared away a good deal besides; & **sent** *this* Copy, written *all out* (with alterations &c. ***re-***

quiring ***judgment***) in **one** day & a half!— — I sent it last night, and am in weekly expectation of the **Tolling Bell**—& death warrant—

This is all my **Lunnon** news—. Send me some from the ***Banks*** of ***Cam,*** as the Poets delight to speak, especially George Dyer[11]—who has no other name nor idea nor definition of Cambridge, = namely, its being a market town, sending members to Parliament, never entered into his definition. **It was & is, simply,** the banks of the Cam, or the fair **Cam.— As Oxford** is the Banks of the Isis, or the fair Isis—— ———

Yours in all humility
most illustrious Trismegist,
C Lamb

(read on, there's more at the bottom)—[12]

You ask me about the farmer's Boy—. Dont you think the fellow who wrote it (who is a shoemaker)—has a *poor* **mind—?** Dont you find he is always silly about ***poor Giles*** & those abject kind of phrases, which mark a man that looks up to **wealth?**— None of Burns's Poet-dignity— —. What do you think?— I have just open'd him—. But he makes me sick. Dyer knows the Shoemaker (a damn'd stupid hound in Company) but George introduce[d] & promises to introduce him, indiscriminately to **all his friends** & all combinations

MS: Huntington Library. Pub.: Talfourd (1837), I, 183–188; Sala, I, 352–355; Purnell, I, 352–355; Fitzgerald, II, 186–189; Hazlitt, I, 270–272; Ainger (1888), I, 145–148; Ainger (1900), I, 221–225; Macdonald, I, 176–179; Ainger (1904), I, 157–160; Harper, II, 272–275; Lucas (1905), VI, 191–193; Lucas (1912), V, 193–196; Lucas (1935), I, 220–222. Address: **Mr. Manning/Mr Crisp's/near St Mary's/Cambridge.** Postmark: November 3, 1800.

1. "What is Archimedes thinking?"

2. " 'Obstacles in the way' . . . 'clusters hanging too high?' "

3. For "Observe."

4. The statistician John Rickman (1771–1840) was born at Newburn, Northumberland, the only son of the Reverend Mr. Thomas Rickman (d. 1809) and the former Miss Beaumont. Rickman entered Guildford Grammar School in 1781. He proceeded in 1788 first to Magdalen College and then to Lincoln College, Oxford. Discouraged from taking church orders, he in 1792 took only his degree and returned to the house of his father, who from 1780 held the livings of Ash, in Surrey, and Stourpaine, in Dorset, and who in 1796 retired to Christchurch, in Hampshire. There Rickman in 1797 met Southey, who was residing at Burton close by. Southey probably intensified Rickman's desire to leave the isolation of the village. He came to London in April 1800 with some literary aspirations and a letter of introduction from Southey to Dyer, who perhaps helped him to settle at 33 Southampton Buildings and did secure for him the editorship, which Rickman held until 1801, of the *Commercial, Agricultural, and Manufacturers' Magazine.* In about December 1800 a paper he had written in 1796 called "Thoughts

on the Utility and Facility of a General Enumeration of the People of the British Empire" was brought by a mutual acquaintance to the attention of Charles Abbot, later first Baron Colchester (1757–1829). Abbot offered Rickman the supervision of the census returns for Great Britain and employment as his secretary after Parliament, on December 30, 1800, passed the first Population Act, which Abbot had introduced. Rickman joined Abbot in Dublin Castle and was made deputy keeper of the privy seal when, in 1801, Abbot was made chief secretary for Ireland. Rickman refused a lucrative permanent office so that he might return to London as the speaker's secretary when, in February 1802, Abbot became speaker of the House of Commons. By April Rickman moved into the official house provided for him in New Palace Yard, Westminster. He continued his work on the census, originating procedures and preparing the reports that had been published in 1801 and would be published in 1811, 1821, and 1831. He also prepared reports on poor-law returns, education, church rates, and taxation. In 1803 he was appointed the secretary to two commissions for constructing roads, churches, and the Caledonian Canal in Scotland. In 1823 he was appointed to a similar commission. He was elevated to second clerk assistant to the House of Commons in 1814 and to first clerk assistant in 1820 or 1821, a post he held until he died, at his home since 1835, at 35 Duke Street, Westminster. He published statistical and agricultural papers in the *Commercial, Agricultural, and Manufacturers' Magazine* from 1799 through 1801, pamphlets on the poor laws in England and Ireland in 1832 and 1833, studies on life annuities in the *Medical Gazette* between 1835 and 1837, *Historical Curiosities Relating to St. Margaret's Church, Westminster* in 1837, and a "Treatise on the Antiquity of Stonehenge and Abury" in *Archaeologia* in 1840. He edited the *Speeches of the Right Hon. Charles Abbot . . . in Communicating Thanks of the House of Commons to Military Commanders, 1807–1816* in 1829 and the autobiography of the engineer Thomas Telford (1757–1834) in 1838. He became a fellow of the Royal Society in 1815 and an honorary member of the Société Française de Statistique Universelle and the Institute of Civil Engineers in 1833 and 1835. In 1805 he was married to Susannah (d. 1836), the daughter of Joseph Postlethwaite of Harting, Sussex. She bore him William Charles, the author of *Biographical Memoir of John Rickman* (1841); Ann (b. 1808), later Mrs. Lefroy; Frances, later Mrs. Hone; and Martha (d. 1810), the youngest, whose death Mary Lamb mentions in her letter to Sarah Stoddart Hazlitt of March 30, 1810, in Vol. III. The most thorough account of him is *Rickman*. But about his works see the unnumbered pages at the end of *Biographical Memoir.*

5. Altered from *Hamlet,* III, ii, 388.

6. Xenophon (ca. 430–354 B.C.), the Greek historian and philosophical essayist. Richard Porson (1759–1808), following, was a renowned editor of Euripides and from 1792 regius professor of Greek at Cambridge.

7. Lamb forgot to add "read" (or something like it) when he corrected his statement.

8. "Treats of man" (Martial, *Epigrams,* X, 4).

9. As a noun replaced by "alloy."

10. See Letter 56, at the reference to note 1.

11. Dyer would write *History of the University and Colleges of Cambridge, Including Notices Relating to the Founders and Eminent Men* (1814), *Address to the Subscribers to the Privileges* (1823), and *Privileges of the University of Cambridge* (1824).

12. Below the address.

87. *C. L. to Manning*

[November 29, 1800]

Dear Manning,

I have received a Very kind invitation from Lloyd and Sophia, to go and spend a month with them at the Lakes.[1] Now it fortunately happens, (which is so seldom the case!) that I have spare cash by me enough to answer the expences of so long a journey; and am determined to get away from the office by some means. The purpose of this letter is to request of you (my dear friend) that you will not take it unkind, if I decline my proposed visit to Cambridge *for the present.* Perhaps I shall be able to take Cambridge *in my way,* going or coming. I need not describe to you the expectations which such an one as myself, pent up all my life in a dirty city,[2] have formed of a tour to the *Lakes.* Consider, Grassmere! Ambleside! Wordsworth! Coleridge! I hope you will.

Hills, woods, Lakes and mountains, to the Eternal Devil. I will eat snipes with thee, Thomas Manning.[3] Only confess, confess a *Bite.*—

P. S. I think you named the *16th.*— But was it not modest of Lloyd to send such an invitation? It shews his knowledge of *money,* and *time.* I would be loth to think, he meant "Ironic satire sidelong sklented On my poor Pursie."

Burns

For my part, with reverence to my friends northward, I must confess that I am not romance-bit about *Nature.* The earth, and sea, and sky (when all is said) is but as a house to dwell in. If the inmates be courteous, and good liquors flow like the conduits at an old coronation, if they can talk sensibly and feel properly, I have no need to stand staring upon the gilded Looking glass (that strained my friend's purse strings in the purchase) nor his 5 shilling print over the mantle Piece of old Nabbs the Carrier[4] (which only betray's his false taste)—. Just as important to me (in a sense) is all the furniture of my world. Eye-pampering but satisfys no heart. Streets, streets, streets, markets, theatres, churches, Covent Gardens, Shops sparkling with pretty faces of industrious milliners, neat sempstresses, Ladies cheapening, Gentlemen behind counters lying, Authors in the street with spectacles, George Dyers (you may know them by their gait)[5] Lamps lit at night, Pastry cook & Silver smith shops, Beautiful Quakers of Pentonville, noise of coaches, drousy cry of mechanic watchmen at night, with Bucks reeling home drunk if you happen to wake at midnight, cries of fire & stop thief, Inns of court (with their learned air and halls and Butteries just like Cambridge colleges), old Book stalls, Jeremy Taylors, Burtons on melancholy, and Religio Medici's on every stall—. These are thy Pleasures O London with-the-many-sins—O City abounding in whores—for these may Keswick and her Giant Brood go hang.

C L

MS: Huntington Library. Pub.: Talfourd (1837), I, 181–183; Sala, I, 355–357; Purnell, I, 355–357; Fitzgerald, II, 189–191; Hazlitt, I, 273–274; Ainger (1888), I, 148–149; Ainger (1900), I, 225–227; Macdonald, I, 179–180; Ainger (1904), I, 160–161; Harper, II, 276–277; Lucas (1905), VI, 194–195; Lucas (1912), V, 196–197; Lucas (1935), I, 223–224. Address: Mr Manning/Mr Crisp's/near St. Mary's/Cambridge. Postmark: November 29, 1800.

1. Specifically, in Ambleside, where the Lloyds had just removed from Olton Green. See the *Lloyd-Manning Letters,* p. 56.

2. Cf. Coleridge's "This Lime-tree Bower My Prison," line 30, and "Frost at Midnight," line 52.

3. "The Snipes shall present themselves to you, ready roasted—*you* shall take the *digestible* parts, and *I*'ll take the long bills. Don't come before the 16th." So reads Manning's invitation of November 28. In his letter of December 12 Manning admitted that Lamb's Lakes story took him in completely, until he turned to the next page. (See the *Manning-Lamb Letters,* pp. 40 and 43.) The *"16th"* and *"Burns,"* below, are underscored twice, the latter possibly because Manning mentioned in his letter of November 28 glancing through Currie's edition of Burns's works. The quotation is an adaptation of "To William Simpson of Ochiltree," lines 9–10. Burns's *sklented* means "squinted."

4. Conjecturally, the Lloyds' Birmingham carrier, possibly known to Lamb and Manning.

5. *Julius Caesar,* I, iii, 132. The "Beautiful Quakers of Pentonville," below, surely includes Hester Savory (1777–1803), the daughter of Joseph, a goldsmith in the Strand, and from July 1802 the wife of the merchant Charles Stoke Dudley. Lamb never spoke to her but silently fell in love with her while he was living in Pentonville. In 1803 he wrote "Hester," or "Hester Savory," on the event of her death. See Vol. II, Letter 143, and *Works,* V, 30–31, for the poem and *Works,* V, facing p. 298, for her likeness. See "The Londoner" (*Works,* I, 39–40) for Lamb's public expression of love for the city.

88. *C. L. to William Godwin*

Thursday morning [December 4, 1800]

Dear Sir

I send this speedily after the Heels of Cooper[1] (O! the dainty expression!) to say that Mary is obliged to stay at home on Su[n]day to receive a female friend, from whom I am equally glad to escape. So that we shall be by ourselves. I write, because it *may* make *some* diffrence in your marketting &c—

C L

I am sorry to put you to the expence of Two Pence Poste. But I calculate thus; if Mary comes she will

eat Beef	2 plates	4d	
Batter Pudding	1 do.———	2	
Beer	a pint———	2	
Wine	3 glasses———	11	I drink no wine!
chestnuts after dinner———		2	
Tea and Supper at moderate calcn———		9	
		2.6	

from which deduct —————— 2 postage

You are clear gainer by her not coming —— 2.4———

MS: Lord Abinger, Bures, Suffolk; transcribed from the microfilm of the Abinger Collection in the William R. Perkins Library, Duke University, Durham, N.C. Pub.: Hazlitt, I, 275–276; Ainger (1888), I, 149–150; Ainger (1900), I, 227–228; Macdonald, I, 180–181; Ainger (1904), I, 161–162; Harper, II, 278; Lucas (1905), VI, 196; Lucas (1912), V, 198; Lucas (1935), I, 224–225. Address: Mr Godwin/Polygon/Somer's Town. Date, by Godwin: Dec. 4. Postmark: December 4, 1800.

1. Godwin's maidservant (*Godwin,* II, 36). Possibly she was a relative of Dr. Thomas Cooper (d. 1787) and his widow, Mary Grace, a cousin of Godwin's mother who had been forced to go into service and to rely on relatives to raise her two sons and daughter after the death of her husband. Godwin accepted the care and education of her elder son, Thomas Abthorpe Cooper (1776–1849), who became an actor and a theatrical manager in America and England.

89. *C. L. to Godwin*

Wedn. morn [December 10, 1800]

Dear Sir,

I expected a good deal of pleasure from your company tomorrow; but I am sorry, I must beg of you to excuse me. I have been confined ever since I saw you with one of the severest colds I ever experienced, occasioned by being in the night air on *Sunday,* and on the following day *very foolishly*— ——. I am neither in health nor spirits to meet company— —. I hope and trust I shall get out on *Saturday night.* .[1] You will add to your many favors by transmitting to me as early as possible, as many *tickets* as conveniently you can spare—

Yours truly—
C Lamb

(turn over)

I have been plotting how to *abridge* the Epiloge—. But I cannot see that any lines can be spared, retaining the *connection,* except these two, which are better out

Why should I instance &c—
The sick man's purpose &c—[2]

and then the following line must run thus—

The truth by *an example* best is shewn—

Excuse this *important* postscript—

MS: Lord Abinger. Pub.: Hazlitt, I, 276–277; Ainger (1888), I, 150; Ainger (1900), I, 228–229; Macdonald, I, 181–182; Ainger (1904), I, 162; Harper, II, 281–282; Lucas (1905), VI, 198; Lucas (1912), V, 200; Lucas (1935), I, 225–226. Address: Mr Godwin/Polygon/Somers Town. Date, by Godwin: Dec. 11. Postmark: December 10, 1800.

1. To attend the performance of Godwin's "Antonio: Or, the Soldier's Return," for which Lamb wrote the Epilogue. (See the next letter and *Works,* V, 121–122.) It opened and closed at Drury Lane on Saturday, December 13, and gave Lamb an evening to recall in "The Old Actors" (*Works,* II, 291–294). Godwin remained convinced of its merits and before the year was out published it, with Lamb's assistance in its revisions but without its Prologue or Epilogue, as *Antonio: A Tragedy in Five Acts.* See *Godwin,* II, 36–55, for a full discussion of the play.

2. Lines 16 and 17. The penultimate word in this letter is underscored twice.

90. *C. L. to Manning*

Saturday 4 oClock
[December 13, 1800]

I have receiv'd your letter[1] *this moment,* not having been at the office—. I have just time to scribble down the Epilogue.— To your Epistle I will just reply, that I will certainly come to Cambridge before January is out,[2]—I'll come *when I can*— —. You shall have an emended copy of my play Early next week. . Mary thanks you, but her hand writing is too **feminine** to be exposed to a Cambridge Gentleman— —tho' I endeavour to persuade her that you understand **algebra,** & must understand her hand——

The play *is*[3] the man's you wot of—, but for God's sake (who would Not like to have so pious a *professor's* work *damned*)—do not mention it——it is to come out in a **feign'd** name, as one Tobins—. I will omit the introductory Lanes, which connect it with the Play, and give you the concluding Tale which is the mass & bulk of the Epilog—. **The** ***Name*** **is** ***Jack Incident.*** It is about promise-breaking—. You will see it all, if you read the *Papers*—

Jack, of dramatic genius justly vain,
Purchas'd a renter's share at Drury Lane,
A prudent man in every other matter,

Known at his Club room for an honest hatter;
Humane & courteous, led a civil life,
And has been seldom known to beat his wife;
But **Jack** is now grown quite another man,
Frequents the **Green room,** knows the plot & plan of each new piece,
And has been seen to talk with **Sheridan!**
In at the play house just at 6 he pops,
And never quits it till the curtain drops,
Is never absent on the *Author's night,*
Knows Actresses & actors too—by sight;
So humble, that with **Suett**[4] he'll confer,
Or take a pipe with plain **Jack Banister.**—
Nay with an Author has been known so **free,**
He once suggested a **Catastrophe**—
In short, John dabbled till his head was turnd;
His wife remonstrated, his neighbours mourn'd,
His customers were dropping off apace,
And Jack's Affairs began to **wear** a piteous face.
One night his wife began a curtain lecture;
"My dearest Johnny, husband, spouse, protector,
"Take pity on your helpless babes & me,
"Save us from ruin, you from bankruptcy—
"Look to your business, leave these cursed plays,
"And try again your **old** industrious ways—"—

Jack, who was always scar'd at the Gazettee,
And had some bits of **scull** uninjur'd yet,
Promis'd amendment, vow'd his wife spake reason,
"He would not see another play that season"—
Three stubborn fortnights Jack his promise kept,
Was late & early in his shop, eat, slept,
And walk'd & talk'd, like ordinary men,—
No ***wit;*** but John the hatter once again—
Visits his Club:— When lo! one *fatal night*
His wife with horror view'd the wellknown sight,
John's *hat, wig, snuffbox*; well she knew his tricks—
And **Jack** decamping at the hour of **six**—

Just at the counter's edge a playbill lay,
Announcing that **Pizarro** was the play.—
"O Johnny, Johnny, this is your old doing."—
Quoth Jack "Why, what the devil storm's a brewing?
"About a harmless play why all this *fright*?
"I'll go & see it, if it's but for spite—
"Zounds woman! ***Nelson's**** to be there tonight"—

turn Over when you have read this—

N. B. this was intended for Jack Banister to speak; but the sage managers have chosen Miss ***Heard,***[5] except Miss Tidswell the **worst** actress Ever seen *or* ***heard*** — — —

Now I remember, I have promis'd the loan of my play—. I will lend it ***instantly*** and you shall get it (pon honor!) by this day week————

I must go & **dress** for the **Boxes!** 1st night———

finding I have time, I transcribe the **Rest**— observe, you have read the last first. it begins thus.— **The Names** I took from a little outline: G: gave me—. I have not read the Play!

Ladies, ye've seen how Guzman's consort died,
Poor victim of a Spaniard Brother's pride,
When Spanish honor thro' the world was blown,
And Spanish Beauty for the Best was know.—†
In that romantic, unenlighten'd time,
A *breach* of *promise*‡ was a sort of crime—
Which of y[ou] handsome English ladies here,
But deems the penance bloody & severe?—
A whimsical old **Saragossa**§ fashion,
That a dead father's dying inclination
Should *live*, to thwart a *living* daughter's passion||
Unjustly on the sex *we*# men exclaim,
Rail at *your*# vices & commit the same—
Man is a promise-breaker from the Womb,
And goes a promise breaker to the tomb— —
What need we instance here the lover's vow,
The sick man's purpose, or the great man's bow?—**
The Truth by few examples best is shewn—

Instead of many, which are better known,
Take poor **Jack** ***Incident*** that's dead & gone——
Jack &c. &c &c———

Now you have it all—how do you like it? I am going to hear it **recited! ! ! !——**
do'nt spill the **Cream** upon this Letter——[6]

*a good clap trap—. Nelson has exhibited two or 3 times at both theatres——— & advertiz'd himself— [Lamb writes of Horatio Nelson.—Ed.]
†four *easy* lines
‡for which the *heroine died*—
§in *spain*! !
||2 *neat* lines
#or *you* or *our* as *they* have alter'd it
**antithesis! !

MS: Huntington Library. Pub.: Talfourd (1837), I, 193–196; Sala, I, 357–360; Purnell, I, 357–360; Fitzgerald, II, 191–193; Hazlitt, I, 277–279; Ainger (1888), I, 151–153; Ainger (1900), II, 1–4; Macdonald, I, 182–183; Ainger (1904), I, 163–165; Harper, II, 282–285; Lucas (1905), VI, 199–200; Lucas (1912), V, 201–203; Lucas (1935), I, 226–228. Address: Mr Manning/Mr Crisp's/near St. Mary's/Cambridge. Postmark: December 13, 1800.

1. Of December 12 (*Manning-Lamb Letters*, pp. 42–46), in which Manning, replying in part to a letter (unrecovered) of Lamb's written since November 29, asked Lamb to visit him in January to permit Lamb time to rid himself of his cold. Manning also asked for a copy of the Epilogue to "Antonio" and a transcription in Lamb's and Mary's hands of "Pride's Cure."

2. A canceled line follows.

3. Underscored twice. "Professor," following, is Lamb's persistent title for Godwin. Godwin, fearing popular prejudice against him because of his reputation for heterodoxy, had it announced that "Antonio" was by John Tobin (1770–1804), who would become the dramatist of *The Honey Moon* (1805), *Curfew* (1807), *School for Authors* (1808), and other works, all published posthumously. Tobin, to maintain the deception, attended the rehearsals. "*Incident*," below, is also underscored twice.

4. Richard Suett (1755–1805), a popular comic actor, as was John Bannister (1760–1836), next. Bannister was additionally the acting manager of Drury Lane from 1802 to 1803. Lamb mentioned both in "On Some of the Old Actors" (*Works*, II, esp. 138 and 139).

5. Elizabeth Heard was reared for the stage at Drury Lane, from which she was dismissed in 1801. She also played at the Haymarket and, after 1801, in Newcastle. She was the daughter of William Heard (fl. 1778)—the dramatist of *The Snuff-box; or, a Trip to Bath* (1775) and *Valentine's Day* (1776) and the author of *A Sentimental Journey to Bath, Bristol, and Their Environs; a Descriptive Poem. To Which Are Added Miscellaneous Pieces* (1778)—and of his

wife, Ann (1750?–1797), who had preceded her daughter as a member of the Drury Lane company. Charlotte Tidswell (b. 1757?), following, a close and lifelong associate of the tragedian Edmund Kean, first appeared at Drury Lane in 1783 and retired from it in 1822 after a career playing modest parts. She was allegedly the daughter of an army officer and became an actress when his death compelled her to seek employment.

6. A reference to a drawing in Manning's letter of December 12, which is not reproduced but explained by Manning as a "Literary table, alias littered; letter lying in front, from Mister Lamb."

91. *C. L. to Godwin*

Late o' Sunday nig[ht, December 14, 1800]

Dear Sir—

I have performed my office in a slovenly way—but judge for me—. I sat down at 6 oClock and never left reading (and I read out to Mary) your play till 10—in this sitting I noted down lines as they occurd, exactly as you will read my rough paper—. Do not be frighten'd at the Bulk of my remarks, for they are almost all upon **single Lines,** which put together do not amount to an hundred, and many of them merely verbal— —. I had but one object in view, abridgement for **compression sake— —.** I have used a dogmatical language (which is truly ludicrous, when the trivial nature of my remarks is considerd)——**and remember, my office was to hunt out faults— —.** You may fairly abridge one half of them, as a fair deduction for the infirmities of **Error** and a single reading— —which leaves only fifty objections, most of them merely against words, in no short play— —. remembr, you constituted me **Executioner,** and a hangman has been seldom seen to be asham'd of his profession before Master Sheriff— —. **We'll *Talk*** of the Beauties (of which I am more than ever [su]re), when we meet—

Yours truly
C L

I wil[l] barely add, as you are on the very point of printing, that in my opinion **neither prologue nor Epilogue** should accompany the play—**it can only serve** to remind your readers of its fate— —. ***both* suppose an audience,** and, that **jest** being gone, must convert into burlesque—. **Nor would *I*** (but therein custom & **decorum** must be a law) print the Actors names—. Some things must be kept out of **sight——**

I have done, and I have but a few square Inches of paper to fill up— — —

I am emboldened by a little jorum of punch (vastly good) to Say, that next to *one man* I *am the most hurt* at **our** ill success——the **Breast of Hecuba,** where she did suckle **Hector,** look'd not to be more lovely than **Marshall's** forehead when it spit forth sweat, at Critic-swords contending——.[1] I remember two honest Lines by Marvel (whose Poems by the way I am just going to possess)—

> "And every fragrant Mower's heat—Shew'[d like an
> Alexan]d[er's sweat."]

MS: Lord Abinger. Pub.: Hazlitt, I, 280–281; Ainger (1888), I, 153–154; Ainger (1900), II, 4–6; Macdonald, I, 184–185; Ainger (1904), I, 165–166; Harper, II, 285–286; Lucas (1905), VI, 201–202; Lucas (1912), V, 204; Lucas (1935), I, 233–234. Date, by Godwin: Dec. 14. Lamb and Godwin's old friend James Marshal—he became Godwin's amanuensis and literary agent and Lamb's M. in "The Old Actors" (see *Shelley and His Circle,* I, 436–437, and *Works,* II, 292–294)—took the shaken Godwin off to Lamb's rooms after the play to console him about its failure, consider half-heartedly its revision for a second presentation, and advise him to publish it under his own name. Lamb retained the manuscript and sent his suggestions for it to Godwin in the next letter and on the "rough paper" that accompanied this one. That paper is gone, but the following paragraph from it is in *Godwin,* II, 49–50: " 'Enviable' is a very bad word. I allude to 'Enviable right to bless us.' For instance, Burns [in "Despondency: An Ode," line 57—see also Letter 76, below the reference to note 6], comparing the ills of manhood with the state of infancy, says, 'Oh! enviable early days'; here 'tis good, because the passion lay in comparison. Excuse my insulting your judgment with an illustration. I believe I only wanted to beg in the name of a favourite Bardie, or at most to confirm my own judgment." Godwin struck out the line.

1. Adapted from *Coriolanus,* I, iii, 40–43. The quotation closing the letter is from Andrew Marvell's "Upon Appleton House, to My Lord Fairfax," lines 427–428.

92. *C. L. Godwin*

[December ?15, 1800]

Queries. Whether the best conclusion would not be a solemn judicial pleading, appointed by the king, before himself in person, of Antonio as proxy for Roderigo, and Guzman for himself—the forms and ordering of it to be highly solemn and grand. For this purpose (allowing it,) the king must be reserved, and not have committed his royal dignity by descending to previous conference with Antonio, but must refer from the beginning to this settlement. He must sit in dignity as a high royal arbiter. Whether this would admit of spiritual interpositions, cardinals, &c.—appeals to the Pope, and haughty rejection of his interposition by Antonio—(this merely by the way).

The pleadings must be conducted by short speeches—replies, taunts, and bitter recriminations by Antonio, in his rough style. In the midst of the undecided cause, may not a messenger break up the proceedings by an account of Roderigo's death (no improbable or far-fetch'd event), and the whole conclude with an affecting and awful invocation of Antonio upon Roderigo's spirit, now no longer dependent upon earthly tribunals or a froward woman's will, &c., &c.

Almanza's daughter is now free, &c.[1]

This might be made *very affecting*. Better nothing follow after; if anything, she must step forward and resolve to take the veil. In this case the whole story of the former nunnery *must* be omitted. But, I think, better leave the final conclusion to the imagination of the spectator. Probably the violence of confining her in a convent is not necessary; Antonio's own castle would be sufficient.

To relieve the former part of the Play, could not some sensible images, some work for the Eye, be introduced? A gallery of Pictures, Almanza's ancestors, to which Antonio might affectingly point his sister, one by one, with anecdote, &c.[2]

At all events, with the present want of action, the Play must not extend above four Acts, unless it is quite new modell'd. The proposed alterations might all be effected in a few weeks.

Solemn judicial pleadings always go off well, as in Henry the 8th, Merchant of Venice, and perhaps Othello.[3]

MS: unrecovered. Text: Lucas (1935), I, 232–233. Also pub.: Harper, II, 279–280; Lucas (1905), VI, 196–197; Lucas (1912), V, 199. This letter may be the "specious proposition" mentioned near the end of the next letter.

1. Neither this line nor the story of "the former nunnery," below, is in the published play, though there are references to a nunnery and a cloister in its fourth and fifth acts.

2. Swinburne wrote of this paragraph in *The Athenaeum* of May 13, 1876: "a singular anticipation of one of the most famous passages in the work of the greatest master of our own age, the scene of the portraits in [Victor Hugo's] 'Hernani.' . . . I know of no coincidence more pleasantly and strangely notable than this between the gentle genius of the loveliest among English essayists and the tragic invention of the loftiest among French poets."

3. *Henry VIII,* II, iv; *The Merchant of Venice,* IV, i; and *Othello,* I, iii.

93. *C. L. to Manning*

[December 15, 1800]

We are damned!—

not the facetious Epilogue itself—could save us.— For, as the Editor of the Morning Post, quicksighted Gentleman, hath this morning truly observed (I beg pardon if I falsify his *words,* their profound *sense* I am sure I retain) both prologue & epilogue were worthy of accompanying such a piece, and indeed (mark the profundity, Mister Manning) were receivd with proper indignation by such of the audience only, as thought either worth attending to.— —[1] **Professor,** thy glories wax dim— —. Again the incomparable Author of the True Briton declareth in *his* paper, (bearing same date) that the Epilogue was an indifferent attempt at humour and character, & failed in both.— I forbear to mention the other papers, because I have not read them— —. **O Professor,** how different thy feelings now (quantum mutatus ab illo Professore, qui in agris Philosophiæ tantas victorias acquisivisti)[2]—how different thy proud feelings but one little week ago—thy anticipation of thy nine nights—those visionary claps, which have soothed thy soul, by day, and thy dreams by night— —. Calling in accidentally on the Professor, while he was out, I was usher'd into the study, and my nose quickly (most sagacious always) pointed me to four Tokens, lying loose upon thy Table, Professor, which indicated thy violent and Satanical Pride of heart—. Imprimis there caught mine eye a list of six persons thy friends, whom thou didst meditate inviting to a sumptous dinner on the Thursday, anticipating the profits of thy Saturday's play to answer charges; I was in the honor'd file—. next, a stronger evidence of thy violent and almost Satanical pride, lay a List of all the morning papers (from the Morning Chronicle[3] downwards to the Porcupine) with the places of their respective offices, where thou wast meditating to insert, and did insert, an elaborate sketch of the story of thy Play; stones in thy Enemy's hand to bruise thee with, and severely wast thou bruis'd O Professor; nor do I know what oil to pour into thy wounds:— **next,** which convinced me, to a dead conviction of thy pride, violent and almost Satanical pride, lay a list of Books, which thy un-tragedy-favourd pocket could never answer, Dodsleys Old Plays, Malone's Shakespere[4] (still harping upon thy Play, thy Philosophy abandoned meanwhile to Christians and superstitious minds) nay I believe (if I can believe my memory) that the Ambitious Encyclopædia itself was part of thy meditated acquisitions, but many a play book was there; all these visions are *damned;* and thou, Professor, must read Shakspere, in future out of a common Edition; & hark 'ye, pray read him to a little better purpose—. Last and strongest against thee (in colours manifest as the Hand upon Belshazar's wall)[5] lay a volume of Poems by C. Lloyd and C. Lamb.— Thy heart misgave thee, that thy Assistant might possibly not have talent enough to furnish thee an Epilogue.— — Manning, all these Things come over my mind, all the gratulations that would have thickend upon him, & even some have glanced aside upon his humble friend, the vanity—and the fame—and the profits (the Professor is £500 ideal money out of pocket by this failure besides £200 he would have got for the copy wright, and the Professor is never much beforehand with the world, what he gets is all by the sweat of his brow, and dint of brain, for the Professor though a sure man is also a slow). and now to muse upon thy alterd physiognomy, thy pale and squalid appearance (a kind of *blue sickness* about the eye lids) & thy crest fallen, and thy proud demand of £200 from thy bookseller[6] changed to an uncertainty of his taking it all, or giving thee full £50)— the **Professor** has won my heart by this *his* mournful catastrophe—

You remember Marshall, who dined with him at my house!— I met him in the lobby immediately after the damnation of the Professor's play, and he looked to me like an angel; his face was lengthen'd and **all over sweat;** I never saw such a care-fraught visage. I could have hug'd him, I loved him so intensely— —"From every pore of him a Perfume fell."—[7] I have seen that man in many situations, and from my soul I think that a more godlike **honest** soul exists not in this world— — —. the professor's poor nerves trembling with the recent shock, he hurried him away to my house to supper, and there we comforted him as well as we could. He came to consult me about a change of catastrophe— —but alas the piece was condemned long before that crisis. I at first humour'd him with a specious proposition, but have since joind his true friends in advising him to give it up. He did it with a pang; and is to print it as *his*.

L

MS: Huntington Library. Pub.: Talfourd (1837), I, 198–202; Sala, I, 360–363; Purnell, I, 360–363; Fitzgerald, II, 193–196; Hazlitt, I, 282–284; Ainger (1888), I, 154–156; Ainger (1900), II, 6–9; Macdonald, I, 185–187; Ainger (1904), I, 166–168; Harper, II, 287–290; Lucas (1905), VI, 203–204; Lucas (1912), V, 205–207; Lucas (1935), I, 230–231. Address: Mr Manning/Mr Crisp's/near St. Mary's/Cambridge. Postmark: December 16, 1800.

1. "A prologue and epilogue were spoken by Mr. C[harles (1775–1854)] Kemble and Miss Heard," concludes the review in the *Morning Post* of December 15; "both productions well suited to the piece, too bad to pass without censure, except when they pass without observation." The December 15 issue of the *True Briton,* referred to below, whose editor from 1793 to 1806 was the author and journalist John Heriot (1760–1833), is not available.

2. "How changed from that Professor who gained such great triumphs in the fields of Philosophy"—an adaptation of Virgil, *Aeneid,* II, 274–275.

3. The December 15 number mauls the play and condemns the Epilogue as "a trite and not humourous description of a tradesman, who neglects his shop to go to the Play" and as having "no more connection with the Tragedy than with the battle of Blenheim." The review in *The Porcupine* of December 15 (the essayist, agriculturist, and radical politician William Cobbett [1763–1835] published the newspaper from 1800 to 1801), begins, "So gross an imposition on the public judgment has, perhaps, never been obtruded on the stage as the Tragedy of Antonio." Miss Heard "in pitiful taking," the review ends, "staggered on with evident emotion, to recite a pitiful Epilogue. Compassion listened to her with patience, but had not a single plaudit to throw away."

4. Edmund Malone (1741–1812), ed., *The Plays and Poems of William Shakspeare* (1790). The phrase "Ambitious Encyclopædia," below, may refer to what came to be called the First Variorum edition of Shakespeare's works, on which Malone worked from 1796 until his death and the younger James Boswell (1778–1822) completed and had published in twenty-one volumes in 1821.

5. In Daniel 5:5. The reference following is to *Blank Verse.*

6. George Robinson (1737–1801), the senior member of G. G. J. and J. Robinson of London. The firm published *Antonio: A Tragedy in Five Acts* on December 22, 1800. See *Shelley and His Circle,* I, 245, for that date and the information that "there exists a copy of *Antonio* in which Lamb has written detailed suggestions for revision (on perhaps half of the pages) and accompanied them with a note on the half title to Godwin. The note indicates that the annotations were made immediately after publication. . . . His [Lamb's] remarks are directed toward a second edition, which, incidentally, never appeared."

7. Nathaniel Lee, *The Rival Queens,* I, iii, 44 (in some editions I, 373), a line Lamb also included in "The Old Actors" (*Works,* II, 292).

94. *C. L. to Manning*

[December ?19, 1800]

Dear Manning——

I have scratched out a good deal, as you will see.— Generally, what I have rejected was either *false* in *feeling,* or a violation of character, mostly of the first sort. I will here just instance in the concluding few lines of the dying Lover's story, which completely contradicted his character of *silent* & *unreproachful*—. I hesitated a good while what copy to send you, and at last resolved to send the *worst, because* you are familiar with it & *can* make it out; and a stranger would find so much difficulty in doing it, that it would give him more pain than pleasure. This is compounded precisely of the two persons' hands, you requested it should be—

Yours sincerely
C Lamb

Mind, this goes for a **Letter.**—— (acknowledge it ***directly,*** if only in ten words)

(I shall want to **hear** this comes safe)

MS: Mr. Francis Kettaneh, New York. Pub.: Ainger (1900), II, 262; Harper, II, 294; Lucas (1905), VI, 205; Lucas (1912), V, 208; Lucas (1935), I, 235–236. Manning's reply, of December 20 (*Manning-Lamb Letters,* pp. 47–49), establishes approximately the dates of this letter and the next. They accompanied the transcription of "Pride's Cure" (also owned by Mr. Kettaneh and described in *Works,* V, 356–368) that Lamb promised Manning in Letter 90.

95. *C. L. to Manning*

[December ?19, 1800]

I send you all of Coleridge's letters to me, which I have preserv'd;[1] Some of them are upon the subject of my play—. I also send you Kemble's two letters, and and the Prompter's courteous Epistle; with a curious critique on Pride's cure by a young Physician[2] from *Edinbro',* who modestly suggests quite another kind of a plot—— these are monuments of my disappointmt—which I like to preserve——. in Coleridge's letters you will find a good deal of amusement, to see genuine Talent struggling against a pompous display of it—. I also send you the Professor's letter to me, (careful Professor, to conceal his *name* even from his correspondent)—'ere yet the Professor's pride was cured—. o! monstrous & almost satanical **Pride—**

You will carefully keep all (except the Scotch Doctor's (*which burn*)) in statu quo, till I come to claim mine own

C Lamb

There is another Letter[3] in the inside cover of the Book, opposite the *blank leaf,* that *was.*

MS: Huntington Library. Pub.: Talfourd (1837), I, 211–212; Sala, I, 371–372; Purnell, I, 371–372; Fitzgerald, II, 204–205; Hazlitt, I, 304–305; Ainger (1888), I, 174; Ainger (1900), II, 51–52; Macdonald, I, 210–211; Ainger (1904), I, 198; Harper, II, 293; Lucas (1905), VI, 205; Lucas (1912), V, 207–208; Lucas (1935), I, 235. Address: For/Mister Manning/Teacher of the mathematics/ and the black arts.

1. Among the many letters Coleridge wrote to Lamb before 1801, only the texts of two—of September 28, 1796, and early May 1798—are preserved in *Coleridge's Letters,* I, 238–239 and 403–405. The first (see above, Letter 7, note 2) was transcribed from a published text, and the second from a transcription by Dorothy Wordsworth. An early transcription of the first, containing "important variants" from the text in *Coleridge's Letters,* is, as item 339, listed and briefly described in Sotheby's catalogue of October 9, 1973.

2. Unidentified. "*Edinbro'*" is underscored twice.

3. The preceding letter, which was inside the boards holding the play.

96. *C. L. to Manning*

London

[Saturday,] the 27th Decr 1800

At length George Dyer's Phrenesis has come to a crisis, he is raging and furiously mad.— I waited upon the Heathen Thursday was a sevn'ight. . . The first symptom which struck my eye, and gave me incontrovertible proof of the fatal truth was a pair of Nankeen Pantaloons, four times too big for him, which the said Heathen did pertinaciously affirm to be **new.**— They were absolutely ingrained with the accumulated dirt of ages. But he affirmed them to be clean. He was going to a visit a Lady that was nice about those things, and that's the reason he wore nankeen that day—. And then he danced and capered, and fidgeted, and pulled up his pantaloons, and hugged his intolerable flannel vestment closer about his poetic Loins, anon he gave it loose to the Zephyrs which plentifully insinuate their tiny bodys thro' every crevice, door, window, or wainscoat, expressly formed for the exclusion of such Impertinents—then he caught at a proof sheet, and catched up a Laundresse's bill instead, made a dart at Bloomfield's poems, and threw them in agony aside—. I could not bring him to one direct reply, he could not maintain his jumping mind in a right line for the tithe of a moment by Clifford's Inn Clock—he must go to the Printer's immediately—the most unlucky accident—he had struck off five hundred impressions of his Poems,[1] which were ready for delivery to subscribers—and the Preface must all be expunged—there were 80

Pages of Preface, and not till that morning he had discovered that in the very first page of said preface he had set out with a principle of criticism fundamentally wrong, which vitiated all his following reasoning—the preface must be expunged, altho' it cost him £30— —the lowest calculation taking in paper & printing—. In vain have his real friends remonstrated against this . . Midsummer madness—. George is as obstinate as a primitive **Xtian**—and wards and parrys off all our thrusts with one unanswerable fence—"Sir, its of great consequence that the *world* is not ***mislead***"—.———

As for the other Professor, he has actually begun to **dive** into Tavernier and Chardin's ***Persian*** **Travels**[2] for a story, to form a new drama *for the* sweet tooth of this fastidious age— — ——

Has not Bethlehem College a fair action for non-residence against such professors?— Are Poets so *few* in *this age,* that ***He*** must write Poetry?— Is *morals* a subject so exhausted, that he must quit that line? Is the metaphysic **Well** (without a bottom) drained dry?— — — If I can guess at the wicked Pride of the Professor's heart, I would take a shrewd wager, that he disdains ever again to dip his pen in ***Prose.***— Adieu ye splendid theories! farewell dreams of Political Justice! Lawsuits, where I[3] was counsel for Archbishop Fenelon *versus* my own mother in the famous **fire** cause!—— — ———

Vanish from my mind, Professors one and all— ——. I have metal more attractive on foot——

Man of many snipes,

I will sup with **thee,** Deo volente, et diabolo nolente,[4] on Monday night the **fifth** of **January** in the new year, and crush a cup to the Infant Century———

A Word or two of my Progress— —. Embark at six oClock in the morning, with a fresh gale, on a Cambridge one-decker, very cold till eight at night, Land at St. Mary's light house, Muffins and Coffee upon Table (or any other curious production of Turkey or both **Indies**)—. Snipes exactly at nine. Punch to commence at ten, *with argument*; difference of opinion is expected to take place about eleven, perfect unanimity, with some haziness and dimness, before twelve—. **N. B.** My single affection is not so singly wedded to Snipes, but the curious and Epicurean ***Eye would*** also take a pleasure in beholding a delicate & well chosen assortment of Teals, Ortolans, the unctious and palate soothing flesh of geese wild and tame, night'ngale's brains, the sensorium of a young sucking pig, or any other Xmas dish, which I leave to the judgment of you & the Cook of Gonvill[e.][5]

C Lamb

MS: Huntington Library. Pub.: Talfourd (1837), I, 202–203; Talfourd (1848), I, 126–128; Sala, I, 363–365; Purnell, I, 363–365; Fitzgerald, II, 196–198; Hazlitt, I, 284–286; Ainger (1888), I, 157–158; Ainger (1900), II, 9–12; Macdonald, I, 187–189; Ainger (1904), I, 169–170; Harper, II, 290–293; Lucas (1905), VI, 206–208; Lucas (1912), V, 209–210; Lucas (1935), I, 236–238. Address: Mr Manning/Mr Crisp's/near St. Mary's/Cambridge. Postmark: December 27, 1800.

1. See Letter 77, note 2.

2. *Les six voyages de J[ean] B[aptiste] Tavernier [1605–1689]* (1676) and *The Travels of Sir John Chardin [1643–1713] into Persia and the East Indies* (1686) for material for "Abbas, King of Persia." Godwin had started the play at Coleridge's suggestion, completed it in September 1801, and offered it to Thomas Harris (d. 1820), a manager and proprietor of Covent Garden. Harris refused it, but proposed to pay Godwin for a "domestic plain story" (Vol. II, Letter 111). On September 23 Sheridan and John Philip Kemble refused it for Drury Lane. Yet even before that Godwin had accepted the likelihood that it would never be performed. He considered Harris' proposal and turned to the composition of "Faulkener, a Tragedy in Prose." It opened at Drury Lane after all, but not until December 16, 1807, and was published the same year as *Faulkener: A Tragedy*. A canceled line follows this paragraph.

3. Godwin, that is, who in *An Enquiry concerning the Principles of Political Justice*, Book II, ch. ii, imagined the French writer and archbishop of Cambrai François de Salignac de la Mothe Fénelon (1651–1715), a chambermaid, and the chambermaid as Godwin's mother caught in a fire in the archbishop's palace. Godwin then argued the merits of each as the one to be rescued if only one could be saved. The conclusion of the next paragraph is a compound of *Hamlet*, III, ii, 109–110—"No, good mother, here's metal more attractive"—and the stage direction "[*Lying down at Ophelia's feet.*]"

4. "God willing, and the devil not willing."

5. Gonville and Caius College.

97. *C. L. to Charles Lloyd, the younger*

[January ?24, 1801]

[Dear Lloyd,]

I am desperate because I have not heard from you.

[Yours ever
C Lamb]

MS: unrecovered. Text: *Lloyd-Manning Letters*, p. 62. This note, apparently in triplicate, is my reconstruction from a postscript by Sophia Lloyd in the letter from her husband, Charles, to Manning of January 26: "Praeter hanc, adsunt tres epist: a *Lamb,* breves, et similes. hoc solummodo continent. 'actus sum in desperationem quod nihil a te audierim' " ("in addition, have come three letters from *Lamb,* short, and alike. they merely contain the words [translated as the text of Letter 97]").

98. *C. L. to William Wordsworth*

[January 30, 1801]

Thanks for your **Letter** and **Present.**—[1] I had already borrowed your second volume—. What most please me are, the Song of Lucy. . . . *Simon's sickly daughter* in the Sexton made me *cry.*— Next to these are the description of the continuous **Echoes** in the story of Joanna's laugh, where the mountains and all the scenery absolutely seem alive—and that fine Shakesperian character of the Happy Man, in the Brothers,

> that creeps about the fields,
> Following his fancies by the hour, to bring
> Tears down his cheek, or solitary smiles
> Into his face, **until the Setting Sun**
> **Write Fool upon his forehead.—**

I will mention one more: the delicate and curious feeling in the wish for the Cumberland Beggar, that he may ha[ve] about him the melody of Birds, altho' he hear them not.— Here the mind knowingly passes a fiction upon herself, first substituting her own feelings for the Beggar's, and, in the same breath detecting the fallacy, will not part with the wish.— — The **Poets** Epitaph is disfigured, to my taste by the vulgar satire upon parsons and lawyers in the beginning, and the coarse epithet of pin point[2] in the 6th stanza.— All the rest is eminently good, and your own—. I will just add that it appears to me a fault in the Beggar, that the instructions conveyed in it are too direct and like a lecture: they dont slide into the mind of the reader, while he is imagining no such matter.— An intelligent reader finds a sort of insult in being told, I will teach you how to think upon this subject. This fault, if I am right, is in a ten thousandth worse degree to be found in **Sterne** and many many novelists & modern poets, who continually put a sign post up to shew **where you are to feel.** They set out with assuming their readers to be stupid. Very different from

Robinson Crusoe, the Vicar of Wakefie[l]d, Roderick Random,[3] and other beautiful bare narratives.— There is implied an unwritten compact between Author and reader; I will tell you a story, and I suppose you will understand it.— Modern Novels "St. Leons" and the like are full of such flowers as these "Let not my reader suppose"—"Imagine, **if you can**"—modest!—&c.— I will here have done with praise and blame. I have written so much, only that you may not think I have passed over your book without observation.— — I am sorry that Coleridge has christened his Ancient Marinere "a poet's Reverie"[4]—it is as bad as Bottom the Weaver's declaration that **he is** not a Lion but only the scenical representation of a Lion. What new idea is gained by this Title, but one subsersive of all credit, which the Tale should force upon us, of its truth?— For me, I was never so affected with any human Tale. After first reading it, I was totally possessed with it for many days.— I dislike all the miraculous part of it, but the feelings of the man under the operation of such scenery dragged me along like Tom Piper's magic Whistle.— I totally differ from your idea that the Marinere should have had a character and profession.—[5] This is a Beauty in Gulliver's Travels, where the mind is kept in a placid state of little wonderments; but the **Ancient Marinere** undergoes such **Trials,** as overwhelm and bury all individuality or memory of what he was.— Like the state of a man in a **Bad dream,** one terrible peculiarity of which is, that all consciousness of personality is **gone.**— Your other observation is I think as well a little unfounded: the **Marinere** from being conversant in supernatural events ***has***[6] acquired a supernatural and strange **cast** of *phrase,* **eye,** appearance &c. which frighten the wedding guest.— You will excuse my remarks, because I am hurt and vexed that you should think it necessary, with a prose apology, to open they[7] eyes of dead men that cannot see— — —. To sum up a general opinion of the second vol.—I do not **feel** any one poem in it so forcibly as the Ancient Marinere, the Mad mother, and the Lines at Tintern Abbey in the **first.**— — I could, too, have wished that The Critical preface had appeared in a separate treatise.— All its dogmas are true and just and most of them new, *as* criticism.— But they associate a *diminishing* idea with the Poems which follow, as having been written for **Experiments** on the public taste, more than having sprung (as they must have done) from living and daily circumstances.— —[8] I am prolix, because I am gratifyed in the opportunity of writing to you, and I dont well know when to leave off.— I ought before this to have reply'd to your very kind invitation into Cumberland.— With you and your Sister I could gang any where. But I am afraid whether I shall ever be able to afford so desperate a Journey.— Separate from the pleasure of your company, I dont mu[ch] care if I never see a mountain in my life.— I have passed all my days in London, until I have formed as many and intense local attachments, as any of you **Mountaineers** can have done with dead nature. . The Lighted shops of the Strand and Fleet Street, the innumerable trades, tradesmen and customers, coaches, waggons, play houses, all the bustle and wickedness round about Covent Garden, the very women of the Town, the Watchmen, drunken scenes, rattles;—life awake, if you awake, at all hours of the night, the impossibility of being dull in Fleet Street, the crowds, the very dirt & mud, the Sun shining upon houses and pavements, the print shops, the **old Book** stalls, parsons cheap'ning books, coffee houses, steams of soups from kitchens, the pantomimes, London itself, a pantomime and a masquerade, all these things work themselves into my mind and feed me without a power of satiating me. The wonder of these sights impells me into night-walks about her crowded streets, and I often shed tears in the motley Strand from fullness of joy at so much **Life**— —. All these emotions must be strange to you. So are your rural emotions to me.— But consider, what must I have been doing all my life, not to have lent great portions of my heart with usury to such scenes?———[9]

My attachments are all local, purely local—. I have no passion (or have had none since I was in love, and then it was the spurious engendering of poetry & books) to groves and vallies.— The rooms where I was born, the furniture which has been before my eyes all my life, a book case which has followed me about, (like a faithful dog, only exceeding him in knowledge) wherever I have moved—old chairs, old tables, streets, squares, where I have sunned myself, my old school,— these are my mistresses—have I not enough, without your mountains?— I do not envy you. I should pity you, did I not know, that the Mind will make friends of any thing. Your sun & moon and skys and hills & lakes affect me no more, or scarcely come to me in more venerable characters, than as a gilded room with tapestry and tapers, where I might live with handsome visible objects.— I consider the clouds above me but as a **roof** beautifully painted, but unable to satisfy the mind, and at last, like the pictures of the apartment of a Connoisseur, unable to afford him any longer a pleasure. So **fading** upon me from disuse, have been the Beauties of Nature, as they have been confinedly called; so ever fresh & green and warm are all the inventions of men and assemblies of men in this great city—. I should certainly have laughed with dear Joanna.—[10]

Give my kindest love, *and my sister's,* to Dorothy & yourself. And a kiss from me to little Barbara Lewthwaite.— —

C Lamb

Thank you for Liking my Play! !—

MS: The University of Texas Library, Austin, Texas. Pub.: Talfourd (1837), I, 212–215; Talfourd (1848), I, 144–147; Sala, I, 234–239; Purnell, I, 234–239; Fitzgerald, II, 69–74; Hazlitt, I, 266–268 and 292–293; Ainger (1888), I, 162–166; Ainger (1900), II, 17–22; Macdonald, I, 190–193; Ainger (1904), I, 174–178; Harper, II, 294–300; Lucas (1905), VI, 208–212; Lucas (1912), V, 211–214; Lucas (1935), I, 239–242. Address: Mr. Wordsworth/Grasmere/near Kendal/Westmoreland. Postmark: January 30, 1801.

1. Perhaps only the second volume of the second (1800) edition of *Lyrical Ballads*—Lamb writes of the second volume in Letters 100 and 101—but perhaps both volumes and Lamb in the following sentence wrote "volume" for "edition." In either case he has both volumes before him and begins by expressing his preference for "Song [: She dwelt among th' untrodden ways]"; "To a Sexton," line 14; "To Joanna," lines 53–65; and "The Brothers," lines 108–112. Lamb then mentions one more: "The Old Cumberland Beggar," lines 184–185.

2. In "A Poet's Epitaph," line 24. Wordsworth later changed the line from "Thy pin-point of a soul away!" to "Thy ever-dwindling soul, away!"

3. By Daniel Defoe, Oliver Goldsmith, Tobias Smollett. Mentioned below is Godwin's *St. Leon: A Tale of the Sixteenth Century* (1799).

4. The subtitle was canceled on page 5 of the revised copy of *Lyrical Ballads* of 1800 that the printer used in setting the third (1802) edition. The subtitle was, however, retained on the half-title of the third edition and in the fourth (1805) edition, but omitted thereafter. For Bottom's declaration, following, see *A Midsummer Night's Dream,* III, i, 36–46.

5. Wordsworth expressed the idea, along with praise for the poem, in his "Note to the Ancient Mariner," in *Lyrical Ballads* of 1800: "The Poem of my Friend has indeed great defects; first, that the principal person has no distinct character, either in his profession of Mariner, or as a human being who having been long under the controul of supernatural impressions might be supposed himself to partake of something supernatural: secondly, that he does not act, but is continually acted upon: thirdly, that the events having no necessary connection do not produce each other; and lastly, that the imagery is somewhat too laboriously accumulated" (*Lyrical Ballads: Wordsworth and Coleridge: The Text of the 1798 Edition with the Additional 1800 Poems and the Prefaces,* ed. R. L. Brett and A. R. Jones [rev. ed.; London: Methuen, 1965], pp. 276–277).

6. Underscored twice.

7. Should be "the." In 1815 Wordsworth changed the title of "The Mad Mother," mentioned below, to "Her Eyes Are Wild."

8. The Preface opens so: "The first Volume of these Poems has already been submitted to general persusal. It was published, as an experiment, which, I hoped, might be of some use to ascertain, how far, by fitting to metrical arrangement a selection of the real language of men in a state of vivid sensation, that sort of pleasure and that quantity of pleasure may be imparted, which a Poet may rationally endeavour to impart" (*Wordsworth's Poetical Works* [1940–1949], II, 384).

9. The question, barely modified, reappears in Lamb's reformulations of the passages above and below on the country and the city in "The Londoner" (*Works,* I, 40). Lamb employed "usury" in a similar fresh context in "The Two Races of Men" (*Works,* II, 26). See also Letter 100, its first paragraph, and Vol. II, Letter 127.

10. In "To Joanna," lines 52–53, Joanna laughed when she beheld the poet's eyes ravished by the glories of a summer morning along the banks of the Rotha. Lamb's departing kiss is to the little girl in "The Pet-lamb: A Pastoral." Although it is doubtful, Wordsworth may have told Lamb that he took the names in both poems from those of persons he knew—in the first from Joanna Hutchinson (1780–1843), who became Wordsworth's sister-in-law, and in the second from a beautiful child, then of Grasmere, who in 1843 was living in Ambleside. (See *Wordsworth's Poetical Works* [1940–1949], II, 487; and I, 364.) The third sentence of Letter 101 almost proves that the postscript here is meant to be as sarcastic as it sounds. The letter that Lamb probably sent with "Pride's Cure" could have been the one that disappeared shortly after its arrival and that Wordsworth, in his letter to Edward Moxon of January 12, 1835), called "much the most interesting we ever received" (*Wordsworths' Letters,* V, 723).

99. *C. L. to Manning*

Tuesday 3 Feb [1801]

Manning,

what is the matter?— my mind misgives me desperately, that you take something amiss.— I commissioned Gutch to give you a letter[1] on Saturday; but it has produced no reply.— Relieve me from a troublesome uncertainty by *but one line*

Yours ever
C Lamb

MS: Huntington Library. Pub.: Lucas (1935), I, 243. Address: Mr. Manning/ Mr Crisp's/Cambridge. Postmark: February 3, 1801.

1. Unrecovered. In his answer of February 24 (*Manning-Lamb Letters,* pp. 51–52) to that letter, this note, and Letter 101, Manning explained that he had only been away from Cambridge and prevented from writing immediately upon his return.

100. *C. L. to Robert Lloyd*

[February 7, 1801]

dear Robert,

I shall expect you to bring me a brimful account of the pleasure which Walton has given you, when you come to town.— It must square with your mind. The delightful innocence and healthfulness of the Anglers mind will have blown upon yours like a Zephyr.— Dont you already feel your spirit *filled* with the scenes?—the banks of rivers—the cowslip beds—the pastoral scenes—the neat alehouses—and hostesses and milkmaids, as far exceeding **Virgil** and **Pope,** as the Holy Living is beyond Thomas a Kempis.—[1] **Are** not the eating and drinking joys painted to the Life?—do they not inspire you with an immortal hunger?— — **Are** not you ambitious of being made an Angler?— What edition have you got? is it **Hawkins's** with plates of Piscator &c? That sells very dear. I have only been able to purchase the last Edition without the old Plates, which pleased my childhood;—the plates being worn out, & the old Edition difficult & expensive to procure.— — (The complete Angler is the only Treatise written in Dialogues that is worth a halfpenny.— Many elegant dialogues have been written (such as Bishop Berkley's Minute philosopher) but in all of them the Interlocutors are merely abstract arguments personify'd; not living dramatic characters, as in Walton; where *every thing* is *alive*; the fishes are absolutely *charactered*;—and birds and animals are as interesting as men & women.)— — I need not be at much pains to get the Holy Livings.— We can procure them in ten minutes search at any stall or shop in London—. By your engaging one for Priscilla, it should seem *she* will be in Town—is that the case?— I thought she was fix'd at the Lakes.— —[2] I perfectly understand the nature of your solitariness at Birm.—and wish I could divide myself, "like a bribed haunch" between London & it.— But courage!— You will soon be emancipated, & (it may be) have a frequent power of visiting this great place.—. (Let them talk of Lakes and mountains and romantic dales all that fantastic stuff;—give me a ramble by night, in the winter nights in London—the Lamps lit—the pavements of the motley **Strand** crouded with to and fro passengers—the shops all brilliant, and stuffed with obliging customers & obliged tradesmen—give me **the old Bookstalls of London—a walk in the bright Piazzas of Covent garden.**— I defy a man to be dull in such places—)̀ perfect Mahometan paradises upon Earth!— I have lent out my heart with usury to such scenes from my childhood up.— and have cried with fullness of joy at the multitudinous scenes of Life in the crouded streets of ever dear London—I wish you could **fix here.**— I dont know if you quite comprehend my low Urban Taste;—but depend upon it that a man of any feeling will have given his heart and his love in childhood & in boyhood to **any** scenes where he has been bred, as we[l]l to **dirty streets** (& smoky walls as they are called) as to green Lanes "where live nibbling sheep"[3] & to the everlasting hills and the Lakes & ocean.— **A mob of men is better than a flock of sheep**— —and a crowd of happy faces justling into the playhouse at the hour of six is a more beautiful spectacle to man than the shepherd driving his **"silly" sheep to fold**—— ——

Come to London & learn to sympathize with my unrural notions.— — Wordsworth has published a second vol. Lyrical Balads.— Most of them very good—but not so good as **first** vol.— What more can I tell you?— I believe I told you I have been to see *Manning*.— He is a dainty chiel.— A man of great **Power.**— An enchanter almost.— Far beyond **Coleridge** or any man in **power of impressing**—when he gets you alone, he can act the wonders of Egypt.— **Only** he is lazy & does not always put forth all his strength—; if he did, I know no man of genius at all comparable to him—[4]

Yours as ever
C L

MS: Huntington Library. Pub.: Ainger (1900), II, 22–25; Macdonald, I, 194–196; Ainger (1904), I, 178–180; Harper, I, facsimile, and II, 300–303; Lucas (1935), I, 243–245. Address: Robt. Lloyd/Charles Lloyd's/Birmingham. Postmark: February 7, 1801.

1. As, that is, Jeremy Taylor's *The Rule and Exercises of Holy Living* is beyond Thomas à Kempis' *De imitatione Christi.* Mentioned below is the edition of Izaak Walton's *The Compleat Angler* of 1760 by Sir John Hawkins (1719–1789), the Middlesex magistrate, writer on music, and biographer, editor, and executor of Dr. Johnson. Mentioned also is George Berkeley's *Alciphron, or the Minute Philosopher.*

2. She was, with her brother Charles and his family. The quotation in the following sentence—"bribed" means "poached"—is a corruption of *The Merry Wives of Windsor,* V, v, 24.

3. *The Tempest,* IV, i, 62. Lamb used the expression "silly sheep" (below) also

in "The Londoner" (*Works,* I, 39). He perhaps took it from *III Henry VI,* II, v, 43, or from Edward Young's *The Complaint; or, Night Thoughts,* IX, 1761.

4. As late as 1824 Lamb declared to Crabb Robinson that Manning was "the most *wonderful* man he ever knew, more extraordinary than Wordsworth or Coleridge" (*H. C. R. on Books and Writers,* I, 308).

101. *C. L. to Manning*

[February 15, 1801]

I had need be cautious henceforward what opinion I give of the Lyrical Balads.— All the north of England are in a turmoil. Cumberland and Westmorland have already declared a state of war.— I lately received from Wordsw. a copy of the second volume, accompanied by an acknowledgment of having received from me many months since a copy of a certain Tragedy, with excuses for not having made any acknowledgment sooner, it being owing to an "almost insurmountable aversion from Letter writing."— This letter I answered in due form and time, and enumerated several of the p[ass]ages which had most affected me, adding, unfortunately, that no single piece had moved me so forcibly as the Ancient Marinere, the Mad Mother, or the Lines at Tintern Abbey. The Post did not sleep a moment. I received almost instantaneously a long letter of four sweating pages from my **reluctant Letterwriter,** the purport of which was, that he was sorry his 2d vol. had not given me more pleasure (Devil a hint did I give that it had *not pleased me*) and "was compelled to wish that my range of **Sensibility** was more extended, being obliged to believe that I should receive large influxes of happiness & happy Thoughts" (I suppose from the L. B.—) With a deal of stuff about a certain **"Union of Tenderness & Imagination,** which in the sense he used Imag. was not the characteristic of Shakesp. but which Milton possessed in a degree far exceeding other Poets: which **Union,** as the highest species of Poetry, and chiefly deserving that name, He was most proud to aspire to"—then illustrating the said Union by two quotations from his own 2d vol. (which I had been so unfortunate as to miss)—. 1st Specimen—A father addresses his Son—

When thou
First cams't into the world, as it befalls
To new born Infants, thou didst sleep away

Two days: ***And Blessings from thy father's tongue***
Then fell upon thee.[1]

The lines were thus undermark'd & then followed "This Passage as combining in an extraordinary degree that union of Imagination & Tenderness, which I am speaking of, I consider as one of the Best I ever wrote."——

2d Specimen.— A Youth after years of absence revisits his native place, and thinks (as most people do) that there has been strange alteration in his absence— —

And that the rocks
And Everlasting Hills themselves were chang'd——[2]

You see both these are good Poetry: but after one has been reading Shaksp. twenty of the best years of one's life, to have a fellow start up, and prate about some unknown quality, which Shakspere possess'd in a degree inferior to Milton and somebody else! !— — This was not to be *all* my castigation.— Coleridge, who had not written to me some months before, starts up from his bed of sickness, to reprove me for my hardy presumption: four long pages, equally sweaty, and more tedious, came from him: assuring me, that, when the works of a man of true Genius, such as W. undoubtedly was, do not please me at first sight, I should suspect the fault to lie "in me & not in them"—&c. &c. &c. &c. &c.—— What am I to do with such people?— I certainly shall write them a very merry Letter.—.—.———[3]

Writing to *you,* I ⟨must⟩ may say, that the 2d vol. has no such pieces as the 3 I enumerated.— It is full of original thinking and an observing mind, but it does not often make you laugh or cry.— It too artfully aims at simplicity of expression. And you sometimes doubt if simplicity be not a cover for Poverty. The best Piece[4] in it I will send you, being *short*—I have grievously offended my friends in the North by declaring my undue preference. But I need not fear you—

She dwelt among the untrodden ways
Beside the Springs of **Dove,**
A maid whom there were few to praise,
And very few to love.—

A Violet, by a mossy stone
Half hidden from the eye;

Fair as a star, when only one
Is shining in the sky.—

She lived unknown; & few could know,
When **Lucy** ceas'd to be.
But she is in the grave, and Oh!
The difference to me.—

This is choice and genuine, and so are many many more. But one does not like to have 'em ramm'd down one's throat— "Pray take it—its very good—let me help you—eat faster."—.—.

At length George Dyer's 1st vol.[5] is come to a birth.— One volume of three.— Subscribers being *allowed* by the Prospectus to pay for all at once (tho its very doubtful if the rest ever come to any thing, this having been already some years getting out) I paid two Guineas for you and myself, which entitle us to the whole.— I will send you your copy, if you are in a *great hurry*. Meantime you owe me a **Guinea.** George skipped about like a **pea** with its arse scorched, at the receipt of so much **Cash.**— To give you one specimen of the beautiful absurdity of the **Notes,** which defys imitation, take one. "Discrimination is not the *aim* of the present volume. It will be more strictly attended to in the next."—[6] One of the Sonnets purports to have been written in **Bedlam!** This for a man to ***own.***—!— The rest are addrest to Science, Genius, Melancholy, &c.—two to the River Cam.—an ode to the Nightingale. Another to Howard, beginning, **Spirit** of meek Philanthropy.— One is entitled the Madman, "being collected by the author from several madhouses"; it begins, **Yes, yes,** tis **He.**— A long poetical Satire is inscribed to John Disney D. D. **His Wife And Daughter! ! !**—

Now to my own affairs—. I have not taken that Thing[7] to Colman, but I have proceeded one step in the business. I have enquir'd his address, and am promis'd it in a few days.— Meantime 3 Acts and a half are finished gallopping, of a Play on a Persian Story, which I must father in April.— But far, very far, below Antonio in composition. O Jeptha, judge of Israel, what a fool I was.—

C Lamb

MS: Folger Shakespeare Library. Pub.: Ainger (1900), II, 25–30; Ainger (1904), I, 180–183; Harper, II, 303–307; Lucas (1905), VI, 212–214; Lucas (1912), V, 215–217; Lucas (1935), I, 245–248. Address: Mr Thos. Manning/ Diss/Norfolk. Postmark: February 15, 1801.

1. "Michael: A Pastoral Poem," lines 339–343. Wordsworth's letters to Lamb referred to here (I should in this instance point out) are not recovered. Coleridge's letter, mentioned below, is not recovered. Lamb's to Wordsworth is Letter 98.
2. "The Brothers," lines 98–99.
3. Unrecovered, though Lamb may not have written it. A canceled line and three-quarters follow "vol.," below.
4. The poem, known by its opening line, Lamb gives in its entirety.
5. *Poems* (1801). See Letter 77, note 2.
6. Page 332. The poems Lamb mentions in the following sentences are "Written in Bedlam: On Seeing a Beautiful Young Female Maniac"; "On Science"; "On Genius. On Taking Leave of Dr. Priestley, When Preparing to Go to America"; "To Melancholy"; "To the River Cam" and "On an Approaching Spring. Written on the Banks of the Cam. To Thomas Northmore [1766–1851], formerly of Emmanuel College, Cambridge"; "To the Nightingale"; "Written on the Death of John Howard [1726?–1790], at His Villa at Cardington, in Bedfordshire"; "The Madman. Collected by the Author from Several Characters, Seen in Different Madhouses"; and "Poetic Sympathies. To Dr. [John (1746–1816)] Disney, His Wife, and Daughter."
7. Presumably "Pride's Cure." The dramatist George Colman, the younger (1762–1836), managed the Haymarket from 1789 to 1813. The first play mentioned below is Godwin's "Abbas, King of Persia." (See Letter 96, note 2.) Lamb's concluding sentence is *Hamlet,* II, ii, 403–404, modified.

102. *C. L. to Manning*

[Friday, February 27? 1801]

You masters of Logic[1] ought to know—(Logic is nothing more than a knowledge of *words,* as the Greek Etymon implys)—that all words are no more to be taken in the literal sense at all times, than a promise given to a Taylor.— When I exprest an apprehension that you were mortally **offended,** I meant no more than by the application of a certain formula of efficacious sounds, which had *done* in similar cases before, to rouse a sense of decency in you, and a remembrance of what was due to me! !— You Masters of Logic should advert to this phenomenon in human speech, before you arraign the usage of us **Dramatic Geniuses— —. Imagination** is a good blood mare & goes well, but the misfortune is she has too many paths before her.— Tis true, I might have imaged to myself, that you had trundled your frail carcase to Norfolk = I might also, and did imagine, that you had ***not***—but that you were lazy, or inventing new properties in a triangle, and for that purpose moulding and squeezing Landlord Crisp's 3 corner'd Beaver into phantastic experimental forms; or that Archimedes was meditating to repulse the **French,** in case of a Cambridge Invasion, by a geometric hurling of **Folios** on their red caps; or peradventure that you were in extremities, in great wants, & just set out for Trinity Bogs, when my Letters came—. In short, my Genius! (which is a short word now adays for what-a-great-man-am-I!) was absolutely stifled and overlaid with its own Riches.— **Truth is one** and **poor** like the cruse of Elijah's Widow,[2] Imagination is the Bald-face that multiplys its oil. ;—and thou the old crack'd *Salvy* pipkin that could not believe it could be put to such purposes.— Dull pipkin, to have Elijah for thy **Cook**——. Imbecil recipient of so **fat** a miracle———

I send you George Dyers Poems, the **richest** production of the Lyrical muse *this* ***Century*** can justly boast, for Wordsworth's L. B. were published or at least written before Xmas.— Please to advert to Pages 291 to 296 for the most astonishing account of where Shakspeare's Muse has been all this while.—[3] I thought she had been dead and buried in Stratford Church, with the young man *that kept her company*— ——. But it seems, like the Devil

> buried in Cole Harbour
> Some say she's risen again,
> Gone prentice to a Barber———

N. B.—

I dont charge any thing for the additional Manuscript **Notes,** which are the joint productions of myself and a learned Translator of Schiller,——Stoddart Esq*r*—[4]

N. B. the 2d.——

I should not have blotted your **Book**—but I had sent my own out to be bound, as I was in duty bound.— A Liberal Criticism upon the several pieces Lyrical, Heroical, Amatory, and Satirical, would be acceptable.—.———[5]

So, you dont think there's a **Word's-**worth of good Poetry in the Great L. B.!— I dare'nt put the dreaded Syllables at their just length, for my ***Arse tickles red*** from the northern castigation—. I send you the **Three Letters,**[6] which I beg you to return along with those former Letters (which I hope you are not going to print, by your detention)—. But dont be in a hurry to send them—. When you come to Town, will do.— **Apropos** of coming to Town!— Last Sunday was a fortnight as I was *coming to town* from the Professor's, inspired with new **Rum,**

I tumbled down and broke my **nose.** I drink nothing stronger than malt-liquors.—

I am going to change my Lodgings, having received a hint that it would be agreeable, at our Lady's next feast.—[7] I have partly fixed upon most delectable Rooms, which look out (when you stand a Tip toe) over the Thames & Surrey Hills; at the upper end of King's Bench walks in the **Temple.**— There I shall have all the privacy of a house without the encumbrance, and shall be able to lock my friends out as often as I desire to hold free converse with my immortal mind, for my present lodgings resemble a minister's levee, I have so encreased my acquaintance (as they call 'em) since I have resided in Town. Like the ***Town*** **Mouse,** that had tasted a little of urbane manners, I long to be nibbling my own cheese by my dear self without mouse traps & time-traps.— By my new plan I shall be as **airy,** up 4 pair of stairs, as in the country; & in a garden in the midst of enchanting more than Mahometan paradise **London,** whose dirtiest drab-frequented alley, and her lowest bowing Tradesman, I would not exchange for Skiddaw, Helvellyin, James, Walter, and the Parson[8] in the bargain——. O! her Lamps of a night! her rich goldsmiths, print shops, toy shops, mercers, hardwaremen, pastry cooks!— St. Paul's ch. yard, the Strand! Exeter Change!—[9] Charing Cross, with the man *upon* a black horse!—— These are thy Gods O London——. A'nt you mightily moped in the banks of the Cam.?—— had not you better come and set up here?— You ca'nt think what a difference. All the streets and pavements are pure gold, I warrant you.— **At least** I know an **Alchymy** that turns her mud into that metal—a mind that loves to be at home in **Crowds**———

Tis half past 12 oClock & all sober peop[l]e ought to be a bed—

C Lamb—(as you may guess)

Between you & me the L. Balads are but *drowsy **performances.***—

MS: Huntington Library. Pub.: Talfourd (1837), I, 165–169; Sala, I, 336–339; Purnell, I, 336–339; Fitzgerald, II, 170–173; Hazlitt, I, 294–297; Ainger (1888), I, 166–169; Ainger (1900), II, 30–33; Macdonald, I, 196–198; Ainger (1904), I, 183–186; Harper, III, 9–12; Lucas (1905), VI, 215–216; Lucas (1912), V, 218–220; Lucas (1935), I, 249–251. Address: Mr Manning. This letter could be dated anytime between February 26 or 27, when Lamb would have received Manning's letter postmarked February 25, and March 12 or 13, which would still have permitted Manning's response of March 14. But Lamb's anxiousness to hear from Manning and Manning's apology in a later letter for again delaying to write suggest the date assigned. See the *Manning-Lamb Letters,* pp. 51–52 and 54–55.

1. Lamb's counter epithet to Manning's "You *Dramatic Writers*" (*Manning-Lamb Letters,* p. 51).

2. The cruse never failed to pour oil. (See 1 Kings 17:12–16.) A salvy pipkin, mentioned below, is an earthenware vessel for holding oil or fat.

3. In the wings of the German stage with Schiller, Kotzebue, and Goethe—according to Dyer's "Poetic Sympathies" and its notes—and from time to time in the British countryside with such as Erasmus Darwin, Cowper, John Wolcot, Samuel Rogers, Thomas Campbell, Southey, Wordsworth, Coleridge, Lloyd, Bloomfield, the Cottles, and even Lamb.

4. See Letter 3, note 28.

5. Manning thought Dyer's translations "very good" and the notes *"all good,* & some very interesting, e.g., 'Shakespear was born at Stratford &c'—an anecdote of that Great Bard, very little known, I wish Dyer had mentioned it oftener—I do not find that tis inserted in more than two notes." He thought the second volume of *Lyrical Ballads* "utterly absurd from one end to the other" and "had rather sit spinning all day than prosing over such uninteresting accounts of uninteresting things" (*Manning-Lamb Letters,* pp. 54 and 52).

6. The two letters from Wordsworth and the letter from Coleridge to Lamb described in Letter 101. Those "former letters," following, are presumably Coleridge's to Lamb that Lamb sent to Manning with Letter 95.

7. On Lady Day, March 25, Lamb and Mary moved to 16 Mitre Court Buildings, Inner Temple.

8. In Wordsworth's "The Brothers."

9. Exeter Change, before it was razed in 1829 or 1830, stood near 356 Strand and held bookstalls, offices, and a menagerie. The next fragment is drawn from this jingle:

> As I was going by Charing Cross,
> I saw a black man upon a black horse;
> They told me it was King Charles the First.
> Oh, dear! my heart was ready to burst!
>
> [*Rainbow in the Sky,* ed. Louis Untermeyer (New York: Harcourt, Brace, 1935), p. 23]

INDEX OF NAMES

Boldface numbers refer to key pages.

The Letters of
Charles and Mary Anne Lamb

Designed by R. E. Rosenbaum.
Composed by York Composition Company, Inc.,
in 11 point Intertype Baskerville, 2 points leaded,
with display lines in monotype Baskerville.
Printed letterpress from type by York Composition Company
on Warren's Olde Style, 60 pound basis,
with the Cornell University Press watermark.
Illustrations printed offset by Art Craft of Ithaca.
Bound by Vail-Ballou Press
in Joanna bookcloth
and stamped in All-Purpose foil.